Managing NFS and NIS

Managing NFS and NIS

Hal Stern

O'Reilly & Associates, Inc.

Cambridge • *Köln* • *Paris* • *Sebastopol* • *Tokyo*

Managing NFS and NIS
by Hal Stern

Copyright © 1991 O'Reilly & Associates, Inc. All rights reserved.
Printed in the United States of America.

Editor: Mike Loukides

Printing History:

June 1991:	First Edition.
April 1992:	Minor corrections.

This book is printed on acid-free paper with 85% recycled content, 15% post-consumer
waste. O'Reilly & Associates is committed to using paper with the highest recycled
content available consistent with high quality.

ISBN: 0-937175-75-7 [1/98]

Table of Contents

Figures

Tables

Preface

Who This Book is For
Versions
Organization
Conventions Used in this Book
Acknowledgments
We'd Like to Hear From You

Ten years ago, most computer centers had a few large computers shared by several hundred users. The "computing environment" was usually a room containing dozens of terminals. All users worked in the same place, with one set of disks, one user account information file, and one view of all resources. Local area networks have made terminal rooms much less common. Today, a "computing environment" almost always refers to distributed computing, where users have workstations on their desks and shared resources are provided by special-purpose systems such as file, compute, and print servers. Each workstation requires redundant configuration files, including user information, network host addresses, and local and shared remote filesystem information.

A mechanism to provide consistent access to all files and configuration information ensures that all users have access to the "right" machines, and that once they have logged in they will see a set of files that is both familiar and complete. This consistency must be provided in a way that is transparent to the users; that is, a user should not know that a filesystem is located on a remote fileserver. The transparent view of resources must be consistent across all machines and also consistent with the way things work in a non-networked environment. In a networked computing environment, it's usually up to the system administrator to manage both the machines on the network (including centralized servers) as well as the network itself. Managing the network means ensuring that the network is transparent to users rather than an impediment to their work.

The Network File System (NFS) and the Network Information Service (NIS)* provide mechanisms for solving "consistent and transparent" access problems. The NFS and NIS protocols were developed by Sun Microsystems and are now licensed to about 300 vendors and universities. NIS centralizes commonly replicated configuration files, such as the password file, on a single host. It eliminates duplicate copies of user and system information and allows the system administrator to make changes from one place. NFS makes remote filesystems appear to be local, as if they were on disks attached to the local host. With NFS, all machines can share a single set of files, eliminating duplicate copies of files on different machines in the network. Using NFS and NIS together greatly simplifies the management of various combinations of machines, users, and filesystems.

NFS provides network and filesystem transparency because it hides the actual, physical location of the filesystem. A user's files could be on a local disk, on a shared disk on a fileserver, or even on a machine located across a wide-area network. As a user, you're most content when you see the same files on all machines. Just having the files available, though, doesn't mean that you can access them if your user information isn't correct. Missing or inconsistent user and group information will break UNIX file permission checking. This is where NIS complements NFS, by adding consistency to the information used to build and describe the shared filesystems. A user can sit down in front of any workstation in his or her group that is running NIS and be reasonably assured that he or she can log in, find his or her home directory, and access tools such as compilers, window systems, and publishing packages. In addition to making life easier for the users, NFS and NIS simplify the tasks of system administrators, by centralizing the management of configuration information and of disk resources.

NFS can be used to create very complex filesystems, taking components from many different servers on the network. It is possible to overwhelm users by providing "everything everywhere," so simplicity should rule network design. Just as a database programmer constructs views of a database to present only the relevant fields to an application, the user community should see a logical collection of files, user account information, and system services from each viewpoint in the computing environment. Simplicity often satisfies the largest number of users, and it makes the system administrator's job easier.

---

*NIS was formerly called the "Yellow Pages". While many commands and directory names retain the *yp* prefix, the formal name of the set of services has been changed to avoid conflicting with registered trademarks.

Who This Book is For

This book is of interest to system administrators and network managers who are installing or planning new NFS and NIS networks, or debugging and tuning existing networks and servers. It is also aimed at the network user who will be building tools and applications that use NIS services, or who are interested in the mechanics that hold the network together.

We'll assume that you are familiar with the basics of UNIX system administration and TCP/IP networking. Terms that are commonly misused or particular to a discussion will be defined as needed. Where appropriate, an explanation of a low-level phenomenon such as Ethernet congestion will be provided if it is important to a more general discussion such as NFS performance on a congested network. Models for these phenomena will be drawn from everyday examples rather than their more rigorous mathematical and statistical roots.

This book focuses on the way NFS and NIS work, and how to use them to solve common problems in a distributed computing environment. Use this book in conjunction with your vendor's documentation, since utilities and their options will vary by implementation. This book explains what the configuration files and utilities do, and how their options affect performance and system administration issues. By walking through the steps comprising a complex operation, or by detailing each step in the debugging process, we hope to shed light on techniques for effective management of distributed computing environments. There are very few absolute constraints or thresholds that are universally applicable, so we refrain from stating them. This book should help you to determine the fair utilization and performance constraints for your network.

Versions

This book is based on the SunOS 4.1 implementations of NFS and NIS. When used without a version number, "SunOS" refers to the SunOS 4.1 UNIX operating system and its derivatives. In this sense, "SunOS" refers to the operating system for SPARC-based machines. NFS- and NIS-related tools did not change significantly between SunOS 4.0 and SunOS 4.1, but functions that are specific to SunOS 4.1 will be noted. Some of the NFS discussions apply to SunOS 3.5 and earlier releases, but SunOS 4.0 introduced many new features: diskless client support using NFS, new exporting rules, the automounter, and a new virtual memory management system.

The discussion of PC/NFS is based on PC/NFS 3.5. Any feature that is particular to PC/NFS 3.5 or behaves differently in earlier releases is noted.

Organization

This book is divided into two sections. The first nine chapters contain explanations of the implementation and operation of NFS and NIS. Chapters 10 through 14 cover advanced administrative and debugging techniques, performance analysis, and tuning. Building on the introductory material, the second section of the book delves into low-level details such as the effects of network partitioning hardware and the various steps in a remote procedure call. The material in this section is directly applicable to the ongoing maintenance and debugging of a network.

Here's the chapter-by-chapter breakdown:

Chapter 1, *Networking Fundamentals*, provides an introduction to the underlying network protocols and services used by NFS and NIS.

Chapter 2, *Network Information Service Operation*, discusses the architecture of NIS and its operation on both NIS servers and NIS clients. The focus is on how to set up NIS and its implementation features that affect network planning and initial configuration.

Chapter 3, *System Management Using the Network Information Service*, discusses operational aspects of NIS that are important to network administrators. This chapter explores common NIS administration techniques, including map management, setting up multiple NIS domains, and using NIS with domain name services.

Chapter 4, *Building Applications with NIS*, shows how to use NIS as a distributed database system, creating your own NIS maps to manage a telephone list and to grant restricted access to specific services. It contains several examples ranging from shell scripts to C programs that use the NIS client programming library.

Chapter 5, *System Administration and the Network File System*, covers basic NFS operations such as mounting and exporting filesystems, and using symbolic links within NFS.

Chapter 6, *Network File System Design and Operation*, explains the architecture of NFS and the underlying virtual file system. It also discusses implementation details that affect performance, such as file attribute and data caching.

Chapter 7, *Diskless Clients*, is all about diskless clients. It also presents debugging techniques for clients that fail to boot successfully.

Chapter 8, *Network Security*, explores network security. Issues such as restricting access to hosts and filesystems form the basis for this chapter. We'll also go into how to make NFS more secure, including a discussion of setting up Sun's Secure NFS.

Chapter 9, *Centralizing Mail Services with NFS and NIS*, covers the impact of NFS on electronic mail services and suggests ways to consolidate mail delivery functions in a network. Tips for handling user aliases, wide-area mailing lists and mail forwarding are included.

Chapter 10, *Diagnostic and Administrative Tools*, describes the administrative and diagnostic tools that are applied to the network and its systems as a whole. This chapter concentrates on the network and on interactions between hosts on the network, instead of the per-machine issues presented in earlier chapters. Tools and techniques are described for analyzing each layer in the protocol stack, from the Ethernet to the NFS and NIS applications.

Chapter 11, *Debugging Network Problems*, is a collection of debugging stories, and shows how the tools described in the previous chapter are applied in some real-world situations.

Chapter 12, *Performance Analysis and Tuning*, covers performance tuning and analysis of machines and the network. It discusses network partitioning using bridges and routers, with a focus on NFS performance optimization. Server parameter tuning, NFS mount parameter adjustments, and client-side issues are explored in detail in this chapter as well.

Chapter 13, *The Automounter*, discusses the automounter, a powerful but sometimes confusing tool that integrates NIS administrative techniques and NFS filesystem management.

Chapter 14, *PC/NFS*, covers PC/NFS, a client-side implementation of NFS for DOS machines.

Appendix A, *Transmission Line Theory*, contains a low-level description of transmission line theory, the basis for Ethernet termination and many other physical constraints of the Ethernet.

Appendix B, *IP Packet Routing*, explains how IP packets are forwarded to other networks. It is additional background information for discussions of performance and network configuration.

Appendix C, *NFS Problem Diagnosis*, summarizes NFS problem diagnosis using the NFS statistics utility and the error messages printed by clients experiencing NFS failures.

Appendix D, *NFS Benchmarks*, contains information on NFS traffic generation for benchmarking.

Conventions Used in this Book

The following conventions are used in this book:

Italic
is used for hostnames. System and library calls are in italic, with parentheses to indicate that they are C routines; for example, *gethostent()*. Italic is also used to emphasize new terms and concepts when they are introduced and to highlight comments in an example.

Bold
is used for UNIX pathnames, filenames, commands, and command lines when they appear in the body of a paragraph.

`Constant Width`
is used in examples to show the contents of files or the output from commands.

`Constant Bold`
is used in examples to show commands or other text that should be typed literally by the user. For example, **rm foo** means to type "rm foo" exactly as it appears in the text or example.

`Constant Italic`
is used in examples to show variables for which a context-specific substitution should be made. The variable `filename`, for example, would be replaced by some actual filename.

Quotes
are used to identify system messages that appear in the body of a paragraph.

%
is the C shell prompt.

#
is the Bourne shell prompt.

[ ]
surround optional values in a description of program syntax. (The brackets themselves should never be typed.)

. . .
stands for text (usually computer output) that's been omitted for clarity or to save space.

The notation CTRL-X or ^X indicates use of *control* characters. It means hold down the CONTROL key while typing the character "x". We denote other keys similarly (e.g., RETURN indicates a carriage return).

All command examples are followed by a RETURN unless otherwise indicated.

Acknowledgments

Writing about NFS and NIS was not easy, because their implementations changed quite rapidly while I was writing. NFS and NIS were introduced in 1985, which makes them old in the technology timescale. While the protocols have not changed, we have seen many new NFS and NIS features such as NFS write accelerators, caching techniques, and specialized NFS server architecture. There are now almost 300 implementations of NFS, and some campus networks have several hundred nodes sharing files and configuration information.

This book would not have been completed without the help of many people. I'd like to thank Brent Callaghan, Chuck Kollars, Neal Nuckolls, and Janice McLaughlin (all of Sun Microsystems); Kevin Sheehan (Kalli Consulting); Vicki Lewolt Schulman (Auspex Systems); and Dave Hitz (H&L Software) for their never ending stream of answers to questions about issues large and small. Bill Melohn (Sun) provided the foundation for the discussion of computer viruses. The discussion of NFS performance tuning and network configuration is based on work done with Peter Galvin and Rick Sabourin at Brown University. Several of the examples of NIS and NFS configuration were taken from a system administrator's guide to NFS and NIS written by Mike Loukides for Multiflow Computer Company.

The finished manuscript was reviewed by Chuck Kollars, Mike Marotta, Ed Milstein, and Brent Callaghan (Sun); Dave Hitz (H&L Software); Larry Rogers (Princeton University); Vicky Lewold Schulman (Auspex); Simson Garfinkel (NeXTWorld); and Mike Loukides and Tim O'Reilly (ORA). This book has benefited in many ways from their insights, comments, and corrections. The production group of O'Reilly & Associates, especially Kismet McDonough, also deserves my gratitude for applying the finishing touches to this book. I owe a tremendous thanks to Mike Loukides of O'Reilly and Associates who helped undo four years of liberal arts education and associated writing habits. It is much to Mike's credit that this book does not read like a treatise on Dostoevsky's *Crime and Punishment*.*

---

*I think I will cause my freshman composition lecturer pain equal to the credit given to Mike, since she assured me that reading and writing about *Crime and Punishment* would prepare me for writing assignments the rest of my life. I have yet to see how, except possibly when I was exploring performance issues.

We'd Like to Hear From You

We have tested and verified all of the information in this book to the best of our ability, but you may find that features have changed (or even that we have made mistakes!). Please let us know about any errors you find, as well as your suggestions for future editions, by writing:

```
O'Reilly & Associates, Inc.
101 Morris Street
Sebastopol, CA 95472
1-800-998-9938 (in the US or Canada)
1-707-829-0515 (international/local)
1-707-829-0104 (FAX)
```

You can also send us messages electronically. To be put on the mailing list or request a catalog, send email to:

info@oreilly.com   (via the Internet)

To ask technical questions or comment on the book, send email to:

bookquestions@oreilly.com   (via the Internet)

1

Networking Fundamentals

Networking Overview
Physical and Data Link Layers
Network Layer
Transport Layer
The Session and Presentation Layers

The Network Information System (NIS) and Network File System (NFS) are services that allow you to build distributed computing systems that are both consistent in their appearance and transparent in the way files and data are shared.

- NIS provides a distributed database system for common configuration files. NIS servers manage copies of the database files, and NIS clients request information from the servers instead of using their own, local copies of these files. For example, the **/etc/hosts** file is managed by NIS. A few NIS servers manage copies of the information in the hosts file, and all NIS clients ask these servers for host address information instead of looking in their own **/etc/hosts** file. Once NIS is running, it is no longer necessary to manage every **/etc/hosts** file on every machine in the network—simply updating the NIS servers ensures that all machines will be able to retrieve the new configuraton file information.

- NFS is a distributed filesystem. An NFS server has one or more filesystems that are mounted by NFS clients; to the NFS clients, the remote disks look like local disks. NFS filesystems are mounted using the standard UNIX **mount** command, and all UNIX utilities work just as well with NFS-mounted files as they do with files on local disks. NFS makes system administration easier because it eliminates the need to maintain multiple copies of files on several machines: all NFS clients share the single copy of the file on the NFS server. NFS also makes life easier for users: instead of logging on to many different systems and moving files from one system to another, a user can stay on one system and access all the files that he or she needs within one consistent file tree.

This book contains detailed descriptions of these services, including configuration information, network design and planning considerations, and debugging, tuning, and analysis tips. If you are going to be installing a new network, expanding or fixing an existing network, or looking for mechanisms to manage data in a distributed environment, you should find this book helpful.

Many people consider NFS to be the heart of a distributed computing environment, because it manages the resource users are most concerned about: their files. However, a distributed filesystem such as NFS will not function properly if hosts cannot agree on configuration information such as user names and host addresses. The primary function of NIS is managing configuration information and making it consistent on all machines in the network. NIS provides the framework in which to use NFS. Once the framework is in place, you add users and their files into it, knowing that essential configuration information is available to every host. Therefore, we will look at NIS first (in Chapters 2 through 4); we'll follow that with a discussion of NFS, in Chapters 5 and following.

Networking Overview

Before discussing either NFS or NIS, we'll provide a brief overview of network services.

Both NFS and NIS are high-level networking protocols, built on several lower-level protocols. In order to understand the way the high-level protocols function, you need to know how the underlying services work. The lower-level network protocols are quite complex, and several books have been written about them without even touching on NFS and NIS services. Therefore, this chapter contains only a brief outline of the network services used by NFS and NIS.

Network protocols are typically described in terms of a layered model, in which the protocols are "stacked" on top of each other. Data coming into a machine is passed from the lowest-level protocol up to the highest, and data sent to other hosts moves down the protocol stack. The layered model is a useful description because it allows network services to be defined in terms of their functions, rather than their specific implementations. New protocols can be substituted at lower levels without affecting the higher-level protocols, as long as these new protocols behave in the same manner as those that were replaced.

The standard model for networking protocols and distributed applications is the International Organization for Standardization (ISO) 7-layer model shown in Table 1-1.

Table 1-1. The ISO 7-layer Model

Layer	Name	Physical Layer
7	Application	NFS and NIS
6	Presentation	XDR
5	Session	RPC
4	Transport	TCP or UDP
3	Network	IP
2	Data Link	Ethernet
1	Physical	

Purists will note that the TCP/IP protocols do not precisely fit the specifications for the services in the ISO model. The functions performed by each layer, however, correspond very closely to the functions of each part of the TCP/IP protocol suite, and provide a good framework for visualizing how the various protocols fit together.

The lower levels have a well-defined job to do, and the higher levels rely on them to perform it independently of the particular medium or implementation. While TCP/IP most frequently is run over Ethernet, it can also be used with a synchronous serial line or fiber optic network. Different implementations of the first two network layers are used, but the higher-level protocols are unchanged. Consider an NFS server that uses all six lower protocol layers: it has no knowledge of the physical cabling connecting it to its clients. The server just worries about its NFS protocols and counts on the lower layers to do their job as well.

Throughout this book, the *network stack* or *protocol stack* refers to this layering of services. *Layer* or *level* will refer to one specific part of the stack and its relationship to its upper and lower neighbors. Understanding the basic structure of the network services on which NFS and NIS are built is essential for designing and configuring large networks, as well as debugging problems. A failure or overly tight constraint in a lower-level protocol affects the operation of all protocols above it. If the physical network cannot handle the load placed on it by all of the desktop workstations and servers, then NFS and NIS will not function properly. Even though NFS or NIS will appear "broken," the real issue is with a lower level in the network stack.

The following sections briefly describe the function of each layer and the mapping of NFS and NIS into them. Many books have been written about the ISO 7-layer model, TCP/IP, and Ethernet, so their treatment here is intentionally light. If you find this discussion of networking fundamentals too basic, feel free to skip over this chapter.

Physical and Data Link Layers

The physical and data link layers of the network protocol stack together define a machine's *network interface*. From a software perspective, the network interface defines how the Ethernet device driver gets packets from or to the network. The physical layer describes the way data is actually transmitted on the network medium. The data link layer defines how these streams of bits are put together into manageable chunks of data.

Ethernet is the best known implementation of the physical and data link layers. The Ethernet specification describes how bits are encoded on the cable and also how stations on the network detect the beginning and end of a transmission. We'll stick to Ethernet topics throughout this discussion, since it is the most popular network medium in networks using NFS and NIS.

Ethernet can be run over a variety of media, including thinnet, thicknet, and unshielded twisted-pair (UTP) cables. All Ethernet media are functionally equivalent—they differ only in terms of their convenience, cost of installation, and maintenance. Converters from one media to another operate at the physical layer, making a clean electrical connection between two different kinds of cable. Unless you have access to high-speed test equipment, the physical and data link layers are not that interesting when they are functioning normally. However, failures in them can have strange, intermittent effects on NFS and NIS operation. Some examples of these spectacular failures are given in "Improper Network Termination," in Chapter 11, *Debugging Network Problems*.

Frames and Network Interfaces

The data link layer defines the format of data on the network. A series of bits, with a definite beginning and end, constitutes a network *frame*, commonly called a *packet*. A proper data link layer packet has checksum and network-specific addressing information in it so that each host on the network can recognize it as a valid (or invalid) frame and determine if the packet is addressed to it. The largest packet that can be sent through the data link layer defines the *Maximum Transmission Unit*, or MTU, of the network.

All hosts have at least one network interface, although any host connected to an Ethernet has at least two: the *Ethernet interface* and the *loopback interface*. The Ethernet interface handles the physical and logical connection to the outside world, while the loopback interface allows a host to send packets to itself. If a packet's destination is the local host, the data link layer chooses to "send" it via the loopback, rather than Ethernet, interface. The loopback device simply turns the packet around and enqueues it at the bottom of the protocol stack as if it were just received from the Ethernet.

You may find it helpful to think of the protocol layers as passing packets upstream and downstream in envelopes, where the packet envelope contains some protocol-specific header information but hides the remainder of the packet contents. As data messages are passed from the top most protocol layer down to the physical layer, the messages are put into envelopes of increasing size. Each layer takes the entire message and envelope from the layer above and adds its own information, creating a new message that is slightly larger than the original. When a packet is received, the data link layer strips off its envelope and passes the result up to the network layer, which similarly removes its header information from the packet and passes it up the stack again.

Ethernet Addresses

Associated with the data link layer is a method for addressing hosts on the network. Every machine on an Ethernet has a unique, 48-bit address called its *Ethernet address* or *Media Access Control (MAC) address*. Vendors making network-ready equipment ensure that every machine in the world has a unique MAC address. 24-bit prefixes for MAC addresses are assigned to hardware vendors, and each vendor is responsible for the uniqueness of the lower 24 bits. MAC addresses are usually represented as colon-separated pairs of hex digits:

```
8:0:20:ae:6:1f
```

Note that MAC addresses identify a *host*, and a host with multiple network interfaces may (or should) use the same MAC address on each.

Part of the data link layer's protocol-specific header are the packet's source and destination MAC addresses. Each protocol layer supports the notion of a *broadcast*, which is a packet or set of packets that must be sent to all hosts on the network. The broadcast MAC address is:

```
ff:ff:ff:ff:ff:ff
```

All network interfaces recognize this wildcard MAC address as a broadcast address, and pass the packet up to a higher-level protocol handler.

Network Layer

At the data link layer, things are fairly simple. Machines agree on the format of packets and a standard 48-bit host addressing scheme. However, the packet format and encoding vary with different physical layers: Ethernet has one set of characteristics, while an X.25-based satellite network has another. Because there are many physical networks, there should ideally be a standard interface scheme so that it isn't necessary to re-implement protocols on top of each physical network and its peculiar interfaces. This is where the network layer fits in. The higher-level protocols, such as TCP (at the transport layer), don't need to know any details about the physical network that is in use. As mentioned before, TCP runs over Ethernet, fiber optic network, or other media; the TCP protocols don't care about the physical connection because it is represented by a well-defined network layer interface.

The network layer protocol of primary interest to NFS and NIS is the Internetwork Protocol, or IP. As its name implies, IP is responsible for getting packets between hosts on one or more networks. Its job is to make a best effort to get the data from point A to point B. IP makes no guarantees about getting all of the data to the destination, or the order in which the data arrives—these details are left for higher-level protocols to worry about.

On a local area network, IP has a fairly simple job, since it just moves packets from a higher-level protocol down to the data link layer. In a set of connected networks, however, IP is responsible for determining how to get data from its source to the correct destination network. The process of directing datagrams to another network is called *routing*; it is one of the primary functions of the IP protocol. Appendix B, *IP Packet Routing*, contains a detailed description of how IP performs routing.

Datagrams and Packets

IP deals with data in chunks called *datagrams*. The terms packet and datagram are often used interchangeably, although a packet is a data link-layer object and a datagram is network layer object. In many cases, particularly when using IP on Ethernet, a datagram and packet refer to the same chunk of data. There's no guarantee that the physical link layer can handle a packet of the network layer's size. As previously mentioned, the largest packet than can be handled by the physical link layer is called the Maximum Transmission Unit, or MTU, of the network media. If the media's MTU is smaller than the network's packet size, then the network layer has to break large datagrams down into packet-sized chunks that the data link and physical layers can digest. This process is called *fragmentation*. The host receiving a fragmented datagram reassembles the pieces in the correct order. For example, an X.25 network may have an MTU as small as 128 bytes, so a 1518-byte IP datagram would have to be fragmented into many smaller network packets to be sent over the X.25 link. For the scope of this book, we'll use packet to describe both the IP and the data link-layer objects, since NFS is most commonly run on Ethernet rather than over wide-area networks with smaller MTUs. However, the distinction will be made when necessary, such as when discussing NFS traffic over a wide area point-to-point link.

IP Host Addresses

The internetwork protocol identifies hosts with a 32-bit number called an *IP address* or a *host address*. To avoid confusion with MAC addresses (which are machine or *station* addresses), the term IP address will be used to designate this kind of address. IP addresses are written as four dot-separated decimal numbers between 0-255:

```
192.9.200.1
```

IP addresses must be unique among all connected machines. Connected machines in this case are any hosts that you can get to over a network or connected set of networks, including your local area network, remote offices joined by the company's wide-area network, or even the entire Internet community. For a standalone system or a small office that is not connected (via an IP network) to the outside world, IP addresses can be chosen using any convenient scheme, such as the vendor's default settings. If your network is connected to the Internet, you have to get a range of IP addresses assigned to your machines through a central network administration authority. If you are planning on joining the Internet at some future time, it's a good idea to get an Internet address from the Network Information Center for your organization before you begin installing your network. We won't go into this further in this book.

The IP address uniqueness requirement differs from that for MAC addresses. IP addresses are unique only on connected networks, but machine MAC addresses are unique in the world, independent of any connectivity. Part of the reason for the difference in the uniqueness requirement is that IP addresses are 32 bits, while MAC addresses are 48 bits, so mapping every possible MAC address into an IP address requires some overlap. Of course, not every machine on an Ethernet is running IP protocols, so the many-to-one mapping isn't as bad as the numbers might indicate. There are a variety of reasons why the IP address is only 32 bits, while the MAC address is 48 bits, most of which are historical.

Since the network and data link layers use different addressing schemes, some system is needed to convert or map the IP addresses to MAC addresses. Transport-layer services and user processes use IP addresses to identify hosts, but packets that go out on the network need MAC addresses. The Address Resolution Protocol (ARP) is used to convert the 32-bit IP address of a host into its 48-bit MAC address. When a host wants to map an IP address to a MAC address, it broadcasts an ARP request on the network, asking for the host using the IP address to respond. The host that sees its own IP address in the request returns its MAC address to the sender. With a MAC address, the sending host can transmit a packet on the Ethernet and know that the receiving host will recognize it.

IP Address Classes

Each IP address has a *network number* and a *host number*. Network numbers are assigned to organizations by the Network Information Center at the Stanford Research Institute. The host number identifies a particular machine on an organization's network. IP addresses are divided into *classes* that determine which parts of the address make up the network and host numbers, as demonstrated in Table 1-2.

Table 1-2. IP Address Classes

Address Class	First Octet Value	Network Number Octets	Host Number Octets	Address Form	Number of Hosts
Class A	1-126	1	3	N.H.H.H	254*254*254 (about 16 million)
Class B	128-191	2	2	N.N.H.H	254*254 (about 64,000)
Class C	192-223	3	1	N.N.N.H	254

Each *N* represents part of the network number and each *H* is part of the address's host number. There are 254 values for each host number octet. The 8-bit octet has 256 possible values, but 0 and 255 are reserved for forming broadcast addresses.

Network numbers with first octet values of 224-254 are reserved for future use. The network numbers 0, 127, and 255 are also reserved.

- 0 is used as a place holder in forming a network number, and in some cases, for IP broadcast addresses.

- 127 is for a host's loopback interface.

- 255 is used for IP broadcast addresses.

Note that there are only 126 Class A network numbers, but well over two million Class C networks. It is almost impossible to get a Class A network number, and few organizations (aside from entire networks or countries) have enough hosts to justify a Class A address. Most companies and universities request Class B or Class C addresses. A medium-sized company, with several hundred machines, can request several Class C network numbers, putting up to 254 hosts on each network. The distinction between the network and host number portion of an IP address is important when setting up IP broadcast addresses.

Transport Layer

The transport layer has two major jobs: it must subdivide user-sized data buffers into network layer sized datagrams, and it must enforce any desired transmission control such as reliable delivery. Two transport protocols that sit on top of IP are the Transmission Control Protocol (TCP) and the User Datagram Protocol (UDP), which offer different delivery guarantees.

TCP and UDP

TCP is best known as the first half of TCP/IP; as discussed in this and the preceding sections, the acronyms refer to two distinct services. TCP provides reliable, sequenced delivery of packets. It is ideally suited for connection-oriented communication, such as a remote login or a file transfer. Missing packets during a log-in session is both frustrating and dangerous—what happens if **rm *.o** gets truncated to **rm ***? TCP-based services are generally geared toward long-lived network connections, and TCP is used in any case when ordered datagram delivery is a requirement. There is overhead in TCP for keeping track of packet delivery order and the parts of the data stream that must be resent. This is *state* information. It's not part of the data stream, but rather describes the state of the connection and the data transfer. Maintaining this information for each connection makes TCP an inherently *stateful* protocol.

UDP is a no-frills transport protocol: it sends large datagrams to a remote host, but it makes no assurances about their delivery or the order in which they are delivered. UDP is best for connectionless communication in which no context is needed to send packets to a remote host. Broadcast-oriented services use UDP, as do those in which repeated, out of sequence, or missed requests have no harmful side effects. Since no state is maintained for UDP transmission, it is ideal for repeated, short operations such as the Remote Procedure Call protocol.

Reliable and unreliable delivery is the primary distinction between TCP and UDP. TCP will always try to replace a packet that gets lost on the network, but UDP doesn't care. UDP packets can arrive in any order. If there is a network bottleneck that drops packets, UDP packets may not arrive at all. It's up to the application built on UDP to determine that a packet was lost, and to resend it if necessary. The state maintained by TCP has a fixed cost associated with it, making UDP a faster protocol. The price paid for speed (in UDP) is unreliability and added complexity to the higher level applications that must handle lost packets.

NIS and NFS are built on top of UDP because of its speed and statelessness. While the performance advantages of a fast protocol are obvious, the stateless nature of UDP is equally important. Without state information in either the client or server, crash recovery is greatly simplified.

Port Numbers

A host may have many TCP and UDP connections at any time. Connections to a host are distinguished by a *port number*, which serves as a sort of mailbox number for incoming datagrams. There may be many processes using TCP and UDP on a single machine, and the port numbers distinguish these processes for incoming packets. When a user program opens a TCP or UDP socket, it gets connected to a port on the local host. The application may specify the port, usually when trying to reach some service with a well-defined port number, or it may allow the operating system to fill in the port number with the next available free port number.

When a packet is received and passed to the TCP or UDP handler, it gets directed to the interested user process on the basis of the destination port number in the packet. The quadruple of:

```
source IP address, source port, destination IP address, destination port
```

uniquely identifies every interhost connection in the network. While many processes may be talking to the process that handles remote log-in requests (therefore their packets have the same destination IP addresses and port numbers), they will have unique pairs of source IP addresses and port numbers. The destination port number determines which of the many processes using TCP or UDP gets the data.

Port numbers below 1024 are reserved for the processes executing with superuser privileges, while ports 1024 and above may be used by any user. This enforces some measure of security by preventing random user applications from accessing ports used by servers.

The Session and Presentation Layers

The session and presentation layers define the creation and lifetime of network connections and the format of data sent over these connections. Sessions may be built on top of any supported transport protocol—log-in sessions use TCP, while services that broadcast information about the local host use UDP. The session protocol used by both NFS and NIS is the Remote Procedure Call (RPC).

The Client-Server Model

RPC provides a mechanism for one host to make a procedure call that appears to be part of the local process but is really executed on another machine on the network. Typically, the host on which the procedure call is executed has resources that are not available on the calling host. This distribution of computing services imposes a client/server relationship on the two hosts: the host owning the resource is a server for that resource, and the calling host becomes a client of the server when it needs access to the resource. The resource might be a centralized configuration file (NIS) or a shared filesystem (NFS).

Instead of executing the procedure on the local host, the RPC system bundles up the arguments passed to the procedure into a network datagram. The exact bundling method is determined by the presentation layer, described in the next section. The RPC client creates a session by locating the appropriate server and sending the datagram to a process on the server that can execute the RPC. On the server, the arguments are unpacked, the server executes the result, packages the result (if any), and sends it back to the client. Back on the client side, the reply is converted into a return value for the procedure call, and the user application is re-entered as if a local procedure call had completed. This is the end of the "session," as defined in the ISO model.

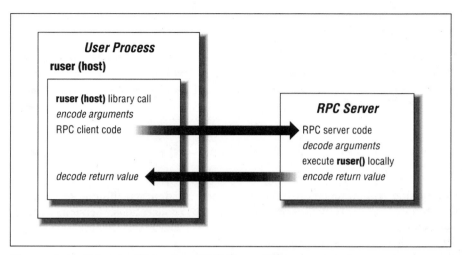

Figure 1-1. Remote Procedure Call Execution

RPC services may be built on either TCP or UDP transports, although most are UDP-oriented because they are centered around short-lived requests. Using UDP also forces the RPC call to contain enough context information for its execution independent of any other RPC requests, since UDP packets may arrive in any order, if at all.

When an RPC call is made, the client may specify a timeout period in which the call must complete. If the server is overloaded or has crashed, or if the request is lost in transit to the server, the remote call may not be executed before the timeout period expires. The action taken upon an RPC timeout varies by application; some resend the RPC call, while others may look for another server. Detailed mechanics of making an RPC call can be found in "RPC Mechanics," in Chapter 10, *Diagnostic and Administrative Tools.*

External Data Representation

At first look, the data presentation layer seems like overkill. Data is data, and if the client and server processes were written to the same specification, they should agree on the format of the data—so why bother with a presentation protocol? While a presentation layer may not be needed in a purely homogeneous network, it is required in a heterogeneous network to unify differences in data representation. These differences are outlined in the following list.

•   Data byte ordering. Does the most significant byte of an integer go in the odd- or even-numbered byte?

- Compiler behavior. Do odd-sized quantities get padded out to even-byte boundaries? How are unions handled?

- Floating point numbers. What standard is used for encoding floating point numbers?

- Arrays and strings. How do you transmit variable sized objects, such as arrays and strings?

Again, a presentation protocol would not be necessary if datagrams consisted only of byte-oriented data. However, applications that use RPC expect a system call-like interface, including support for structures and data types more complex than byte streams. The presentation layer provides services for encoding and decoding argument buffers that may then be passed down to RPC for transmission to the client or server.

The External Data Representation (XDR) protocol was developed by Sun Microsystems and is used by NIS and NFS at the presentation layer. XDR is built on the notion of an immutable network byte ordering, called the *canonical form.* It isn't really important what the canonical form is—your system may or may not use the same byte ordering and structure packing conventions. The canonical form simply allows network hosts to exchange structured data (as opposed to streams of bytes) independently of any peculiarities of a particular machine. All data structures are converted into the network byte ordering and padded appropriately.

The rule of XDR is "sender makes local canonical; receiver makes canonical local." Any data that goes over the network is in canonical form.* A host sending data on the network converts it to canonical form, and the host that receives the data converts it back into its local representation. A different way to implement the presentation layer might be "receiver makes local." In this case, the sender does nothing to the local data, and the receiver must deduce the packing and encoding technique and convert it into the local equivalent. While this scheme may send less data over the network—since it is not subject to additional padding—it places the burden of incorporating a new hardware architecture on the receiving side, rather than on the new machine. This doesn't seem like a major distinction, but consider having to change all existing, fielded software to handle the new machine's structure-packing conventions. It's usually worth the overhead of converting to and from canonical form to ensure that all new machines will be able to "plug in" to the network without any software changes.

---

*The canonical form matches the byte ordering of the Motorola and SPARC family of microprocessors, so that these processors do not have to perform any byte swapping to translate to or from canonical form.

The XDR and RPC layers complete the foundation necessary for a client/server distributed computing relationship. Both NFS and NIS are client/server applications, which means they sit at the top layer of the protocol stack and use the XDR and RPC services. To complete this introduction to network services, we'll take a look at the two mechanisms used to start and maintain servers for various network services.

Internet and RPC Server Configuration

The XDR and RPC services are useful for applications that need to exchange data structures over the network. Each new RPC request contains all required information in its XDR-encoded arguments, just as a local procedure call gets its inputs from passed-in arguments. RPC services are usually *connectionless* services because RPC requests do not require the creation of a long-lived network connection between the client and server. The client communicates with the server to send its request and receive a reply, but there is no connection or environment for the communication.

There are many other network services, such as **telnet and ftp,** that are commonly referred to as the Internet or ARPA services. They are part of the original suite of utilities designed for use on the ARPAnet (now officially the Internet). Internet services are generally based on the TCP protocol and are *connection-oriented—* the service client establishes a connection to a server, and data is then exchanged in the form of a well-ordered byte stream. There is no need for RPC or XDR services, since the data is byte-oriented, and the service defines its own protocols for handling the data stream. The **telnet** service, for example, has its own protocol for querying the server about end-of-line, terminal type, and flow control conventions.

Note that RPC services are not required to be connectionless. RPC can be run over TCP, in a connection-oriented fashion. The TCP transport protocol may be used with RPC services whenever a large amount of data needs to be transferred. The Network Information Service, for example, uses UDP (in connectionless mode) for most of its operations, but switches to TCP whenever it needs to transfer an entire database from one machine to another.

All Internet services are managed by a super-daemon called **inetd** that accepts requests for connections to servers and starts instances of those servers on an as-needed basis. Rather than having many server processes, or *daemons,* running on each host, **inetd** starts them as requests arrive. Clients contact the **inetd** daemon on well-known port numbers for each service. These port numbers are published in the **/etc/services** file.

inetd sets up a one-to-one relationship between service clients and server-side daemons. Every **rlogin** shell, for example, has a client side **rlogin** process (that calls **inetd** upon invocation) and a server-side **in.rlogind** daemon that was started by **inetd**. In this regard, **inetd** and the services it supports are *multi-threaded*: they can service multiple clients at the same time, creating a new separate connection (and state information) for each client. A new server instance, or thread, is initiated by each request for that service, but a single daemon handles all incoming requests at once.

Only traffic specific to a single session moves over the connection between a client and its server. When the client is done with the service, it asks the server to terminate its connection, and the server daemon cleans up and exits. If the server prematurely ends the connection due to a crash, for example, the client drops its end of the connection as well.

RPC services can't afford the overhead of using **inetd**. The standard **inetd** based services, like **telnet**, tend to be used for a long time, so the cost of talking to **inetd** and having it start a new server process is spread out over the lifetime of the connection. RPC calls are short in duration, lasting at most the time required to perform a disk operation.

RPC servers are generally started during the boot process and run as long as the machine is up. While the time required to start a new server process may be small compared to the time a remote log-in or **rsh** session exists, this overhead is simply too large for efficient RPC operation. As a result, RPC servers are *single-threaded*: there is one server process for the RPC service, and it executes remote requests from all clients one at a time. To achieve better performance, two or more copies of the same RPC server may be started, but each server instance still handles only one request at a time. There may be many clients of the RPC server, but their requests intermingle in the RPC server queue and are processed in the order in which they are received.

Instead of using pre-assigned ports and a super-server, RPC servers are designated by service number. The file **/etc/rpc** contains a list of RPC servers and their program numbers. Each program may contain many procedures. The NFS program, for example, contains more than a dozen procedures, one for each filesystem operation such as "read block," "write block," "create file," "make symbolic link," and so on. RPC services still must use TCP/UDP port numbers to fit the underlying protocols, so the mapping of RPC program numbers to port numbers is handled by the **portmap** daemon.

When an RPC server initializes, it registers its service with the portmapper. The RPC server tells the portmapper which ports it will listen on for incoming requests, rather than having the portmapper listen for it, in **inetd** fashion. An RPC client contacts the portmapper daemon on the server to determine the port number used by the RPC server, or it may ask the portmapper to call the server indirectly on its behalf. In either case, the first RPC call from a client to a server must be made with the portmapper running. If the portmapper dies, clients will be unable to locate RPC daemons services on the server. A server without a running port-mapper effectively stops serving NIS, NFS, and other RPC-based applications.

We'll come back to RPC mechanics and debugging techniques in later chapters. For now, this introduction to the configuration and use of RPC services suffices as a foundation for explaining the NFS and NIS applications built on top of them.

2

Network Information Service Operation

Masters, Slaves, and Clients
Basics of NIS Management
Files Managed Under NIS
NIS Design and Implementation
Trace of a Key Match

A major problem in running a distributed computing environment is maintaining separate copies of common configuration files such as the password, group, and hosts files. Ideally, the network should be consistent in its configuration, so that users don't have to worry about where they have accounts or if they'll be able to find a new machine on the network. Preserving consistency, however, means that every change to one of these common files must be propagated to every host on the network. In a small network, this might not be a major chore, but in a computing environment with hundreds or thousands of systems, simple administrative tasks can turn into all-day projects. Furthermore, without an automated tool for making changes, the probability of making mistakes grows with the size of the network and the number of places where changes must be made.

The Network Information System (NIS) addresses these problems. It is a distributed database system that replaces copies of commonly replicated configuration files with a centralized management facility. Instead of having to manage each host's files (like **/etc/hosts**, **/etc/passwd**, **/etc/group**, **/etc/ethers**, and so on), you maintain one database for each file on one central server. Machines that are using NIS retrieve information as needed from these databases. If you add a new system to the network, you can modify one file on a central server and propagate this change to the rest of the network, rather than changing the **hosts** file for each individual host on the network. For a network of two or three systems, the difference may not be crucial; but for a large network with hundreds of systems, NIS is life-saving.

Because NIS enforces consistent views of files on the network, it is suited for files that have no host-specific information in them. The **/etc/fstab** file of filesystems and mount points, for example, is a terrible candidate for management by NIS because it's different on just about every machine. Files that are generally the same on all hosts in a network, such as **/etc/passwd** and **/etc/hosts**, fit the NIS model of a distributed database nicely. Some files, like the **hosts** file, are ignored entirely once NIS is running; NIS provides all "hosts" information from its global database. For other files, like **passwd**, the local file is augmented by the global database, allowing you to mix host-specific information with global information.

In addition to managing configuration files, NIS can be used for any general data file that is accessed on one or more key fields. In a later chapter, we will discuss how to use NIS to manage your own site-specific databases.

This discussion of networking services starts with NIS because it provides the consistency that is a prerequisite for the successful administration of a distributed filesystem. Imagine a network in which you share files from a common server, but you have a different home directory and user ID value on every host. The advantages of the shared filesystem are lost in such a loosely run network: you can't always read or write your files due to permission problems, and you don't get a consistent view of your files between machines because you don't always end up in the same home directory. We'll start with a brief description of the different roles systems play under NIS, and then look at how to install NIS on each type of machine.

Masters, Slaves, and Clients

NIS is built on the client-server model. An NIS server is a host that contains NIS data files, called *maps*. Clients are hosts that request information from these maps. Servers are further divided into master and slave servers: the master server is the true single owner of the map data. Slave NIS servers handle client requests, but they do not modify the NIS maps. The master server is responsible for all map maintenance and distribution to its slave servers. Once an NIS map is built on the master to include a change, the new map file is distributed to all slave servers. NIS clients "see" these changes when they perform queries on the map file—it doesn't matter whether the clients are talking to a master or a slave server, because once the map data is distributed, all NIS servers have the same information.

Before going any futher, let's take a quick and simple look at how this works. Figure 2-1 shows the relationship between masters, slaves, and clients.

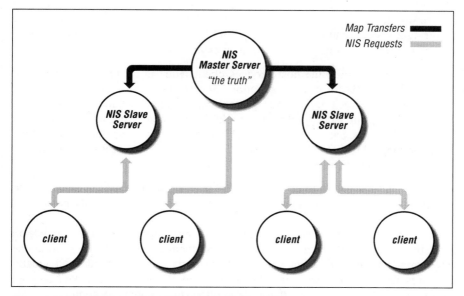

Figure 2-1. NIS masters, slaves, and clients

Consider the *hosts* NIS map, which replaces the **/etc/hosts** files on individual systems. If you're familiar with UNIX adminstration, you know that this file tells the system how to convert hostnames into IP (internet) addresses. When a client needs to look up the internet address of some system, it would normally read the **hosts** file. If NIS is running, however, the client bypasses its **hosts** file, and instead asks an NIS server (either a master or a slave server—it doesn't make any difference) for the information it needs.

Now the other side of the coin: you've added a system, and need to modify the *hosts* NIS map. You only modify the **hosts** file on the "master server"—remember, the master server knows the "truth" about the network.* Once you've made your changes, you can rebuild the NIS database (i.e., the NIS maps) on the master server. The master server then distributes new versions of the NIS maps to the slave servers, which now provide the updated information to the NIS clients.

---

* Remember: when you want to make a global change to the network, you MUST modify the file on the master server. Global changes made to slave servers or clients will, at best, be ignored.

With the distinction between NIS servers and clients firmly established, we can see that each system fits into the NIS scheme in one of three ways:

- Client only. This is typical of desktop workstations, where the system administrator tries to minimize the amount of host-specific tailoring required to bring a system onto the network. As an NIS client, the host gets all of its common configuration information from an extant server.

- Server only. While the host services client requests for map information, it does not use NIS for its own operation. Server-only configuration may be useful when a server must provide global host and password information for the NIS clients, but security concerns prohibit the server from using these same files. However, bypassing the central configuration scheme opens some of the same loopholes that NIS was intended to close. Although it is possible to configure a system to be an NIS server only, we don't recommend it.

- Client and server. In most cases, an NIS server also functions as an NIS client so that its management is streamlined with that of other client-only hosts.

On a client host, NIS is usually an all-or-nothing proposition. It is possible to limit the scope of NIS to a few files that are changed infrequently, such as the /etc/protocols file, but doing so defeats the purpose of using NIS and greatly increases the cost of network management. Once NIS is running, it will be used by all system library functions that refer to maps (files) under NIS control.

Now that we have this client-server model for the major administrative files, we need a way to discuss where and when a particular set of files applies to a given host. It is much too simple-minded for a single set of files to apply to every host on a network; a reasonable system must support different clusters of systems with different administrative requirements. For example, a group of administrative systems and a group of research systems might share the same network. In most cases, these two clusters of systems don't need to share the same administrative information. In some cases, sharing the same administrative files might be harmful.

To allow an administrator to set different policies for different systems, NIS provides the concept of a *domain*. Most precisely, a domain is a set of NIS maps. A client can refer to a map (for example, the *hosts* map) from any of several different domains. Most of the time, however, any given host will only look up data from one set of NIS maps. Therefore, it's common (although not precisely correct) to use the term "domain" to mean "the group of systems that share a set of NIS maps." All systems that need to share common configuration information are put into an NIS domain. Although each system can potentially look up information in any NIS domain, each system is assigned to a "default domain," meaning that the system, by default, looks up information from a particular set of NIS maps. In our example, the research systems would, by default, look at the maps in the *research* domain, rather than the maps from the *accounting* domain; and so on.

It is up to the administrator (or administrators) to decide how many different domains are needed. In Chapter 3, *System Management Using the Network Information Service*, we will give some rules-of-thumb for deciding how many domains are needed. Lest you think this is terribly complex, we'll tell you now: many networks, possibly even most small networks, can get by with a single domain. We will also take a closer look at the precise definition of an NIS domain.

Basics of NIS Management

Now that we have laid a conceptual foundation, let's look at how to set the machinery in motion. Basic NIS management involves setting up NIS servers and enabling NIS on client hosts. Server management includes three tasks:

- Installing a new NIS environment, building both master and slave servers.

- Starting the **ypserv** daemon, which enables the system to act as an NIS server.

- Adding new slave servers when growth of your network or NIS performance requires more server bandwidth.

Enabling NIS on a client requires two tasks:

- Modifying the client's administrative files so that the client can take advantage of NIS.

- Starting the **ypbind** daemon, which allows the client to make NIS requests.

In this section, we'll review the procedures required to initialize NIS, set up slave servers, and configure NIS clients.

Choosing NIS Servers

First, a few words on how to plan your network. One of the most important decisions you will make is which systems will be your NIS servers. Because a client gets almost all of its configuration information from NIS, servers must be highly available in measures of both uptime and request handling bandwidth. If an NIS server stops responding or replies too slowly, the client tries to find another, less-loaded server. While this is an argument for at least one slave server for each master server, it supports an equally strong case for building NIS on reliable hosts.

An interruption in NIS service affects all NIS clients if no other servers are available. Even if another server is available, clients will suffer periodic slowdowns as they recognize the current server is down and hunt for a new one.

Use your judgment in defining "highly available." You know what machines have troublesome hardware or are likely to be commandeered for a trade show, and would therefore make poor NIS servers. Request handling bandwidth is much harder to measure, because it is a product of network loading, CPU utilization, and disk activity. In later chapters, we'll come back to choosing the number of NIS servers and identifying signs that you have too few servers.

A second imperative for NIS servers is synchronization. Clients may get their NIS information from any server, so all servers must have copies of every map file to ensure proper NIS operation. Furthermore, the data in each map on the slave servers must agree with that on the master server, so that NIS clients cannot get out-of-date or stale data. NIS contains several mechanisms for making changes to map files and distributing these changes to all NIS servers on a regular basis.

Installing the NIS Master Server

We'll assume that you've already done your planning and decided that you need a single NIS domain, which will be called *bedrock*.* Before going any further, make sure you've set the NIS domain name on the master server using **domainname**. We'll install a server for an NIS domain named *bedrock*:

```
newmaster# domainname bedrock
```

A line like this will usually appear in the **/etc/rc.local** file for every host (server and client) in the domain. A **domainname** line (probably reading **domainname noname**)† will already be in **/etc/rc.local** if you have loaded the NIS software on your system. Setting the domainname if you aren't using NIS is harmless.

After establishing the domain's name, you should go over all the system's administrative files with a fine-toothed comb: make sure they contain only the entries you want, no more, and no less. It is important for your network to start with correct map information. Which administrative files NIS cares about varies, but generally includes the information shown in Table 2-1.

---

* The multiple-domain case is really no different than this; you just have to remember which systems belong to which domain.

† There's a laudable tendency to rewrite the **/etc/rc** files so that they never need to be touched. On such systems, the **domainname** command will look like this:

```
domainname `cat /etc/defaultdomain`
```

To set the domain name, just put it in the file **/etc/defaultdomain** and reboot.

Table 2-1. Files Managed by NIS

File	Contains
/etc/bootparams	Information about diskless nodes.
/etc/ethers	Ethernet numbers (MAC addresses).
/etc/group	User groups.
/etc/hosts	Hostnames and IP addresses.
/etc/aliases	Aliases and mailing lists for the mail system.
/etc/netgroup	Netgroup definitions (used by NIS).
/etc/netmasks	Network "masks."
/etc/networks	Network addresses.
/etc/passwd	User names, user IDs, and passwords.
/etc/protocols	Network protocol names and numbers.
/etc/rpc	Remote procedure call program numbers.
/etc/services	Network port numbers and service names.

With the exception of **netgroup,** these are all standard UNIX administrative files. Once NIS is running, it will replace or supplement all of these files. **/etc/netgroup** is a new administrative file that is only consulted via the NIS database. Before creating it, see the section "Netgroups" later in this chapter.

Make sure that your **/etc/passwd** file on the master server does *not* include the entry:

```
+::0:0::
```

This entry is used by NIS client hosts to indicate that they want to include NIS map information in their password files. On the NIS master server, all entries in the **/etc/passwd** file get put into the *passwd* NIS map. If you leave this NIS "marker" in the master server's **/etc/passwd** file, your NIS password file map will contain an entry for a user named +. If you do leave the entry in the password file, be sure to put an asterisk (*****) in the password field so that this "user" will not have a valid password:

```
+:*:0:0::
```

Note that this will not work under all operating systems, in particular you must not use an asterisk in SunOS 4.0 or later. If you cannot fill the password field of the NIS "marker" entry, make sure you remove this entry if you decide not to run NIS at some future point.

If you are using NIS to manage any local files (company phone lists, etc.), you must also make sure that your local source files are up-to-date. Once you have established the domain's name and "purified" the master server's source files, you're ready to initialize a master server. To do so, you will use the **ypinit** utility. To create a new master server, become the superuser on the host and invoke **ypinit** with the **–m** flag:

satin # /usr/sbin/ypinit

```
newmaster# /usr/etc/yp/ypinit -m
```

ypinit builds the domain subdirectory of **/var/yp** or **/etc/yp** for the current default domain. Note that the **ypinit** utility lives in **/usr/etc/yp**, so you should use its full pathname if you don't have this directory in your search path. In this example, **ypinit** creates **/var/yp/bedrock**.

After building the domain subdirectory, **ypinit** builds a complete set of administrative maps for your system and places them in this directory. The first map created by **ypinit –m** is the *ypservers* map. **ypinit** will ask you for a list of hosts that will be running NIS. The hosts named in the *ypservers* map do not have to be running NIS at that time, but they should become NIS servers before the first modifications are made to NIS maps.

You should have only one master server per NIS domain. If you need additional server horsepower, add NIS slave servers in the same domain. There is nothing in **ypinit** that checks for the existence of another master server, so it's possible to create two masters accidentally in the same domain. Having more than one master confuses procedures that contact the NIS master, such as map transfers and NIS password file updates.

Once **ypinit** finishes, you should start NIS service by manually giving the command **ypserv** or by rebooting the server host. The relevant part of **/etc/rc.local** normally looks like this:

```
if [ -f /usr/etc/ypserv -a -d /var/yp/`domainname` ]; then
    ypserv;                     echo -n ' ypserv'
fi
```

Note that you probably don't need to touch this line at all. It has probably been a part of your **rc.local** file since you bought the system. **ypserv** has been effectively disabled because the NIS map directory (**/var/yp/'domainname'**) doesn't exist. Among other things, running **ypinit** created this directory, allowing the system to become an NIS server. In some cases, the shell commands to start the NIS server daemon are just commented out and must be uncommented to enable NIS service. The startup logic may require modifications if a server is a client of one domain but serves another; this situation sometimes occurs when a host is on multiple networks. Issues surrounding multiple domains are left for the next chapter.

You are now ready to add new slave servers or to set up NIS clients. Note that NIS *must* be running on a master server before you can proceed.

Installing NIS Slave Servers

Slave servers are also initialized using **ypinit**. Instead of specifying the –m option, use –s and the name of the NIS master server:

```
newslave# /usr/etc/yp/ypinit -s newmaster
```

The new slave server should have had its NIS domain name set with **domainname** and the NIS master *newmaster* must have been initialized and running NIS.

The NIS master server listed on the command line also must be reachable from the new slave server, if there are no other NIS slave servers for this domain running on the local network. This means that the master and slave must be on the same IP network, so that IP broadcasts from the new slave will be heard by the master. If the master and slave are on two different IP networks, you can still perform the initialization if you set up the slave as an NIS client, and use **ypset** to explicitly point it at the NIS master (see "Modifying Client Bindings," in Chapter 10, *Diagnostic and Administrative Tools*).

When you initialize a new slave server, it transfers the data from the master server's map files and builds its own copies of the maps. No ASCII source files are used to build the NIS maps on a slave server—only the information already in the master server's maps. If the slave has information in ASCII configuration files that belongs in the NIS maps, make sure the master NIS server has a copy of this data before beginning the NIS installation. For example, having password file entries only on an NIS slave server will not add them to the NIS *passwd* map. The map source files on the master server must contain *all* map information, since it is the only host that constructs map files from their sources.

Adding Slave Servers Later

In general, it is a good idea to initialize your NIS slave servers as soon as possible after building the master server, so that there are no inconsistencies between the *ypservers* map and the hosts that are really running NIS. Once the initial installation is complete, though, you can add slave servers at any time. If you add an NIS slave server that was not listed in the *ypservers* map, you must add its hostname to this map so that it receives NIS map updates.

To edit *ypservers*, dump out its old contents with **ypcat**, add the new slave server name, and rebuild the map using **makedbm**. This procedure should be done on the NIS master server:

```
master# ypcat -k ypservers > /tmp/ypservers
Edit /tmp/ypservers to add new server name
master# cd /var/yp
master# cat /tmp/ypservers | makedbm - /var/yp/`domainname`/ypservers
```

The new NIS slave server will then receive map updates from the master server.

Once you've changed the master *ypservers* map, you can run **ypinit –s** on the slave (to initialize it) and **ypserv** (to start actual NIS service).

Enabling NIS on Client Hosts

Once you have one or more NIS servers running **ypserv**, you can set up NIS clients that query them. Make sure you do not enable NIS on any clients until you have at least one NIS server up and running. If no servers are available, the host that attempts to run as an NIS client will hang.

To enable NIS on a client host, you must do three things:

1. Make sure that configuration files on the client include NIS "marker" entries so that NIS map information will be added to the local files.

2. Set the NIS domain name on the client, using the **domainname** utility.

3. Start the **ypbind** daemon, which is responsible for locating NIS servers and maintaining bindings of domain names to servers.

Once NIS is running, references to the basic administrative files are handled in two fundamentally different ways:

- The NIS database *replaces* some files. Local copies of replaced files (**ethers, hosts, netmasks, netgroups,* networks, protocols, rpc,** and **services**) are ignored as soon as the **ypbind** daemon is started (to enable NIS).

- Some files are *augmented*, or *appended* to, by NIS. Files that are appended, or augmented, by NIS are consulted before the NIS maps are queried. The appended files are **passwd, bootparams, group,** and **aliases**. These files are read first, and if an appropriate entry isn't found in the local file, the corresponding NIS map is consulted. For example, when a user logs in, an NIS client will first look up the user's login name in the local **passwd** file; if it does not find anything that matches, it will refer to the NIS *passwd* map.

Although the replaced files aren't consulted once NIS is running, they shouldn't be deleted entirely. In particular, the **/etc/hosts** file is used by an NIS client during the boot process, before it starts NIS, but is ignored as soon as NIS is running. The NIS client needs a "runt" **hosts** file during the boot process so that it can get

---

* The **netgroups** file is a special case. Netgroups are only meaningful when NIS is running, in which case the *netgroups* map (rather than the file) is consulted. The **netgroups** file is therefore only used to build the *netgroups* map; it is never "consulted" in its own right.

configure itself and get NIS running. Administrators usually truncate **hosts** to the absolute minimum: entries for the host itself and the "loopback" address. Diskless nodes need additional entries for the node's boot server and the server for the diskless node's **/usr** filesystem. Trimming the **hosts** file to these minimal entries is a good idea because, for historical reasons, many systems have extremely long host tables. Other files, like **rpc, services,** and **protocols,** could probably be eliminated, but it's safest to leave the files distributed with your system untouched; these will certainly have enough information to get your system booted safely, particularly if NIS stops running for some reason. However, you can make any local additions to these files on the master server alone. You don't need to bother keeping the slaves and clients "up to date."

We'll take a much closer look at the files managed by NIS and the mechanisms used to manage appended files in the section "Files Managed Under NIS." Meanwhile, we'll assume that you have modified these files correctly and proceed with NIS setup.

The NIS domain name is usually set inside the **/etc/rc.local** boot script, followed by an invocation of **ypbind**:

```
domainname bedrock
...
if [ -d /var/yp ]; then
        ypbind;      echo -n ' ypbind'
fi
```

The invocation of **domainname** sets the default domain name for the NIS client. In this example, **ypbind** is started only if the directory **/var/yp** exists. This directory is used by **ypbind** for temporary files. You can also start **ypbind** manually, after setting the NIS domain name:

```
client# domainname bedrock
client# ypbind
```

NIS Masters as Clients

Now is a good time to think about whether or not the NIS master server should also be an NIS client. This may not seem prudent—after all, you might want to restrict access to the master server, and that may not be possible if the master server's **passwd** file is a complete master list for the network.

We recommend that all NIS servers be clients. Many bizarre side effects can result from creating a server that doesn't have access to all of the network's information. If the NIS master server is also the mail delivery host, using an alternative password that does not include the NIS password map file will break mail delivery. Not all users will be known to the system, so deliverable mail will be returned. Furthermore, some user's home directories and **.forward** files (used for mail forwarding) will not be found if their local password file entries contradict the NIS maps. The costs of managing a server without NIS exceed the limited security this configuration offers.

How do you restrict access on an NIS server? If the server must be made secure by reducing the password file to a bare minimum, then the NIS password file map can be generated from an alternative password file, such as **passwd.global**. (This requires modifying the NIS **Makefile**; we'll discuss how in "Using Alternate Map Source Files," in Chapter 3, *System Management Using NIS*.) **passwd.global** would be the all-inclusive, net-wide password file. The server's password file, **/etc/passwd**, remains intact, but you can still use NIS to manage it: you can include the entire NIS map or you can use netgroups (which we'll discuss later in the chapter) to implement more restricted access.

Finally, note that most sites probably don't need this extra security. In this case, the master server simply uses the "plain" **/etc/passwd** file to build the NIS map.

Files Managed Under NIS

Now that we've walked through the set-up procedure, we will discuss how the NIS maps relate to the files that they replace. In particular, we'll discuss how to modify the files that are appended by NIS so they can take advantage of NIS features. We will also pay special attention to the *netgroups* NIS map, a confusing but nevertheless important part of the overall picture.

Table 2-2 lists the most common files managed by NIS. Not all vendors use NIS for all of these files, so it is best to check your documentation for a list of NIS-supported files.

Table 2-2. Summary of NIS Maps

Map Name	Nickname	Access By	Contains	Integration
bootparams		Hostname	/etc/bootparams	Append
ethers.byname	ethers	Hostname	/etc/ethers	Replace
ethers.byaddr		MAC address	/etc/ethers	Replace
group.byname	group	Group name	/etc/group	Append
group.bygid		Group ID	/etc/group	Append
hosts.byname	hosts	Hostname	/etc/hosts	Replace
hosts.byaddr		IP address	/etc/hosts	Replace
mail.aliases	aliases	Alias name	/etc/aliases	Append
mail.byaddr		Expanded alias	/etc/aliases	Append
netgroup.byhost		Hostname	/etc/netgroup	Replace
netgroup.byuser		Username	/etc/netgroup	Replace
netid.byname		Username	UID & GID info	Derived
netmasks.byaddr		IP address	/etc/netmasks	Replace
networks.byname		Network name	/etc/networks	Replace
networks.byaddr		IP address	/etc/networks	Replace
passwd.byname	passwd	Username	/etc/passwd	Append
passwd.byuid		User ID	/etc/passwd	Append
protocols.bynumber	protocols	Port number	/etc/protocols	Replace
protocols.byname		Protocol name	/etc/protocols	Replace
rpc.bynumber		RPC number	/etc/rpc	Replace
services.byname	services	Service name	/etc/services	Replace
ypservers		Hostname	NIS server names	Replace

It's now time to face up to some distortions we've been making for the sake of simplicity. We've assumed that there's a one-to-one correspondence between files and maps. In fact, there are usually several maps for each file. A map really corresponds to a particular way of accessing a file: for example, the *passwd.byname* map looks up data in the password database by username. There's also a *passwd.byuid* that looks up users according to their user ID number. There could be (but there aren't) additional maps that looked up users on the basis of their group ID number, home directory, or even their choice of log-in shell. To make things a bit easier, the most commonly used maps have "nicknames," which correspond directly to the name of the original file: for example, the nickname for *passwd.byname* is simply *passwd*. Using nicknames as if they were map names rarely causes problems—but it's important to realize that there is a distinction. It's also important to realize the "nicknames" are only recognized by two NIS utilities: **ypmatch** and **ypcat**.

Another distortion: this is the first time we've seen the *netid.byname* map. This map is not based on any single source file, but instead is derived from information in the group, password, and hosts files. It contains one entry for each user in the password file. The data associated with the username is a list of every group to which the user belongs. The *netid* is used to determine group memberships quickly when a user logs in. Instead of reading the entire *group* map, searching for the user's name, the **login** process performs a single map lookup on the *netid* map. You usually don't have to worry about this map—it will be built for you as needed—but you should be aware that it exists.

Working with the Maps

Earlier, we introduced the concept of replaced files and appended files. Now, we'll discuss how to work with these files. First, some review: these are important concepts, so repetition is helpful. If a map *replaces* the local file, the file is ignored once NIS is running. Aside from making sure that misplaced optimism doesn't lead you to delete the files that were distributed with your system, there's nothing interesting that you can do with these replaced files. We won't have anything further to say about them.

Conversely, local files that are *appended* to by NIS maps are always consulted first, even if NIS is running. The password file is a good example of a file augmented by NIS. You may want to give some users access to one or two machines, and not include them in the NIS password map. The solution to this problem is to put these users into the local **passwd** file, but not into the master **passwd** file on the master server. The local password file is always read before **getpwuid()** goes to an NIS server. Password-file reading routines find locally defined users as well as those in the NIS map, and the search order of "local, then NIS" allows local password file entries to override values in the NIS map. Similarly, the local aliases file can be used to override entries in the NIS mail aliases map, setting up machine-specific expansion of one or more aliases.

There is yet another group of files that can be augmented with data from NIS. These files are not managed by NIS directly, but to which you can add special entries referring to the NIS database (in particular, the *netgroups* map). Such files include **hosts.equiv** and **.rhosts**. We won't discuss these files in this chapter; we will treat them as the need arises. For example, we will discuss **hosts.equiv** in Chapter 8, *Network Security*.

Now we're going to discuss the special *netgroups* map. This new database is the basis for the most useful extensions to the standard administrative files; it is what prevents NIS from becoming a rigid, inflexible system. After our discussion of netgroups, we will pay special attention to the appended files.

Netgroups

In addition to the standard password, group, and host file databases, NIS introduces a new database for creating sets of users and hosts called the *netgroup* map. The user and hostname fields are used to define groups (of hosts or users) for administrative purposes. For example, to define a subset of the users in the *passwd* map that should be given access to a specific machine, you can create a netgroup for those users.

A netgroup is a set of triples of the form:

```
(hostname, username, domain name)
```

A single netgroup contains one or more of these triples. Host and usernames have their usual meanings, but a domain name in this instance refers to the NIS domain in which the netgroup is valid. If an entry in the triple is left blank, that field becomes a wildcard. If the entry is specified as a dash (–), the field can take no value.

Netgroups are typically used to augment other maps and files; for example, adding a selected group of users to the password file. The definitions and behavior of netgroups are confusing because their syntax doesn't exactly match the way the netgroup information is used. Even though the netgroup syntax allows you to specify user and host names in the same triple, user and hostnames are rarely used *together*. For example, when a netgroup is used to add users to an NIS-managed password file, only the usernames are taken from the netgroup. The hostnames are ignored, because hostnames have no place in the password file. Similarly, when using a netgroup to grant filesystem access permissions to a set of NFS clients, only the hostname fields in the netgroup are used. Usernames are ignored in this case, which means a hostname will be included in the list even if – is used as the username in its triple.

Some examples are helpful:

```
source (-,stern,nesales), (-,julie,nesales), (-,peter,nesales)
trusted-hosts (bitatron,,), (corvette,,)
trusted-users (bitatron,stern,), (corvette,johnc,)
dangerous-users (,jimc,), (,dave,)
```

In the first example, *source* is a group of three users; in this respect, the netgroup is similar to an entry in **/etc/group**. The *source* netgroup above grants no specific permissions, although it could be included in the password file for the source archive machine, granting selected users access to that host. The second example shows a definition for a set of hosts, and would be of no use in a password file. In the third example, *stern* and *johnc* are members of the *trusted-users* group when it is parsed for usernames. Hosts *bitatron* and *corvette* are members of *trusted-users* when it is parsed for hostnames. Note that there is no interpretation of the netgroup that associates user *stern* with host *bitatron*. In the fourth example, *dave* and *jimc* are members of *dangerous-users*, but no hosts are included in this group. The domain name field is used when multiple NIS domains exist on the same network and it is necessary to create a group that is valid in only one or the other domain.

These groups are very different from those in **/etc/group**. The group file (or equivalent NIS map) explicitly grants permissions to users while the netgroup mechanism simply creates shorthand notations or nicknames. A netgroup can be used in many places where a user or hostname would appear, such as the password file or in the list of hosts that can access an NFS filesystem.

You can also build netgroups from other netgroups. For example, you could create the netgroup *hosts-n-users* from the following entry:

```
hosts-n-users trusted-hosts, trusted-users
```

This netgroup contains all the members of both *trusted-hosts* and *trusted-users*.

By using netgroups carefully, you can create special-purpose groups that can be "managed" separately. For example, you could create a group of "administrators" that can easily be added to the password list of every machine, or a group of "visitors" who are only added to the password files of certain machines.

A final note about netgroups: they are accessible *only* through NIS. The library routines that have been modified to use NIS maps have also been educated about the uses of the netgroup map, and use the *netgroup, password,* and *host* maps together. If NIS is not running, netgroups are not defined. This implies that any **netgroup** file on an NIS client is ignored, because the NIS netgroup map replaces the local file. A local netgroup file does nothing at all. The uses of netgroups will be revisited as a security mechanism.

Integrating NIS Maps with Local Files

For files that are augmented by NIS maps, you typically strip the local file to the minimum number of entries needed for bootstrap or single-user operation. You then add in entries that are valid only on the local host—for example, a user with an account on only one machine—and then integrate NIS services by adding special entries that refer to the NIS map files.

The plus sign (+) is the NIS "magic token." It is used to indicate when an NIS map, or part of a map, should be included in a file that is augmented by NIS. The plus sign marker really directs the routines that read NIS-managed configuration files to leave the local file alone and perform NIS RPC calls to the NIS server for additional information. The + is inserted into the configuration file as a normal entry, usually requiring some colon separators to make it fit the syntax of the file.

For example, consider the **/etc/group** file. We can use NIS to add to the **group** information on any host, because the NIS *group* map is appended to the local **/etc/group** file. This means that we can strip the **group** file to a few (possibly zero) system-specific entries; then we add a special + entry to insert the contents of the *groups* map, as follows:

```
ps-staff:*:20:stern,julie,peter
sysadm:*:21:stern,johnc
+:*:*
```

On many systems, the final + line would be the sole **/etc/group** file.

NOTE

Note that the NIS entry is +:*:*, not simply +. This is a security precaution. Should NIS stop running for some reason, the asterisks prevent + from becoming a valid group that could be used in unpredictable ways. You should take similar precautions when modifying the **passwd** file.

If the + token is omitted, the **/etc/group** file is the sole source of group information; this is sometimes useful in a heterogeneous server environment where different vendors' default group names and values have many clashes.

The *aliases* map is handled similarly. To integrate the **/etc/aliases** file into NIS, you only need strip the file to a minimal set of system-specific entries, and then add a + to the end of the file:

```
# end of local alias list
last-local-mail-alias george@bigfeet
# insert NIS entries
+
```

Syntactically, this is all you can do with the *aliases* map. Practically speaking, NIS and NFS can greatly simplify mail management. These issues are discussed in Chapter 9, *Centralizing Mail Services with NFS*.

And, finally, the **bootparams** file is similar to the **aliases** and **group** files. Adding a + as the last line of the file tells the system to read the global *bootparams* database after it has finished processing the local **bootparams** file.

NIS and Password Administration

Integrating NIS information into the **group** and **aliases** files is relatively simple and inflexible: it's an all-or-nothing affair. For the **passwd** file, integrating NIS information is much more flexible, but correspondingly more complex. We'll start with the simplest case.

The simplest way to integrate the NIS map into the **passwd** file is to add the entire map. To do so, trim the **passwd** file to a minimal group of system-specific entries, and add a + entry to the end of the file, as follows:

```
root:passwd:0:1:Operator:/:/bin/csh
daemon:*:1:1::/:
sys:*:2:2::/:/bin/csh
bin:*:3:3::/bin:
uucp:*:4:8::/var/spool/uucppublic:
+:*:0:0:::
```

This is exactly the same as what we did to the **group** file. The last line appends the entire NIS *passwd* map to the client's password file. The * in the password field prevents the + from becoming a valid username if NIS is *not* running. The zeros are placeholders for the user ID and group ID values, and the remaining colons are used to match the required format of **passwd** file entries.

Within the password file, there are several more selective methods for including NIS information:

- **+user** includes the NIS *passwd* map entry for **user**. For example:

  ```
  +stern:*:
  +julie:*:
  ```

  adds NIS password file entries for the two specified users to the password file.

- The *passwd* map lets you merge fields from an entry in the client's **passwd** file with fields from the global database. You can merge a local and NIS map entry using an entry like:

  ```
  +stern:*:0:0:Hal Stern - Guest:::
  ```

The UID and GID fields are taken from the NIS map entry for user *stern*, but the *gecos* (full name) field in this definition overrides the NIS map. This feature will be discussed further in the next section. An asterisk (*) is used in the password field in this entry so that it is not possible to log in as +*stern*, without a password, if NIS is not running.

- **+@netgroup** includes NIS password map entries for the users in the named netgroup; host information in the netgroup is ignored. For example, consider the netgroup defined as:

```
trusted-users (bitatron,stern,), (corvette,johnc,)
```

and inserted into the password file via the special NIS entry:

```
+@trusted-users
```

This includes the NIS password file entries for the users in netgroup *trusted-users*. Only the users in the netgroup—*stern* and *johnc*—are taken from the password file. The hostnames associated with these users have no effect on the password file entries. For example, it is *not* the case that *stern* will be included in the password file only when logging in from host *bitatron*. Netgroups in this case are really just a simple mechanism for granting selective access to subsets of the user community without having to modify individual hosts' password files each time a user is added to the group. Adding a user to the netgroup automatically includes him or her in the appropriate password files.

- **–user** or **–@netgroup** removes the NIS password entry for **user** and the users in **netgroup**, respectively. The line that subtracts the user must appear before any other **/etc/passwd** file entry that includes the user—either by including the entire NIS map, or including a netgroup containing the user as a member. For example, if user *johnc* is a member of netgroup *trusted-users*, the following **/etc/passwd** file excerpt will not remove *johnc* from the **/etc/passwd** file:

```
+@trusted-users
-johnc:*:12389:20::
+:*:0:0:::
```

Once the routines that read the password file's find a match for *johnc*, they stop parsing the file. This means that the *-johnc* entry will never be found, because the netgroup *trusted-users* includes this user.

The password file entry must contain the username, UID, and group ID. For example:

```
-johnc:*:12389:20::
-@dangerous-users
+:*:0:0:::
```

appends the entire NIS password file map to the local password file, but effectively removes password entries for user *johnc*, and users in the *dangerous-users* netgroup (*jimc* and *dave*).

We will also see the +@ and –@ notations in other files that can refer to the *netgroups* database.

Overriding the NIS Maps

When NIS consults a local file before reading one of its maps, the local file can override any key and value pair in the NIS map. Routines that do key lookup stop searching when the first match is found; finding a match in the local file prevents the routine from issuing an NIS lookup request. For example, local overrides can be used with the aliases map to redirect a user's mail on certain machines, or to resolve alias name conflicts between an established local user and a new alias in the NIS map.

The Password Map

The password file offers the most flexibility for merging local changes into NIS map entries. The NIS map always supplies the UID and GID for the given username, but local entries in the full username, shell, and home directory fields will override the defaults in the NIS map:

```
+stern:*:0:0:Hal Stern:/home/thud/stern:/bin/csh
```

In this entry, the UID and GID are filled in with dummy values; the NIS map contains the real values. Zeros just make the line fit the syntax of the **passwd** file. The explicit entries in the full name (*gecos*) field and home directory field override the values in the NIS map. This scheme is useful for users who require distinct home directories on several machines, and need to be placed in these directories upon login for proper execution of shell profile scripts. A uniform UID and GID are associated with the username on all hosts, so the user enjoys consistent file access privileges across machines.

Note that the only way to match a username with a UID different from that in the NIS map is to have a complete password file entry in the local password file. For example:

```
stern:password:1234:10:Hal Stern:/home/thud/stern:/bin/csh
+@trusted-users
```

assigns UID 1234 to *stern* on this host, even if the NIS map has a different value. This entry does not refer to NIS at all, so it "hides" the NIS *passwd* map entry for user *stern*. To be effective, the local password file entry must appear in the **passwd** file *before* another entry that would have taken the entry for *stern* from the NIS map—this is the same restriction that applies to user subtraction. For example, consider a password file containing the *trusted-users* netgroup (which contains *stern* as a member) and a complete entry for *stern*:

```
+@trusted-users
stern:password:1234:10:Hal Stern:/home/thud/stern/:/bin/csh
```

This combination of NIS and local entries does not have the desired effect: the password file entry for *stern* will be taken from the NIS map, because including the netgroup *trusted-users* includes an entry for *stern*. The routines that read the password file will use the first entry for a user.

The restriction on UID overrides is due to the **passwd.byuid** NIS map. Since this map uses the UID value as a key, it is non-trivial to determine whether another, different key clashes with the NIS map entry or even accesses a different user's entry. To avoid this problem, the NIS map entry's UID is taken to be the "truth" in all cases.

Password file overrides should be used sparingly. You may want to use them to specify different default shells on a per-machine basis. For example, if you have the Korn shell available on some machines, you can override the default shell for those users who prefer it on those hosts that support the Korn shell. However, creating non-global UID and GID values creates the very same administrative headaches that NIS was intended to cure.

The Aliases Map

In addition to the password file, the aliases file is augmented by an NIS map and can therefore use local overrides. An entry in **/etc/aliases** overrides a corresponding entry in the NIS alias map; there is no way to merge a single alias in the local aliases file with an NIS map entry. By using the local file to override entries in the global *aliases* map, you can create a common alias that gets interpreted differently on each host, allowing host-specific delivery of mail addressed to the alias. For example, creating a local alias named *problems* allows users to use:

```
% mail problems
```

to report system trouble. The NIS map would contain the default expansion of the alias, but machines that have their own (or different) system administrators would set up a local alias expansion to override the NIS default. This example is covered in more detail in "Merging NIS and Local Aliases," in Chapter 9, *Centralizing Mail Services with NFS*.

NIS Design and Implementation

At this point, we've run through most of what you need to know to get NIS running. You know how to configure a master server, a slave server, and a client; and you know how to modify the **passwd, group,** and **aliases** files to take advantage of the global NIS database. With this background out of the way, we'll look at how NIS works. Along the way, we will give more precise definitions of terms that, until now, we have been using fairly loosely. Understanding how NIS works is essential to successful debugging. It is also crucial to planning your NIS network.

NIS is built on the RPC protocol, and uses the UDP transport to move requests from the client host to the server. NIS services are integrated into the standard UNIX library calls so that they remain transparent to processes that reference NIS-managed files. If you have a process that reads **/etc/passwd**, most of the queries about that file will be handled by NIS RPC calls to an NIS server. The library calling interface used by the application does not change at all, but the implementations of library routines such as *getpwuid*() that read the **/etc/passwd** file are modified to refer to NIS or to NIS and local files. The application using *getpwuid*() is oblivious to the change in its implementation.

Therefore, when you enable NIS, you don't have to change any existing software. A vendor that supports NIS has already modified all of the relevant library calls to have them make NIS RPC calls in addition to looking at local files where relevant. Any process that used to do lookups in the host table still works; it just does something different in the depths of the library calls.

Map Files

Configuration files managed by NIS are converted into keyword and value pair tables called *maps*. We've been using the term "map" all along, as if a map were equivalent to the ASCII files that it replaces or augments. For example, we have said that the *passwd* NIS map is appended to the NIS client's **/etc/passwd** file. Now it's time to understand what a map file really is.

NIS maps are constructed from DBM database files. DBM is the database system that is built into BSD UNIX implementations; if it is not normally shipped as part of your UNIX system, your vendor will supply it as part of the NIS implementation. Under DBM, a database consists of a set of keys and associated values organized in a table with fast lookup capabilities. Every key and value pair may be located using at most two filesystem accesses, making DBM an efficient storage mechanism for NIS maps. A common way to use the password file, for example, is to locate an entry by user ID number, or UID. Using the flat **/etc/passwd** file, a linear search is required, while the same value can be retrieved from a DBM file with a single lookup. This performance improvement in data location offsets the overhead of performing a remote procedure call over the network.

Each DBM database, and therefore each NIS map, comprises two files: a hashtable accessed bitmap of indices and a data file. The index file has the **.dir** extension and the data file uses **.pag**. A database called **addresses** would be stored in:

addresses.dir	*index file*
addresses.pag	*data file*

A complete map contains both files.

Consecutive records are not packed in the data file; they are arranged in hashed order and may have empty blocks between them. As a result, the DBM data file may appear to be up to four times as large as the data that it contains. The UNIX operating system allows a file to have holes in it that are created when the file's write pointer is advanced beyond the end of the file using *lseek()*. Filesystem data blocks are allocated only for those parts of the file containing data. The empty blocks are not allocated, and the file is only as large as the total number of used filesystem blocks and fragments.

The holes in DBM files make them difficult to manipulate using standard UNIX utilities. If you try to copy an NIS map using **cp**, or move it across a filesystem boundary with **mv**, the new file will have the holes expanded into zero-filled disk blocks. When **cp** reads the file, it doesn't expect to find holes, so it reads sequentially from the first byte until the end-of-file is found. Blocks that are not allocated are read back as zeros, and written to the new file as all zeros as well. This has the unfortunate side effect of making the copied DBM files consume much more disk space than the hole-filled files. Furthermore, NIS maps will not be usable on a machine of another architecture: if you build your maps on a SPARC machine, you can't copy them to a Motorola-based machine. Map files are not ASCII files. For the administrator, the practical consequence is that you must always use NIS tools (like **ypxfr** and **yppush**, discussed later in this chapter) to move maps from one machine to another.

Map Naming

ASCII files are converted into DBM files by selecting the key field and separating it from the value field by spaces or a tab. The **makedbm** utility builds the **.dir** and **.pag** files from ASCII input files. A limitation of the DBM system is that it supports only one key per value, so files that are accessed by more than one field value require an NIS map for each key field. With a flat ASCII file, you can read the records sequentially and perform comparisons on any field in the record. However, DBM files are indexed databases, so only one field—the key—is used for comparisons. If you need to search the database in two different ways, using two fields, then you must use two NIS maps or must implement one of the searches as a linear walk through all of the records in the NIS map.

The password file is a good example of an ASCII file that is searched on multiple fields. The *getpwnam()* library call opens the password file and looks for the entry for a specific username. Equal in popularity is the *getpwuid()* library routine, which searches the database looking for the given user ID value. While *getpwnam()* is used by **login** and **chown**, *getpwuid()* is used by processes that need to match numeric user ID values to names, such as **ls –l**. To accommodate both access methods, the standard set of NIS maps includes two maps derived from the password file: one that uses the username as a key and one that uses the user ID field as a key.

The map names used by NIS indicate the source of the data and the key field. The convention for map naming is:

```
filename.bykeyname
```

The two NIS maps generated from the password file, for example, are *passwd.byname* (used by *getpwnam()*) and *passwd.byuid* (used by *getpwuid()*. These two maps are stored on disk as four files:

```
passwd.byname.dir
passwd.byname.pag
passwd.byuid.dir
passwd.byuid.pag
```

The order of the records in the maps will be different because they have different key fields driving the hash algorithm, but they contain exactly the same sets of entries.

Map Structure

Two extra entries are added to each NIS map by **makedbm**. The master server name for the map is embedded in one entry and the map's *order*, or modification timestamp, is put in the other. These additional entries allow the map to describe itself fully, without requiring NIS to keep map management data. Again, NIS is ignorant of the content of the maps and merely provides an access mechanism. The maps themselves must contain timestamp and ownership information to coordinate updates with the master NIS server.

Some maps are given nicknames based on the original file from which they are derived. Map nicknames exist only within the **ypwhich** and **ypmatch** utilities (see "NIS Tools," in Chapter 10, *Diagnostic and Administrative Tools*) that retrieve information from NIS maps. Nicknames are neither part of the NIS service nor embedded in the maps themselves. They do provide convenient shorthands for referring to popular maps such as the password or hosts files. For example, the map nickname *passwd* refers to the *passwd.byname* map, and the *hosts* nickname refers to the *hosts.byname* map. To locate the password file entry for user *stern* in the *passwd.byname* map, use **ypmatch** with the map nickname:

```
% ypmatch stern passwd
stern:passwd:1461:10:Hal Stern:/home/thud/stern:/bin/csh
```

In this example, **ypmatch** expands the nickname *passwd* to the map name *passwd.byname*, locates the key *stern* in that map, and prints the data value associated with the key.

The library routines that use NIS don't retain any information from the maps. Once a routine looks up a hostname, for example, it passes the data back to the caller and "forgets" about the transaction. Caching in NIS is both impractical and inefficient. It's impractical because there's no place to put the cached data. The client process making the NIS RPC calls can't hold data for the entire host, since the process may have a fairly short lifespan. You could keep recently retrieved information in a daemon process on the client, but this cache daemon would have to perform consistency checks on its data before returning it to a calling process. Checking the consistency of an NIS map entry is nothing more than asking the server if its map was modified since the time the data was cached. However, the consistency check is inefficient: if you have to query the server about the map's modification time, you could just as easily retrieve the desired information from the map itself.

NIS Domains

"Domain" is another term that we have used loosely; now we'll define domains more precisely. Groups of hosts that use the same set of maps form an NIS *domain*. All of the machines in an NIS domain will share the same password, hosts, and group file information. Technically, the maps themselves are grouped together to form a domain, and hosts join one or more of these NIS domains. For all practical purposes, though, an NIS domain includes both a set of maps and the machines using information in those map files.

NIS domains define spheres of system management. A domain is a name applied to a group of NIS maps. The hosts that need to look up information in the maps *bind* themselves to the domain, which involves finding an NIS server that has the maps comprising the domain. It's easy to refer to the hosts that share a set of maps and the set of maps themselves interchangeably as a domain. The important point is that NIS domains are *not* just defined as a group of hosts; NIS domains are defined around a set of maps and the hosts that use these map files. Think of setting up NIS domains as building a set of database definitions. You need to define both the contents of the database and the users or hosts that can access the data in it. When defining NIS domains, you must decide if the data in the NIS maps applies to all hosts in the domain. If not, you may need to define multiple domains. This is equivalent to deciding that you really need two or more groups of databases to meet the requirements of different groups of users and hosts.

As we've seen, the default domain name for a host is set using the **domainname** command:

```
nisclient# domainname nesales
```

This usually appears in the boot scripts; only the superuser can set or change the default domain. Without an argument, **domainname** prints the currently set domain name. Library calls that use NIS always request maps from the default domain, so setting the domain name must be the first step in NIS startup. It is possible for an application to request map information from more than one domain, but assume for now that all requests refer to maps in the current default domain.

Despite the long introduction, a domain is implemented as nothing more than a subdirectory of the top-level NIS directory, usually **/etc/yp** or **/var/yp** (under SunOS). Nothing special is required to create a new domain—you simply assign it a name and then put maps into it using the server initialization procedures described below. The map files for a domain are placed in its subdirectory:

```
/var/yp/domainname/mapname
```

You can create multiple domains by repeating the initialization using different NIS domain names. Each new domain initialization creates a new subdirectory in the NIS map directory **/var/yp**. An NIS server provides service for every domain represented by a subdirectory in **/var/yp**. If multiple subdirectories exist, the NIS server answers binding requests for all of them. You do not have to tell NIS which domains to serve explicitly—it figures this out by looking at the structure of its map directory.

It's possible to treat NIS as another administrative tool. However, it's more flexible than a simple configuration file management system. NIS resembles a database management system with multiple tables. As long as the NIS server can locate map information with well-known file naming and key lookup conventions, the contents of the map files are immaterial to the server. A relational database system such as Ingres provides the framework of schemas and views, but it doesn't care what the schemas look like or what data is in the tables. Similarly, the NIS system provides a framework for locating information in map files, but the information in the files and the existence or lack of map files themselves is not of consequence to the NIS server. There is no minimal set of map files necessary to define a domain. While this places the responsibility for map synchronization on the system manager, it also affords the flexibility of adding locally defined maps to the system that are managed and accessed in a well-known manner.

Internet Domains Versus NIS Domains

The term "domain" is used in different ways by different services. In the Internet community, a domain refers to a group of hosts that are managed by an Internet-work name service. These domains are defined strictly in terms of a group of hosts under common management, and are tied to organizations and their hierarchies. These domains include entire corporations or divisions, and may encompass several logical TCP/IP networks. The Internet domain **east.sun.com**, for example, spans six organizations spread over at least 15 states.

Domains in the NIS world differ from Internet name service domains in several ways. NIS domains exist only in the scheme of local network management and are usually driven by physical limits or political "machine ownership" issues. Because of the network broadcasts used in domain binding, an NIS domain frequently covers only a single network. There may be several NIS domains on one network, all managed by the same system administrator. Again, it is the set of maps and the hosts that use the maps that define an NIS domain, rather than a particular network partitioning. In general, you may find many NIS domains in an Internet name service domain; the name service's hostname database is built from the hostname maps in the individual NIS domains. Integration of NIS and name services is covered in "Domain Name Servers," in Chapter 3, *System Management Using NIS*. From here on, "domain" refers to an NIS domain unless explicitly noted.

The ypserv Daemon

NIS service is provided by a single daemon, **ypserv**, that handles all client requests. It's simple to tell whether a system is an NIS server: just look to see whether or not **ypserv** is running. In this section we'll look at the RPC procedures implemented as part of the NIS protocol and the facilities used to transfer maps from master to slave servers.

Three sets of procedure calls make up the NIS protocol: client lookups, map maintenance calls, and NIS internal calls. Lookup requests are key-driven, and return one record from the DBM file per call. There are four kinds of lookups: match (single key), get-first, get-next, and get-all records. The get-first and get-next requests are used to scan the NIS map linearly, although keys are returned in a random order. "First" refers to the first key encountered in the data file based on hash table ordering, not the first key from the ASCII source file placed into the map.

Map maintenance calls are used when negotiating a map transfer between master and slave servers, although they may be made by user applications as well. The get-master function returns the master server for a map and the get-order request returns the timestamp from the last generation of the map file. Both values are available as records in the NIS maps. Finally, the NIS internal calls are used to effect a map transfer and answer requests for service to a domain. An NIS server replies only positively to a service request; if it cannot serve the named domain it will not send a reply.

The server daemon does not have any intrinsic knowledge of what domains it serves or which maps are available in those domains. It answers a request for service if the domain has a subdirectory in the NIS server directory. That is, a request for service to domain *polygon* will be answered if the **/var/yp/polygon** directory exists. This directory may be empty, or may not contain a full complement of maps, but the server still answers a service request if the map directory exists. There is no NIS RPC procedure to inquire about the existence of a map on a server; a "no such map" error is returned on a failed lookup request for the missing map. This underscores the need for every NIS server to have a full set of map files—the NIS mechanism itself can't tell when a map is missing until an NIS client asks for information from it.

If the log file **/var/yp/ypserv.log** exists when **ypserv** is started, error and warning messages will be written to this file. If an NIS server receives a service request for a domain it cannot serve, it logs messages such as:

```
ypserv: Domain financials not supported (broadcast)
```

indicating that it ignored a broadcast request for an unknown domain. If each server handles only its default domain, binding attempts overheard from other domains generate large numbers of these log messages. Running multiple NIS domains on a single IP network is best done if every server can handle every domain, or if you turn off logging. If not, you will be overwhelmed with these informational error messages that do nothing but grow the log file.

ypserv keeps the file open while it is running, so a large log file must be cleaned up by truncating it:

```
# cat /dev/null > /var/yp/ypserv.log
```

Removing the file with **rm** clears the directory entry, but does not free the disk space because the **ypserv** process still has the file open. If you have multiple domains with distinct servers on a single network, you probably shouldn't enable NIS logging.

The ypbind Daemon

The **ypbind** daemon is central to NIS client operation. Whenever any system is running **ypbind**, it is an NIS client—no matter what else it is doing. Therefore, it will be worth our effort to spend some time thinking about **ypbind**.

When **ypbind** first starts, it finds a server for the host's default domain. The process of locating a server is called *binding* the domain. If processes request service from other domains, **ypbind** attempts to locate servers for them as needed. **ypbind** broadcasts a request for service for each NIS domain that it uses. If the NIS server chosen for a domain crashes or begins to respond slowly due to a high load, **ypbind** dissolves its binding and broadcasts another request for service. The NIS timeout period varies by implementation, but is usually between two and three minutes. Each client can be bound to several domains at once; **ypbind** manages these bindings and locates servers on demand for each newly referenced NIS domain.

A client in the NIS server-client relationship is not just a host, but a process on that host that needs NIS map information. Every client process must be bound to a server, and they do so by asking **ypbind** to locate a server on their behalf. **ypbind** keeps track of the server to which it is currently directing requests, so new client binding requests can be answered without having to send another broadcast for service. **ypbind** continues to use its current server until it is explicitly told, as the result of an NIS RPC timeout, that the current server is not providing prompt service. After an RPC timeout, **ypbind** will broadcast the next binding request in an attempt to locate a faster NIS server. Because all client processes go through **ypbind**, we usually don't make a distinction between the client processes and the host on which they are running—the host itself is called the NIS client.

Once **ypbind** has created a binding between a client and a server, it never talks to the server again. When a client process requests a binding, **ypbind** simply hands back the name of the server to which the queries should be directed. Once a process has bound to a server, it can use that binding until an error occurs (such as a server crash or failure to respond). A process does *not* bind its domain before each NIS RPC call.

Domain bindings are shown by **ypwhich**:

```
% domainname
nesales
% ypwhich
wahoo
```

Here, **ypwhich** reports the currently bound server for the named domain. If the default or the named domain is not bound, **ypwhich** reports an error:

```
% ypwhich -d financials
ypbind: Domain financials not bound.
```

An NIS client can be put back in standalone operation by taking the invocation of **ypbind** out of the boot scripts. This can be done by commenting out the lines that start **ypbind**, renaming the **ypbind** executable, or removing the scratch directory /etc/yp or /var/yp used by **ypbind**. The last option should be used *only* on client-only machines, otherwise you run the risk of destroying maps in the NIS directory. You can stop NIS on a client by killing the **ypbind** daemon:

```
client# ps -agux | fgrep ypbind
bin         62  0.0  0.0   40    0 ?  IW   Apr 21  0:00 ypbind
root     29185  0.0  0.8  144  248 p0 S    08:39   0:00 fgrep ypbind
client# kill -9 62
```

If NIS is disabled, the NIS markers in NIS-appended files are ignored. Make sure that the former client has enough information in its local files to survive without NIS. Turning off NIS for a diskless workstation is a disaster if the hostname of the NFS server with its root filesystem doesn't appear in its local /etc/hosts file. In general, step gingerly when disabling NIS service, and check the contents of the critical files (particularly **password**, **hosts**, and **group**) before you reboot.

NIS Server as an NIS Client

Previously, we recommended that NIS servers also be NIS clients. This has a number of important effects on the network's behavior. When NIS servers are booted, they may bind to each other instead of to themselves. A server that is booting executes a sequence of commands that keep it fairly busy; other hosts may be likely to hear the server's **ypbind** broadcast and return a valid binding before it hears its own broadcast. The first host to answer the broadcast is bound, so multiple NIS servers usually end up cross-binding—they bind to each other instead of themselves.

If servers are also NIS clients, then having only one master and one slave server creates a window in which the entire network pauses if either server goes down. If the servers have bound to each other, and one crashes, the other server rebinds to itself after a short timeout. In the interim, however, the "live" server is probably not doing useful work because it's waiting for an NIS server to respond. Increasing the number of slave servers decreases the probability that a single server crash hangs other NIS servers and consequently hangs their bound clients. In addition, running more than two NIS servers prevents all NIS clients from rebinding to the same server when an NIS server becomes unavailable.

Trace of a Key Match

Now we've seen how all of the pieces of NIS work by themselves. In reality, of course, the clients and servers must work together with a well-defined sequence of events. To fit all of the client- and server-side functionality into a time-sequenced picture, here is a walk through the *getpwuid()* library call. The inter-action of library routines and NIS daemons is shown in Figure 2-2.

1. A user runs **ls –l**, and the **ls** process needs to find the username corresponding to the UID of each file's owner. In this case, **ls –l** calls *getpwuid(11461)* to find the password file entry—and therefore username—for UID 11461.

2. The local password file looks like this:

   ```
   root:passwd:0:1:Operator:/:/bin/csh
   daemon:*:1:1::/:
   sys:*:2:2::/:/bin/csh
   bin:*:3:3::/bin:
   uucp:*:4:8::/var/spool/uucppublic:
   +:*:0:0:::
   ```

   The local file is checked first, but there is no UID 11461 in it. However, there is a plus sign (+) at the end of the file, including the entire NIS password map. *getpwuid()* decides it needs to go to NIS for the password file entry.

3. *getpwuid()* grabs the default domain name, and binds the current process to a server for this domain. The bind can be done explicitly by calling an NIS library routine, or it may be done implicitly when the first NIS lookup request is issued. In either case, **ypbind** provides a server binding for the named domain. If the default domain is used, **ypbind** returns the current binding after pinging the bound server. However, the calling process may have speci-fied another domain, forcing **ypbind** to locate a server for it. The client may have bindings to several domains at any time, all of which are managed by the single **ypbind** process.

4. The client process calls the NIS lookup RPC with *key=11461* and *map=passwd.byuid*. The request is bundled up and sent to the **ypserv** process on the bound server.

5. The server does a DBM key lookup and returns a password file entry, if one is found. The record is passed back to the *getpwuid()* routine, where it is returned to the calling application.

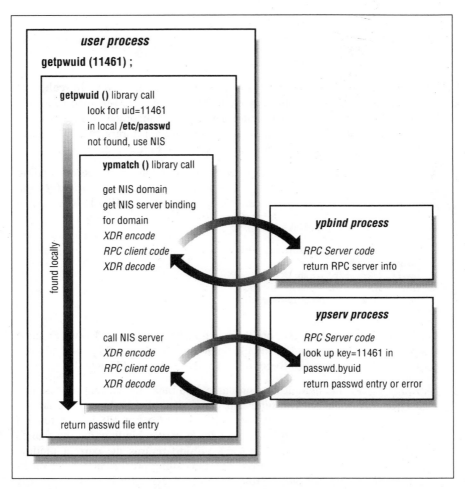

Figure 2-2. Trace of the getpwuid() Library Call

The server can return a number of errors on a lookup request. Obviously, the specified key might not exist in the DBM file, or the map file itself might not be present on the server. At a lower level, the RPC might generate an error if it times out before the server responds with an error or data; this would indicate that the server did not receive the request or could not process it quickly enough. Whenever an RPC call returns a timeout error, the low-level NIS RPC routine instructs **ypbind** to dissolve the process's binding for the domain.

NIS RPC calls continue trying the remote server after a timeout error. This happens transparently to the user-level application calling the NIS RPC routine; for example, **ls** has no idea that one of its calls to *getpwuid*() resulted in an RPC timeout. The **ls** command just patiently waits for the *getpwuid()* call to return, and the RPC code called by *getpwuid()* negotiates with **ypbind** to get the domain rebound and to retry the request.

Before retrying the NIS RPC that timed out, the client process (again, within some low-level library code) must get the domain rebound. Remember that **ypbind** keeps track of its current domain binding, and returns the currently bound server for a domain whenever a process asks to be bound. This theory of operation is a little too simplistic, since it would result in a client being immediately rebound to a server that just caused an RPC timeout. Instead, **ypbind** does a health check by pinging the NIS server before returning its name for the current domain binding. This ensures that the server has not crashed or is not the cause of the RPC failure. An RPC timeout could have been caused when the NIS packet was lost on the network or if the server was too heavily loaded to promptly handle the request. NIS RPC calls use the UDP protocol, so the network transport layer makes no guarantees about delivering NIS requests to the server—it's possible that some requests never reach the NIS server on their first transmission. Any condition that causes an RPC to time out is hopefully temporary, and **ypbind** should find the server responsive again on the next ping. **ypbind** will try to reach the currently bound server for several minutes before it decides that the server has died.

When the server health check fails, **ypbind** broadcasts a new request for NIS service for the domain. When a binding is dissolved because a host is overloaded or crashes, the rebinding generally locates a different NIS server, effecting a simple load balancing scheme. If no replies are received for the rebinding request, messages of the form:

```
NIS: server not responding for domain "nesales"; still trying
```

appear on the console as **ypbind** continues looking for a server. At this point, the NIS client is only partially functional; any process that needs information from an NIS map will wait on the return of a valid domain binding.

Most processes need to check permissions using UIDs, find a hostname associated with an IP address, or make some other reference to NIS-managed data if they are doing anything other than purely CPU-bound work. A machine that is using NIS will not run for long once it loses its binding to an NIS server. It remains partially dead until a server appears on the network and answers **ypbind**'s broadcast requests for service. The need for reliable NIS service cannot be stressed enough. In the next chapter we'll look at ways of using and configuring the service efficiently.

3

System Management Using NIS

NIS Network Design
Managing Map Files
Advanced NIS Server Administration
Managing Multiple Domains
Domain Name Servers

We've seen how NIS operates on master servers, slave servers, and clients, and how clients get map information from the servers. Just knowing how NIS works, however, does not lead to its efficient use. NIS servers must be configured so that map information remains consistent on all servers, and the number of servers and the load on each server should be evaluated so that there is not a user-noticeable penalty for referring to the NIS maps.

Ideally, NIS streamlines system administration tasks by allowing you to update configuration files on many machines by making changes on a single host. When designing a network to use NIS, you must ensure that its performance cost, measured by all users doing "normal" activities, does not exceed its advantages. This chapter explains how to how to design an NIS network, update and distribute NIS map data, manage multiple NIS domains, and integrate NIS hostname services with the Domain Name service.

NIS Network Design

At this point, you should be able to set up NIS on master and slave servers and have a good understanding of how map changes are propagated from master to slave servers. Before creating a new NIS network, you should think about the number of domains and servers you will need. NIS network design entails deciding the number of domains, the number of servers for each domain, and the domain names. Once the framework has been established, installation and ongoing maintenance of the NIS servers is fairly straightforward.

Dividing a Network Into Domains

The number of NIS domains that you need depends upon the division of your computing resources. The two most common divisions—administrative and network—give rise to two rules of thumb:

- Use a separate NIS domain for any separate group of systems that has its own network. Because NIS domains are bound by a broadcast from the client's **ypbind** process, at least one master or slave NIS server must be on that client's local network.

- Use a separate NIS domain for each group of systems that has its own system administrator. The job of maintaining a system also includes maintaining its configuration information, wherever it may exist.

Large groups of users sharing network resources may warrant a separate NIS domain if the users may be cleanly separated into two or more groups. The degree to which users in the groups share information should decide whether you should split them into different NIS domains. These large groups of users usually correspond very closely to the organizational groups within your company, and the level of information sharing within the group and between groups is fairly well defined.

A good example is that of a large university, where the physics and chemistry departments have their own networked computing environments. Information sharing within each department will be common, but inter-department sharing is minimal. The physics department isn't that interested in the machine names used by the chemistry department. The two departments will almost definitely be in two distinct NIS domains if they are not on the same network, or do not have the same system administrator (each probably gets one of its graduate students to assume this job). Assume, though, that they share an administrator and a network—why create two NIS domains? The real motivation is to clearly mark the lines along which information is commonly shared. Setting up different NIS domains also keeps users in one department from using machines in another department.

Conversely, the need to create splinter groups of a few users for access to some machines should not warrant an independent NIS domain. Netgroups are better suited to handle this problem, because they create subsets of a domain, rather than an entirely new domain. A good example of a splinter group is the system administration staff—they may be given logins on central servers, while the bulk of the user community is not. Putting the system administrators in another domain generally creates more problems than the new domain was intended to solve.

Domain Names

Choosing domain names is not nearly as difficult as gauging the number of domains needed. Just about any naming convention can be used provided that domain names are unique. You can choose to apply the name of the group as the NIS domain name; for example, you could use *history*, *politics*, and *comp-sci* to name the departments in a university.

If you are setting up multiple NIS domains that are based on hierarchical divisions, you may want to use a multi-level naming scheme with dot-separated name components:

```
cslab.comp-sci
staff.comp-sci
profs.history
grad.history
```

The first two domain names would apply to the "lab" machines and the departmental staff machines in the computer science department, while the two *.history* domain names separate the professors and graduate students in that department.

Multi-level domain names are useful if you will be using an Internet Domain Name Service. You can assign NIS domain names based on the Name Service domain names, so that every domain name is unique and also identifies how the additional Name Service is related to NIS. Integration of Internet name services and NIS is covered at the end of this chapter.

Number of NIS Servers per Domain

The number of servers per NIS domain is determined by the size of the domain and the aggregate service requirements for it, the level of failure protection required, and any physical network constraints that might affect client binding patterns. As a general rule, there should be at least two servers per domain: one master and one slave. The dual-server model offers basic protection if one server crashes, since clients of that server will rebind to the second server. With a solitary server, the operation of the network hinges on the health of the NIS server, creating both a performance bottleneck and a single point of failure in the network.

Increasing the number of NIS servers per domain reduces the impact of any one server crashing. With more servers, each one is likely to have fewer clients binding to it, assuming that the clients are equally likely to bind to any server. When a server crashes, fewer clients will be affected. Spreading the load out over several hosts may also reduce the number of domain rebindings that occur during unusually long server response times. If the load is divided evenly, this should level out variations in the NIS server response time due to server crashes and reboots.

There is no golden rule for allocating n servers for every m NIS clients. The total NIS service load depends on the type of work done on each machine and the relative speeds of client and server. A faster machine generates more NIS requests in a given time window than a slower one, if both machines are doing work that makes equal use of NIS. Some interactive usage patterns generate more NIS traffic than work that is CPU-intensive. A user who is continually listing files, compiling source code, and reading mail will make more use of password file entries and mail aliases than one who runs a text editor most of the time.

The bottom line is that very few types of work generate endless streams of NIS requests; most work makes casual references to the NIS maps separated by at most several seconds (compare this to disk accesses, which are usually separated by milliseconds). Generally, 30-40 NIS clients per server is an upper limit if the clients and servers are roughly the same speed. Faster clients need a lower client/server ratio, while a server that is faster than its clients might support 50 or more NIS clients. The best way to gauge server usage is to watch for **ypbind** broadcasts for domain bindings, indicating that clients are timing out waiting for NIS service. Methods for observing broadcasts are discussed in "Displaying and Analyzing Client Bindings," in Chapter 10, *Diagnostic and Administrative Tools*.

Finally, the number of servers required may depend on the physical structure of the network. If you have decided to use four NIS servers, for example, and have two network segments joined by a bridge or repeater, make sure you divide the NIS servers equally on both sides of the network partitioning hardware. If you put only one NIS server on one side of a bridge or repeater, then clients on that side will almost always bind to this server. The delay experienced by the **ypbind** broadcast packet in traversing the bridge is close to any server-related delay, so that the NIS server on the same side of the bridge will answer a client's request before a server on the opposite side of the bridge, even if the closer server is more heavily loaded than the one across the bridge. With this configuration, you have undone the benefits of multiple NIS servers, since clients on the one-server side of the bridge bind to the same server in most cases. Locating lop-sided NIS server bindings are discussed in "Displaying and Analyzing Client Bindings," in Chapter 10, *Diagnostic and Administrative Tools*.

Managing Map Files

Keeping map files updated on all servers is essential to the proper operation of NIS. There are two mechanisms for updating map files: using **make** and the NIS **Makefile**, which pushes maps from the master server to the slave servers, and the **ypxfr** utility, which pulls maps from the master server. This section starts with a look at how map file updates are made, and how they get distributed to slave servers.

Having a single point of administration makes it easier to propagate configuration changes through the network, but it also means that you may have more than one person changing the same file. If there are several system administrators maintaining the NIS maps, they need to coordinate their efforts, or you will find that one person removes NIS map entries added by another. Using a source code control system, such as SCCS or RCS, in conjunction with NIS often solves this problem. In the second part of this section, we'll see how to use alternate map source files and source code control systems with NIS.

Map Distribution

Master and slave servers are distinguished by their ability to effect permanent changes to NIS maps. Changes may be made to an NIS map on a slave server, but the next map transfer from the master will overlay this change. Modify maps *only* on the master server, and push them from the master server to its slave servers. On the NIS master server, edit the source file for the map using your favorite text editor. Source files for NIS maps are listed in Table 2-1. Then go to the NIS map directory and build the new map using **make**, as shown below:

```
# vi /etc/hosts
# cd /var/yp
# make
...New hosts map is built and distributed...
```

Without any arguments, **make** builds all maps that are out-of-date with respect to their ASCII source files. When more than one map is built from the same ASCII file, for example, the *passwd.byname* and *passwd.byuid* maps built from /etc/passwd, they are all built when **make** is invoked.

When a map is rebuilt, the **yppush** utility is used to check the order number of the same map on each NIS server. If the maps are out-of-date, **yppush** transfers the map to the slave servers, using the server names in the **ypservers** map. Scripts to rebuild maps and push them to slave servers are part of the NIS **Makefile**, which is covered in "Map File Dependencies."

Map transfers done on demand after source file modifications may not always complete successfully. The NIS slave server may be down, or the transfer may time out due to severe congestion or server host loading. To ensure that maps do not remain out-of-date for a long time (until the next NIS map update), NIS uses the **ypxfr** utility to transfer a map to a slave server. The slave transfers the map after checking the timestamp on its copy; if the master's copy has been modified more recently the slave server will replace its copy of the map with the one it transfers from the server. It is possible to force a map transfer to a slave server, ignoring the slave's timestamp, which is useful if a map gets corrupted and must be replaced. Under SunOS, an additional master server daemon called **ypxfrd** is used to speed up map transfer operations, but the map distribution utilities resort to the old method if they cannot reach **ypxfrd** on the server.

The map transfer—both in **yppush** and in **ypxfr**—is performed by requesting that the slave server walk through all keys in the modified map and build a map containing these keys. This seems quite counterintuitive, since you would hope that a map transfer amounts to nothing more than the master server sending the map to the slave server. However, NIS was designed to be used in a heterogenous environment, so the master server's DBM file format may not correspond to that used by the slave server. DBM files are tightly tied to the byte ordering and file block allocation rules of the server system, and a DBM file must be created on the system that indexes it. Slave servers, therefore, have to enumerate the entries in an NIS map and rebuild the map from them, using their own local conventions for DBM file construction. When the slave server has rebuilt the map, it replaces its existing copy of the map with the new one. Schedules for transferring maps to slave servers and scripts to be run out of **cron** are provided in the next section.

Regular Map Transfers

Relying on demand-driven updates is overly optimistic, since a server may be down when the master is updated. NIS includes the **ypxfr** tool to perform periodic transfers of maps to slave servers, keeping them synchronized with the master server even if they miss an occasional **yppush**. The **ypxfr** utility will only transfer a map if the slave's copy is out-of-date with respect to the master's map.

Unlike **yppush**, **ypxfr** runs on the slave. **ypxfr** contacts the master server for a map, enumerates the entries in the map, and rebuilds a private copy of the map. If the map is built successfully, **ypxfr** replaces the slave server's copy of the map with the newly created one. Note that doing a **yppush** from the NIS master essentially involves asking each slave server to perform a **ypxfr** operation if the slave's copy of the map is out-of-date. The difference between **yppush** and **ypxfr** (besides the servers on which they are run) is that **ypxfr** retrieves a map even if the slave server does not have a copy of it, while **yppush** requires that the slave server have the map in order to check its modification time.

ypxfr map updates should be scheduled out of **cron** based on how often the maps change. The *passwd* and *aliases* maps change most frequently, and could be transferred once an hour. Other maps, like the *services* and *rpc* maps, tend to be static and can be updated once a day. The standard mechanism for invoking **ypxfr** out of **cron** is to create two or more scripts based on transfer frequency, and to call **ypxfr** from the scripts. The maps included in the **ypxfr_1perhour** script are those that are likely to be modified several times during the day, while those in **ypxfr_1perday** may change once every few days:

```
ypxfr_1perhour script:
/usr/etc/yp/ypxfr passwd.byuid
/usr/etc/yp/ypxfr passwd.byname
/usr/etc/yp/ypxfr aliases.byname
/usr/etc/yp/ypxfr mail.aliases

ypxfr_1perday script:
/usr/etc/yp/ypxfr services.byname
/usr/etc/yp/ypxfr protocols.byname

crontab entry:
0 * * * * ypxfr_1perhour
0 0 * * * ypxfr_1perday
```

ypxfr logs its activity on the slave servers if the log file **/var/yp/ypxfr.log** exists when **ypxfr** starts.

Map File Dependencies

Dependencies of NIS maps on ASCII source files are maintained by the NIS **Makefile**, located in the NIS directory **/var/yp** or **/etc/yp** on the master server. The **Makefile** dependencies are built around timestamp files named after their respective source files. For example, the timestamp file for the NIS maps built from the password file is **passwd.time**, and the timestamp for the hosts maps is kept in **hosts.time**.

The timestamp files are empty because only their modification dates are of interest. The **make** utility is used to build maps according to the rules in the **Makefile**, and **make** compares file modification times to determine which targets need to be rebuilt. For example, **make** compares the timestamp on the **passwd.time** file and that of the ASCII **/etc/passwd** file, and rebuilds the NIS *passwd* map if the ASCII source file was modified since the last time the NIS *passwd* map was built.

After editing a map source file, building the map (and any other maps that may depend on it) is done with **make**:

```
# cd /var/yp
# make passwd        Rebuilds only password map.
# make               Rebuilds all maps that are out-of-date.
```

If the source file has been modified more recently than the timestamp file, **make** notes that the dependency in the **Makefile** is not met and executes the commands to regenerate the NIS map. In most cases, map regeneration requires that the ASCII file be stripped of comments, fed to **makedbm** for conversion to DBM format, and then pushed to all slave servers using **yppush**.

Be careful when building a few selected maps; if other maps depend on the modified map, then you may distribute incomplete map information. For example, SunOS uses the *netid* map to combine password and group information. The *netid* map is used by log-in shells to determine user credentials: for every user, it lists all of the groups that user as a member. The *netid* map depends on both the **/etc/passwd** and **/etc/group** files, so when either one is changed, the *netid* map should be rebuilt.

But let's say you make a change to the **/etc/groups** file, and decide to just rebuild and distribute the *group* map:

```
nismaster# cd /var/yp
nismaster# make group
```

The commands in this example do not update the *netid* map, because the *netid* map doesn't depend on the *group* map at all. The *netid* map depends on the **/etc/group** file—as does the *group* map—but in the previous example, you would have instructed **make** to build only the *group* map. If you build the *group* map without updating the *netid* map, users will become very confused about their group memberships: their log-in shells will read *netid* and get old group information, even though the NIS map source files *appear* correct.

The best solution to this problem is to build all maps that are out-of-date by using **make** with no arguments:

```
nismaster# cd /var/yp
nismaster# make
```

Once the map is built, the NIS **Makefile** distributes it, using **yppush**, to the slave servers named in the *ypservers* map. **yppush** walks through the list of NIS servers and performs an RPC call to each slave server to check the timestamp on the map to be transferred. If the map is out-of-date, **yppush** uses another RPC call to the slave server to initiate a transfer of the map.

A map that is corrupted or was not successfully transferred to all slave servers can be explicitly rebuilt and repushed by removing its timestamp file on the master server:

```
master# cd /var/yp
master# rm hosts.time
master# make hosts
```

This procedure should be used if a map was built when the NIS master server's time was set incorrectly, creating a map that becomes out-of-date when the time is reset. If you need to perform a complete reconstruction of all NIS maps, for any reason, remove all of the timestamp files and run **make**:

```
master# cd /var/yp
master# rm *.time
master# make
```

This extreme step is best reserved for testing the map distribution mechanism, or recovering from corruption of the NIS map directory.

Password File Updates

The exception to the **yppush** push-on-demand strategy is the *passwd* map. Users need to be able to change their passwords without system manager intervention. The hosts file, for example, is changed by the superuser and then pushed to other servers when it is rebuilt. In contrast, when you change your password, you (as a non-privileged user) modify the local password file. To change a password in an NIS map, the change must be made on the master server and distributed to all slave servers in order to be seen back on the client host where you made the change.

yppasswd is a user utility that is similar to the **passwd** program, but it changes the user's password in the original source file on the NIS master server. **yppasswd** usually forces the password map to be rebuilt, although at sites choosing not to rebuild the map on demand, the new password will not be distributed until the next map transfer. **yppasswd** is used like **passwd,** but it reports the server name on which the modifications are made. Here is an example:

```
[wahoo]% yppasswd
Changing NIS password for stern on mahimahi.
Old password:
New password:
Retype new password:
NIS entry changed on mahimahi
```

Some versions of **passwd** check to see if the password file is managed by NIS, and invoke **yppasswd** if this is the case. Check your vendor's documentation for procedures particular to your system.

NIS provides read-only access to its maps. There is nothing in the NIS protocol that allows a client to rewrite the data for a key. To accept changes to maps, a server distinct from the NIS server is required that modifies the source file for the map and then rebuilds the NIS map from the modified ASCII file. To handle incoming **yppasswd** change requests, the master server must run the **yppasswdd** daemon (note the second "d" in the daemon's name). This RPC daemon gets started in the **/etc/rc.local** boot script on the master NIS server only:

```
if [ -f /usr/etc/rpc.yppasswdd ]; then
        /usr/etc/rpc.yppasswdd /etc/passwd -m passwd DIR=/var/yp
        echo "Starting yppasswdd"
fi
```

The host making a password map change locates the master server by asking for the master of the NIS *passwd* map, and the **yppasswdd** daemon acts as a gateway between the user's host and a **passwd**-like utility on the master server. The location of the master server's password file and options to build a new map after each update are given as command-line arguments to **yppasswdd,** as shown in the previous example.

The first argument is the name of the master server's source for the password map; it may be the default **/etc/passwd** or it may point to an alternative password file. The arguments after the **−m** option are passed to **make** in the NIS directory on the master server. In this example, the commands:

```
# ( cd /var/yp; make passwd DIR=/var/yp )
```

are executed by **yppasswdd** after each change to the master's password source file.

Source Code Control For Map Files

With multiple system administrators and a single point of administration, it is possible for conflicting or unexplained changes to NIS maps to wreak havoc with the network. The best way to control modifications to maps and to track the change history of map source files is to put them under a source code control system such as SCCS.

SCCS manages any ASCII text file that contains at least one SCCS information macro, or keyword. Source code files usually contain the SCCS headers in a comment or in a global string that gets compiled into an executable. Putting SCCS keywords into comments in the /etc/hosts and /etc/aliases files allows them to be put under SCCS control as well:

```
header to be added to file:
#        /etc/hosts header
#        %M%        %I%              %H% %T%
#        %W%


keywords filled in after getting file from SCCS:
#        /etc/hosts header
#        hosts        1.32          12/29/90 16:37:52
#        @(#)hosts           1.32
```

Once the headers have been added to the map source files, put them under SCCS administration:

```
nismaster# cd /etc
nismaster# mkdir SCCS
nismaster# sccs admin -ialiases aliases
nismaster# sccs admin -ihosts hosts
nismaster# sccs get aliases hosts
```

The copies of the files that are checked out of SCCS control are read-only. Someone making a casual change to a map is forced to go and check it out of SCCS properly before doing so. Using SCCS, each change to a file is documented before the file gets put back under SCCS control. If you always return a file to SCCS before it is converted into an NIS map, the SCCS control file forms an audit trail for configuration changes:

```
nismaster# cd /etc
nismaster# sccs prs hosts
D 1.31 90/12/12 08:52:35 root 31 30      00001/00001/00117
MRs:
COMMENTS:
added new host for info-center group
```

```
D 1.30 90/12/10 07:19:04 root 30 29      00001/00001/00117
MRs:
COMMENTS:
changed bosox-fddi to jetstar-fddi

D 1.29 90/11/08 11:03:47 root 29 28      00011/00011/00107
MRs:
COMMENTS:
commented out the porting lab systems.
```

If any change to the hosts or aliases file breaks, SCCS can be used to find the exact lines that were changed and the time the change was made (for confirmation that the modification caused the network problems).

The two disadvantages to using SCCS for NIS maps are that all changes must be made as root and that it won't work for the password file. The superuser must perform all file checkouts and modifications, unless the underlying file permissions are changed to make the files writeable by non-privileged users. If all changes are made by *root*, then the SCCS logs do not contain information about the user making the change. The password file falls outside of SCCS control because its contents will be modified by users changing their passwords, without being able to check the file out of SCCS first.

Using Alternate Map Source Files

You may decide to use non-standard source files for various NIS maps on the master server, especially if the master server is not going to be an NIS client. Alternatively, you may need to modify the standard NIS **Makefile** to build your own NIS maps. Approaches to both of these problems are discussed in this section.

Some system administrators prefer to build the NIS password map from a file other than **/etc/passwd**, giving them finer control over access to the server. Separating the host's and the NIS password files is also advantageous if there are password file entries on the server (such as those for dial-in UUCP) that shouldn't be made available on all NIS clients. To avoid distributing UUCP password file entries to all NIS clients, the NIS password file should be kept separately from **/etc/passwd** on the master server. The master can include private UUCP password file entries and can embed the entire NIS map file using a plus sign at the end of the file.

If the NIS password map is decoupled from the master server's password file, then the NIS **Makefile** should be modified to reflect the new dependency. The **passwd.time** target depends on the location of the new password file, and the

Makefile action calling **makedbm** should be updated to read the new file instead of the default:

```
passwd.time: $(DIR)/passwd.global
        @(awk 'BEGIN { FS=":"; OFS="\t"; } \
          /^[a-zA-Z0-9_]/ { print $$1, $$0 }'\
        $(DIR)/passwd.global ) \
        | $(MAKEDBM) - $(YPDBDIR)/$(DOM)/passwd.byname;
        @(awk 'BEGIN { FS=":"; OFS="\t"; } \
          /^[a-zA-Z0-9_]/ { printf("%-10d ", $$3); print $$0 }'\
        $(DIR)/passwd.global ) \
        | $(MAKEDBM) - $(YPDBDIR)/$(DOM)/passwd.byuid;
        @touch passwd.time;
        @echo "updated passwd";
```

In this example, the password maps are built from **/etc/passwd.global**, instead of the default **/etc/passwd**.

Advanced NIS Server Administration

Once NIS is installed and running, you may find that you need to remove or rearrange your NIS servers to accommodate an increased load on one server. For example, if you attach several printers to an NIS server and use it as a print server, it may no longer make a good NIS server if most of its bandwidth is used for driving the printers. If this server is your master NIS server, you may want to assign NIS master duties to another host. We'll look at these advanced administration problems in this section.

Removing an NIS Slave Server

If you decommission an NIS slave server, or decide to stop running NIS on it because the machine is loaded by other functions, you need to remove it from the *ypserver* map and turn off NIS. If a host is listed in the *ypservers* map but is not running **ypserv**, then attempts to push maps to this host will fail. This will not cause any data corruption or NIS service failures. It will, however, significantly increase the time required to push the NIS maps because **yppush** times out waiting for the former server to respond before trying the next server.

There is no explicit "remove" procedure in the NIS maintenance tools, so you have to do this manually. Start by rebuilding the *ypservers* map on the NIS master server:

```
master# cd /var/yp
master# ypcat -k ypservers | grep -v servername\
    | makedbm - /var/yp/'domainname'/ypservers
```

The **ypcat** command line prints the entries in the current *ypservers* map, then removes the entry for the desired server using **grep -v**. This shortened list of servers is given to **makedbm**, which rebuilds the *ypservers* map. If the decommissioned server is not being shut down permanently, make sure you remove the NIS maps in /var/yp on the former server so that the machine doesn't start **ypserv** on its next boot and provide out-of-date map information to the network. Many strange problems result if an NIS server is left running with old maps: the server will respond to requests, but may provide incorrect information to the client. After removing the maps and rebuilding *ypservers*, reboot the former NIS server and check to make sure that **ypserv** is not running. You may also want to force a map distribution at this point to test the new *ypservers* map. The **yppush** commands used in the map distribution should not include the former NIS server.

Changing NIS Master Servers

The procedure described above only works for slave servers. There are some additional dependencies on the master server that must be removed before an NIS master can be removed. To switch NIS master service to another host, you must rebuild all NIS maps to reflect the name of the new master host, update the *ypservers* map if the old master is being taken out of service, and distribute the new maps (with the new master server record) to all slave servers. Here are the steps used to change master NIS servers.

1. Build the new master host as a slave server, initializing its domain directory and filling it with copies of the current maps. Each map must be rebuilt on the new master, which requires the NIS **Makefile** and map source files from the old master. Copy the source files and the NIS **Makefile** to the new master, and then rebuild all of the maps—but do not attempt to push them to other slave servers:

```
newmaster# cd /var/yp
newmaster# rm *.time
newmaster# make NOPUSH=1
```

Removing all of the timestamp files forces every map to be rebuilt; passing **NOPUSH=1** to **make** prevents the maps from being pushed to other servers. At this point, you have NIS maps that contain master host records pointing to the new NIS master host.

2. Install copies of the new master server's maps on the old master server. Transferring the new maps to existing NIS servers is made more difficult because of the process used by **yppush**: when a map is pushed to a slave server via the *transfer-map* NIS RPC call, the slave server consults *its own* copy of the map to determine the master server from which it should load a new copy. This is an NIS security feature: it prevents someone from creating an NIS master server and forcing maps onto the valid slave servers using **yppush**. The slave servers will look to their current NIS master server for map data, rather than accepting it from the renegade NIS master server.

In the process of changing master servers, the slave servers' maps will point to the old master server. To work around **yppush**, first move the new maps to the old master server using **ypxfr**:

```
oldmaster# ypxfr -h newmaster -f passwd.byuid
oldmaster# ypxfr -h newmaster -f passwd.byname
oldmaster# ypxfr -h newmaster -f hosts.byname
```

The **-h newmaster** option tells the old master server to grab the map from the new master server, and the **-f** flag forces a transfer even if the local version is not out of order with the new map. Every NIS map must be transferred to the old master server. When this step is complete, the old master server's maps all point to the new master server.

3. On the old master server, distribute copies of the new maps to all NIS slave servers using **yppush**:

```
oldmaster# yppush passwd.byuid
oldmaster# yppush passwd.byname
oldmaster# yppush hosts.byname
```

yppush forces the slave servers to look at their old maps, find the master server (still the old master), and copy the current map from the master server. Because the map itself contains the pointer record to the master server, transferring the entire map automatically updates the slave servers' maps to point to the new master server.

4. If the old master server is being removed from NIS service, rebuild the **ypservers** map.

Many of the steps above can be automated using shell scripts or simple rule additions to the NIS **Makefile**, requiring less effort than it might seem. For example, you can merge steps 2 and 3 in a single shell script that transfers maps from the new master to the old master, and then pushes each map to all of the slave servers. Run this script on the old master server:

```
#! /bin/sh
MAPS="passwd.byuid passwd.byname hosts.byname ..."
NEWMASTER=newmaster
for map in $MAPS
do
        echo moving $map
        ypxfr -h $NEWMASTER -f $map
        yppush $map
done
```

The alternative to this method is to rebuild the entire NIS system from scratch, starting with the master server. In the process of building the system, NIS service on the network will be interrupted as slave servers are torn down and rebuilt with new maps.

Managing Multiple Domains

A single NIS server may be a slave of more than one master server, if it is providing service to multiple domains. In addition, a server may be a master for one domain and a slave of another. Multi-master relationships are set up when NIS is installed on each of the master servers. In the course of building the *ypservers* map, the slave servers handling multiple domains are named in the *ypservers* map for each domain.

When multiple domains are used with independent NIS servers (each serving only one domain), it is sometimes necessary to keep one or more of the maps in these domains in perfect synchronization. Domains with different password and group files, for example, might still want to share global alias and host maps to simplify administration. Adding a new user to either domain would make the user's mail aliases appear in the global alias file, to be shared by both domains. Figure 3-1 shows three NIS domains that share some maps and keep private copies of others.

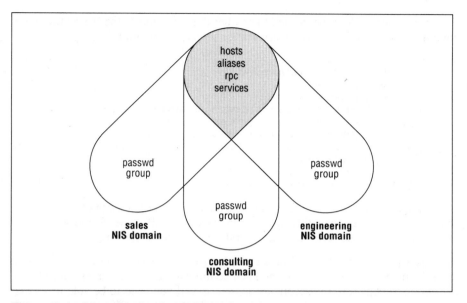

Figure 3-1. Map sharing in multiple domains

The *hosts* and *aliases* maps are shared between the NIS domains so that any changes to them are reflected on all NIS clients in all domains. The *passwd* and *group* files are managed on a per-domain basis so that new users or groups in one domain do not automatically appear in the other domains: this gives the system administrators fine control over user access to machines and files in each NIS domain.

A much simpler case is the argument for having a single **/etc/rpc** file and an **/etc/services** file across all domains in an organization. As locally developed or third party software that relies on these additional services is distributed to new networks, the required configuration changes will be in place. This scenario is most common when multiple NIS domains are run on a single network with less than one system administrator per domain.

Sharing maps across domains involves setting up a master/slave relationship between the two NIS master servers. The map transfer can be done periodically out of **cron** on the "slave" master server, or the true master server for the map can push the modified source file to the secondary master after each modification. The latter method offers the advantages of keeping the map source files synchronized and keeping the NIS maps current as soon as changes are made, but it requires that the superuser have remote execution permissions on the secondary NIS master server.

To force a source file to be pushed to another domain, modify the NIS **Makefile** to copy the source file to the secondary master server, and rebuild the map there:

```
hosts.time:        ....
        rebuild hosts.byname and hosts.byaddr
        @touch hosts.time;
        @echo "updated hosts";
        @if [ ! $(NOPUSH) ]; then $(YPPUSH) -d $(DOM) hosts.byname; fi
        @if [ ! $(NOPUSH) ]; then $(YPPUSH) -d $(DOM) hosts.byaddr; fi
        @if [ ! $(NOPUSH) ]; then echo "pushed hosts"; fi
        @echo "copying hosts file to NIS server ono"
        @rcp /etc/hosts ono:/etc/hosts
        @echo "updating NIS maps on ono"
        @rsh ono "( cd /var/yp; make hosts )"
```

The commands in the **Makefile** are preceded by at signs (@) to suppress command echo when **make** is executing them. **rcp** moves the file over to the secondary master server, and the script invoked by **rsh** rebuilds the maps on server *ono*.

Superuser privileges are not always extended from one NIS server to another, and this scheme only works if the **rsh** and **rcp** commands can be executed. In order to get the maps copied to the secondary master server, you need to be able to access that server as *root*. The alternative is to leave the source files out-of-date and simply move the map file to the secondary master and have it distributed to slave servers in the second domain.

The following script can be run out of **cron** on the secondary master server to pick up the host maps from NIS server *mahimahi*, the master server for domain *nesales*:

```
#! /bin/sh
/usr/etc/yp/ypxfr -h mahimahi -s nesales hosts.byname
/usr/etc/yp/ypxfr -h mahimahi -s nesales hosts.byaddr
/usr/etc/yp/yppush -d `domainname` hosts.byname
/usr/etc/yp/yppush -d `domainname` hosts.byaddr
```

The **ypxfr** commands get the maps from the primary master server, and then the **yppush** commands distribute them in the local, secondary NIS domain. The **-h** option to **ypxfr** specifies the hostname from which to initiate the transfer, and overrides the map's master record. The **-s** option indicates the domain from which the map is to be taken. Note that in this approach, the hosts map points to *mahimahi* as the master in *both* domains. If the **rcp**-based transfer is used, then the hosts map in each domain points to the master server in that domain. The master server record in the map always indicates the host containing a source file from which the map can be rebuilt.

Domain Name Servers

The hostname management provided by NIS can be integrated with an Internet Domain Name Service (DNS), or the DNS facilities can be used to replace the NIS host map in its entirety. We'll avoid a full-length discussion of setting up a name server. That process depends on the type of name server supported by your vendor, and is best described by your vendor's documentation. Instead, this section concentrates on differences between the scope of the two hostname services and support for DNS with and without NIS. Note that the implementation of Domain Name Services provided by your vendor may not be called DNS. If the Berkeley InterNetwork Domain (BIND) name service or one of its derivatives is used, the service is usually called BIND.

DNS versus NIS

The Domain Name Service provides a hierarchical hostname management system that spans the entire Internet. Each level in the hierarchy designates authoritative name servers that contain maps of host names and IP addresses, similar to the NIS hosts map but on a larger scale. The DNS server for a large Name Service domain would have hosts information merged from dozens of NIS domains. First among the advantages of DNS is its ability to decentralize responsibility for the maintenance of hostname-to-IP address mappings and the resulting domain name qualification that is used to differentiate identically named hosts.

Decentralized name management means that each organization running a Name Service domain—whether it is a subdivision of a corporation or an entire company—can maintain its own host information without having to notify some central authority of changes in its local configuration. Host information is published through the authoritative name server for that domain, and hosts in other Name Service domains retrieve information from the name server when needed. Every domain knows how to reach the next highest level in the name space hierarchy, and it can generally find most of its peer name servers within the same organization. If a name server does not know how to reach the name server for another domain, it can ask the next higher level domain name server for assistance.

For example, Princeton University is part of the educational, or **.edu** domain. The domain name for the entire university is **princeton.edu**, and it is further divided by department:

```
cs.princeton.edu
politics.princeton.edu
history.princeton.edu
```

and so on. Each of the name servers for the departmental Name Service domains knows how to reach most of the others; therefore each department can run its own systems without having to notify a campus-wide network manager of any changes to host information. There is also a name server for the entire **princeton.edu** domain that points to lower-level name servers for incoming queries and locates other domains in **.edu**, **.com**, or **.gov** for outbound requests.

In a world in which every machine name must be unique, all of the good names are taken very quickly. DNS allows each domain to have a distinct name space, so that two domains may have hosts with the same name: the Name Service domain suffix distinguishes them on a higher level in the hierarchy. This is a job that cannot be performed by NIS, since the concatenation of **/etc/hosts** files from several different domains would result in hostname clashes. If the NIS domains are left independent, there is no global naming authority, because NIS lacks a mechanism for cross-domain hostname queries.

DNS Integration with NIS

Hostnames are managed in a hierarchy. Each host manages its own name, so the hosts are the "leaf nodes" in this management tree. Hosts are grouped together into NIS or DNS domains, creating a two-level tree. DNS domains may be further grouped together by company, department or physical location, adding more levels to the management hierarchy. NIS fits into the DNS management scheme at the lowest level in this hierarchy.

Within a single DNS domain, there may be many physical networks with several system administrators. NIS provides a system for the independent management of these small networks; NIS host map information can be combined to form the DNS host file. There are three ways to integrate NIS with DNS:

- Run NIS without DNS, which is the default. Even if you are running DNS, routines that use NIS ignore DNS servers unless you make the changes described below.

- Use the NIS maps first, then go to DNS for hostnames that aren't managed by NIS. This is done using a special flag in the NIS hosts map.

- Ignore NIS for hostnames, and use only DNS. Using DNS without NIS requires rebuilding the library routines that look up hostnames so that they no longer make NIS library calls.

In DEC's Ultrix operating system, you can specify the order in which the local **/etc/hosts** file, the NIS map, and the DNS name servers are queried for host information. We'll see how to specify the order of services in the section "Multiple Service Integration."

NIS is forced to query DNS for hostnames not found in the hosts map if the map is built with the "Internetwork Domain" token. The NIS-then-DNS algorithm is embedded in the implementation of the *gethostbyname()* and *gethostent()* library routines as well as **ypserv**. The library code always checks NIS if it is running and the NIS server consults the domain name server. This means that individual NIS clients don't need to know about the DNS; only the NIS servers will be calling DNS for non-local hostnames.

In the NIS **Makefile**, add the **–b** flag to the **makedbm** script for the *hosts.byname* and *hosts.byaddr* maps. If a hostname is not found in the NIS map, this cookie instructs NIS to look up the name with the domain name server. Instead of immediately returning an error indicating that the hostname key was not found, **ypserv** asks the DNS server to look up the hostname. If DNS cannot find the name, then **ypserv** returns an error to the client. However, if the DNS server locates the hostname, it returns the IP address information to **ypserv**, and **ypserv** returns it to the client. Integration of NIS and DNS is completely invisible to the client in terms of calling interfaces: all of the work is done by **ypserv** on the NIS server.

NIS servers locate DNS servers through the *resolver* interface, which relies on information in the **/etc/resolv.conf** configuration file. The resolver configuration file should point to a the master NIS server (which is probably also a DNS server) and then to other DNS authorities:

```
nameserver 130.1.52.28
nameserver 130.1.1.15
```

The *nameserver* keyword is used to identify the IP address of a DNS server. The servers are listed by IP address, since hostnames are dependent on the very mechanism being configured by this file. Set up a **resolv.conf** file on every NIS slave server, and on the NIS master server if it is not also running a DNS server.

DNS Without NIS

Given that DNS is a full-service hostname management system, some network managers choose to eliminate the NIS hosts map file and use pure DNS service for hostnames and IP addresses. A new version of *gethostent*() is required that skips the NIS query and directly calls the DNS *resolver* routines for hostname lookups. Check with your vendor for instructions on how to dissect **libc.a** and insert a new library routine into it. If you disable NIS host name management and use DNS alone, you'll need to set up a **resolv.conf** file on *every* host in the network, so that they can find DNS servers.

The main argument for using DNS only is that it consolidates hostname management under one distributed service, instead of having it split across two services. The drawbacks to this approach are that each host is then dependent upon both an NIS and a DNS server for normal operation (if NIS is running), and a reliable DNS server or sufficient resolver information is required to make each small network self-supporting. Widespread use of DNS to replace NIS host maps suffers from the same server availability problems that NIS does—the entire network is dependent upon reliable and well behaved servers.

NIS and DNS Domain Names

If an Internet Domain Name Service is used in conjunction with NIS, it is helpful to tie the NIS domain names to the DNS domain name. Deriving NIS domain names from the DNS domain name links the two management schemes: the DNS-derived portion of the NIS domain name indicates where the NIS domain looks for its hostname information. Joining NIS and DNS domain names also makes sense if you have a single DNS domain that spans several physical locations. Each office will have its own networks, and its own NIS domains, so using the DNS domain name in the NIS domain name indicates how these locations fit into the "big picture."

For example, the Polygon Company uses the DNS domain name **polygon.com**. It has four NIS domains in its main office, which uses the **polygon.com** DNS domain name. The NIS domain names use the DNS domain name as a suffix:

```
bos-engin.polygon.com
philly-engin.polygon.com
finance.polygon.com
sales.polygon.com
```

The SunOS version of **sendmail** assumes that an NIS domain name with three or more components was derived from a DNS domain name. That is, if your NIS domain name is **bos-engin.polygon.com**, then **sendmail** uses **.polygon.com** as your DNS domain name by default. There may be many NIS domains in this DNS domain; **sendmail** strips off the leading component to form the DNS domain name. If the NIS domain name contains a leading plus sign, or starts with a dot, then the SunOS **sendmail** assumes that the NIS domain name is the *same as* the DNS domain name. This is a useful convention if you have exactly one NIS domain per DNS domain. For example, if DNS domain **sales.polygon.com** contains just one NIS domain, then it is convenient to tie the NIS domain name to the DNS domain name:

```
+sales.polygon.com
```

However, if there are multiple NIS domains within the DNS domain—several sales offices in different cities, for example—then the NIS domain names should reflect the subdivision of the DNS domain, as shown in Table 3-1.

Table 3-1. Subdividing a DNS Domain into NIS Domains

NIS Domain	DNS Domain
boston.sales.polygon.com	.sales.polygon.com
philly.sales.polygon.com	.sales.polygon.com
rahway.sales.polygon.com	.sales.polygon.com
waltham.engin.polygon.com	.engin.polygon.com
alameda.engin.polygon.com	.engin.polygon.com

Because the NIS domain name contains four dot-separated components, **sendmail** drops the first component and uses the remainder as a DNS domain name. This allows all of the sales offices to be treated as a single administrative unit for mail and hostname management, even though they require distinct NIS domains.

Domain Aliases

Some systems impose a fairly small limit on the length of a domain name. If you've chosen a long NIS domain name, say *nesales.East.Sun.COM*, then implementations of NIS that restrict the length of a domain name will not be able to bind to a server. For example, Sun's PC/NFS has a 14-character domain name length limit, which may be insufficient for a domain name that echos several levels of Internet domain hierarchy.

You could build a second NIS domain with a shorter name and duplicate the maps from the first domain, but this leaves you with twice the administrative work. An easier solution to this problem is to create a domain name alias for the longer name by making a symbolic link in the NIS server directory **/var/yp** on each server host:

```
master# cd /var/yp
master# ln -s nesales.East.Sun.COM nesales
```

NIS servers in the fully qualified domain respond to requests for service for the truncated domain name because they believe they have a set of maps for the specified domain. It is of no consequence that the "directory" is really a link to another domain's directory. This trick can also be used to force two distinct NIS domains to share exactly the same set of maps.

In a simple network, your domain names are likely to be short and easily managed. However, if you integrate Domain Name Services with NIS, and choose NIS domain names based on name service domains, you may end up with fairly long, multi-component names such as **grad.history.princeton.edu**. Using symbolic links to create aliases for long names may be necessary to make all of your NIS clients find NIS servers.

Multiple Service Integration

Library routines in DEC's Ultrix operating system can retrieve information from the BIND domain name service, NIS, and local configuration files. The configuration file **/etc/svc.conf** specifies the search order for information found in NIS maps:

```
hosts=local,yp,bind
passwd=local,yp
```

In this example, hostnames and addresses are taken from the local **/etc/hosts** file, then from the NIS (*yp*) map, then from the BIND name service. This search pattern differs from the usual NIS-and-DNS ordering, because the NIS *hosts* map replaces the local **/etc/hosts** file once NIS is running. Each host needs its own copy of **/etc/svc.conf**.

What Next?

The Network Information Service provides an easy-to-manage general purpose distributed database system. When used in conjunction with a source code control system and local tools, it solves many problems with configuration file management by providing audit trails and a single point of administration. The single biggest advantage of NIS is that it adds consistency to a network. Getting all hosts to agree on usernames, **uid/gid** values, and host addresses is a prerequisite for adding other distributed services such as the Network File System.

4

Building Applications with NIS

Locally Defined Maps
Using NIS For Information Distribution
The NIS Client Library

The Network Information System is frequently considered purely a system administration tool. While it centralizes management of commonly replicated files, it does so using a distributed database mechanism that is accessible to the user through UNIX utilities and system calls. Knowing how NIS clients and servers define and access these databases, we can now go on and look at building custom applications that use NIS services.

There are three approaches to integrating NIS with an application. The easiest mechanism is to use the **ypmatch** and **ypcat** tools that are part of the suite of NIS client tools. Simple applications such as electronic Rolodexes or telephone lists can be built entirely from these tools. More advanced applications use the NIS-specific tools to extend or emulate some of the functionality of a UNIX utility, such as **rdist**. Finally, you can access any map in the NIS domain from within a C program using the NIS client library. While this is the most complex type of NIS programming, it also gives you the most flexibility. In this chapter, we'll look at examples of each kind of application.

Locally Defined Maps

System administration entails management of much more than user ID and host IP address numbers. There is a large volume of information that usually gets put into ASCII files: software license keys, telephone lists, host serial numbers, and service contract numbers, for starters. Anything that you would put into a text file and doesn't change from host to host is a good candidate for management with NIS.

Before deciding to create a new map, think about the ways in which the data is accessed. You should ensure that the data and its access patterns map into the NIS client-server relationship. Your personal telephone list probably doesn't belong in an NIS map because it would have only one client (you) accessing it, and there is no reason to share it with other clients (other users). On the other hand, the company-wide telephone list makes a good NIS map, since you can then build telephone number look-up scripts around it and use the NIS map in any other application that looks up phone numbers.

To convert an ASCII file into an NIS map, you need to know three things:

- Location and format of the source file. This defines where the map data comes from and how it will be converted into a DBM file.

- Fields that are used as keys on the data. This determines how many NIS maps you need to service requests for map data. If there's more than one common access method then you need to have multiple NIS maps derived from the same ASCII file.

- Relative frequency of change of the data. Knowing how often the map is updated is required so that you can include map updates in the appropriate **ypxfr** scripts.

The first step in creating a new NIS map is to convert the ASCII file into a DBM database file.

Building NIS Maps From ASCII Files

One NIS map must be created for each key on which the file is indexed. For example, the password file is searched by both username and numeric user ID (UID), so it requires building two NIS maps from the same ASCII file. If applications using the new map will use more than one access method, building multiple maps from the source file improves the efficiency of NIS lookups. Restricting the application to a single look-up mechanism may force it to use linear search through the NIS map if it needs to match a field other than the key field. With the password file, if the only NIS map were *passwd.byname*, then locating a user by UID value would require searching the entire NIS map, comparing UID field values with the desired key. Having the *passwd.byuid* map allows UID-driven look-ups to be completed in a single operation.

For this discussion, we'll look at converting an ASCII telephone list into a set of NIS maps. The ASCII source file is **/etc/telephone**, and it is organized as a colon-separated list of names and one or more telephone numbers. We assume that the file has some comments in it, where comment lines begin with a pound sign (#) as they do in shell scripts. In addition, any text after a # on a line is taken to be a comment. An excerpt from **/etc/telephone** is:

```
# Bitatron engineers
Hal Stern:617-555-1234:617-555-2000
John Cosentino:617-555-7890          # no secondary phone
```

To turn the ASCII file into an NIS map, it must be prepared for input to **makedbm**. The two steps in DBM preparation are to strip out comment lines and comments at the end of lines and to produce a file with lines of the form:

```
key          value
```

where *key* contains no white space and a space or tab separate the key and value items. DBM treats comment lines as valid entries and multiple comment lines may appear as entries with the same key. We'll use a **sed** script to remove entire comment lines and comments that start in the middle of a line, such as the comment in the last line of the previous example.

The white space requirement is slightly harder to meet, since most entries will have white space in between the person's first and last names. To use the person's name as a key in the NIS map, we will need to remove white space from the names. When building the map, we'll substitute underscores for spaces when creating the NIS map. Again, **sed** is a good tool for this kind of change.

Now that we know how to convert the ASCII file into DBM input, we need to determine how many NIS maps will be created from the ASCII file. To be able to look up information based on the person's name as well as their number, two maps are needed: *phones.byname* and *phones.bynumber*. In addition to requiring multiple maps, some applications need to have multiple DBM file records created for each source file entry. The telephone list is a good example of both require-ments.

The *phones.byname* map looks very similar to the original ASCII file, although spaces in names will be replaced by underscores:

```
Hal_Stern              Hal_Stern:617-555-1234:617-555-2000
John_Cosentino         John_Cosentino:617-555-7890
```

Since each person may have multiple phone numbers, the *phones.bynumber* map has multiple entries for each corresponding line in the **/etc/telephone** source file. The *phones.bynumber* map, therefore, has two entries for Hal Stern, but only one for John Cosentino:

```
617-555-1234           Hal_Stern:617-555-1234:617-555-2000
617-555-2000           Hal_Stern:617-555-1234:617-555-2000
617-555-7890           John_Cosentino:617-555-7890
```

Note that the value fields in both records for Hal Stern are identical; we'll assume in this example that we're just copying the entire database record into the value field.

Once you know which fields are used as keys for each map, and how the fields should be arranged in the data value portion of the map, you're ready to define the conversion mechanism. Since NIS maps are built and updated through the NIS **Makefile**, the rules for building a new map must be included in the **Makefile**.

Modifying the NIS Makefile

Three sections must be modified in the NIS **Makefile** to include the new NIS maps: the list of default targets, the list of map name dependencies, and the set of rules for building maps. Each NIS **Makefile** has a list of targets that will be built if **make** is invoked with no arguments. If the new map should be built in this "default" case, add its name to the definition for target *all*:

```
all: passwd group hosts ethers networks rpc services protocols \
     netgroup bootparams aliases netid netmasks phones
```

Add the following **Makefile** definition to the long section containing rules for rebuilding the maps. The first line is the map dependency, which may be placed with other map dependencies at the end of the **Makefile**:

```
phones: phones.time
phones.time: $(DIR)/telephone
        @sed -e "/^#/d" -e s/#.*$$// -e "s/ /_/g" $(DIR)/telephone | \
            awk 'BEGIN {FS=":"; OFS="\t"} \
                    {for (i = 2; i <= NF; i++) print $$i, $$0}' | \
            $(MAKEDBM) - $(YPDBDIR)/$(DOM)/phones.bynumber
        @sed -e "/^#/d" -e s/#.*$$// -e "s/ /_/g" $(DIR)/telephone | \
            awk 'BEGIN {FS=":"; OFS="\t"} \
                    {print $$1, $$0}' | \
            $(MAKEDBM) - $(YPDBDIR)/$(DOM)/phones.byname
```

```
@touch phones.time;
@echo "updated phones";
@if [ ! $(NOPUSH) ]; then $(YPPUSH) -d $(DOM) phones.byname; fi
@if [ ! $(NOPUSH) ]; then $(YPPUSH) -d $(DOM) phones.byaddr; fi
@if [ ! $(NOPUSH) ]; then echo "pushed phones"; fi
```

The **sed** scripts strip out entire comment lines and comments that run to the end of a line. The **"s/ /_/g"** editing clause also converts all spaces to underscores, removing white space that might confuse the DBM conversion. The **awk** script for *phones.bynumber* map builds a list of telephone numbers and original file lines. If an entry in **/etc/telephone** contains more than one number, the script generates multiple entries in the **phones.bynumber** map. This handles the case described above, where one person has multiple telephone numbers listed.

The **awk** script for *phones.byname* just pulls the key field—the name—and prepends it to each line of the file, separated by a tab. Again, we're using the entire line of the file as the value portion of the database record, and just adding the key field in front for DBM file conversion. The double dollar signs ($$) within the **awk** scripts keep **make** from interpreting them as **Makefile** macro expansions.

Relational database systems usually require that key fields be unique. DBM is no exception. Each record is inserted into the database using its key; if the key already exists in the data then the new record overwrites the one that was there. This is why we *must* remove white space from the keys in our telephone database, otherwise two employees with the same first name would collapse into a single DBM record in the NIS map file, as shown in the following example:

```
Hal Stern:617-555-1234:617-555-2000
Hal Pollack:617-555-8070
```

If this input file is used, and the name field is used as the key (with spaces intact), then both records try to use the key *Hal*. The record inserted for *Hal Pollack* will overwrite the first one created for *Hal Stern*, because both use the same key. Converting spaces to underscores makes the two keys unique and adds two distinct records to the database.

In the *phones.name* map, we have multiple data items in a single value field—all of the phone numbers for *Hal Stern*, for example, are in the single record with this key. The job of turning the NIS data value into something legible is left for the user-level utility in this application. This approach isn't that different from the handling of the password file, where NIS hands back a complete password file entry and the local library call converts it into a *passwd* structure for use within a C program. Before doing any data lookups, we have to get the map installed on all servers in the NIS domain.

Installing and Maintaining the Map

Distributing a new NIS map requires that you build the map on the master server, distribute initial copies to the slave servers, and include the map in the regular **ypxfr** transfer scripts. Building the new map on the master server is trivial, since it uses the rules we just added to the NIS **Makefile**:

```
master# cd /var/yp
master# make -DNOPUSH phones.byname phones.bynumber
```

The **–DNOPUSH** option gets interpreted when building the maps, and it prevents the master server from attempting to distribute the maps to the slave servers. The **yppush** utility hangs if a slave server cannot access a map, and at this point in the map creation the slave servers don't even have a copy of the map to try to access. Therefore, attempting a **yppush** before the slave servers are given a copy of the map will cause the NIS **make** to fail and **yppush** to hang. Using **–DNOPUSH** simply builds the map files on the master server; later, we can pick them up explicitly on the slave servers.

On each slave server, get the map from the master server using **ypxfr**:

```
slave# cd /var/yp
slave# ypxfr -h master phones.byname
```

The **–h master** option tells the new slave server where to find the map; once it has the map the master server record in the NIS map points to the master server for future **ypxfr** transfers. Whenever you create new maps, you have to tell the existing slave servers about them explicitly. Installing a new slave server does not require these steps to transfer locally defined maps to the new server. The slave installation script builds a list of all maps currently managed by the master server—default and locally defined maps.

The phonelist Application

Now that we have the NIS maps built and distributed, we need some applications to make the data available to users. The two simplest ways of getting data out of NIS maps are the **ypcat** and **ypmatch** tools. **ypmatch** locates a key in an NIS map and prints the data value associated with that key:

```
% ypmatch bitatron hosts.byname
131.40.52.152    bitatron
```

ypcat is similar to **ypmatch**: it dumps all of the data values in the entire NIS map. Use **ypcat** when you need to search the NIS map on a field other than the key:

```
% ypcat passwd.byname | grep /home/thud
his:Ye3FeskoSu1S2p3:1279:10:Howard Solomon:/home/thud/his:/bin/csh
stern:C7ErYscoc6bgA:1461:10:Hal Stern     :/home/thud/stern:/bin/csh
jan:ef6jgaMan9Kadw7:9641:10:Jan LeVine     :/home/thud/jan:/bin/csh
cosentin:U1gQe33tkJ:2831:10:John Cosentino:/home/thud/cosentin:/bin/csh
```

In this example, we searched the NIS password map for all lines containing **/home/thud**, giving us a list of users with home directories on this filesystem. **ypmatch** and **ypcat** will be discussed further in "NIS Tools," in Chapter 10, *Diagnostic and Administrative Tools*, but this brief introduction is sufficient to explain the operation of the tools we'll develop here.

The new telephone database can be searched with simple aliases built on **ypmatch**:

```
alias number "ypmatch `echo \!* | sed -e 's/ /_/g'` phones.byname \
        | sed -e 's/:/         /' -e 's/_/ /g'"
alias name "ypmatch `echo \!* | sed -e 's/ /-/g'` phones.bynumbers \
        | sed -e 's/:/         /'"
```

The **ypmatch** part of the alias takes the arguments on the command line and concatenates them using underscores instead of spaces between words; then the key formed by space-replacement is matched against the NIS map file. Output from **ypmatch** is post-processed by the **sed** scripts that convert colon separators into tabs, making the output easier to read. These output filters also remove the underscores we added during NIS map creation and key matching, replacing them with spaces again.

number prints all telephone numbers for the named person; **name** finds the person associated with a telephone number.

```
% number Hal Stern
Hal Stern       617-555-1234    617-555-2000
% name 617 555 1234
Hal Stern       617-555-1234    617-555-2000
```

The telephone list could be made to match names in a case-insensitive manner by building **phones.byname** with **makedbm –l**. The **–l** option forces **makdbm** to fold all keys into lowercase:

```
excerpt from NIS Makefile:
@sed -e "/^#/d" -e s/#.*$$// -e "s/ /_/g" $(DIR)/telephone | \
        awk 'BEGIN {FS=":"; OFS="\t"} \
                {print $$1, $$0}' | \
        $(MAKEDBM) -l - $(YPDBDIR)/$(DOM)/phones.byname
```

```
% number Hal Stern
Hal Stern        617-555-1234    617-555-2000
% number hal stern
Hal Stern        617-555-1234    617-555-2000
```

The difficult part of using a telephone database such as this one is that you have to know how to spell someone's name before you can locate their number. It's often more useful to be able to perform **grep**-like pattern searches on the database. Using **ypcat**, we can take our telephone database and do exactly that:

```
% ypcat phones.byname | grep Hal
Hal Stern:617-555-1234:617-555-2000
```

Using **ypmatch** is faster to find a single name, since the NIS database is accessed exactly once while **ypcat** dumps every entry in the map file. However, using **ypcat** allows you to apply other UNIX filters such as **grep** to handle inexact matching or other types of lookups.

Using NIS For Information Distribution

The telephone database is a fairly simple and common NIS application. In this section, we'll use NIS to take a different approach to configuration file distribution. Instead of distributing the entire configuration file to every host on the network, the clients will retrieve those parts of the file in which they are interested. We'll be merging the functionality of the **rdist** file distribution tool and **grep** to perform host-specific file management from a single point of administration.

There are two cases in which client-driven file distribution is preferable to server-driven distribution: when clients must have private information exclusive of other hosts, and when extending root permissions for **rcp** or **rdist** compromises other security measures in place on the network. Using NIS solves both problems: you keep all data in a single place, and clients pick and choose those data values they need. The process is client-driven, so there is no need for allowing networked superuser access.

Consider a file containing software package licenses. Each line in the file contains a hostname, the package name, and some encrypted license key. Machines using the packages must have valid license files, with one line for each package licensed. However, the license file should contain information only for the local host; adding information for hundreds of other machines makes the package start-up much slower as it parses hundreds (or thousands) of lines looking for the relevant license key. A solution is to create a central NIS map with complete license information for all hosts. Each client then extracts its record and "explodes it" to form its relevant portion of the licenses file.

The package license file requires that we put the hostname, package name, and key on a single line, with one line for each installed package. The per-host license file, which is saved in **/etc/licenses**, looks like this:

```
bitatron:dos-emulator:abcdef
bitatron:spreadsheet:ghijkl
```

To simplify administration of the master license database and to make generation of the NIS map easier, we'll merge lines for a host onto a single line in the master NIS map source file. The ASCII master license file, **/etc/license.master**, has all of the information in colon-separated fields, with each line containing all package/key pairs for a single host:

```
# hostname : package name : key : package name : key
bitatron:dos-emulator:abcdef:spreadsheet:ghijkl
corvette:dos-emulator:mkdlok
```

Now we can build an NIS map using the hostname as the key field, since the source file contains exactly one line for each host. The NIS **Makefile** excerpt looks similar to that used for the telephone database:

```
licenses: licenses.time
licenses.time: $(DIR)/licenses.master
        @sed -e "/^#/d" -e s/#.*$$// $(DIR)/licenses.master | \
                awk 'BEGIN {FS=":"; OFS="\t"} \
                        {print $$1, $$0}' | \
                $(MAKEDBM) - $(YPDBDIR)/$(DOM)/licenses.byname
        @touch licenses.time;
        @echo "updated licenses";
        @if [ ! $(NOPUSH) ]; then $(YPPUSH) -d $(DOM) licenses.byname; fi
        @if [ ! $(NOPUSH) ]; then echo "pushed licenses"; fi
```

Since we only access the license file by hostname, we only need one NIS map for it. The key is the first field in the file; the data value is the entire record. Finding all of the package information for a host involves doing a single **ypmatch** on this map, using the hostname as the key value.

To distribute the license file and convert it into the proper format, run the following script out of **cron**, on each client, once a night:

```
#! /bin/sh
ypmatch `hostname` licenses.byname | \
        awk -F':' '{for (i = 2; i <= NF; i+=2) print $i, $(i+1)}' | \
        sed -e "s/^/`hostname`:/" -e "s/ /:/" > /etc/licenses
```

The first line locates the local host's license information in the NIS map and pipes it into an **awk** script, which prints the package names and license keys in pairs, one pair per line. The final **sed** script inserts the hostname at the beginning of each line and puts colon separators in between the package names and license keys. The output of the whole pipe is dropped into **/etc/licenses**, completing the configuration file distribution.

The NIS Client Library

The shell scripts described so far are useful for managing configuration information or simple text databases. One of the real strengths of using NIS as a database management system is the NIS client library, which provides a C language interface to the library and system calls used by **ypmatch** and **ypcat**. Using the client library, you can integrate NIS services with other applications.

In previous chapters, we saw how the plus sign (+) token in many system configuration files included the contents of an NIS map. The mechanism that interprets + to mean "read an NIS map" is contained in the standard C library routines that read these files; when they see the NIS token they make NIS client library calls. If you insert the + marker in other files, it won't have any effect unless the routines that read these files have been modified to use NIS services as well. For example, inserting + at the end of **/etc/printcap** does *not* make the line printing system look at any NIS-managed **printcap** files. It is up to you, as a tools developer, to define both the syntax of using NIS map files and the semantics of the data in map files.

Integrating NIS Services Into Applications

Setting up an application to talk to an NIS server is easy once you have all of the data. To retrieve map data, you need an NIS domain name, an NIS map name, and the key for the map. Integrating NIS services well requires that you first consider how the NIS data and any local data will interact: how will the NIS map data be included? Will the local file be referenced or overridden completely by NIS? The best answer to these questions is to maintain consistency in the use of NIS, both by custom applications and by standard tools and procedures used by system administrators.

The functions in the NIS client library closely resemble the user-level utilities that perform similar functions:

yp_get_default_domain()

> Gets the current NIS domain name, set by **domainname** at boot time. Applications may choose to use the current client domain name, or they may bind to another domain.

yp_bind()

> Binds the named domain (passed as an argument) to a server. Recall that the **ypbind** process maintains client-server bindings and handles multiple domains if processes on the client request the services of more than one domain.

yp_match()	Matches a key in a named map. It is the heart of the **ypmatch** utility.
yp_get_first()	Retrieves the first key (in DBM file order) from the NIS map. It is the beginning of the **ypcat** tool.
yp_get_next()	Picks up where *yp_get_first()* left off and gets the next key from the NIS map. The order in which the keys are retrieved depends upon how DBM put them into its hash table, so there is no guaranteed order of the records. Walking through all entries in an NIS map is required only if you need to match multiple records in the database (on non-key fields, since the keys are unique) or if the key fields are not suitable as search criteria.

The NIS client library also defines a few NIS-specific **errno** values, reflecting possible error conditions encountered during NIS map access:

YPERR_DOMAIN	No server could be found for the named domain. This usually means that either the programmer has passed an invalid domainname to an NIS routine, or all of the NIS servers in the network are down.
YPERR_MAP	The named map doesn't exist in the NIS domain. This is usually because the programmer missed a suffix on a map file name.
YPERR_KEY	The specific key does not exist in the database.
YPERR_NOMORE	When walking through the NIS map, this error occurs when the last record has been read.

The key is passed in *yp_match()* calls to the server along with the key length. Key data is stored in character arrays and is treated as a vector of 8-bit values rather than a null-terminated string. Any arbitrary binary value can be used as a key, but you must take care that a binary key is byte-order independent on hosts of different architectures.

Example: The Stock Quote Service

At Sun, we have a stock quote service that is paid for out of contributions by its users. If you don't pay for the service, you can't use it. To enforce this policy, the stock quote retrieval tools were modified to match usernames against an NIS map of valid contributors and to print spirited messages for anyone not in the map.

The code fragment below shows how the quote service identifies valid users before displaying any interesting information. It uses uses the current NIS domain name—the default domain name—and a map called *stock.byname*:

```c
#include <stdio.h>
#include <ctype.h>
#include <netdb.h>
#include <pwd.h>

main(argc, argv)
        int argc;
        char *argv[];
{
        char *domainname;
        char  username[16];
        char  *mapentry;
        int    yperr;
        int    entrylen;
        struct passwd *getpwuid();
        struct passwd *pw;

        pw = getpwuid(getuid());
        strcpy(username,  pw->pw_name);
        yp_get_default_domain(&domainname);
        yp_bind(domainname);
        yperr = yp_match(domainname, "stock.byname", username, strlen(username),
                       &mapentry, &entrylen);
        if (yperr == YPERR_KEY) {
                printf("You are not an authorized quote system user.\n");
                printf("You can change this for the low price of $5.\n");
                exit(1);
        }
        if (yperr) {
                printf("There is a problem with the stock user map.\n");
                printf("Please call your system administrator for help\n");
                exit(1);
        }
        /* quote retrieval code goes here */
}
```

This code fragment starts by getting the current user's log-in name via *getpwuid()*, which itself calls NIS to read the password map. It then grabs the default domain name (set by **domainname** at boot time), and then requests a binding to the NIS server for the domain. There is no requirement that the default domain be used, but if you've added maps according to the examples above then your maps are part of the default domain.

The username is then matched as a key in the *stock.byname* map. Keys are interpreted as 8-bit values that may include zeros, so a length is passed along with the key to designate the actual number of bytes to match in the key. While it's possible to use binary data in NIS map keys, be sure that clients accessing the data agree on the format of the key data. If you have both big-endian and little-endian machines reading NIS maps, don't use a 2-byte integer as a map key, because the two hosts don't pack the key buffer the same way. The key is a stream of bytes, not integers, so be sure you load it byte-by-byte. Copying an integer (or anything else besides character data) into the key field will make your code non-portable.

If the user is a paid contributor, then *yp_match*() returns a success and the quote retrieval proceeds normally. If, however, YPERR_KEY is returned, the user is not in the stock user's NIS map and is politely told to send money. For simplicity, some additional error checking is left out of this example. The *yp_match*() call, for example, could return YPERR_MAP, indicating that the *stock.byname* NIS map either isn't in the domain at all or isn't present on the currently bound NIS server.

When building applications that use NIS, consider the cost of performing NIS RPCs for each access to the database. If you can retrieve the data once, or think that the data will be static during the lifetime of your application, retrieve it from the NIS map and then store it within the application. RPC servers are limited by the number of CPU cycles or disk throughput available to them on the server host, but RPC clients are generally not restricted in the number of calls they may make to any servers. A few misbehaved clients can degrade performance of one or more RPC servers on the network, affecting both NFS and NIS. Client behavior problems will be covered in more detail as we explore the operation of the Network File System.

5

System Administration Using the Network Filesystem

Setting up NFS
Exporting Filesystems
Mounting Filesystems
Symbolic Links
Naming Schemes

The Network File System (NFS) is a distributed file system that provides transparent access to remote disks. Just as NIS allows you to centralize administration of user and host information, NFS allows you to centralize administration of disks. Instead of duplicating common directories such as **/usr/local** on every system, NFS provides a single copy of the directory that is shared by all systems on the network. To a host running NFS, remote filesystems are indistinguishable from local ones. For the user, NFS means that he or she doesn't have to log into other systems to access files. There is no need to use **rcp** or tapes to move files onto the local system. Once NFS has been set up properly, users should be able to do all their work on their local system; remote files (data and executables) will appear to be "local" to their own system. NFS and NIS are frequently used together: NIS makes sure that configuration information is propagated to all hosts, and NFS ensures that the files a user needs are accessible from these hosts.

NFS is also built on the RPC protocol and imposes a client-server relationship on the hosts that use it. An NFS server is a host that owns one or more filesystems and makes them available on the network; NFS clients mount filesystems from one or more servers. This follows the normal client-server model where the server owns a resource that is used by the client. In the case of NFS, the resource is a physical disk drive that is shared by all clients of the server.

There are two aspects to system administration using NFS: choosing a filesystem naming and mounting scheme, and then configuring the servers and clients to adhere to this scheme. The goal of any naming scheme should be to use network transparency wisely. Being able to mount filesystems from any server is useful only if the files are presented in a manner that is consistent with what the users' expectations are.

If NFS has been set up correctly, it should be transparent to the user. For example, if locally developed applications were found in **/usr/local/bin** before NFS was installed, they should continue to be found there when NFS is running, whether **/usr/local/bin** is on a local filesystem or a remote one. To the user, the actual disk holding **/usr/local/bin** isn't important as long as the executables are accessible and built for the right machine architecture. If users must change their environments to locate files accessed through NFS, they will probably dislike the new network architecture because it changes the way things work.

An environment with many NFS servers and hundreds of clients can quickly become overwhelming in terms of management complexity. Successful system administration of a large NFS network requires adding some intelligence to the standard procedures. The cost of consistency on the network should not be a large administrative overhead. One tool that greatly eases the task of running an NFS network is the *automounter*, which applies NIS management to NFS configuration. This chapter starts with a quick look at how to get NFS up and running on clients and servers, and then explores NFS naming schemes and common filesystem planning problems. We'll cover the automounter in detail in Chapter 13, *The Automounter*.

Setting up NFS

Setting up NFS on clients and servers involves starting the daemons that handle the NFS RPC protocol, starting additional daemons for auxiliary services such as file locking, and then simply exporting filesystems from the NFS servers and mounting them on the clients.

On an NFS client, you need to have the **biod, rpc.lockd,** and **rpc.statd** daemons running in order to use NFS. These daemons are generally started in the boot scripts:

```
if [ -f /usr/etc/biod ]; then
        biod 4;                     echo -n ' biod'
fi

if [ -f /usr/etc/rpc.statd ]; then
        rpc.statd &                 echo -n ' statd'
fi

if [ -f /usr/etc/rpc.lockd ]; then
        rpc.lockd &                 echo -n ' lockd'
fi
```

On your system, **biod** may be started only if there are NFS filesystem entries in the **/etc/fstab**, or if you enable NFS through a boot configuration file. Check your vendor's documentation for the proper invocation of the NFS client daemons.

The **biod** daemons perform block I/O operations for NFS clients, performing some simple read-ahead and write-behind performance optimization. You run multiple instances of **biod** so that each client process can have multiple NFS requests outstanding at any time. We'll take a closer look at the **biod** process later on.

The **rpc.lockd** and **rpc.statd** daemons handle file locking and lock recovery on the client. These locking daemons also run on an NFS server, and the client-side daemons coordinate file locking on the NFS server through their server-side counterparts. We'll come back to file locking later when we discuss how NFS handles state information.

On an NFS server, NFS services are started with the **nfsd** and **rpc.mountd** daemons, as well as the file locking daemons used on the client. You should see the NFS server daemons started in the boot scripts:

```
if [ -f /etc/exports ]; then
        > /etc/xtab
        exportfs -a
        nfsd 8
        echo -n ' nfsd'
        rpc.mountd -n
fi
```

The **/etc/exports** file determines which filesystems the NFS server will allow clients to mount via NFS. In this script file excerpt, the NFS server daemons are not started unless the host exports NFS filesystems in the **/etc/exports** file. If there are filesystems to be made available for NFS service the machine initializes the export list with them and starts the NFS daemons. As with the client-side, check your vendor's documentation or the boot scripts themselves for details on how the various server daemons are started.

The **nfsd** daemon accepts NFS RPC requests and executes them on the server. A server runs multiple copies of the daemon so that it can handle several RPC requests at once. Varying the number of daemons on a server is a performance tuning issue that will be discussed in "NFS Server Daemons," in Chapter 12, *Performance Analysis and Tuning*. The **rpc.mountd** daemon handles client mount requests. The mount protocol is not part of NFS and requires its own daemon to convert mount information on the client into pathnames on the server.

Exporting Filesystems

Usually, a host decides to become an NFS server if it has filesystems to export to the network. A server does not explicitly advertise these filesystems; instead, it keeps a list of currently exported filesystems and associated access restrictions in a file and compares incoming NFS mount requests to entries in this table. It is up to the server to decide if a filesystem can be mounted by a client. You may change the rules at any time by rebuilding its exported filesystem table.

The exported filesystem table is initialized from the **/etc/exports** file. The superuser may export other filesystems once the server is up and running, so the **exports** file and the actual list of currently exported filesystems are maintained separately. When a fileserver boots, it checks for the existence of **/etc/exports** and runs **exportfs** on it to make filesystems available for client use. On many systems, the presence of **/etc/exports** is the condition used to start the NFS server daemons **nfsd** and **rpc.mountd**.

Rules for Exporting Filesystems

There are four rules for making a server's filesystem available to NFS:

1. Any filesystem, or proper subset of a filesystem, can be exported from a server. A proper subset of a filesystem is a file or directory tree that starts below the mount point of the filesystem. For example, if **/usr** is a filesystem, and the **/usr/local** directory is part of that filesystem, then **/usr/local** is a proper subset of **/usr**.

2. You cannot export any subdirectory of an exported filesystem unless the subdirectory is on a different physical device.

3. You cannot export any parent directory of an exported filesystem unless the parent is on a different physical device.

4. You can only export local filesystems.

The first rule allows you to export selected portions of a large filesystem. You can export and mount a single file, a feature that is used by diskless clients. The second and third rules seem both redundant and confusing, but are in place to enforce the selective views imposed by exporting a subdirectory of a filesystem.

The second rule allows you to export **/usr/local/bin** when **/usr/local** is already exported from the same server only if **/usr/local/bin** is on a different disk. For example, if your server mounts these filesystems using **/etc/fstab** entries like:

```
/dev/sd0g       /usr/local          4.2 rw 1 3
/dev/sd1d       /usr/local/bin      4.2 rw 1 3
```

then exporting both of them is allowed, since the exported directories reside on different filesystems. If, however, **bin** was a subdirectory of **/usr/local**, then it could not be exported in conjunction with its parent.

The third rule is the converse of the second. If you have a subdirectory exported, you cannot also export its parent unless they are on different filesystems. In the previous example, if **/usr/local/bin** is already exported, then **/usr/local** can only be exported if it is on a different filesystem. This rule prevents entire filesystems from being exported on the fly when the system administrator has carefully chosen to export a selected set of subdirectories.

Together, the second and third rules say that you can only export a local filesystem one way. Once you export a subdirectory of it, you can't go and export the whole thing; and once you've made the whole thing public you can't go and restrict the export list to a subdirectory or two.

One way to check the validity of subdirectory exports is to use the **df** command to determine on which local filesystem the current directory resides. If you find that the parent directory and its subdirectory appear in the output of **df**, then they are on separate filesystems and it is safe to export them both.

Exporting subdirectories is similar to creating views on a relational database. You choose the portions of the database that a user needs to see, hiding information that is extraneous or sensitive. In NFS, exporting a subdirectory of a filesystem is useful if the entire filesystem contains subdirectories with names that might confuse users, or if the filesystem contains several parallel directory trees of which only one is useful to the user.

Exporting Options

The **/etc/exports** file contains a list of filesystems that a server exports and any restrictions or export options for each.

Options are preceded with a dash and are separated by commas:

```
/home/users
/usr/local      -rw=corvette
/usr/tools      -ro,access=bitatron:corvette:vacation
```

Table 5-1. NFS Export Options

Option	Function
rw=_host:host_	Limit hosts that can write to the filesystem.
ro	Prevent any host from writing to the filesystem.
access=_host:host_	Restrict access to the named hosts.
root=_host:host_	Grant root access to the named hosts.
anon=_uid_	Map anonymous users to _uid_.
secure	Force clients to use Secure RPC to access this filesystem.

There are several options that modify the way a filesystem is exported to the network:

ro   Prevent NFS clients from writing to the filesystem. This option is not checked when the client mounts the filesystem; the NFS server cannot determine which options were specified by the client when it performed the NFS mount. Read-only restrictions are enforced when a client performs an operation on an NFS filesystem: if the client has mounted the filesystem with read and write permissions, but the server specified **ro** when exporting it, any attempt by the client to write to the filesystem will fail, with "Read-only filesystem" or "Permission denied" messages.

rw=_host_   Limit the set of hosts that may write to the filesystem to the named host or hosts. If no hostname is given, then any NFS client may write to the filesystem.

access=_host_   Allow only the named host or hosts to access the filesystem. Hosts that are not in this list will not be able to mount the filesystem at all.

anon=*uid*   Map anonymous, or unknown, users to *uid*. Anonymous users are those that do not present valid credentials in their NFS requests. Note that an anonymous user is *not* one that does not appear in the server's password file or NIS *passwd* map. If no credentials at all are included with the NFS request, it is treated as an anonymous request. Secure NFS and PC/NFS clients can submit requests from unknown users if the proper user validation is not completed; we'll look at both of these problems in later chapters. "Unknown User Mapping," in Chapter 8, *Network Security*, discusses the *anon* option in more detail.

root=*host*   Grant superuser access to the named host or hosts. To enforce basic network security, superuser privileges are not extended over the network. The *root* option allows you to selectively grant root access to a filesystem. This is another security feature that will be covered in "Superuser Mapping," in Chapter 8.

Your system may support additional options, so check your vendor's manual pages for **exportfs(8)** and **exports(5)**.

Mounting Filesystems

NFS clients can mount any filesystem, or part of a filesystem, that has been exported from an NFS server. The filesystem can be listed in the client's **/etc/fstab** file, or it can be mounted explicitly using the **mount(8)** command. NFS filesystems appear to be "normal" filesystems on the client, which means that they can be mounted on any directory on the client. It's possible to mount an NFS filesystem over all or part of another filesystem, since the directories used as mount points appear the same no matter where they actually reside. When you mount a filesystem on top of another one, you obscure whatever is "under" the mount point. NFS clients see the most recent view of the filesystem. These potentially confusing issues will be the foundation for the discussion of NFS naming schemes later in this chapter.

Using /etc/fstab

Adding entries to **/etc/fstab** is the most common way to mount NFS filesystems. Once the entry has been added to the **fstab** file, the client mounts it on every reboot. There are several features that distinguish NFS filesystems in the **fstab** file:

- The "device name" field is replaced with a *server:filesystem* specification, where the filesystem name is a pathname (not a device name) on the server.

- The filesystem type is *nfs*, not *4.2* as for local filesystems.

- The **fsck** pass and sequence numbers are both 0.

- The options field can contain a variety of NFS-specific mount options, covered in the next section, "Using mount."

Some typical **fstab** entries for NFS filesystems are:

```
ono:/home/ono          /home/ono          nfs rw,bg,hard  0 0
onaga:/home/onaga      /home/onaga        nfs rw,bg,hard  0 0
wahoo:/var/spool/mail  /var/spool/mail    nfs rw,bg,hard  0 0
```

Of course, each vendor is free to vary the server and filesystem name syntax, and your manual set should provide the best sample **fstab** entries. In Ultrix, for example, filesystem and hostnames are represented like mail addresses and the fields are separated by colons, not by white space:

```
/usr/nemo@nemo:/usr/nemo:rw:0:0:nfs:rw,bg,hard:
```

Using mount

While entries in the **fstab** file are useful for creating a long-lived NFS environment, sometimes you need to mount a filesystem right away or mount it temporarily while you copy files from it. The **mount** command allows you to perform an NFS filesystem mount that remains active until you explicitly unmount the filesystem using **umount**, or until the client is rebooted.

As an example of using **mount**, consider building and testing a new **/usr/local** directory. On an NFS client, you already have the "old" **/usr/local**, either on a local or NFS mounted filesystem. Let's say you have built a new version of **/usr/local** on NFS server *wahoo*, and want to test it on this NFS client. Mount the new filesystem on top of the existing **/usr/local**:

```
# mount wahoo:/usr/local /usr/local
```

Anything in the old **/usr/local** is hidden by the new mount point, so you can debug your new **/usr/local** as if it were mounted at boot time.

From the command line, **mount** uses a server name and filesystem name syntax similar to that of the **fstab** file. **mount** assumes that the type is **nfs** if a hostname appears in the device specification:

```
# mount ono:/home/ono /home/ono -o rw,bg,hard
```

The server filesystem name must be an absolute pathname (starting with a leading /), but it need not exactly match the name of a filesystem exported from the server. The only restriction on server filesystem names is that they must contain a valid, exported server filesystem name as a prefix. This means that you can mount a subdirectory of an exported filesystem, as long as you specify the entire pathname to the subdirectory in either the **fstab** file or on the **mount** command line.

For example, to mount a particular home directory from **/home/ono**, you do not have to mount the entire filesystem. Picking up the interesting subdirectory may make the local filesystem hierarchy simpler and less cluttered with extra directories. To mount a subdirectory of a server's exported filesystem, just specify the pathname to that directory in the **fstab** file:

```
ono:/home/ono/stern        /home/ono/stern      nfs rw,bg,hard  0 0
```

Even though server *ono* exports all of **/home/ono**, you can choose to handle some smaller portion of the entire filesystem.

Mount Options

NFS mount options are as varied as the vendors themselves. There are a few well-known and widely-supported options, and others that are added to support additional NFS features or to integrate secure remote procedure call systems. As with everything else that is vendor-specific, your system's manual set provides a complete list of supported mount options. Check the manual pages for both **mount(8)** and **fstab(5)**.

The common NFS mount options are:

rw/ro   **rw** mounts a filesystem read-write; this is the default. If **ro** is specified, the filesystem is mounted read-only. Use the **ro** option if the server enforces write protection for various filesystems.

bg   Retry a failed mount attempt in the background, allowing the foreground **mount** process to continue. We'll discuss this option further in the next section.

hard/soft   By default, NFS filesystems are **hard** mounted, and operations on them are retried until they are acknowledged by the server. If the

soft option is specified, an NFS RPC call returns a timeout error if it fails the number of times specified by the **retrans** option.

retrans/timeo   The **retrans** option specifies the number of times to repeat an RPC request before returning a timeout error on a soft mounted filesystem. The **timeo** parameter varies the RPC timeout period and is given in tenths of a second:

```
onaga:/home/onaga  /home/onaga  nfs rw,retrans=6,timeo=11  0 0
```

intr   Normally, NFS operations are not interruptible and continue until an RPC error occurs or they are completed successfully. If a server is down and a client is waiting for an RPC call to complete, the process making the RPC call hangs until the server responds. With the **intr** option, the user can interrupt NFS RPC calls and force the RPC layer to return an error.

The **intr**, **retrans**, **timeo**, **hard**, and **soft** options will be discussed in in the section "Client Tuning," in Chapter 12, *Performance Analysis and Tuning*, since they are directly responsible for altering clients' performance in periods of peak server loading.

Backgrounding Mounts

The mount protocol used by clients is subject to the same RPC timeouts as individual NFS RPC calls. When a client cannot mount an NFS filesystem during the allotted RPC execution time, it retries the RPC operation up to the count specified by the **retry** mount option. If the **bg** mount option is used, **mount** starts another process that continues trying to mount the filesystem in the background, allowing the **mount** command to consider that request complete and to attempt the next mount operation. If **bg** is not specified, **mount** blocks waiting for the remote file server to recover, or until the mount retry count has been reached. The default value of 10,000 may cause a single mount to hang for several hours before **mount** gives up on the file server.

You cannot background the mount of any system-critical filesystem such as the root (/) or **/usr** filesystem on a diskless client. If you need the filesystem to run the system, you must allow the mount to complete in the foreground. Similarly, if you require some applications from an NFS mounted partition during the boot process—let's say you start up a license server in **/etc/rc.local**—you should hard mount the filesystem with these executables so that you are not left with a half-functioning machine. Any filesystem that is not critical to the system's operation can be mounted with the **bg** option. Use of background mounts allows your network to recover more gracefully from widespread problems such as power failures.

When two servers are clients of each other, the **bg** option must be used in at least one of the server's **/etc/fstab** files. When both servers boot at the same time, as the result of a power failure, for example, one usually tries to mount the other's filesystems before they have been exported and before NFS is started. If both servers use foreground mounts only, then a deadlock is possible when they wait on each other to recover as NFS servers. Using **bg** allows the first mount attempt to fail and be put into the background. When both servers finally complete booting, the backgrounded mounts complete successfully.

The retry count was chosen to be large enough to guarantee that a client makes a sufficiently good effort to mount a filesystem from a crashed or hung server. However, if some event causes client and server to reboot at the same time, and the client cannot complete the mount before the retry count is exhausted, the client will not mount the filesystem even when the remote server comes back online. If you have a power failure early in the weekend, and all clients come up but a server is down, you may have to manually remount filesystems on clients that have reached their limit of mount retries.

Hard and Soft Mounts

The **hard** and **soft** mount options determine how a client behaves when the server is excessively loaded for a long period, or when it crashes. By default, all NFS filesystems are mounted **hard**, which means that an RPC call that times out will be retried indefinitely until a response is received from the server. This makes the NFS server look as much like a local disk as possible—the request that needs to go to disk completes at some point in the future. An NFS server that crashes looks like a disk that is very, very slow.

A side effect of hard-mounting NFS filesystems is that processes block (or "hang") in a high-priority disk wait state until their NFS RPC calls complete. If an NFS server goes down, the clients using its filesystems hang if they reference these filesystems before the server recovers. Using **intr** in conjunction with the **hard** mount option allows users to interrupt system calls that are blocked waiting on a crashed server. The system call is interrupted when the process making the call receives a signal, usually sent by the user typing CTRL-C or using the **kill** command.

When an NFS filesystem is **soft** mounted, repeated RPC call failures eventually cause the NFS operation to fail as well. Instead of emulating a painfully slow disk, a server exporting a soft-mounted filesystem looks like a failing disk when it crashes: system calls referencing the soft-mounted NFS filesystem return errors. Sometimes the errors can be ignored or are preferable to blocking at high priority; for example, if you were doing an **ls –l** when the NFS server crashed, you wouldn't really care if the **ls** command returned an error as long as your system didn't hang.

The other side to this "failing disk" analogy is that you *never* want to write data to an unreliable device, nor do you want to try to load executables from it. You should not use the **soft** option on any filesystem that is writeable, nor on any filesystem from which you load executables. NFS only guarantees the consistency of data after a server crash if the NFS filesystem was hard-mounted by the client.

We'll come back to hard- and soft-mount issues in when we discuss modifying client behavior in the face of slow NFS servers.

Resolving Mount Problems

There are several things that can go wrong when attempting to mount an NFS filesystem. The most obvious failure of **mount** is when it cannot find the server, remote filesystem, or local mount point; you get the usual assortment of errors such as "No such host" and "No such file or directory." However, you may also get more cryptic messages like:

```
client# mount orion:/home/orion /home/orion
mount: orion:/home/orion on /home/orion: No such device.
```

If either the local or remote filesystem was specified incorrectly, you would expect a message about a nonexistent file or directory. The *device* hint in this error indicates that NFS is not configured into the client's kernel. The *device* in question is more of a pseudo-device—it's the interface to the NFS vnode operations. If the NFS client code is not in the kernel, this interface does not exist and any attempts to use it return invalid device messages. We won't discuss how to build a kernel; check your documentation for the proper procedures and options that need to be included to support NFS.

Probably the most common message on NFS clients is "NFS server not responding." An NFS client will attempt to complete an RPC call up to the number of times specified by the **retrans** option. Once the retry limit has been reached, the "not responding" message appears on the system's console (or in the console window), followed by a message indicating that the server has responded to the client's RPC requests:

```
NFS server bitatron not responding, still trying
```

or:

```
NFS server bitatron OK
```

These "not responding" messages may mean that the server is heavily loaded and cannot respond to NFS requests before the client has had numerous RPC timeouts, or they may indicate that the server has crashed. The NFS client cannot tell the difference between the two, because it has no knowledge of why its NFS RPC calls are not being handled. If NFS clients begin printing "not responding" messages, a server have may have crashed, or you may be experiencing a burst of activity causing poor server performance.

A less common but more confusing error message is "stale file handle." Because NFS allows multiple clients to share the same directory, it opens up a window in which one client can delete files or directories that are being referenced by another NFS client of the same server. When the second client goes to reference the deleted directory, the NFS server can no longer find it on disk, and marks the handle, or pointer, to this directory "invalid." The exact causes of stale file handles and suggestions for avoiding them are described in "Stale File Handles," in Chapter 12, *Performance Analysis and Tuning*.

If there is a problem with the server's NFS configuration, your attempt to mount filesystems from it will result in RPC errors when **mount** cannot reach the portmapper on the server. If you get RPC timeouts, then the remote host may have lost its portmapper service or the **rpc.mountd** daemon may have exited prematurely. Use **ps** to locate these processes:

```
server% ps -agux | fgrep mountd
stern     252  0.0  0.8  144  248 p0 S   15:30  0:00 fgrep mountd
root      112  0.0  0.7   88  224 ?  S   12:17  0:04 rpc.mountd
server% ps -agux | fgrep portmap
root       55  0.0  0.0   80    0 ?  IW  12:17  0:00 portmap
stern     254  0.0  0.8  144  248 p0 S   15:30  0:00 fgrep portmap
```

You should see both the **rpc.mountd** and the **portmap** processes running on the NFS server.

If **mount** promptly reports "MOUNT_PROG not registered," this means that the **rpc.mountd** daemon never started up and registered itself. In this case, make sure that **rpc.mountd** is getting started at boot time on the NFS server, by checking the **/etc/rc.local** script.

Another **mountd**-related problem is two **rpc.mountd** daemons competing for the same RPC service number. With one mount daemon started in the boot scripts and one configured into **/etc/inetd.conf**, the second instance of the server daemon will not be able to register its RPC service number with the portmapper. Since the **inetd**-spawned process is usually the second to appear, it repeatedly exits and restarts until **inetd** realizes that the server cannot be started and disables the service. The NFS RPC daemons should be started from the boot scripts and not from **inetd**, due to the overhead of spawning processes from the **inetd** server (see "Internet and RPC Server Configuration," in Chapter 1, *Networking Fundamentals*).

There is also a detection mechanism for attempts to make "transitive," or multi-hop, NFS mounts. You can only use NFS to mount another system's local filesystem as one of your NFS filesystems. You can't mount another system's NFS-mounted filesystems. That is, if **/home/bob** is local on *serverb*, then all machines on the network must mount **/home/bob** from *serverb*. If a client attempts to mount a remotely mounted directory on the server, the mount fails with a multi-hop error message:

```
mount: marble:/home/bob on /home/bob: Too many levels of remote in path
```

"Too many levels" means more than one—the filesystem on the server is itself NFS mounted. You cannot nest NFS mounts by mounting through an intermediate fileserver. There are two practical sides to this restriction:

- Allowing multi-hop mounts would defeat the host-based permission checking used by NFS. If a *server* limits access to a filesystem to a few clients, then one of these client should not be allowed to NFS mount the filesystem and make it available to other, non-trusted systems. Preventing multi-hop mounts makes the server owning the filesystem the single authority governing its use—no other machine can circumvent the access policies set by the NFS server owning a filesystem.

- Any machine used as an intermediate server in a multi-hop mount becomes a very inefficient "gateway" between the NFS client and the server owning the filesystem.

We've seen how to export NFS filesystems on a network, and how NFS clients mount them. With this basic explanation of NFS usage, we'll look at how NFS mounts are combined with symbolic links to create more complex—and sometimes confusing—client filesystem structures.

Symbolic Links

Symbolic links are both useful and confusing when used with NFS-mounted filesystems. They can be used to "shape" a filesystem arbitrarily, giving the system administrator freedom to organize filesystems and pathnames in convenient ways. When used badly, symbolic links have unexpected and unwanted side effects, including poor performance and "missing" files or directories. In this section, we'll discuss the many effects that symbolic links can have on NFS.

Symbolic links differ from hard links in several ways, but the salient distinction is that hard links duplicate directory entries, while symbolic links are new directory entries of a special type. Using a hard link to a file is no different from using the original file, but referencing a symbolic link requires reading the link to find out where it points and then referencing that file or directory. It is possible to create a loop of symbolic links, but the kernel routines that read the links and build up pathnames eventually return an error when too many links have been traversed in a single pathname.

Resolving Symbolic Links in NFS

When an NFS client does a *stat*() of a directory entry and finds it is a symbolic link, it issues an RPC call to read the link (on the server) and determine where the link points. This is the equivalent of doing a local *readlink*() system call to examine the contents of a symbolic link. The server returns a pathname that is interpreted on the client, not on the server.

The pathname may point to a directory that the client has mounted, or it may not make sense on the client. If you uncover a link that was made on the server that points to a filesystem not exported from the server, you will have either trouble or confusion if you resolve the link. If the link accidentally points to a valid file or directory on the client, the results are often unpredictable and sometimes unwanted. If the link points to something non-existent on the client, an attempt to use it produces an error.

An example here helps explain how links can point in unwanted directions. Let's say that you install a new publishing package, **marker,** in the **tools** filesystem on an NFS server. Once it's loaded, you realize that you need to free some space on the **/tools** filesystem, so you move the font directory used by **marker** to the /usr filesystem, and make a symbolic link to redirect the **fonts** subdirectory to its new location:

```
# mkdir /usr/marker
# cd /tools/marker
# tar cf - fonts | ( cd /usr/marker; tar xbBfp 20 - )
# rm -rf fonts
# ln -s /usr/marker/fonts fonts
```

The **tar** command copies the entire directory tree from the current directory to **/usr/marker** (see the manual page for **tar(1)** for a more detailed explanation).

On the server, the redirection imposed by the symbolic link is invisible to users. However, an NFS client that mounts **/tools/marker** and tries to use it will be in for a surprise when the client tries to find the **fonts** subdirectory. The client looks at **/tools/marker/fonts**, realizes that it's a symbolic link, and asks the NFS server to read the link. The NFS server returns the link's target—**/usr/marker/fonts**—and the client tries to open this directory instead. On the client, however, this directory *does not exist*. It was created for convenience on the server, but breaks the NFS clients that use it. To fix this problem, you must create the same symbolic link on all of the clients, and ensure that the clients can locate the target of the link.

Think of symbolic links as you would files on an NFS server. The server does not interpret the contents of files, nor does it do anything with the contents of a link except pass it back to the user process that issued the *readlink* RPC. Symbolic links are treated as if they existed on the local host, and they are interpreted relative to the client's filesystem hierarchy.

Absolute and Relative Pathnames

Symbolic links can point to an absolute pathname (one beginning with /) or a pathname relative to the link's path. Relative symbolic link targets are resolved relative to the place at which the link appears in the client's filesystem, not the server's, so it is possible for a relative link to point at a nonexistent file or directory on the client. Consider this server for **/usr/local**:

```
% cd /usr/local/bin
% ls -l
total 1
lrwxrwxrwx  1 root           16 Jun  8 1990 a2ps -> ../bin.mips/a2ps
lrwxrwxrwx  1 root           12 Jun  8 1990 mp -> ../bin.mips/mp
```

If you mount just **/usr/local/bin** from this server, you will not be able to use any of the executables in it unless you have them in the directory **/usr/local/bin.mips**.

Using symbolic links to reduce the number of directories in a pathname is beneficial only if users are not tempted to **cd** from one link to another:

```
# ln -s /home/minnow/fred /u/fred
# ln -s /home/alewife/lucy /u/lucy
```

The unsuspecting user tries to use the path-compressed names, but finds that relative pathnames aren't relative to the link directory:

```
% cd /u/fred
% cd ../lucy
../lucy: No such file or directory
```

A user may be bewildered by this behavior. According to the **/u** directory, **fred** and **lucy** are subdirectories of a common parent. In reality, they aren't. The symbolic links hide the real locations of the **fred** and **lucy** directories, which do not have a common parent. Using symbolic links to shorten pathnames in this fashion is not always the most efficient solution to the problem; NFS mounts can often be used to produce the same filesystem naming conventions.

Mount Points, Exports, and Links

Symbolic links have strange effects on mounting and exporting filesystems. A good general rule to remember is that filesystem operations apply to the target of a link, not to the link itself. The symbolic link is just a pointer to the real operand.

If you mount a filesystem on a symbolic link, the actual mount occurs on the directory pointed to by the link. The following sequence of operations produces the same net result:

```
# mkdir /home/hal
# ln -s /home/hal /usr/hal
# mount bitatron:/home/hal /usr/hal
```

as this sequence does:

```
# mkdir /home/hal
# mount bitatron:/home/hal /home/hal
# ln -s /home/hal /usr/hal
```

The filesystem is mounted on the directory **/home/hal** and the symbolic link **/usr/hal** has the mount point as its target. You should make sure that the directory pointed to by the link is on a filesystem that is mounted read/write and that performing the mount will not obscure any required filesystem underneath the symbolic link target.

Exporting a symbolic link from a server follows similar rules. The filesystem or subtree of a filesystem that is really exported is the one pointed to by the symbolic link. If the parent of the link's target has already been exported, or a subtree of it is exported, the attempt to export the link fails.

More interesting than exporting a symbolic link is mounting one from the server. Mounting a link from a server is not the same thing as mounting a filesystem containing a symbolic link. The latter means that there is a symbolic link somewhere in the filesystem mounted using NFS. The former case implies that the server pathname used to locate the remote filesystem is a link and directs the mount somewhere else. The client mounts the directory pointed to by the link. As shown in Figure 5-1, if **/usr/man** is a symbolic link to **/usr/share/man**, then this **mount** command:

```
# mount bitatron:/usr/share/man /mnt
```

does the same thing as this mount command:

```
# mount bitatron:/usr/man   /mnt
```

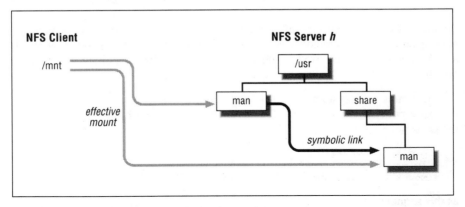

Figure 5-1. Mounting a server's symbolic link

A potential problem arises if the symbolic link and the directory it points to are on different filesystems: it's possible that the server has exported the link's filesystem but not the filesystem containing the link's target. In this example, **/usr/man** and **/usr/share/man** could be in two distinct filesystems, which would require two entries in the server's **exports** file.

Naming Schemes

Simple, efficient naming schemes make the difference between a filesystem that is well organized and a pleasure to use, and a filesystem that you are constantly fighting against. In this section, we'll look at ways of using mount points and symbolic links to create simple, consistent naming schemes on all NFS clients. NFS provides the mechanism for making distributed filesystems transparent to the user, but it has no inherent guidelines for creating easy to use and easier to manage filesystem hierarchies. There are few global rules, and each network will adopt conventions based on the number of servers, the kinds of files handled by those servers, and any peculiar naming requirements of locally developed or third party software.

As a system administrator, you should first decide how the various NFS fileservers fit together on a client before assigning filesystem names and filling them with software or users. Here are some ideas and suggestions for choosing NFS naming schemes:

- Use **/home/**_hostname_ for user home directories. The hostname indicates the server where the files are located. This seems contrary to the location transparency goals of NFS, but it makes network administration and **/etc/fstab** generation much easier.

- As an alternative, use the simpler **/home/**_username_ naming scheme to mount each user's home directory. This makes it easier to deal with servers that have several filesystems of home directories, without having to fabricate names to fit the **/home/**_hostname_ model. The disadvantage to this approach is that it requires a larger **/etc/fstab** file, with one entry for each user's home directory. If you use the NFS automounter, this naming scheme is more easily managed than the hostname-oriented one. Directories that follow any regular naming scheme are easily managed by the automounter, as discussed in Chapter 13, *The Automounter*.

- Use the same pathnames on the client as on the server so that it is easier to find and fix problems on the server. If you call your local software tools directory **/toolbox** on the NFS server, mount it as **/toolbox** on the clients as well.

- Keep growth in mind. Having a single third-party software filesystem may be the most effective (or only) solution immediately, but over the next year you may need to add a second or third filesystem to make room for more tools. To provide adequate performance, you may want to put each filesystem on a different server, distributing the load. If you choose a naming scheme that cannot be extended, you will end up renaming things later on and having to support the "old style" names.

In the third party tools directory example, you could separate tools into subdirectories group by function: **/tools/epubs** for page composition and publishing software, and **/tools/cae** for engineering tools. If either directory grows enough to warrant its own filesystem, you can move the subdirectory to a new server and preserve the existing naming scheme by simply mounting both subdirectories on clients:

Before: single tools depository
```
# mount toolbox:/tools  /tools
```

After: multiple filesystems
```
# mount toolbox:/tools/epubs /tools/epubs
# mount backpack:/tools/cae /tools/cae
```

The next two sections cover examples of common filesystem naming problems and some approaches to solving them.

Solving the /usr/local Puzzle

Assume you have a network with many different kinds of workstations: SPARC workstations, Motorola-based workstations, UNIX PC's, and so on. Of course, each kind of workstation has its own set of executables. The executables may be built from the same source files, but you need a different binary for each machine architecture. How do you arrange the filesystem so that each system has a **/usr/local/bin** directory (and, by extension, other executable directories) that contains only the executables that are appropriate for its architecture? How do you "hide" the executables that aren't appropriate, so there's no chance that a user will mistakenly try to execute them? This is the **"/usr/local"** puzzle: creating an "architecture neutral" executable directory.

Implementing an architecture-neutral **/usr/local/bin** is probably one of the first challenges posed to the system administrator of a heterogeneous network. Everybody wants the standard set of tools, such as emacs, PostScript filters, mail pretty printers, and the requisite telephone list utility. Ideally, there should be one **bin** directory for each architecture, and when a user looks in **/usr/local/bin** on any machine, he or she should find the proper executables. Hiding the machine architecture is a good job for symbolic links.

One solution is to name the individual binary directories with the machine type as a suffix and then mount the proper one on **/usr/local/bin**:

```
On server toolbox:
# cd /usr/local
# ls
bin.mips    bin.sun3    bin.sun4    bin.vax

On client:
# mount toolbox:/usr/local/bin.`arch` /usr/local/bin
```

The **mount** command determines the architecture of the local host and grabs the correct binary directory from the server.

This scheme is sufficient if you only have binaries in your local depository, but most sites add manual pages, source code, and other ASCII files that are shared across client architectures. There is no need to maintain multiple copies of these files. To accommodate a mixture of shared ASCII and binary files, use two mounts of the same filesystem: the first mount sets up the framework of directories, and puts the shared file directories in their proper place. The second mount deposits the proper binary directory on top of **/usr/local/bin**:

```
On server toolbox:
# cd /usr/local
# ls
bin         bin.mips    bin.sun3    bin.sun4
bin.vax     man         share       src

On client:
# mount toolbox:/usr/local /usr/local
# mount toolbox:/usr/local/bin.`arch` /usr/local/bin
```

At first glance, the previous example appears to violate the NFS rules prohibiting the export of a directory and any of its subdirectories. However, there is only one exported filesystem on server *toolbox*, namely, **/usr/local**. The clients mount different parts of this exported filesystem on top of one another. NFS allows a client to mount any part of an exported filesystem, on any directory.

To save disk space with the two-mount approach, populate **/usr/local/bin** on the server with the proper executables, and make the **bin.***arch* directory a symbolic link to **bin**. This allows clients of the same architecture as the server to get by with only one mount.

If you keep *all* executables—scripts and compiled applications—in the **bin** directories, you still have a problem with duplication. At some sites, scripts may account for more than half of the toois in **/usr/local/bin**, and having to copy them into each architecture-specific **bin** directory makes this solution less pleasing.

A more robust solution to the problem is to divide shell scripts and executables into two directories: scripts go in **/usr/local/share** while compiled executables live in the familiar **/usr/local/bin**. This makes **share** a peer of the **/usr/local/man** and **src** directories, both of which contain architecture-neutral ASCII files. To adapt to the fully architecture-neutral **/usr/local/bin**, users need to put both **/usr/local/bin** and **/usr/local/share** in their search paths, although this is a small price to pay for the guarantee that all tools are accessible from all systems.

There is one problem with mounting one filesystem on top of another: if the server for these filesystems goes down, you will not be able to unmount them until the server recovers. When you unmount a filesystem, it gets information about all of the directories above it. If the filesystem is not mounted on top of another NFS filesystem, this isn't a problem: all of the directory information is on the NFS client. However, the hierarchy of mounts used in the **/usr/local/bin** example presents a problem. One of the directories that an unmount operation would need to check is located on the server that crashed. An attempt to unmount the **/usr/local/bin** directory will hang because it tries to get information about the **/usr/local** mount point—and the server for that mount point is the one that crashed. Similarly, if you try to unmount the **/usr/local** filesystem, this attempt will fail because the **/usr/local/bin** directory is in use: it has a filesystem mounted on it.

A User Switchboard

Scattering user home directories across several file servers forces users to associate home directory names with usernames. The C and Korn shells' tilde (˜) notation locates a home directory, but it is frequently necessary to have an absolute pathname to a user's home directory for use in shells or applications that do not perform tilde expansion. In other cases, a simple naming scheme is needed for project directories that do not have usernames assigned to them. A directory of symbolic links functioning as a switchboard solves the problem but creates an unnecessary load for the server with this directory.

Consider making a symbolic link in NFS filesystem **/u** that points to each user's home directory. Even with hostnames in the pathnames, the **/u** notation allows users to find any other home directory or project directory with a simple naming convention:

```
% ls -l /u
total 5
lrwxrwxrwx  1 root           17 Jun  8 1990 fred -> /home/minnow/fred
lrwxrwxrwx  1 root           18 Jun  8 1990 lucy -> /home/alewife/lucy
lrwxrwxrwx  1 root           18 Jun  8 1990 wilma -> /home/minnow/wilma
lrwxrwxrwx  1 root           16 Jun  8 1990 source -> /home/cod/source
```

Every client in the network mounts /u and uses it as a table of pointers to user and project home directories. The problem with this set up is that every single reference to a file prefixed with /u sends two NFS requests to the server exporting /u: one NFS request reads the directory entry and another reads the link itself. In periods of peak usage such as project builds, the additional load placed on the /u server will be noticeable.

As an alternative, consider placing /u on every system and distributing the symbolic links each night using **rdist** or a shell script that uses **tar** to copy the links to each remote system:

```
#! /bin/sh

for h in minnow alewife cod tuna mahimahi
do
        tar cf - /u | rsh $h "tar xbBpf 20 -"
done
```

The script duplicates the entire /u directory each night, but this may require less total time than building a distribution script and executing it regularly. The best solution for the user switchboard problem is to use the automounter, as described in Chapter 13, *The Automounter*.

This user switchboard example shows how NFS can be used to add transparency to the network but still leave it with some rough edges. The more uniform naming conventions are, the easier the network is to use. Up to this point, we've focused on how to configure NFS and NIS to perform the functions you want. In the next chapter, we'll take a closer look at the design and implementation of NFS services.

6

Network File System Design and Operation

Virtual File Systems and Virtual Nodes
NFS Protocol and Implementation
NFS Daemons
Caching
File Locking
NFS Futures

It's possible to install and use the Network File System without too much knowledge of how it is implemented or why various design decisions were made. But if you need to debug problems, or analyze patterns of NFS usage to suggest performance optimizations, you will need to know more about the inside workings of the NFS protocol and the daemons that implement it. With an understanding of how and why NFS does the things it does, you can more readily determine why it is broken or slow—probably the two most common complaints in any large NFS network.

Like NIS, NFS is implemented as a set of RPC procedures that use External Data Representation (XDR) encoding to pass arguments between client and server. A filesystem mounted using NFS provides two levels of transparency:

- The filesystem appears to be resident on a disk attached to the local system, and all of the filesystem entries—files and directories—are viewed the same way, whether local or remote. NFS hides the location of the file on the network.

- NFS-mounted filesystems contain no information about the file server from which they are mounted. The NFS file server may be of a different architecture or running an entirely different operating system with a radically different filesystem structure. For example, a Sun running SunOS can mount an NFS filesystem from a VAX/VMS system or an IBM MVS mainframe, using NFS server implementations for each of these systems. NFS hides differences in the underlying remote filesystem structure and makes the remote filesystem appear to be of the exact same structure as that of the client.

NFS achieves the first level of transparency by defining a generic set of file system operations that are performed on a *Virtual File System* (VFS). The second level comes from the definition of *virtual nodes*, which are related to the more familiar UNIX filesystem *inode* structures but hide the actual structure of the physical file system beneath them. The set of all procedures that can be performed on files is the vnode interface definition. The vnode and VFS specifications together define the NFS protocol.

Virtual File Systems and Virtual Nodes

The Virtual File System allows a client system to access many different types of filesystems as if they were all attached locally. VFS hides the differences in implementations under a consistent interface. On a UNIX NFS client, the VFS interface makes all NFS filesystems look like UNIX filesystems, even if they are exported from IBM MVS or VAX/VMS servers. The VFS interface is really nothing more than a switchboard for filesystem- and file-oriented operations, as shown in Figure 6-1.

Actions that operate on entire filesystems, such as getting the amount of free space left in the filesystem, are called *VFS operations*; calls that operate on files or directories are *vnode operations*. On the server side, implementing a VFS entails taking the generic VFS and vnode operations and converting them into the appropriate actions on the real, underlying filesystem. This conversion happens invisibly to the NFS client process. It made a straightforward system call, which the client-side VFS turned into a vnode operation, and the server then converted into an equivalent operation on its filesystem.

For example, the *chown()* system call has an analogous operator in the vnode interface that sets the attributes of a file, as does the *stat()* system call that retrieves these attributes. There is not a strict one-to-one relationship of UNIX system calls to vnode operations. The *write()* system call uses several filesystem calls to get a file's attributes, and append or modify blocks in the file. Some vnode operations are not defined on certain types of filesystems. The DOS file

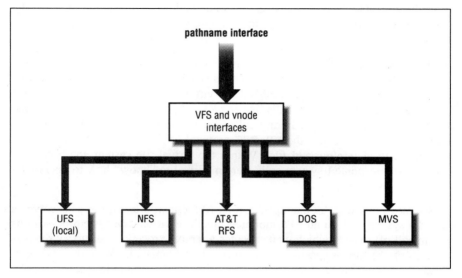

Figure 6-1. Virtual File System Interfaces

system, for example, doesn't have an equivalent of symbolic links, so an NFS file server running on a DOS machine rejects any attempts to use the vnode operation to create a symbolic link.

So far we have defined an interface to some file system objects, but not the mechanism used to "name" objects in the system. In a local UNIX system call, these object names are file descriptors, which uniquely identify a file within the scope of a process. The counterparts of file descriptors in NFS are file *handles*, which are opaque "pointers" to files on the remote system. An opaque handle is of no value to the client because it can only be interpreted in the context of the remote filesystem. When you want to make a system call on a file, you first get a file descriptor for it. To make an NFS call (in the kernel) you must get a file handle for the vnode. It is up to the virtual file system layer to translate user-level file descriptors into kernel-level file handles. File handles and their creation will be covered in more depth in the next section.

NFS Protocol and Implementation

NFS is an RPC based protocol, with a client-server relationship between the machine having the filesystem to be distributed and the machine wanting access to that filesystem. NFS server daemons, called **nfsd** daemons, run on the server and accept RPC calls from clients. NFS servers also run the **rpc.mountd** daemon to handle filesystem mount requests and some pathname translation. On an NFS client, the **biod** daemon is usually run to improve NFS performance, but it is not required.

On the client, each process using NFS files is a client of the server. The client's system calls that access NFS-mounted files make RPC calls to the NFS servers from which these files were mounted. The virtual file system really just extends the operation of basic system calls like *read*() and *write*(), similar to the way that NIS extends the operation of library calls like *getpwuid*(). In NIS, the *getpwuid*() routine knows how to use the NIS RPC protocol to locate user information that isn't in the local **/etc/passwd** file. Within the virtual file system, the basic file- and filesystem-oriented system calls were modified to "know" how to operate on non-local filesystems.

Let's look at this with an example. On an NFS client, a user process executes a *chmod*() system call on an NFS-mounted file. The virtual file system passes this system call off to NFS, which then executes a remote procedure call to set the permissions on the file, as specified in the process's system call. When the RPC completes, the system call returns to the user process. This example is fairly simple, because it doesn't involve any block I/O to get file data to or from the NFS server. When blocks of files are moved around, the **biod** daemons get involved to improve NFS performance. This section covers the protocols used by NFS and features of its implementation that were driven by performance or transparency goals.

NFS RPC Procedures

The NFS RPC protocol contains 16 procedures, each of which operates on either a file or a filesystem object. The basic procedures performed on an NFS server can be grouped into directory operations, file operations, link operations, and filesystem operations. Directory operations include *mkdir* and *rmdir*, which create and destroy directories like their UNIX system call equivalents. *readdir* reads a directory, using an opaque directory pointer to perform sequential reads of the same directory. Other directory-oriented procedures are *rename* and *remove*, which operate on entries in a directory the same way the **mv** and **rm** commands do. *create* makes a new directory entry for a file.

The *lookup* operation is the heart of the pathname-to-file handle translation mechanism. *lookup* finds a named directory entry and returns a file handle pointing to it. The *open*() system call uses *lookup*() extensively: it breaks a pathname down into its components and locates each component in its parent directory. For example, *open*() would handle the pathname **/home/thud/stern** by performing three operations:

- Look up **home** in the root directory (/).

- Look up **thud** in **/home**.

- Look up **stern** in **/home/thud**.

File operations are very closely associated with UNIX system calls: *read* and *write* move data to and from the NFS client, and *getattr* and *setattr* get or modify the file's attributes. In a UNIX filesystem, these attributes are stored in the file's inode, but file attributes are mapped to whatever system is used by the NFS server. Link operations include *link*, which creates a hard link on the server, and *symlink* and *readlink* which create and read the values of symbolic links, respectively. Finally, *statfs* is a filesystem operation that returns information about the mounted filesystem that might be needed by **df**, for example.

Other filesystem operations include mounting and unmounting a filesystem, but these are handled through the NFS **rpc.mountd** server rather than the **nfsd** RPC daemon. Mount operations are separated from the NFS protocol because mount points revolve around pathnames, and pathname syntax is peculiar to each operating system. UNIX and VMS, for example, do not use the same syntax to specify the path to a file. The mount protocol is responsible for turning the client's file pathname into information that NFS can use to locate the file in future operations.

From the descriptions above, it is fairly clear how the basic UNIX system calls map into NFS RPC calls. It is important to note that the NFS RPC protocol and the vnode interface are two different things. The vnode interface defines a set of operating system services that are used to access all filesystems, NFS or local. Vnodes simply generalize the interface to file objects. There are many routines in the vnode interface that correspond directly to procedures in the NFS protocol, but the vnode interface also contains implementations of operating system services such as mapping file blocks and buffer cache management.

The NFS RPC protocol is a specific realization of one of these vnode interfaces. It is used to perform specific vnode operations on remote files. Using the vnode interface, new filesystem types may be plugged into the operating system by adding kernel routines that perform the necessary vnode operations on objects in that filesystem.

Statelessness and Crash Recovery

The NFS protocol is stateless, meaning that there is no need to maintain information about the protocol on the server. The client keeps track of all information required to send requests to the server, but the server has no information about previous NFS requests, or how various NFS requests relate to each other. Remember the differences between the TCP and UDP protocols: UDP is a stateless protocol that can lose packets or deliver them out of order; TCP is a stateful protocol that guarantees that packets arrive and are delivered in order. The hosts using TCP must remember connection state information to recognize when part of a transmission was lost.

The choice of a stateless protocol has several implications for the design and implementation of NFS:

- NFS RPC requests must completely describe the operation to be performed. When writing a file block, for example, the write operation must contain a file handle, the offset into the file, and the length of the write operation. This is distinctly different from the UNIX *write()* system call, which writes a buffer to wherever the current file descriptor's write pointer directs it. The state contained in the file descriptor does not exist on the NFS server.

- Most NFS requests are *idempotent*, which means that an NFS client may send the same request one or more times without any harmful side effects. The net result of these duplicate requests is the same. For example, reading a specific block from a file is idempotent: the same data is returned from each operation.

  Obviously, some operations are not idempotent: removing a file can't be repeated without side effects, because a second attempt to remove the file will fail if the first one succeeded. Most NFS servers make all requests idempotent by recording recently performed operations. A duplicate request that matches one of the recently performed requests is thrown away by the NFS server.*

- Because requests can be repeated and state information is prohibited, NFS uses the unreliable User Datagram Protocol (UDP) to transport its RPC requests. UDP itself is stateless, promising neither a guaranteed packet delivery or a specific delivery order. NFS servers notify clients when an RPC call completes by sending the client an acknowledgement, also using UDP.

---

*Not all implementations of NFS have this duplicate request cache. Current releases of SunOS, Ultrix, and other current operating systems implement the cache to improve the performance and "correctness" of NFS. A few, older implementations of NFS do not reject non-idempotent, duplicate requests. This produces some strange and often incorrect results when requests are retransmitted. An NFS client that sends the same *remove* operation to such a server may find that the designated file was removed, but the RPC call returns the "No such file or directory" error.

The primary motivation for choosing a stateless protocol was to minimize the burden of crash recovery. Unlike a database system, which must verify transaction logs and look for incomplete operations, NFS has no explicit crash recovery mechanism. Because no state is maintained, the server may reboot and begin accepting client NFS requests again as if nothing had happened. Similarly, when clients reboot, the server does not need to know anything about them. Each NFS request contains enough information to be completed without any reference to state on the client or server.

Request Retransmission

NFS RPC requests are sent from a client to the server one at a time. A single client process will not issue another RPC call until the current call in progress completes and has been acknowledged by the NFS server. In this respect NFS RPC calls are like system calls—a process cannot continue with the next system call until the current one completes. A single client host may have several RPC calls in progress at any time, coming from several processes, but each process ensures that its file operations are well ordered by waiting for their acknowledgements. Using the NFS block I/O **biod** daemons makes this a little more complicated, but for now it's helpful to think of each process sending a stream of NFS requests, one at a time.

When a client makes an RPC request, it sets a timeout period during which the server must service and acknowledge it. If the server doesn't get the request because it was lost along the way, or because the server is too overloaded to complete the request within the timeout period, the client *retransmits* the request. Requests are idempotent (if the server has a duplicate request cache), so no harm is done if the server executes the same request twice—when the NFS client gets a second confirmation from the RPC request, the client discards it.

NFS clients continue to retransmit requests until the request completes, either with an acknowledgement from the server or an error from the RPC layer. If an NFS server crashes, clients continue retransmitting requests until the server reboots and can service them again. When the server is up again, NFS clients continue as if nothing happened. NFS clients cannot tell the difference between a server that has crashed and one that is very slow. This raises some important issues for tuning NFS servers and networks, which will be visited in "Slow Server Compensation," in Chapter 12, *Performance Analysis and Tuning*.

The duplicate request cache on NFS servers usually contains a few hundred entries—the last few seconds (at most) of NFS requests on a busy server. This cache is limited in size to establish a "window" in which non-idempotent NFS requests are considered duplicates caused by retransmission rather than distinct requests. For example, if you execute:

```
% rm foo
```

on an NFS client, the client may need to send two or more *remove* requests to the NFS server before it receives an acknowledgment. It's up to the NFS server to weed out the duplicate *remove* requests, even if they are a second or so apart. However, if you execute **rm foo** on Monday, and then on Tuesday you execute the same command in the same directory (where the file has already been removed), you would be very surprised if **rm** did not return an error. Executing this "duplicate request" a day later should produce this familiar error:

```
% rm foo
rm: foo: No such file or directory
```

Duplicate request caching is limited to window that is "short" compared to the time between successive user requests.

Preserving UNIX Filesystem Semantics

The VFS makes all filesystems appear homogeneous to user processes. There is a single UNIX system call interface that operates on files, and the VFS and underlying vnode interface translate semantics of these system calls into actions appropriate for each type of underlying filesystem. It's important to stress the difference between *syntax* and *semantics* of system calls. Consistent syntax means that the system calls take the same arguments independent of the underlying filesystem. Semantics refers to what the system calls actually do: preserving semantics across different filesystem types means that a system call will have the same net effect on the files in each filesystem type. *UNIX filesystem semantics* collectively refers to the way in which UNIX files behave when various sequences of system calls are made. For example, opening a file and then unlinking it doesn't cause the file's data blocks to be released until the *close()* system call is made. A new filesystem that wants to maintain UNIX filesystem semantics must support this behavior.

The VFS definition makes it possible to ensure that semantics are preserved for all filesystems, so they all behave in the same manner when UNIX system calls are made on their files. It is easy to use VFS to implement a filesystem with non-UNIX semantics. It's also possible to integrate a filesystem into the VFS interface without supporting all of the UNIX semantics; for example, you can put DOS filesystems under VFS, but you can't create UNIX-like symbolic links on them because the native DOS filesystem doesn't support symbolic links.

In this section, we'll look at how NFS deals with UNIX filesystem semantics, including some of the operations that aren't exactly the same under NFS. NFS has slightly different semantics than the local UNIX filesystem, but it tries to preserve the UNIX semantics. An application that works with a local filesystem works equally well with an NFS mounted filesystem and will not be able to distinguish the two.

Consistency at the vnode interface level makes NFS a powerful tool for creating filesystem hierarchies using many different NFS servers. The **mount** command requires that a filesystem be mounted on a directory; but directories are vnodes themselves. An NFS filesystem can be mounted on any vnode, which means that NFS filesystems can be mounted on top of other NFS filesystems or local filesystems. This is completely consistent with the way in which local disks are mounted on local filesystems. **/home** may be on the root filesystem, and **/home/host** is mounted on top of it. A workstation configured using NFS can create a view of the filesystems on the network that best meets its requirements by mounting these filesystems with a directory naming scheme of its choice.

Maintaining other UNIX file system semantics is not quite as easy. Locking operations, for example, introduce state into a system that was meant to be stateless. This problem is addressed by a separate lock manager daemon. Another bit of UNIX lore that had be preserved was the retention of an open file's data blocks, even when the file's directory entry was removed. Many UNIX utilities including shells and mailers use this "delayed unlink" feature to create temporary files that have no name in the filesystem, and are therefore invisible to probing users.

A complete solution to the problem would require that the server keep open file reference counts for each file and not free the file's data blocks until the reference count decreased to zero. However, this is precisely the kind of state information that makes crash recovery difficult, so NFS was implemented with a client-side solution that handles the common applications of this feature. When a *remove* operation is performed on an open file, the client issues a *rename* NFS RPC instead. The file is renamed to **.nfsXXXX**, where **XXXX** is a suffix to make the filename unique. When the file is eventually closed, the client issues the *remove* operation on the previously unlinked file. Note that there is no need for an "open" or "close" NFS RPC procedure, since "opened" and "closed" are states that are maintained on the client. It is still possible to confuse two clients that attempt to unlink a shared, open NFS-mounted file, since one client will not know that the other has the file open, but it emulates the behavior of a local filesystem sufficiently to eliminate the need to change utilities that rely on it.

Pathnames and File Handles

All NFS operations use file handles to designate the files or directories on which they will be performed. File handles are created on the server and contain information that uniquely identifies the file or directory on the server. The client's NFS *mount* and *lookup* requests retrieve these file handles for existing files. A side effect of making all vnodes homogeneous is that file pathname lookup must be done one component at a time. Each directory in the pathname might be a mount point for another filesystem, so each name look-up request cannot include multiple components. For example, let's look at *clientA* that NFS-mounts the **/usr/local** filesystem and also NFS-mounts a filesystem on **/usr/local/bin**:

```
clientA# mount server1:/usr/local /usr/local
clientA# mount server2:/usr/local/bin.mips /usr/local/bin
```

When the NFS client reaches the **bin** component in the pathname, it realizes that there is an NFS filesystem mounted on this directory, and it sends its lookup requests to *server2* instead of *server1*. If the NFS client passed the whole pathname to *server1*, it might get the wrong answer on its lookup: *server1* has its own **/usr/local/bin** directory that may or may not be the same directory that *clientA* has mounted. While this may seem to be a very expensive series of operations, the kernel keeps a directory name lookup cache (DNLC) that prevents every look-up request from going to an NFS server.

The *lookup* operation takes a filename and a file handle for a directory, and returns a file handle pointing to the named file on the server. How then does the pathname traversal get started, if every *lookup* requires a file handle from a previous pathname resolution? The **mount** operation seeds the look-up process by providing a file handle for the root of the mounted filesystem. Within NFS, the only procedure that accepts full pathnames is the **mount** RPC, which turns the pathname into a file handle for the mounted filesystem.

Let's look at how NFS turns the pathname **/usr/local/bin/emacs** into an NFS file handle, assuming that it's on a filesystem mounted on **/usr/local** from server *wahoo*:

- The NFS client asks the **mountd** daemon on *wahoo* for a file handle for the filesystem the client has mounted on **/usr/local**, using the *server's* pathname that was supplied in the **/etc/fstab** file or **mount** command. That is, if the client has mounted **/usr/local** with the **/etc/fstab** entry:

```
wahoo:/tools/local    /usr/local    nfs ro,hard 0 0
```

then the client will ask *wahoo* for a file handle for the **/tools/local** directory.

- Using the mount point file handle, the client performs a look up operation on the next component in the pathname: **bin**. It sends a *lookup* to *wahoo*, supplying the file handle for the **/usr/local** directory and the name "bin." Server *wahoo* returns another file handle for this directory.

- The client goes to work on the next component in the path, **emacs**. Again, it sends a *lookup* using the file handle for the directory containing **emacs** and the name it is looking for. The file handle returned by the server is used by the client as a "pointer" (on the server) to **/usr/local/bin/emacs** (in the filesystem seen by client) for all future operations on that file.

File handles are opaque to the client. In most NFS implementations on UNIX machines, they are an encoding of the file's inode number, disk device number, and inode generation number. Other implementations, particularly non-UNIX NFS servers that do not have inodes, encode their own native filesystem information in the file handle. In any system, the file handle is in a form that can be disassembled only on the NFS server. The structures contained in the file handle are kept hidden from the client, the same way the structures in an object-oriented system are hidden in the object's implementation routines. In the case of NFS file handles, the data described by the structure doesn't even exist on the client—it's all on the server, where the file handle can be converted into a pointer to local file.

File handles become invalid, or stale, when the inodes to which they point (on the server) are freed or re-used. NFS clients have no way of knowing what other operations may be affecting objects pointed to by their file handles, so there is no way to warn a client in advance that a file handle is invalid. If an RPC call is made with a file handle that is stale, the NFS server returns a *stale file handle* error to the caller. Say that a user on one client removes an NFS-mounted directory and its contents using **rm –rf test**, while another client has a process using **test** as its current working directory. The next time the other process tries to read its working directory, it gets a stale file handle error back from the NFS server:

Client A	*Client B*
cd /home/test	cd /home
	rm -rf test
stat(.)--)Stale file handle	

If one client removes a file and then creates a new file that re-uses the freed inode, other file handles (on other clients) that point to the re-used inode must be marked stale. Inode generation numbers were added to the basic UNIX file system to add a time history to an inode. In addition to the inode number, the file handle must match the current generation number of the inode, or it is marked stale. When the inode is re-used for a new file, its generation number is incremented. Stale file handles become a problem when one user's work tramples on an area in use by another, or when a filesystem on a server is rebuilt from a backup tape. When restoring from a dump tape onto a fresh filesystem, all of the inode generation numbers in the filesystem are set to random numbers. This causes every file handle in use for that filesystem to become stale—every inode pointed to by a pre-restore file handle now probably points to a completely different file on the disk.

Therefore, a quick way to cripple an NFS network is to restore a fileserver from a dump tape without rebooting the NFS clients. When you rebuild the server's filesystems, all of the inode generation numbers are reset; when you load the tape, files end up with different inode numbers and different inode generation numbers than they had on the original filesystem. All NFS client file handles are now invalid because of the new generation numbers and the (random) renumbering of each file's inode. Any attempt to use an open file handle results in stale file handle errors. If you are going to restore an NFS-exported filesystem from tape, unmount it from its clients or reboot the clients.

NFS Daemons

NFS is similar to other RPC services in its use of a server-side daemon (**nfsd**) to process incoming requests. It differs from the typical client-server model in that processes on NFS clients make some RPC calls themselves, and other RPC calls are made by the client block I/O daemon **biod**. NFS also uses multiple copies of each daemon to improve throughput. All of the NFS client and server code is contained in the kernel, instead of in the server daemon executable, a decision also driven by performance requirements.

Server nfsd Daemons

With all of the NFS code in the kernel, why bother with user processes for the daemons? Why not make NFS a purely kernel-to-kernel service, without any user processes? The NFS daemons—both client and server side—make one system call that never returns, and that system call executes the appropriate NFS code in the system's kernel. The process container in which this system executes is necessary for scheduling, multithreading, and providing a user context for the kernel. Multithreading in this case means running multiple copies of the same daemon, so that multiple NFS requests may be handled in parallel on the client and server hosts.

The most pressing need for NFS daemons to exist as processes centers around the need for multithreading NFS RPC requests. Making NFS a purely kernel resident service would require significant work to have the kernel support multiple threads of execution. The alternative to multiple daemons is that an NFS server is forced to handle one NFS request at a time. Running daemons in user-level processes allows the server to have multiple, independent threads of execution, so the server can handle several NFS requests at once. NFS daemons service requests in a pseudo-round robin fashion; whenever a daemon is done with a request it goes to the end of the queue waiting for a new request. Using this scheduling algorithm, a server is always able to accept a new NFS request as long as at least one **nfsd** is waiting in queue. Running multiple copies of the **nfsd** daemon lets a server start multiple disk operations at the same time and handle quick turnaround requests such as *getattr* and *lookup* while disk-bound requests are in progress.

The user context associated with a process also allows the kernel to put one of these execution threads to sleep, waiting for a disk or other system resource. With a pure kernel service, there is no mechanism for making the service wait— another force making it single threaded. The implementation of NFS fits nicely into the kernel's native process scheduling and resource allocation facilities.

Client biod Daemons

On the client side, each process accessing an NFS-mounted filesystem makes its own RPC calls to NFS servers. A single process will be a client of many NFS servers if it is accessing several filesystems on the client. For operations that do not involve block I/O, such as getting the attributes of a file or performing a name lookup, having each process make its own RPC calls provides adequate performance. However, when file blocks are moved between client and server, NFS needs to use the UNIX file buffer cache mechanism to provide throughput similar to that achieved with a local disk. The client-side **biod** daemon is the part of NFS that interacts with the buffer cache.

Before looking at **biod** in detail, some explanation of buffer cache and file cache management is required. The traditional UNIX buffer cache is a portion of the system's memory that is reserved for file blocks that have been recently referenced. When a process is reading from a file, the operating system performs read-ahead on the file and fills the buffer cache with blocks that the process will need in future operations. The result of this "pre-fetch" activity is that not all *read()* system calls require a disk operation: some can be satisfied with data in the buffer cache. Similarly, data that is written to disk is written into the cache first; when the cache fills up, file blocks are flushed out to disk. Again, the buffer cache allows the operating system to bunch up disk requests, instead of making every system call wait for a disk transfer.

SunOS 4.x and System V Release 4 replace the buffer cache with a page mapping system. Instead of transferring files into and out of the buffer cache, the virtual memory management system directly maps files into a process's address space, and treats file accesses like page faults. Any page that is not being used by the system can be taken to cache file pages. The net effect is the same as that of a buffer cache, but the size of the cache is not fixed. The file page cache could be a large percentage of the system's memory if only one or two processes are doing file I/O operations. For this discussion, we'll refer to the in-memory copies of file blocks as the "buffer cache," whether it is implemented as a cache of file pages or as a traditional UNIX buffer cache.

The client-side **biod** daemons improve NFS performance by filling and draining the buffer cache on behalf of NFS clients. When a process reads from an NFS-mounted file, it performs the *read* RPC itself. To pre-fetch data for the buffer cache, the kernel has the **biod** daemons send more *read* RPC requests to the server, *as if* the reading process had requested this data. NFS functions properly without any **biod** daemons on a client—but no read-ahead is done without them, limiting the throughput of the NFS filesystem. When the **biod** daemons are running, the client's kernel can initiate several RPC calls at the same time. If restricted to a single RPC call per process, NFS client performance suffers—sometimes dramatically.

When a client writes to a file, the data is put into the buffer cache. After a complete buffer is filled, the operating system writes out the data in the cache to the filesystem. If the data needs to be written to an NFS server, the kernel makes an RPC call to perform the write operation. If there are **biod** daemons available, they make the *write* RPC requests for the client, draining the buffer cache when the cache management system dictates. If no **biod** daemons can make the RPC call, the process calling *write()* performs the RPC call itself. Again, without any **biod** daemons, the kernel can still write to NFS files, but it must do so by forcing each client process to make its own RPC calls. The **biod** daemons allow the client to execute multiple RPC requests at the same time, performing write-behind on behalf of the processes using NFS files.

NFS read and write requests are performed in *NFS buffer* sizes. The buffer size used for disk I/O requests is independent of the network's MTU and the server or client filesystem block size. It is chosen based on the most efficient size handled by the network transport protocol, and is usually 8 kbytes. The NFS protocol process implements this buffering scheme, so that all disk operations are done in larger (and usually more efficient) chunks. When reading from a file, a *read* RPC requests an entire 8-kbyte NFS buffer. The client process may only request a small portion of the buffer, but the buffer cache saves the entire buffer to satisfy future references.

For write requests, the buffer cache batches them until a full NFS buffer has been written. Once a full buffer is ready to be sent to the server, a **biod** daemon picks up the buffer and performs the *write* RPC request. The size of a buffer in the cache and the size of an NFS buffer may not be the same; if the machine has 2-kbyte buffers then four buffers are needed to make up a complete 8-kbyte NFS buffer. The **biod** daemon attempts to combine buffers from consecutive parts of a file in a single RPC call. It groups smaller buffers together to form a single NFS buffer, if it can. If a process is performing sequential write operations on a file, then the **biod** daemons will be able to group buffers together and perform *write* operations with NFS buffer-sized requests. If the process is writing random data, it is likely that NFS writes will occur in buffer cache-sized pieces.

On systems that use page mapping (SunOS and System V Release 4), there is no buffer cache, so the notion of "filling a buffer" isn't quite as clear. Instead, the **biod** daemons are given file pages whenever a write operation crosses a page boundary. The **biod** daemons group consecutive pages together to form a single NFS buffer. This process is called *dirty page clustering*.

If no **biod** daemons are running, or if all of them are busy handling other RPC requests, then the client process performing the *write*() system call executes the RPC itself (as if there were no **biod** daemons at all). A process that is writing large numbers of file blocks enjoys the benefits of having multiple *write* RPC requests performed in parallel: one by each of the **biod** daemons and one that it does itself.

As shown in Figure 6-2, some of the advantages of asynchronous UNIX *write*() operation are retained by this approach. Smaller write requests that do not force an RPC call return to the client right away.

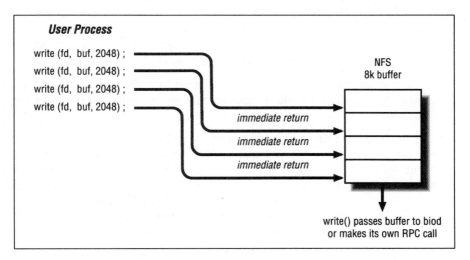

Figure 6-2. NFS buffer writing

Doing the read-ahead and write-behind in NFS buffer-sized chunks imposes a logical block size on the NFS server, but again, the logical block size has nothing to do with the actual filesystem implementation on either the NFS client or server. We'll look at the buffering done by NFS clients when we discuss data caching and

NFS write errors. The next section discusses the interaction of the **biod** daemons and UNIX system calls in more detail.

Kernel NFS Code

The functions performed by the **biod** and **nfsd** daemons provide only part of the boost required to make NFS performance acceptable. The **nfsd** and **biod** are user-level processes, but they contain no user-level code: they make a single system call that goes into the kernel and never returns. All of the **nfsd** and **biod** code—and therefore all of NFS—is in the kernel. The NFS daemon processes are nothing more than scheduling "handles" for these pieces of kernel code.

It is possible to put the NFS client and server code entirely in the **nfsd** and **biod** user processes. Unfortunately, making system calls is relatively expensive in terms of operating system overhead, and moving data to and from user space is also a drain on the system. Implemenenting NFS code outside the kernel, at the user level, would require every NFS RPC to go through a very convoluted sequence of kernel and user process transitions, moving data into and out of the kernel whenever it was received or sent by a machine.

The kernel implementation of the NFS RPC client and server code eliminates all data copying except for the final move of data from the client's kernel back to the user process requesting it, and it eliminates extra transitions out of and into the kernel. To see how the NFS daemons, buffer (or page) cache, and system calls fit together, we'll trace a *read*() system call through the client and server kernels:

- A user process calls *read*() on an NFS mounted file. The process has no way of determining where the file is, since its only pointer to the file is a UNIX file descriptor.

- The VFS maps the file descriptor to a vnode and calls the read operation for the vnode type. Since the VFS type is NFS, the system call invokes the NFS client read routine. In the process of mapping the type to NFS, the file descriptor is also mapped into a file handle for use by NFS. Locally, the client has a virtual node (vnode) that locates this file in its filesystem. The vnode contains a pointer to more specific filesystem information: for a local file, it points to an inode, and for an NFS file, it points to a structure containing an NFS file handle.

- The client read routine checks the local buffer (or page) cache for the data. If it is present, the data is returned right away. It's possible that the data requested in this operation was loaded into the cache by a previous NFS read operation. To make the example interesting, we'll assume that the requested data is not in the client's cache.

- The client process performs an NFS *read* RPC. The read request asks for a complete 8-kbyte NFS buffer. The client process goes to sleep waiting for the RPC request to complete. Note that the client process itself makes the RPC, not the **biod** daemon: the client can't continue execution until the data is returned, so there is nothing gained by having another process perform its RPC. However, the operating system will schedule **biod** daemons to perform read-ahead for this process, getting the next 8-kbyte buffer from the remote file.

- The server receives the RPC packet and schedules an **nfsd** to handle it. The **nfsd** code picks up the packet, determines the RPC call to be made, and initiates the disk operation. All of these are kernel functions, so **nfsd** never leaves the kernel. The **nfsd** process that was scheduled goes to sleep waiting for the disk read to complete, and when it does the kernel schedules it again to send the data and RPC acknowledgement back to the client.

- The reading process on the client wakes up, and takes its data out of the 8-kbyte buffer returned by the NFS *read* RPC request. The data is left in the buffer cache so that future read operations do not have to go over the network. The process's *read()* system call returns, and the process continues execution. At the same time, the read-ahead RPC requests sent by the **biod** daemons are pre-fetching additional buffers of the file. If the process is reading the file sequentially, it will be able to perform many *read()* system calls before it looks for data that is not in the buffer cache.

Obviously, changing the number of NFS daemons and the NFS buffer sizes impacts the behavior of the read-ahead (and write-behind) algorithms. Effects of varying the number of daemons and the NFS buffer sizes will be explored as part of the performance discussion in Chapter 12, *Performance Analysis and Tuning*.

Caching

Caching involves keeping frequently used data "close" to where it is needed, or preloading data in anticipation of future operations. Data read from disks may be cached until a subsequent write makes it invalid, and data written to disk is usually cached so that many consecutive changes to the same file may be written out in a single operation. In NFS, data caching means not having to send an RPC request over the network to a server: the data is cached on the NFS client and can be read out of local memory instead of from a remote disk. Depending upon the filesystem structure and usage, some cache schemes may be prohibited for certain operations to guarantee data integrity or consistency with multiple processes reading or writing the same file. Cache policies in NFS ensure that performance is acceptable while also preventing the introduction of state into the client-server relationship.

File Attribute Caching

Not all filesystem operations touch the data in files; many of them either get or set the attributes of the file such as its length, owner, modification time, and inode number. Because these attribute-only operations are frequent and do not affect the data in a file, they are prime candidates for using cached data. Think of ls –1 as a classic example of an attribute-only operation: it gets information about directories and files, but doesn't look at the contents of the files.

NFS caches file attributes on the client side so that every *getattr* and *setattr* operation does not have to go all the way to the NFS server. When a file's attributes are read, they remain valid on the client for some minimum period of time, typically three seconds. If the client modifies the file (updating its attributes), that change is made in the local copy of the attributes and the cache validity period is extended another minimum time slice. If the file's attributes remain static for some maximum period, nominally 60 seconds, they are flushed from the cache and written back to the server if they have been modified.

The same mechanism is used for directory attributes, although they are given a longer minimum lifespan. The usual defaults for directory attributes are a minimum cache time of 30 seconds and a maximum of 60 seconds. The longer minimum cache period reflects the typical behavior of periods of intense filesystem activity—files themselves are modified almost continuously but directory updates (adding or removing files) happen much less frequently.

Attribute caching allows a client to make a steady stream of updates to a file without having to constantly get and set file attributes on the server. The intermediate attributes are cached, and the net effect of all updates is finally written to the server when the maximum attribute cache period expires. This is the only filesystem data that is not committed to non-volatile storage after being modified. Furthermore, frequently accessed files and directories, such as the current working directory, have their attributes cached on the client so that some NFS operations can be performed without having to make an RPC call.

In the previous section, we saw how the **biod** process fills and drains the NFS client's buffer or page cache. This presents a cache consistency problem: if a **biod** daemon performs read-ahead on a file, and the client accesses that information at some later time, how does the client know that the cached copy of the data is valid? What guarantees are there that another client hasn't changed the file, making the copy of the file's data in the buffer cache invalid?

An NFS client needs to maintain cache consistency with the copy of the file on the NFS server. It uses file attributes to perform the consistency check. The file's modification time is used as a cache validity check; if the cached data is newer than the modification time then it remains valid. As soon as the file's modification time is newer than the time at which **biod** read data, the cached data must be flushed. In page mapped systems, the modification time becomes a "valid bit" for cached pages. If a client reads a file that never gets modified, it can cache the file's pages for as long as needed.

This feature explains the "accelerated make" phenomenon seen on NFS clients when compiling code. The second and successive times that a software module (located on an NFS fileserver) is compiled, the **make** process is faster than the first build. The reason is that the first make reads in header files and causes them to be cached. Subsequent builds of the same modules or other files using the same headers pick up the cached pages instead of having to read them from the NFS server. As long as the header files are not modified, the client's cached pages remain valid. The first compilation requires many more RPC requests to be sent to the server; the second and successive compilations only send RPC requests to read those files that have changed.

The cache consistency checks themselves are by the file attribute cache. When a cache validity check is done, the kernel compares the modification time of the file to the timestamp on its cached pages; normally this would require reading the file's attributes from the NFS server. Since file attributes are kept in the file's inode (which is itself cached on the NFS server), reading file attributes is much less "expensive" than going to disk to read part of the file. However, if the file attributes are not changing frequently, there is no reason to re-read them from the server on every cache validity check. The data cache algorithms use the file attribute cache to speed modification time comparisons.

Keeping previously read data blocks cached on the client does not introduce state into the NFS system, since nothing is being modified on the client caching the data. Long-lived cache data introduces consistency problems if one or more other clients have the file open for writing, which is one of the motivations for limiting the attribute cache validity period. If the attribute cache data never expired, clients that opened files for reading only would never have reason to check the server for possible modifications by other clients. Stateless NFS operation requires each client to be oblivious to all others and to rely on its attribute cache only for ensuring consistency. Of course, if clients are using different attribute cache aging schemes, then machines with longer cache attribute lifetimes will have stale data. Attribute caching and its effects on NFS performance is revisited in "Attribute Caching," in Chapter 12, *Performance Analysis and Tuning*.

Client Data Caching

In the previous section, we looked at the **biod** daemon's management of an NFS client's buffer cache. The **biod** daemons perform read-ahead and write-behind for the NFS client processes. We also saw how NFS moves data in NFS buffers, rather than in page- or buffer cache-sized chunks. The use of NFS buffers allows NFS operations to utilize some of the sequential disk I/O optimizations of UNIX disk device drivers.

Reading in 8-kbyte buffers allows NFS to reduce the cost of getting file blocks from a server. The overhead of performing an RPC call to read just a few bytes from a file is significant compared to the cost of reading that data from the server's disk, so it is to the client's and server's advantage to spread the RPC cost over as many data bytes as possible. If an application sequentially reads data from a file in 128-byte buffers, the first read operation brings over a full 8-kbyte NFS buffer from the file system. If the file is less than 8 kbytes, the entire file is read from the NFS server. The next *read()* picks up data that is in the buffer (or page) cache, and following reads walk through the entire buffer. When the application reads data that is not cached, another full NFS buffer is read from the server. If there are **biod** daemons performing read-ahead on the client, the next buffer may already be present on the NFS client by the time the process needs data from it. Performing reads in NFS buffer-sized operations improves NFS performance significantly by decoupling the client application's system call buffer size and the VFS implementation's buffer size.

Going the other way, small write operations to the same file are buffered until they fill a complete page or buffer. When a full buffer is written, the operating system gives it to a **biod** daemon, and **biod** daemons try to cluster write buffers together so they can be sent in NFS buffer-sized requests. The eventual *write* RPC call is performed synchronous to the **biod** daemon; that is, the **biod** daemon does not continue execution (and start another write or read operation) until the RPC call completes. On the server, the write RPC operation does not return to the client's **biod** process until the file block has been committed to stable, non-volatile storage. All write operations are performed synchronously on the server to ensure that no state information is left in volatile storage, where it would be lost if the server crashed.

There are elements of a write-back cache in **biod**. Queueing small write operations until they can be done in buffer-sized RPC calls leaves the client with data that is not present on a disk, and a client failure before the data is written to the server would leave the server with an old copy of the file. This behavior is similar to that of the UNIX buffer cache or the page cache in memory-mapped systems. If a client is writing to a local file, blocks of the file are cached in memory and are not flushed to disk until the **update** daemon schedules them. If the machine crashes between the time the data is updated in a file cache page and the time that page is flushed to disk, the file on disk is not changed by the write. This is also expected of systems with local disks—applications running at the time of the crash may not leave disk files in well-known states.

Having file blocks cached on the server during writes poses a problem if the server crashes. The client cannot determine which RPC write operations completed before the crash, violating the stateless nature of NFS. Writes cannot be cached on the server side, as this would allow the client to think that the data was properly written when the server is still exposed to losing the cached request during a reboot.

Ensuring that writes are completed before they are acknowledged introduces a major bottleneck for NFS write operations. A single file write operation may require up to three disk writes on the server to update the file's inode, an indirect block pointer, and the data block being written. Each of these server write operations must complete before the NFS *write* RPC returns to the client. Vendors making battery-backed NFS servers write buffers eliminate some of this bottleneck by committing the data to non-volatile, non-disk storage at memory speeds, and then moving data from the NFS write buffer memory to disk in large (64-kbyte) buffers.

Using the buffer cache and allowing **biod** daemons to cluster multiple buffers introduces some problems when several machines are reading from and writing to the same file. To prevent file inconsistency with multiple readers and writers of the same file, NFS institutes a flush-on-close policy: all partially filled NFS buffers are written to the NFS server when a file is closed. This ensures that a process on another NFS client sees all changes to a file that it is opening for reading:

```
Client A              Client B
open ()
write ()
close ()
                      open ()
                      read ()
```

The *read()* system call on *clientB* will see all of the data in a file just written by *clientA*, because *clientA* flushed out all of its buffers for that file when the *close()* system call was made. Note that file consistency is less certain if *clientB* opens the file *before clientA* has closed it. If overlapping read and write operations will be performed on a single file, file locking should be used to prevent cache consistency problems. When a file has been locked, the use of the buffer cache is disabled for that file, making it more of a write-through than a write-back cache. Instead of bundling small NFS requests together, each NFS write request for a locked file is sent to the NFS server immediately.

Server-Side Caching

The client-side caching mechanisms—file attribute and buffer caching—reduce the number of requests that need to be sent to an NFS server. On the server, additional cache policies reduce the time required to service these requests. NFS servers have three caches:

- The inode cache, containing file attributes. Inode entries read from disk are kept in-core for as long as possible. Being able to read and write these attributes in memory, instead of having to go to disk, make the get- and set-attribute NFS requests much faster.

- The directory name lookup cache, or DNLC, containing recently read directory entries. Caching directory entries means that the server does not have to open and re-read directories on every pathname resolution. Directory searching is a fairly expensive operation, since it involves going to disk and searching linearly for a particular name in the directory. The DNLC cache works at the VFS layer, not at the local filesystem layer, so it caches directories entries for all types of filesystems. If you have a CD-ROM drive on your NFS server, and mount it on NFS clients, the DNLC becomes even more important because reading directory entries from the CD-ROM is much slower than reading them from a local hard disk. Server configuration effects that affect both the inode and DNLC cache systems are discussed in "Kernel Configuration," in Chapter 12, *Performance Analysis and Tuning*.

- The server's buffer cache, used for data read from files. As mentioned before, file blocks that are written to NFS servers cannot be cached, and must be written to disk before the client's RPC *write* call can complete. However, the server's buffer or page cache acts as an efficient read cache for NFS clients. The effects of this caching are more pronounced in page-mapped systems, since nearly all of the server's memory can be used as a read cache for file blocks.

Cache mechanisms on NFS clients and servers provide acceptable NFS performance while preserving many—but not all—of the semantics of a local filesystem. If you need finer consistency control when multiple clients are accessing the same files, you need to use file locking.

File Locking

File locking allows one process to gain exclusive access to a file or part of a file, and forces other processes requiring access to the file to wait for the lock to be released. Locking is a stateful operation and does not mesh well with the stateless design of NFS. One of NFS's design goals is to maintain UNIX filesystem semantics on all files, which includes supporting record locks on files.

UNIX locks come in two flavors: BSD-style file locks and System V-style record locks. The BSD locking mechanism implemented in the *flock()* system call exists for local files only, while the more general System V-style locks are implemented through the *fcntl()* system call and the *lockf()* library routine, which uses *fcntl()*. System V locking operations are separated from the NFS protocol and handled by an RPC lock daemon and a status monitoring daemon that recreate and verify state information when either a client or server reboot.

Lock and Status Daemons

The RPC lock daemon, **rpc.lockd**, runs on both the client and server. It handles all lock requests, whether they are for local or remote files. When a lock request is made for an NFS-mounted file, **rpc.lockd** forwards the request to the server's **rpc.lockd**. The lock daemon asks the status monitor daemon, **rpc.statd**, to note that the client has requested a lock and to begin monitoring the client.

The file locking daemon and status monitor daemon keep two directories with lock "reminders" in them: **/etc/sm** and **/etc/sm.bak**. The first directory is used by the status monitor on an NFS server to track the names of hosts that have locked one or more of its files. The files in **/etc/sm** are empty and are used primarily as pointers for lock renegotiation after a server or client crash. When **rpc.statd** is asked to monitor a system, it creates a file with that system's name in **/etc/sm**.

If the system making the lock request must be notified of a server reboot, then an entry is made in **/etc/sm.bak** as well. When the status monitor daemon starts up, it calls the status daemon on all of the systems whose names appear in **/etc/sm.bak** to notify them that the NFS server has rebooted. Each client's status daemons tells its lock daemon that locks may have been lost due to a server crash. The client-side lock daemons resubmit all outstanding lock requests, recreating the file lock state (on the server) that existed before the server crashed.

Client Lock Recovery

If the server's **rpc.statd** cannot reach a client's status daemon to inform it of the crash recovery, it begins printing annoying messages on the server's console:

```
clnttcp_create: RPC: Portmapper failure - rpc: timed out
rpc.statd cannot talk to statd at client
```

These messages indicate that the local **rpc.statd** process could not find the port-mapper on the client to make an RPC call to its status daemon. If the client has also rebooted and is not quite back on the air, the server's status monitor should eventually find the client and update the file lock state. However, if the client was taken down, had its named changed, or was removed from the network altogether, these messages continue until **rpc.statd** is told to stop looking for the missing client.

To silence **rpc.statd**, kill the status daemon process, remove the appropriate file in **/etc/sm.bak**, and restart **rpc.statd**. For example, if server *onaga* cannot find the **statd** daemon on client *noreaster*, remove that client's entry in **/etc/sm.bak**:

```
onaga# ps -agux | fgrep statd
root        133  0.0  0.0   72    0 co IW    07:20  0:01 rpc.statd
root        144  0.0  0.6  136  184 co S     07:23  0:00 fgrep statd
onaga# kill -9 133
onaga# cd /etc/sm.bak
onaga# ls
noreaster
onaga# rm noreaster
onaga# rpc.statd
```

Error messages from **rpc.statd** should be expected whenever an NFS client is removed from the network, or when clients and servers boot at the same time.

Recreating State Information

Because permanent state (state that survives crashes) is maintained on the server host owning the locked file, the server is given the job of asking clients to re-establish their locks when state is lost. Only a server crash removes state from the system, and it is missing state that is impossible to regenerate without some external help.

When a client reboots, it by definition has given up all of its locks, but there is no state *lost*. Some state information may remain on the server and be out-of-date, but this "excess" state is flushed by the server's status monitor. After a client reboot, the server's status daemon notices the inconsistency between the locks held by the server and those the client thinks it holds. It informs the server **rpc.lockd** that locks from the rebooted client need reclaiming. The server's **rpc.lockd** sets a grace period—45 seconds by default—during which the locks must be reclaimed or be lost. When a client reboots, it will not reclaim any locks, because there is no record of the locks in its local **rpc.lockd**. The server releases all of them, removing the old state from the client-server system.

Think of this server-side responsibility as dealing with your checkbook and your local bank branch. You keep one set of records, tracking what your balance is, and the bank maintains its own information about your account. The bank's information is the "truth," no matter how good or bad your recording keeping is.

If you vanish from the earth or stop contacting the bank, then the bank tries to contact you for some finite grace period. After that, the bank releases its records and your money. On the other hand, if the bank were to lose its computer records in a disaster, it could ask you to submit checks and deposit slips to recreate the records of your account.

NFS Futures

While the NFS protocol hasn't changed significantly in several years, its implementations have seen near-constant improvement and extensions:

- Duplicate request caching on the server and more elaborate retransmission algorithms on the client side.

- NFS to AppleShare protocol converters, allowing Macintosh systems to mount NFS filesystems as AppleShare volumes.

- Implementations of the NFS server code under IBM's MVS, DEC's VAX/VMS, and several other non-UNIX platforms.

- Stable-storage NFS write accelerators, using battery-backed memory to provide fast write operations with delayed, safe writes to disk.

- Research into using stateful protocols such as TCP.

- Conversion between the NFS and Andrew File System (AFS) protocols.

## 7

Diskless Clients

NFS Support for Diskless Clients
Setting up a Diskless Client
Diskless Client Boot Process
Managing Client Swap Space
Changing a Client's Name
Troubleshooting
Configuration Options
Client/Server Ratios

This chapter is devoted to diskless clients of SunOS or SunOS derivative servers. Diskless Sun clients need not be served by Sun machines, since many vendors have adopted Sun's diskless boot protocols as part of SunOS or NFS ports. The current Sun diskless client support relies entirely on NFS for root and swap filesystem service and uses NIS maps for host configuration information. Diskless clients are probably the most troublesome part of NFS. It is a nontrivial matter to get a machine with no local resources to come up as a fully functioning member of the network, and the interactions between NIS servers, boot servers, and diskless clients create many ways for the boot procedure to fail.

NFS Support for Diskless Clients

Prior to SunOS 4.0, diskless clients were supported through a separate distributed filesystem protocol called Network Disk, or ND. A single raw disk partition was divided into several logical partitions, each of which had a root or swap filesystem on it. Once ND partitions were created, changing their sizes entailed rebuilding all diskless client nodes from backup or distribution tapes. ND also used a smaller buffer size than NFS, employing 1024-byte buffers for filesystem read and write operations.

In SunOS 4.0, diskless clients are supported entirely through NFS. Two features in the operating system and NFS protocols allowed ND to be replaced: swapping to a file and mounting an NFS filesystem as the root directory. The page-oriented virtual memory management system in SunOS 4.0 treats the swap device like an array of pages, so that files can be used as swap space. Instead of copying memory pages to blocks of a raw partition, the VM system copies them to blocks allocated for the swap file. Swap space added in the filesystem is addressed through a vnode, so it can either be a local UNIX filesystem (UFS) file or an NFS-mounted file. Diskless clients now swap directly to a file on their boot servers, accessed via NFS.

The second change supporting diskless clients is the *mount_root()* VFS operation. This mount request looks like any other to the **rpc.mountd** daemon on the server, but on the client it makes the named filesystem the root device of the machine. Once the root filesystem exists, other filesystems can be mounted on any of its vnodes, so an NFS-mounted root partition is a necessary bootstrap for any filesystem mount operations on a diskless client. With the root filesystem NFS mounted, there was no longer a need for a separate protocol to map root and swap filesystem logical disk blocks into server filesystem blocks, so the ND protocol was removed from the SunOS.

Setting up a Diskless Client

To set up a diskless client, you must have the appropriate operating system software loaded on its boot server. If the client and server are of the same architecture, then they share the **/usr** and **/usr/kvm** filesystems. However, if the client has a different CPU or kernel architecture, the server must contain the relevant **/usr** and/or **/usr/kvm** filesystems for the client. The **/usr** filesystem contains the operating system itself, and will be different for each diskless client CPU architecture. The **/usr/kvm** filesystem contains those executables that depend on both the machine's *kernel architecture* and CPU architecture.

Kernel architecture and CPU architecture are not the same thing; CPU architecture guarantees that binaries are compatible, while kernel architecture compatibility means that page sizes, kernel data structures, and supported devices are the same. You can determine the kernel architecture of a running machine using **arch –k**:

```
% arch -k
sun4c
```

If clients and their server have the same CPU architecture but different kernel architectures, then they can share **/usr** but need different **/usr/kvm** filesystems. Client-specific operating system filesystems, and client root and swap filesystems, are normally placed in **/export** on the server.

Setting up a diskless client is fairly easy if all of the operating system software has already been loaded. For each new diskless client, perform the following steps:

- Give the client a name and an IP address, and add them both to the NIS *hosts* map.

- Set up the boot parameters for the client, including its name and the paths to its root and swap filesystems on the server. The boot server keeps these values in its **/etc/bootparams** file, or in the NIS *bootparams* map. A typical **bootparams** file entry looks like this:

```
buonanotte       root=sunne:/export/root/buonanotte \
                 swap=sunne:/export/swap/buonanotte
```

  The first line indicates the name of the diskless client and the location of its root filesystem, and the second line gives the location of the client's swap filesystem. Note that the swap "filesystem" is really just a single file exported from the server.

- The client system's MAC address and hostname must be added to the NIS *ethers* map, so that it can determine its IP address using the Reverse ARP (RARP) protocol. To find the client's MAC address, power it on without the network cable attached, and look for its MAC address in the power-on diagnostic messages.

- Add an entry for the client to the server's **/tftpboot** directory, so the server knows how to locate a boot block for the client. Diskless client servers use this information to locate the appropriate boot code and to determine if they should answer queries about booting the client.

- Create root and swap filesystems for the client on the boot server. These filesystems must be listed in the server's **/etc/exports** file so they can be NFS mounted. After you update **/etc/exports**, run **exportfs** to have the changes take effect. Most systems restrict access to a diskless client root filesystem to that client. In addition, the filesystem export must allow *root* to operate on the NFS-mounted filesystem for normal system operation. A typical **/etc/exports** entry for a diskless client's root filesystem is:

```
/export/root/vineyard          -access=vineyard,root=vineyard
/export/swap/vineyard          -access=vineyard,root=vineyard
```

The **access** option prevents other diskless clients from accessing this filesystem, while the **root** option ensures that the superuser on the client will be given normal **root** privileges on this filesystem.

The **add_client** installation script creates root and swap filesystems, installs the boot block information on the server, and updates most server configuration files. It is the easiest and safest way to add new diskless clients to the network.

Before adding a client to the network, make sure that you have updated the *ethers*, *hosts*, and *bootparams* maps. Then, use the **add_client** script to complete the rest of the steps outlined above:

```
server# /usr/etc/install/add_client -i
```

The installation script asks you for client information interactively, or you can specify each option on the command line. See the manual page for the elaborate syntax. The default server filesystem naming conventions for diskless client files are shown in Table 7-1.

Table 7-1. Diskless Client Filesystem Locations

Filesystem	Contents
/export/root	Root filesystems.
/export/swap	Swap filesystems.
/export/exec	/usr/bin and /usr/kvm executables.

If all clients have the same kernel architecture as the server, then **/export/exec** will contain symbolic links to the server's **/usr/bin** executables. In a heterogeneous network, executables built for the client's architecture are kept in **/export/exec**.

To configure a server with many disks and many clients, create several directories for root and swap filesystems and distribute them over several disks. For example, on a server with two disks, split the **/export/root** and **/export/swap** filesystems, as shown in Table 7-2.

Table 7-2. Diskless Client Filesystems on Two Disks

Disk	Root Filesystems	Swap Filesystems
0	/export/root1	/export/swap1
1	/export/root2	/export/swap2

Some implementations of the client installation script do not allow you to specify a root or swap filesystem directory other than /**export/root** or /**export/swap**. Perform the installation using the script's defaults, and after the client has been installed, move its root and swap filesystems. After moving the client's filesystems, be sure to update the **bootparams** file and NIS map with the new filesystem locations.

As an alternative to performing an installation and then juggling directories, use symbolic links to point the /**export** subdirectories to the desired disk for this client. To force an installation on /**export/root2** and /**export/swap2**, for example, create the following symbolic links on the diskless client server:

```
server# cd /export
server# ln -s root2 root
server# ln -s swap2 swap
```

Verify that the **bootparams** entries for the client reflect the actual location of its root and swap filesystems, and also check the client's /**etc/fstab** file to be sure it mounts its filesystems from /**export/root2** and /**export/swap2**. If the client's /**etc/fstab** file contains the generic /**export/root** or /**export/swap** pathnames, the client won't be able to boot if these symbolic links point to the wrong subdirectories.

Diskless Client Boot Process

Debugging any sort of diskless client problems requires some knowledge of the boot process. When a diskless client is powered on, it knows absolutely nothing about its configuration. It doesn't know its hostname, since that's established in the boot scripts that it hasn't run yet. It has no concept of IP addresses, because it has no hosts file or hosts NIS map to read. The only piece of information it knows for certain is its 48-bit Ethernet address, which is in hardware on the CPU (or Ethernet interface) board. To be able to boot, a diskless client must convert the 48-bit Ethernet address into more useful information such as a boot server name, a hostname, an IP address, and the location of its root and swap filesystems.

Reverse ARP Requests

The heart of the boot process is mapping 48-bit Ethernet addresses to IP addresses. The Address Resolution Protocol (ARP) is used to locate a 48-bit Ethernet address for a known IP address. Its inverse, Reverse ARP (or RARP), is used by diskless clients to find their IP addresses given their Ethernet addresses. Servers run the **rarpd** daemon to accept and process RARP requests, which are broadcast on the network by diskless clients attempting to boot.

IP addresses are calculated in two steps. The 48-bit Ethernet address received in the RARP is used as a key in the **/etc/ethers** file or *ethers* NIS map. **rarpd** locates the hostname associated with the Ethernet address from the *ethers* map, and uses that name as a key into the *hosts* map to find the appropriate IP address.

For the **rarpd** daemon to operate correctly, it must be able to get packets from the raw network interface. RARP packets are not passed up through the TCP or UDP layers of the protocol stack, so **rarpd** listens on the Network Interface Tap (NIT) device for RARP requests. If **/dev/nit** is not present, or if the NIT driver is not configured into the kernel, **rarpd** exits silently. Make sure that all boot servers are running **rarpd** before examining other possible points of failure. The best way to check is with **ps**, which should show two **rarpd** processes:

```
% ps -agux | fgrep rarpd
root       123  0.0  0.0   56    0 ?  IW   Feb  7  0:00 rarpd ie0
root       124  0.0  0.0   40    0 ?  IW   Feb  7  0:00 rarpd ie0
stern     2967  0.0  0.8  144  248 hf S    01:03   0:00 fgrep rarp
```

rarpd starts a copy of itself, called a *delayed responder*. The main **rarp** daemon and the delayed responder are joined by a pipe. If the main daemon gets a request but decides to delay its response, it passes the request to the delayed responder, which waits a few seconds before sending the response. The primary **rarpd** chooses to send a delayed response if it decides it is not the best candidate to answer the request. To understand how this decision is made, we need to look at the process of converting Ethernet addresses into IP addresses in more detail.

The client broadcasts a RARP request containing its 48-bit Ethernet address and waits for a reply. Using the *ethers* and *hosts* maps, any **rarp** server receiving the request attempts to match it to an IP address for the client. Before sending the reply to the client, the server verifies that it is the best candidate to boot the client by checking the **/tftpboot** directory (more on this soon). If the server has the client's boot parameters but might not be able to boot the client, it delays sending a reply (by giving the request to the delayed responder daemon) so that the correct server replies first. Because RARP requests are broadcast, they are received and processed in somewhat random order by all boot servers on the network. The reply delay compensates for the time skew in reply generation. The server that thinks it can boot the diskless client immediately sends its reply to the client; other machines may also send their replies a short time later.

You may ask "Why should a host other than the client's boot server answer its RARP request?" After all, if the boot server is down the diskless client won't be able to boot even if it does have a hostname and IP address. The primary reason is that the "real" boot server may be very loaded, and it may not respond to the RARP request before the diskless client times out. Allowing other hosts to answer the broadcast prevents the client from getting locked into a cycle of sending a RARP request, timing out, and sending the request again. A related reason for having multiple RARP replies is that the RARP packet may be missed by the client's boot server. This is functionally equivalent to the server not replying to the RARP request promptly: if some host does not provide the correct answer, the client continues to broadcast RARP packets until its boot server is less heavily loaded. Finally, RARP is used for other network services as well as for booting diskless clients, so RARP servers must be able to reply to RARP requests whether they are diskless client boot servers or not.

After receiving any one of the RARP replies, the client knows its IP address, as well as the IP address of a boot server (found by looking in the packet returned by the server). The client announces its IP address with a message of the form:

```
Using IP address 192.9.200.1 = C009C801
```

A valid IP address is only the first step in booting; the client needs to be able to load the boot code if it wants to eventually get a UNIX kernel running.

Getting a Boot Block

A local and remote IP address are all that are needed to download the boot block using a simple file transfer program called **tftp** (for trivial **ftp**). This minimal file transfer utility does no user or password checking and is small enough to fit in the boot PROM. Downloading a boot block to the client is done from the server's **/tftpboot** directory.

The server has no specific knowledge of the architecture of the client issuing a RARP or **tftp** request. It also needs a mechanism for determining if it can boot the client, using only its IP address—the first piece of information the client can discern. The server's **/tftpboot** directory contains boot blocks for each architecture of client support, and a set of symbolic links that point to these boot blocks:

```
[wahoo]% ls -l /tftpboot
total 504
lrwxrwxrwx  1 root            19 Jul 23 16:19 828D0E09 -> boot.sun4
lrwxrwxrwx  1 root            19 Jul 23 16:19 828D0E09.SUN4 -> boot.sun4
lrwxrwxrwx  1 root            19 Jul 23 13:33 828D0E8B -> boot.sun3
```

```
lrwxrwxrwx  1 root               19 Jul 23 13:33 828D0E8B.SUN3 -> boot.sun3
lrwxrwxrwx  1 root               19 Jul 23 13:49 828D0E99 -> boot.sun3
lrwxrwxrwx  1 root               19 Jul 23 13:49 828D0E99.SUN3 -> boot.sun3
-rwxr-xr-x  1 root           104936 Jun  6 1990 boot.sun3
-rwxr-xr-x  1 root           144288 Jun  6 1990 boot.sun4
lrwxrwxrwx  1 root                1 Jun  6 1990 tftpboot -> .
```

The link names are the IP addresses of the clients in hexadecimal. The first client
link—**828D0E09**—corresponds to IP address 130.141.14.9:

```
828D0E09
```
Insert dots to put in IP address format:
```
82.8D.0E.09
```
Convert back to decimal:
```
130.141.14.9
```

Two links exist for each client—one with the IP address in hexadecimal, and one
with the IP address and the machine architecture. The second link is used by
some versions of **tftpboot** that specify their architecture when asking for a boot
block. It doesn't hurt to have both, as long as they point to the correct boot block
for the client.

The previous section stated that a server delays its response to a RARP request if
it doesn't think it's the best candidate to boot the requesting client. The server
makes this determination by matching the client IP address to a link in /**tftpboot**.
If the link exists, the server is the best candidate to boot the client; if the link is
missing, the server delays its response to allow another server to reply first.

The client gets its boot block via **tftp**, sending its request to the server that
answered its RARP request. When the **inetd** daemon on the server receives the
tftp request, it starts an **in.tftpd** daemon that locates the right boot file by following the symbolic link representing the client's IP address. The **tftpd** daemon
downloads the boot block to the client. When the client gets a valid boot block, it
reports the address of its boot server:

```
Booting from tftp server at 192.9.200.2 = C009C802
```

It's possible that the first host to reply to the client's RARP request can't boot
it—it may have had valid *ethers* and *hosts* map entries for the machine but not a
boot block. If the first server chosen by the diskless client does not answer the
tftp request, the client broadcasts this same request. If no server responds, the
machine complains that it cannot find a **tftp** server.

The **tftpd** daemon should be run in secure mode using the **–s** option. This is
usually the default configuration in its /**etc**/**inetd.conf** entry:

```
tftp dgram udp wait root /usr/etc/in.tftpd in.tftpd -s /tftpboot
```

The argument after the **-s** is the directory that **tftp** uses as its root—it does a
chdir() into this directory and then a *chroot*() to make it the root of the filesystem

visible to the **tftp** process. This measure prevents **tftp** from being used to take any file other than a boot block in **tftpboot**.

The last directory entry in **/tftpboot** is a symbolic link to itself, using the current directory entry (**.**) instead of its full pathname. This symbolic link is used for compatibility with older systems that passed a full pathname to **tftp**, such as **/tftpboot/C009C801.SUN3**. Following the symbolic link effectively removes the **/tftpboot** component and allows a secure **tftp** to find the request file in its root directory. Do not remove this symbolic link, or older diskless clients will not be able to download their boot blocks.

Booting a Kernel

Once the boot block is loaded, the diskless client jumps out of its PROM monitor and into the boot code. To do anything useful, **boot** needs a root and swap file-system, preferably with a bootable kernel on the root device. To get this information, **boot** broadcasts a request for boot parameters. The **rpc.bootparamd** RPC server listens for these requests and returns a gift pack filled with the location of the root filesystem, the client's hostname, a default route, an NIS domain name, and the name of the boot server. The filesystem information is kept in **/etc/boot-params** or in the NIS *bootparams* map. The NIS domain name sent to the client is the server's default domain name, and is not part of the *bootparams* map. You cannot mix information for clients in different NIS domains in the same *boot-params* map, because a server in another NIS domain might answer the boot parameter request and supply the wrong NIS domain name for the client.

The diskless client mounts its root filesystem from the named boot server and boots the kernel image found there. The running kernel issues another boot parameter request for the location of the swap filesystem, which is also handled by **rpc.bootparamd**. After configuring root and swap devices, the client begins single user startup and sets its hostname, IP addresses, and NIS domain name from information in its **/etc** files. It is imperative that the names and addresses returned by **rpc.bootparamd** match those in the client's configuration files, which must also match the contents of the NIS maps.

As part of the single user boot, the client mounts its **/usr** filesystem from the server listed in its **/etc/fstab** file. At this point, the client has root and swap file-systems, and looks (to the UNIX kernel) no different than a system booting from a local disk. The diskless client executes its boot script files, and eventually enters multi-user mode and displays a login prompt. Any breakdowns that occur after the **/usr** filesystem is mounted are caused by problems in the boot scripts, not in the diskless client boot process itself.

Managing Boot Parameters

Every diskless client boot server has an /etc/bootparams file. The NIS *bootparams* map is appended to this file if it contains a plus sign (+) at the end. There is no mechanism for including selected parts of the map file in /etc/bootparams; if you include the NIS marker then you include the entire map file.

Here are some suggestions for managing diskless client boot parameters:

- Keep the boot parameters in the *bootparams* map if you are using NIS. Reduce the /etc/bootparams file on diskless client boot servers to just a single plus sign. Obviously, if your NIS master server is also a diskless client server, it will contain a complete /etc/bootparams file.

- If you have diskless clients in more than one NIS domain, make sure you have a separate NIS *bootparams* map for each domain. Do not use the same /etc/bootparams file for all domains, or clients may be given the wrong NIS domain name when they receive their boot information, as described in the previous section).

- On networks with diskless clients from different vendors, make sure that the format of the boot parameter information used by each vendor is the same. If one system's **rpc.bootparamd** daemon returns a boot parameter packet that cannot be understood by another system, you will not be able to use the NIS *bootparams* map. We'll look at the problems caused by differing boot parameter packet formats in "Boot Parameter Confusion," in Chapter 11, *Debugging Network Problems*.

Eliminating copies of the boot parameter information on the other servers reduces the changes that you'll have out-of-date information on boot servers after you've made a configuration change.

Managing Client Swap Space

Once a client is running, it may need more swap space. Generally, allocating four times the physical memory on the client is a good start, with a bare minimum of 24 or 32 Mbytes per client. Power users, or those who open many windows, run many processes in the background, or execute large compute-intensive jobs, may need to have their initial swap allocation increased.

To increase the swap space on a diskless client, you simply create a new swap file for it on the boot server. Shut the client down before removing the existing swap file, or the client will panic when it cannot locate parts of its swap filesystem. To increase the client's swap space, remove the old swap file and create a new one using **mkfile**:

```
First shutdown client honeymoon
# cd /export/swap
# rm honeymoon
# mkfile 25M honeymoon
# ls -l honeymoon
-rw-------T  1 root      26214400 Jan  9 00:38 honeymoon
```

Make sure you do not use the **–n** option to **mkfile**, since this causes the swap file to be incompletely allocated. If the client tries to find a swap block that should have been pre-allocated by **mkfile**, but doesn't exist, the client usually panics and reboots.

There is no need to re-run **exportfs** since filesystems are exported by pathname, which has not changed in this case. When the client reboots, it finds its new and improved swap file. Note that the last bit in the world permission field is T, indicating that "sticky-bit" access is set even though the file has no execute permissions. The **mkfile** utility sets these permissions by default. Enabling the sticky bit on a non-executable file has two effects:

- The virtual memory system does not perform read-ahead of this file's data blocks.

- The filesystem code does not write out inode information or indirect blocks each time the file is modified.

Unlike regular files, no read-ahead should be done for swap files. The virtual memory management system brings in exactly those pages it needs to satisfy page fault conditions, and performing read-ahead for swap files only consumes disk bandwidth on the server.

Eliminating the write operations needed to maintain inode and indirect block information does not present a problem because the diskless client cannot extend its swap filesystem. Only the file modification time field in the inode will change, so this approach trades off an incorrect modification time (on the swap file) for fewer write operations.

Changing a Client's Name

There are many motivations for using diskless clients:

- They are quieter than machines with disks.

- They are easier to administer, since there is no local copy of the operating system that requires updates.

- They are slightly more secure, because there is no local "secret" data.

Diskless clients are sometimes reserved for nontechnical users or new employees who have yet to work their way up the hardware totem pole. If users are given the option of naming their own systems (sometimes as a consolation for receiving workstations used by someone who received a more powerful machine), renaming diskless clients can become a fairly common task.

If you have not changed the default diskless client configuration, it's easiest to shut down the client, remove its root and swap filesystems, and then create a new client, with the new name, using **add_client**. However, if you have made a large number of local changes—modifying configuration files, setting up a name service, and creating mount points—then it may be easier to change the client's name using the existing root and swap filesystems.

Before making any changes, shut down the client system so that you can work on its root filesystem and change NIS maps that affect it. On the NIS master server, you need to make several changes:

- Update **/etc/bootparams** to reflect the new client's name and root and swap filesystem pathnames.

- Add the new hostname to the hosts map in place of the old client name. If any mail aliases include the old hostname, or if the host is embedded in a list of local hostnames, update these files as well.

- Modify the *ethers* NIS map if all hosts are listed in it.

- Rebuild the *bootparams*, *ethers*, and *hosts* maps.

On the client's boot server, complete the renaming process:

- Rename the root and swap filesystems for the client:

```
# cd /export/root
# mv oldname newname
# cd /export/swap
# mv oldname newname
```

- Update the server's list of exported NFS filesystems with the new root and swap pathnames. Also change the **access** and **root** options in **/etc/exports**. After modifying the file, export the newly named filesystems, or re-export all filesystems, so that the client will be able to find them when it reboots.

- In the client's root filesystem, modify its hosts file and boot scripts to reflect the new hostname:

```
# cd /export/root/newname/etc
# vi hosts
# vi rc.boot
```

or:

```
# vi hostname.le0
```

In SunOS 4.1 and later, the hostname is set in a configuration file with the network interface as an extension; for example: **hostname.le0**. It is essential that the host's name and IP address in its own hosts file agree with its entries in the NIS map, or the machine either boots with the wrong IP address or doesn't boot at all.

Aside from shutting the client down, the remainder of this operation could be automated using a script that takes the old and new client names as arguments. The number of changes that were made to NIS maps should indicate a clear benefit of using NIS: without the centralized administration, you would have had to change the **/etc/ethers** and **/etc/bootparams** files on every server, and update **/etc/hosts** on *every* machine on the network.

Troubleshooting

When diskless clients refuse to boot, they do so rather emphatically. Shuffling machines and hostnames to accommodate changes in personnel increases the likelihood that a diskless machine will refuse to boot. Start debugging by verifying that hostnames, IP addresses, and Ethernet addresses are all properly registered on boot and NIS servers. The point at which the boot fails usually indicates where to look next for the problem: machines that cannot even locate a boot block may be getting the wrong boot information, while machines that boot but cannot enter single-user mode may be missing their /usr filesystems.

Missing and Inconsistent Client Information

There are a few pieces of missing host information that are easily tracked down. If a client tries to boot but gets no RARP response, check that the NIS _ethers_ map or the /etc/ethers files on the boot servers contain an entry for the client with the proper MAC address. A client reports RARP failures by complaining that it cannot get its IP address.

Diskless clients that boot part way but hang after mounting their root filesystems may have /etc/hosts files that do not agree with the NIS _ethers_ or _hosts_ maps. It's also possible that the client booted using one name and IP address combination, but chose to use a different name while going through the single-user boot process. Check the boot scripts to be sure that the client is using the proper hostname, and also check that its local /etc/hosts file agrees with the NIS maps.

Other less obvious failures may be due to confusion with the _bootparams_ map and the **rpc.bootparamd** daemon. Since the diskless client broadcasts a request for boot parameters, any host running **rpc.bootparamd** can answer it, and that server may have an incorrect /etc/bootparams file, or it may have bound to an NIS server with an out-of-date map.

Checking Boot Parameters

The **bootparamd** daemon returns a fairly large bundle of values to a diskless client. In addition to the pathnames used for root and swap filesystems, the diskless client gets the name of its boot server and a default route. The boot server takes values from a local /etc/bootparams if it exists, so ensure that local file copies match NIS maps if they are used. Changing the map on the NIS master server will not help a diskless client if its boot server uses only a local copy of the boot parameters file. The _bootparams_ map is appended to the local /etc/bootparams file, so a mistake in the local file will hide the correct information in the NIS map.

You can debug boot parameter problems by enabling debugging on the client or on the boot server. On the client, boot using the –v flag, so you can see the client's boot parameters as it receives them from a **bootparamd** server:

```
> b -v
Requesting Internet address for 8:0:20:0:47:9f
RARP for IP address:
call portmapper: to 255.255.255.255 port 111: prog 100026 vers 1 proc 1
```

```
portmapper reply succeeded (status 0)
got machine_name major domain_name nesales router_address 131.14.52.12
```
ARP for Ethernet address:
```
requesting bootparam getfile from 131.14.52.26
got server_name wahoo server_address 131.14.52.26 server_path /export/root/major
server name 'wahoo'
```

In this example, the client *major* broadcasts a request to RPC program 100026, the **rpc.bootparamd** server, and receives its machine name, NIS domain name, and default route. It then sends a request for additional boot information, and gets back its server name, the server's IP address, and the path to its root filesystem on the server.

By enabling debug mode in **rpc.bootparamd** on the server, you can see the hostname, addresses, and pathnames given to the diskless client. You can turn on **rpc.bootparamd** debugging by killing it on the server and starting it again with the **–d** option:

```
# ps -agux | fgrep bootparam
root      129  0.0  0.0   64     0 ? IW    Feb  7  0:01 rpc.bootparamd
root     3037  0.0  0.8  144   248 hf S    01:26   0:00 fgrep bootparam
# kill 129
# rpc.bootparamd -d
In debug mode
Whoami returning name = major, router address = 131.14.52.12
```

If the server shows strange boot parameters passed to the client, check that the server's **/etc/bootparams** file is correct, and that the boot server's NIS server has up-to-date maps.

If the boot parameters received by the client are incorrect, check that the server answering the request for them has current information. Because requests are broadcast to **rpc.bootparamd**, the server that can reply in the shortest time supplies the information. If the client refuses to boot at all, complaining of:

```
null domain name
invalid domain name
invalid boot parameters
```

or similar problems, verify that the host answering its broadcasts is using the same boot protocol and configuration files. See "Boot Parameter Confusion," in Chapter 11, *Debugging Network Problems*, for an example of invalid boot parameters.

Also ensure that the boot server exports the client's root and swap filesystems with the proper *root* mapping and access restrictions. Both the root and swap filesystems should have the options:

```
-access=client,root=client
```

so that access is limited to the diskless client, and to allow the superuser to write to the filesystems. If the swap filesystem is not exported so that *root* can write to it, the diskless client will not be able to start the **init** process to begin the single user boot.

Missing /usr

After setting the host and domain names and configuring network interfaces in the boot process, a machine mounts its **/usr** filesystem. If there are problems with **/usr**, the boot process either hangs or fails at the first reference to the **/usr** filesystem. The two most common problems are not being able to locate the NFS server for **/usr** and attempting to mount the wrong **/usr**.

NIS cannot be started until after **/usr** is mounted, since client-side daemons like **ypbind** live in **/usr**. Generally, **/usr** is mounted from the boot server, so a diskless client needs its own name and its server's hostname in its **/etc/hosts**. If **/usr** is not mounted from the root/swap filesystem server, the **/usr** server's hostname must appear in the local hosts file as well. You may need as many as four different entries in the "runt" **/etc/hosts** file on a diskless client: its hostname, a localhost entry, the boot server's name, and the name of the **/usr** server.

Heterogeneous client/server environments create another set of problems. Clients of different architectures need their own **/usr** filesystems with executables built for the client's CPU, not the server's. The most obvious problem is when the client mounts the wrong **/usr**. If the executables on it were built for a different CPU, then the first attempt to invoke one of them produces a fairly descriptive error. However, if the **/usr/kvm** filesystem is for the correct CPU architecture but contains the wrong kernel architecture (for example, Sun's *sun4* and *sun4c* variants), then the client boots but certain UNIX utilities will not work. Processes that read the kernel or user address spaces, such as **trace** and **ps**, are the most likely to break.

If you suspect that you're mounting the wrong **/usr**, first check the client's **/etc/fstab** file to see where it gets **/usr**:

```
wahoo:/export/root/spinki              /        nfs rw 0 0
wahoo:/export/exec/sun3.sunos.4.1      /usr     nfs ro 0 0
wahoo:/export/exec/kvm/sun3.sunos.4.1  /usr/kvm nfs ro 0 0
```

In this example, we would check **/export/exec** on the server *wahoo*. The directories in **/export/exec** and **/export/exec/kvm** are named by using the template called *architecture.SunOS-release*. If the client and the server are of the same CPU architecture, and are running the same release of the operating system, the subdirectory in **/export/exec** is a symbolic link to the server's **/usr** directory. If the client and server have the same kernel architecture, then the client's mount point in **/export/exec/kvm** will be a symbolic link as well, pointing to the server's **/usr/kvm** directory. If the client and server do not have the same kernel or CPU architectures, the directories in **/export/exec** contain complete operating system releases.

Three things can go wrong with this link-and-directory scheme:

- The links in **/export/exec** point to the wrong place. This is possible if you changed the architecture of the server but restored **/export** from a backup tape. Make sure that **sun4.sunos.4.1** links only point to **/usr** if the server is a Sun-4 running SunOS 4.1. You'll get "exec format errors" if you mount a **/usr** of the wrong architecture on the client.

- The **/export/exec** directories referenced by the clients don't exist. This is possible if you added a client of a new, different CPU architecture but did not install the appropriate operating system software for it. If you try to mount a directory that doesn't exist, you should see "cannot mount root" errors on the client.

- The client may have the wrong mount point listed in its **/etc/fstab** file. If you did not specify the architecture of the client correctly when using **add_client**, the client's **fstab** file is likely to contain the wrong mount information.

If you are unsure of how a mount and link combination will work, experiment on another diskless client having the same architecture. For example, mount **/export/exec/sun3.sunos.4.1** on **/mnt**, and then try a sample command to be sure you've mounted the right one:

```
client# mount wahoo:/export/exec/sun3.sunos.4.1 /mnt
client# cd /var
client# /mnt/bin/ls
adm             log             net             spool
crash           preserve        tmp             yp
```

If commands are executed properly, then you should be able to mount **/usr** safely on the diskless client in question.

Configuration Options

Adding disks to local clients opens two configuration options. You can use the local disk for swap space, or you can build an entire bootable system on it, and put the root and swap filesystems on the local disk. This latter configuration is called a *dataless* client, and makes sense if the client does not need most of the local disk for a very large swap space. If the client has a large swap partition and uses it frequently, adding a local disk may improve performance by reducing the client's traffic to its boot server. In other instances, the local disk provides private storage for sensitive files.

Dataless clients contain no user or data files on their local disks. Everything on the local disk can be reconstructed from operating system release tapes or from system installation scripts. The local disks are used for the root and swap filesystems, while /usr and all other filesystems are NFS mounted. The dataless architecture provides some performance advantages from both the client and server perspective, particularly when the client has a large swap space.

A significant portion—usually more than 50% and sometimes 90%—of a diskless client's network traffic is caused by reading and writing the root and swap filesystems. Clients with local disks place less of a load on the network and on the boot server by sending their swap traffic to this disk.

Dataless Clients

You may choose to use the dataless client configuration if you have to support a few machines of a new client architecture, and would have to carve the disk space out of the server's /**export** partition. Adding a local disk keeps the server configuration simple and puts all files specific to the new client architecture on the local disks. If you are going to upgrade the operating system frequently, a dataless client makes a good testbed because it does not require any server changes to install the new software. Of course, if you use a dataless client as a proving ground for new operating system releases, you should put its /usr on the local disk as well.

The best network architecture for dataless clients is one in which desktop machines run application sets with large, randomly accessed virtual address spaces. If the machine has a reasonably high level of swapping activity, using a local disk improves performance. Dataless clients may appear to be more expensive per seat than diskless clients, since the diskless machines get root and swap space at "bulk" prices from the server. Small disks used for dataless clients are more expensive per byte than large server disks. On the other hand, in a pure diskless client environment, you must purchase additional disk space to hold the clients' root and swap filesystems. If you allocate some portion of the server's cost as the cost of replacing local disks, the dataless and diskless architectures have much less of a price differential. Be careful when analyzing client/server cost projections. You'll get the fairest numbers when you compare the total cost of the desktop workstation, any local disk, and the desktop's share of the cost of servers providing root, swap, and user filesystems.

When you do add local disks, it's important to choose your disk size carefully. If larger local disks are attached to dataless clients, they become inviting homes for user files that may not be backed up regularly. If you plan to configure dataless clients, use the smallest disk possible to contain the root and swap filesystems, with enough room on the local disk's root partition to contain a very large **/tmp** filesystem. Applications that use enough virtual memory to justify a local disk probably create huge temporary files as well.

Management of dataless nodes is slightly more complex than that of diskless nodes. Even though the local disks contain no user files or tools, they may still have host-specific configuration information in the **/etc** directory, such as software password files. Use care when modifying the private parts of a dataless node so that the entire node can be recreated from a boot tape or archive tape if the local disk must be replaced. You will probably want to create a script that creates spool directories, copies **printcap** files, and creates NFS mount points on the client; you can use this script on dataless or new diskless clients as well. If possible, mount the dataless client spool directories from an NFS server so that the dataless client's disk contains no host-specific information. Ideally, you should not have to do backups of a dataless client.

Swapping on a Local Disk

The presence of a local disk on a diskless client genuinely confuses the kernel's autoconfiguration process. If the generic kernel autoconfiguration is specified (as it usually is in the kernel configuration file), the system searches for a valid root device, starting with the fastest installed disk driver and working its way down to the network. On an older machine, for example, the kernel is likely to check for an SMD disk, a SCSI disk, and then finally decide to put the root and swap filesystems on the network. As soon as a potential root device is found, the kernel attempts to locate the root filesystem on it and continues booting from there.

To boot from the diskless client's server but use the local disk for file storage, the generic kernel configuration must explicitly list the devices to be used for root and swap filesystems. Kernel configuration files are named /sys/*arch*/**conf**/*name*, where *arch* is the kernel architecture of the machine and *name* is the name given to the kernel. For example, the kernel configuration file for the **GENERIC** kernel on a **sun4c** architecture machine is:

```
/sys/sun4c/conf/GENERIC
```

In the kernel configuration file, change the kernel root configuration line.

```
config  vmunix  swap generic
```

becomes:

```
config  vmunix  root on type nfs swap on type nfs
```

Explicitly placing the root and swap filesystems on NFS-mounted devices suppresses the root device search in the autoconfiguration process.

If the local disk is used for swap space only, then the kernel configuration file should note the location of the swap device:

```
config  vmunix  root on type nfs swap on type spec sd0b
```

The swap partition should cover most, if not all of the local disk. The package of boot parameters returned by **bootparamd** may not point to a swap file. The client's configuration file will mount the local disk as the primary swap device.

Client/Server Ratios

The number of clients that can be supported from a single server depends on many variables: the type of work done on each client, the type of disks and network interfaces on the server, the number of clients on the network and the configuration of the clients. Diskless clients used in a software engineering shop do not have the same server requirements as diskless machines used to run documentation group; similarly, when dozens of diskless clients are put onto the same physical network, the network itself becomes a bottleneck before the server does. Instead of adopting a somewhat arbitrary client-server ratio, use the following steps to calculate a rough client-server distribution:

1. Set up a diskless or dataless client on a network with its own server. Put home directories, applications, tools, and other NFS-mounted filesystems on another server, so that the server under test does nothing but handle root and swap filesystem requests from the client. Use only one client for this test so that the server does not become a bottleneck: you want to measure the load imposed by a single client in an unconstrained environment.

2. Run a normal workload on the client, using scripts or a live user to produce a typical traffic pattern. On the server, measure the average traffic generated (over the course of several hours) and also try to measure the peak request rates produced by the client. Use the **nfsstat** utility on the server to determine the number of NFS requests per second that the server handles. **nfsstat** is described in more detail in "NFS Statistics," in Chapter 10, *Diagnostic and Administrative Tools*.

3. Repeat the first two steps for each "type" of client or user: diskless client, dataless client, development engineer, testing/quality assurance lab, documentation writer, and so on. Blend these figures together based on the percentage of each client type to determine the average NFS load imposed by all of the clients.

4. Tune and benchmark the server using the methodologies described in Chapter 12, *Performance Analysis and Tuning*, and Appendix D, *NFS Benchmarking*. The benchmarks should produce an expected upper bound on the number of NFS operations that the server can provide.

5. Divide the server's capacity by the weighted average of the client request rates to determine a coarse client-server ratio. Conversely, you can multiply the weighted number of NFS operations performed by each client by the number of clients to set a goal for the server tuning process.

The ratio produced in this manner should be used as a coarse estimate only. The client-server ratio will be overstated because each diskless client server may handle other responsibilities, such as serving other NFS filesystems, or driving printers. It may also be understated, because it is rare to find an environment in which the average load produced by N hosts is N times the load produced by a single host. Workstation users simply aren't that synchronized. We'll take closer looks at server and client tuning, NFS benchmarking, and performance optimization in later chapters.

8

Network Security

User-oriented Network Security
Password and NIS Security
NFS Security
Secure RPC and Secure NFS
Viruses

The simplicity and transparency provided by NFS and NIS must be weighed against security concerns. Providing access to all files to all users may not be in the best interests of security, particularly if the files contain sensitive or proprietary data. Not all hosts may be considered equally secure or "open," so access may be restricted to certain users. Transparency must be limited when dealing with secured hosts: if you have taken precautions to prevent unauthorized access to a machine, you don't want someone to be able to sit down and use an open window or logged-in terminal to access the secured machine. To enforce access restrictions, you always want password verification for users, which means eliminating some of the network transparency provided by NIS.

This chapter describes mechanisms in NFS and NIS that exist to tighten access restrictions to machines and filesystems. It is not intended to be a complete list of security loopholes and their fixes. The facilities and administrative techniques covered are meant to complement the network transparency provided by NFS and NIS while still enforcing local security measures. For a more detailed treatment of security issues, refer to *Practical UNIX Security*, by Garfinkel and Spafford (O'Reilly & Associates, 1991).

User-oriented Network Security

One area of concern is user access to hosts on the network. Figure 8-1 shows several classes of permissions to consider, reflecting the ways in which a user might access a host from another host on the network.

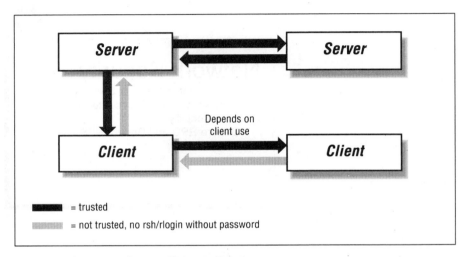

Figure 8-1. Client-Server Remote Logins

Remote logins are not the only concern; remote execution of commands using **rsh** should be considered in the same context. This section only covers log-in restrictions; we'll look at protecting data in NFS filesystems later in this chapter. Local log-in restrictions are defined by the local host's password file, NIS password maps, and the use of netgroups. Across the network, access is determined by the notion of trusted hosts and trusted users.

Trusted Hosts and Trusted Users

Defining a *trusted host* requires two machines: one that will be trusted, and one that is extending the trust to it. The local host *lh* trusts remote host *rh* if users can log into *lh* from *rh* without supplying their passwords. Similarly, a user is trusted if he or she can log into a host from some remote machine without supplying a password. Trust is defined only for the local host; users and machines may be trusted on some systems but not on others.

The relationships between hosts often define the realm of trusted users and trusted hosts. Two NIS or NFS clients, for example, may trust all users and all other client hosts. On the NFS server, only other servers may be trusted hosts and only the system administration staff may be trusted users.

WARNING

The following trusted user and trusted host descriptions apply in an environment in which you do not have to be wary of users or outsiders who will attempt to compromise security. These are basic security measures that fit in with the other network management strategies discussed in this book. If you need to secure your systems against all attacks, then you must consider the effects of having security compromised on any machine in your network. Again, these extensive security mechanisms are discussed in *Practical Unix Security*.

Some of the common patterns of trusting hosts and users are:

Server-Server   Generally, servers trust each other. A few users can be trusted in server-to-server relationships if each server has a password file that contains a subset of the NIS password map, or a password file with no NIS references. To emphasize the previous warning, extending trust between servers means that if one server is compromised, then they all are.

Server-Client   Most clients should trust the servers and users on the servers. A system administrator may need to run performance monitoring daemons on the client from the server and require transparent access to the client. Similarly, the server may be used to distribute files to the clients on a regular basis.

Client-Server   This is probably the most restrictive relationship. Only users who are responsible for managing the servers are generally given transparent access to the servers. Remote access to the server for access to the Berkeley line printer daemon can be controlled through the **/etc/hosts.lpd** file, instead of by trusting client machines on the server.

Client-Client   Client-client relationships depend upon how you have centralized your disk resources. If all files live on one or more fileservers, then client-to-client relationships are generally relaxed. However, if you are using the clients as isolated systems, with some per-client storage containing private data, then client-client relationships look more like those between clients and servers. The scope of the client-client relationships depends upon the sensitivity of the data on the clients: if you don't want other users to see the private data, then you must treat the client machine like a server.

The **/etc/hosts.equiv** and **.rhosts** files (in each user's home directory) define the set of trusted hosts, users, and user-host pairs for each system. Again, trust and transparent access are granted by the machine being accessed remotely, so these configuration files vary from host to host. The **.rhosts** file is maintained by each user and specifies a list of hosts or user-host pairs that are also parsed for determining if a host or user is trusted.

Enabling Transparent Access

Both **rlogin** and **rsh** use the *ruserok()* library routine to bypass the normal log-in and password security mechanism. *ruserok()* determines if the user and hostname given are trusted on the *local* host; it is usually called by the remote daemon for these utilities during its startup. If the user or host are not trusted, then the user must supply a password to log in or get "Permission denied" errors when attempting to use **rsh**. If the remote host trusts the user and host, execution (or login) proceeds without any other verification of the user's identity.

The **hosts.equiv** file contains either hostnames or host-user pairs:

```
hostname [username]
```

If a username follows the hostname, only that combination of user and hostnames is trusted. Netgroup names, in the form *+@group*, may be substituted for either hostnames or user names. As with the password file, using a plus sign (+) for an entry includes the appropriate NIS map: in the first column, the hosts map is included, and in the second column, the password map is included. Entries that grant permission contain the hostname, a host and username, or a netgroup inclusion.

The following is **/etc/hosts.equiv** on host *mahimahi*:

```
wahoo
bitatron +
corvette johnc
+@source-hosts
+@sysadm-hosts +@sysadm-users
```

The first example trusts all users on host *wahoo*. Users on *wahoo* can **rlogin** to **mahimahi** without a password. The second example is similar to the first, except the list of trusted users is restricted to those in the global NIS password database. This isn't a particularly strong restriction, but it does prevent users that have password file entries defined only on *bitatron* from gaining access to other systems.

The third example is the most restrictive. Only user *johnc* is trusted on host *corvette*. Other users on host *corvette* are not trusted, and must supply a password when logging in to *mahimahi*.

The last two entries use netgroups to define lists of hosts and users. The +*@source-hosts* entry trusts all hosts whose names appear in the *source-hosts* netgroup. If usernames are given as part of the netgroup triples, they are ignored. This means that hostname wildcards grant overly generous permissions. If the *source-hosts* netgroup contained (,stern,), then using this netgroup in the first column of **hosts.equiv** effectively opens up the machine to all hosts on the network. If you need to restrict logins to specific users from specific machines you must use either explicit names or netgroups in both the first and second column of **hosts.equiv**.

The last example does exactly this. Instead of trusting one host-username combination, it trusts all combinations of hostnames in *sysadm-hosts* and the usernames in *sysadm-users*. Note that the *usernames* in the first netgroup, and the *hostnames* in the second are completely ignored.

Permission may be revoked by preceding the host or user specification with a minus sign (–):

```
-wahoo
+ -@dangerous-users
```

The first entry denies permission to all users on host *wahoo*. The second example negates all users in the netgroup *dangerous-users* on all machines in the NIS hosts map (referenced by the plus sign (+) in the hosts field). If you want to deny permission to everything in both the hosts and password NIS maps, leave **hosts.equiv** empty.

The **.rhosts** file uses the same syntax as the **hosts.equiv** file, but it is parsed *after* it. The sole exception to this rule is when granting remote permission to *root*. When the superuser attempts to access a remote host, the **hosts.equiv** file is ignored and only the /.**rhosts** file is read. For all other users, the *ruserok()* routine reads **hosts.equiv** and then the user's **.rhosts** file until a match, either positive or negative, is found. If an entry in either file denies permission to a remote user, the file parsing stops at that point, even if an entry further down in the file grants permission to that user and host combination. The first match determines whether the user and host pair is trusted.

Usernames that are not the same on all systems are handled through the user's **.rhosts** file. If you are user *julie* on your desktop machine *vacation*, but have user name *juliec* on host *starter*, you can still get to that remote host transparently by adding a line to your **.rhosts** file on *starter*. Assuming a standard home directory scheme, your **.rhosts** file would be **/home/starter/juliec/.rhosts**, and should contain the name of the machine you are logging in from and your username on the originating machine:

```
vacation julie
```

From *vacation*, you can execute commands on *starter* using:

```
% rsh starter -l juliec "ls -l"
```

or:

```
% rlogin starter -l juliec
```

On *starter*, the *ruserok()* routine looks for a .**rhosts** file for user *juliec*, your username on that system. If no entry in **hosts.equiv** grants you permission (probably the case because you have a different username on that system), then your .**rhosts** file entry maps your local username into its remote equivalent. You can also use netgroups in .**rhosts** files, with the same warnings that apply to using them in /**etc**/**hosts.equiv**.

As a network manager, watch for overly permissive .**rhosts** files. Users may accidentally grant password-free access to any user on the network, or map a foreign user name to their own UNIX username. If you have many password files with private, non-NIS managed entries, watch the use of .**rhosts** files. Merging password files to eliminate non-uniform usernames may be easier than maintaining a constant lookout for unrestricted access granted through an .**rhosts** file.

Using Netgroups

Netgroups have been used in several examples already to show how triples of host, user, and domain names are used in granting access across the network. The best use of netgroups is for the definition of splinter groups of a large NIS domain, where creating a separate NIS domain would not justify the administrative effort required to keep the two domains synchronized.

Because of the variety of ways in which netgroups are applied, their use and administration are sometimes counterintuitive. Perhaps the most common mistake is defining a netgroup with host or usernames not present in the NIS maps or local host and password files. Consider a netgroup that includes a hostname in another NIS domain:

```
remote-hosts    (poi,-,-), (muban,-,-)
```

When a user attempts to **rlogin** from host *poi*, the local server-side daemon attempts to find the hostname corresponding to the IP address of the originating host. If *poi* cannot be found in the NIS *hosts.byaddr* map, then an IP address, instead of a hostname, is passed to **ruserok()**. The verification process fails to match the hostname, even though it appears in the netgroup. Any time information is shared between NIS domains, the appropriate entries must appear in both NIS maps for the netgroup construction to function as expected.

Even though netgroups are specified as host and user pairs, no utility uses both names together. There is no difference between the following two netgroups:

```
group-a          (los, mikel,) (bitatron, stern, )
group-b          (los, -,) (bitatron, -,) (-, mikel, ) (-, stern, )
```

Things that need hostnames—the first column of **hosts.equiv** or NFS export lists—produce the set of hosts {*los, bitatron*} from both netgroups. Similarly, anything that takes a username, such as the password file or the second column of **hosts.equiv**, always finds the set {*mikel, stern*}. You can even mix-and-match these two groups in **hosts.equiv**. All four of the combinations of the two netgroups, when used in both columns of **hosts.equiv**, produce the same net effect: users *stern* and *mikel* are trusted on hosts *bitatron* and *los*.

The triple-based format of the netgroups map clouds the real function of the netgroups. Because all utilities parse either host or usernames, you will find it helpful to define netgroups that contain only host or usernames. It's easier to remember what each group is supposed to do, and the time required to administer a few extra netgroups will be more than made up by time not wasted chasing down strange permission problems that arise from the way the *netgroups* map is used.

An example here helps to show how the *netgroup* map can produce unexpected results. We'll build a netgroup containing a list of users and hosts that we trust on a server named *gate*. Users in the netgroup will be able to log in to *gate*, and hosts in the netgroup will be able to mount filesystems from it. The netgroup definition looks like this:

```
gate-group    (,stern,), (,johnc,), (bitatron, -,), (corvette, -,)
```

In the **/etc/exports** file on *gate*, we'll add an *access* restriction:

```
/home/gate              -access=gate-group
```

No at sign (@) is needed to include the netgroup name in the **/etc/exports** file. The *netgroup* map is searched first for the names in the *access* list, followed by the *hosts* map.

In **/etc/passwd** on *gate*, we'll include the *gate-group* netgroup, but exclude the entire NIS *passwd* map by leaving out the plus sign (+) at the end of the file:

```
root:passwd:0:1:Operator:/:/bin/csh
nobody:*:-2:-2::/:
daemon:*:1:1::/:
sys:*:2:2::/:/bin/csh
bin:*:3:3::/bin:
```

```
uucp:*:4:4::/var/spool/uucppublic:
+@gate-group
```

To test our access controls, we go to a machine not in the netgroup—NFS client *vacation*—and attempt to mount **/home/gate**. We expect that the **mount** will fail with a "Permission denied" error:

```
vacation# mount gate:/home/gate/home/gate
vacation#
```

The mount completes without any errors. Why doesn't this netgroup work as expected?

The answer is in the wildcards left in the host fields in the netgroup entries for users *stern* and *johnc*. Because a wildcard was used in the host field of the netgroup, *all* hosts in the NIS map became part of *gate-group* and were added to the access list for **/home/gate**. When creating this netgroup, our intention was probably to allow users *stern* and *johnc* to log into *gate* from any host on the network, but instead we gave away access rights.

A better way to manage this problem is to define two netgroups, one for the users and one for the hosts, so that wildcards in one definition do not have strange effects on the other. The modified **/etc/netgroup** file looks like this:

```
gate-users:    (,stern,), (,johnc,)
gate-hosts:    (bitatron,,), (corvette,,)
```

In the **/etc/exports** file on *gate*, we use the *gate-hosts* netgroup:

```
/home/gate-access=gate-hosts
```

and in **/etc/passwd**, we use the netgroup *gate-users*. When host information is used, the *gate-hosts* group explicitly defines those hosts in the group; when user-names are needed, the *gate-users* map lists just those users. Even though there are wildcards in each group, those wildcards are in fields that are not referenced when the maps are used in these function-specific ways.

Password and NIS Security

Several volumes could be written about password aging, password guessing programs, and the usual poor choices made for passwords. Again, this book won't describe a complete password security strategy, but here are some common-sense guidelines for password security:

- Watch out for easily guessed passwords. Some obvious bad password choices are: your first name, your last name, your spouse or a sibling's name, the name of your favorite sport, and the kind of car you drive. Unfortunately, enforcing any sort of password approval requires modifying or replacing the standard NIS password management tools.

- Define and repeatedly stress local password requirements to the user community. This is a good first-line defense against someone guessing passwords, or using a password cracking program (a program that tries to guess user passwords using a long list of words). For example, you could state that all passwords had to contain at least six letters, one capital and one non-alphabetic letter.

- Remind users that almost any word in the dictionary can be found by a thorough password cracker.

- Use any available password guessing programs that you find. Having the same weapons as a potential intruder at least levels the playing field.

In this section, we'll look at ways to manage to root password using NIS and to enforce some simple workstation security.

Managing the Root Password with NIS

NIS can be used to solve a common dilemma at sites with advanced, semi-trusted users. Many companies allow users of desktop machines to have the root password on their local hosts to install software, make small modifications, and power down/boot the system without the presence of a system administrator. With a different, user-specific root password on every system, the job of the system administrator quickly becomes a nightmare. Similarly, using the same root password on all systems defeats the purpose of having one if most users know it.

Root privileges on servers should be guarded much more carefully, since too many hands touching host configurations inevitably creates untraceable problems. It is important to stress to semi-trusted users that their lack of root privileges on servers does not reflect a lack of expertise or trust, but merely a desire to exert full control over those machines for which you have full and total responsibility. Any change to a server that impacts the entire network becomes your immediate problem, so you should have jurisdiction over those hosts. A common way to discourage would-be part-time superusers is to require anyone with a server root password to carry the 24-hour emergency beeper at least part of each month.

Some approach is required that allows users to gain superuser access to their own hosts, but not on servers. At the same time, the system administrator must be able to become root on any system at any time to perform day-to-day maintenance.

To solve the second problem, the root password can be managed by NIS. After adding the superuser password file entry to the NIS map, include it in each host's password file:

```
+root::0:0::
```

Grant root access to individual users by creating a local user, such as *lroot*, with **uid=0**, and allow each user to set the secondary root password on his or her desktop machine. Do this only when you manage the root password with NIS, since you may encounter bugs or other oddities that develop when a password file has duplicate user IDs in it.

Instead of creating an additional root user, some sites use a modified version of **su** that consults a "personal" password file. The additional password file has one entry for each user that is allowed to become root, and each user has a unique root password.* With either system, users are able to manage their own systems but will not know the root passwords on any other hosts. The NIS-managed root password ensures that the system administration staff can still gain superuser access to every host.

Making NIS More Secure

Aside from the caveats about trivial passwords, there are a few precautions that can be taken to make NIS more secure:

- If you are trying to keep your NIS maps private to hide hostnames or usernames within your network, do not make any host that is on two or more networks an NIS server. Users on the external networks can forcibly bind to your NIS domain and dump the NIS maps from a server that is also performing routing duties. While the same trick may be performed if the NIS server is inside the router, it can be defeated by disabling IP packet forwarding on the router. Appendix B, *IP Packet Routing*, covers this material in more detail.

- On the master NIS server, separate the server's password file and the NIS password file so that all users in the NIS password file do not automatically gain access to the NIS master server. A set of changes for building a distinct password file was presented in "Using Alternate Map Source Files," in Chapter 3, *System Management Using NIS*.

---

*An **su**-like utility is contained in *UNIX System Administration Handbook*, by Evi Nemeth, Scott Seebass, and Garth Snyder (Prentice-Hall, 1990).

- Periodically check for null passwords using the following **awk** script:

```
#! /bin/sh
( cat /etc/passwd; ypcat passwd ) | awk -F':' '{if ($2 == "") print $1}'
```

The subshell concatenates the local password file and the NIS *passwd* map; the **awk** script prints any username that does not have an entry in the password field of the password map.

- Consider making the consoles of machines insecure, so that they cannot be booted single-user without supplying the root password. In systems with the Berkeley-style **/etc/ttytab** file, remove the token *secure* from the line for **/dev/console**:

```
console "/usr/etc/getty std.9600"      wyse50        on
```

When the system is booted in single-user mode, the single-user shell will not be started until the user supplies the root password. On Sun systems, the boot PROM itself can be used to enforce security. To enforce PROM security, change the **secure** parameter in the PROM to **full**:

```
# eeprom secure=full
```

No PROM commands can be entered without supplying the PROM password; when you change from **secure=none** to **secure=full** you will be prompted for the new PROM password. This is not the same as the root password, and serves as a redundant security check for systems that can be halted and booted by any user with access to the break or reset switches.

CAUTION

There is *no* mechanism for removing the PROM security without the supplying PROM password. If you forget the PROM password after installing it, you must get a new PROM for the machine.

Intruder Alerts

If a user's UID changes while he or she is logged in, many utilities break in esoteric ways. Simple editing mistakes, such as deleting a digit in the UID field of the password file and then distributing the "broken" map file, are the most common source of this problem. Another error which causes a UID mismatch is the replacement of an NIS password file entry with a local password file entry where the two UIDs are not identical. The next time the password file is searched by UID, the user's password file entry will not be found if it no longer contains the correct UID. Similarly, a search by username may turn up a UID that is different than the real or effective user ID of the process performing the search.

The most cryptic message comes from **whoami**, which replies with "Intruder alert" if the effective UID of its process cannot be found in the password file. Other utilities that check the validity of UIDs are **rcp, rlogin**, and **rsh**, all of which generate "who are you?" messages if the user's UID cannot be found in the password map. These messages appear on the terminal or window in which the command was typed, which generally confuses users.

NFS Security

Filesystem security has two aspects: controlling access to and operations on files, and limiting exposure of the contents of the files. Controlling access to remote files involves mapping UNIX file operation semantics into the NFS system, so that certain operations are disallowed if the remote user fails to provide the proper credentials. To avoid giving superuser permissions across the network, additional constraints are put in place for access to files by *root*. Even more stringent NFS security requires proving that the UNIX-style credentials contained in each NFS request are valid; that is, the server must know that the NFS client's request was made by a valid user and not an imposter on the network.

Limiting disclosure of data in a file is more difficult, as it usually involves encrypting the contents of the file. The client application may choose to enforce its own data encryption and store the file on the server in encrypted form. In this case, the client's NFS requests going over the network contain blocks of encrypted data. However, if the file is stored and used in clear text form, NFS requests to read or write the file will contain clear text as well. Sending parts of files over a network is subject to some data exposure concerns. In general, if security would be comprised by any part of a file being disclosed, then the file should not be placed on an NFS-mounted filesystem. You can prevent damage to files by restricting write permissions and enforcing user authentication, but there are few safeguards against someone eavesdropping on your network. NFS has some simple security mechanisms in place today, and the Secure RPC mechanisms described in this chapter ensure that user authentication is made secure as well. This section presents ways of restricting access based on the user credentials presented in NFS requests, and then looks at validating the credentials themselves using Secure RPC.

NFS RPC Authentication

Every NFS request, including mount requests, contains a set of user credentials with a UID and a list of group IDs (GIDs) to which the UID belongs. NFS credentials are the same as those used for accessing local files, that is, if you belong to five groups, your NFS credentials contain your UID and five GIDs. On the NFS server, these credentials are used to perform the permission checks that are part of UNIX file accesses—verifying write permission to remove a file, or execute permission to search directories. There are three areas in which NFS credentials may not match the user's local credential structure: the user is the superuser, the user is in too many groups, or no credentials were supplied (an "anonymous" request). Mapping of root and anonymous users is covered in the next section.

Problems with "too many" groups depend upon the implementation of NFS used by the client and the server, and may be an issue only if they are different (including different revisions of the same operating system). Every NFS implementation has a limit on the number of groups that can be passed in a credentials structure for an NFS RPC. This number usually agrees with the maximum number of groups to which a user may belong, but it may be smaller. Typically, the limit on the number of groups is either 8 or 16. If the client's group limit is larger than the server's, and a user is in more groups than the server allows, then the server's attempt to parse and verify the credential structure will fail, yielding error messages like:

```
RPC: Authentication error
```

Authentication errors may occur when trying to mount a filesystem, in which case the superuser is in too many groups. Errors may also occur when a particular user tries to access files on the NFS server; these errors result from any NFS RPC operation. Pay particular attention to the group file in a heterogeneous environment, where the NIS-managed group map may be appended to a local file with several entries for common users like *root* and *bin*. The only solution is to restrict the number of groups to the smallest value allowed by all systems that are running NFS.

Superuser Mapping

The superuser is not given normal file access permissions to NFS-mounted files. The motivation behind this restriction is that root access should be granted on a per-machine basis. A user who is capable of becoming root on one machine should not necessarily have permission to modify files on a file server. Similarly, a *setuid* program that assumes root privileges may not function properly or as expected if it is allowed to operate on remote files.

To enforce restrictions on superuser access, the root's UID is mapped to the anonymous user *nobody* in the NFS RPC credential structure. The superuser frequently has fewer permissions than a non-privileged user for NFS-mounted filesystems, since *nobody*'s group usually includes no other users. In the password file, *nobody* has a UID of -2, and the group *nogroup* also has a GID of -2. On systems that require non-negative user and group ID values, *nobody* and *nogroup* use 65534, which is a 16-bit unsigned representation of -2. When an executable that is *setuid* runs, its effective user ID is root, which gets mapped to *nobody*. The executable still has permissions on the local system, but it cannot get to remote files unless they have been explicitly exported with root access enabled.

Some implementations of NFS allow the root UID mapping to be defeated by changing the UID used for *nobody* in the server's kernel. Changing the UID for *nobody* from -2 to 0 allows the superuser to access all files exported from the server, which may be less restrictive than desired. The mapping may be changed by simply modifying the UID and GID of the *nobody* user in the server's password file:

```
nobody:*:0:0:Anonymous User::
```

Changing *nobody*'s UID affects every filesystem exported from the server, and should be considered as much an invitation for trouble as providing the root password to users that mount filesystems from the server.

Most NFS servers grant root permission on an exported filesystem on a per-host basis using the **root**=export option. The server exporting a filesystem grants root access to a host or list of hosts by including them in the **/etc/exports** file:

```
/home/work      -root=bitatron:corvette
```

The superuser on hosts *bitatron* and *corvette* is given normal root filesystem privileges on the server's **/home/work** directory. The name of a netgroup may be substituted for a hostname; all of the hosts in the netgroup are granted root access.

Root permissions on a remote filesystem should be extended only when absolutely necessary. While privileged users may find it annoying to have to log into the server owning a filesystem in order to modify something owned by root, this restriction also eliminates many common mistakes. If a system administrator wants to purge **/usr/local** on one host (to rebuild it, for example), executing **rm –rf *** will have disastrous consequences if there is an NFS-mounted filesystem with root permission under **/usr/local**. If **/usr/local/bin** is NFS mounted, then it is possible to wipe out the server's copy of this directory from a client when root permissions are extended over the network.

The only clear-cut case where root permissions should be extended on an NFS filesystem is for the root and swap partitions of a diskless client, where they are mandatory. One other possible scenario in which root permissions are useful is for cross-server mounted filesystems. Assuming that only the system administration staff is given superuser privileges on the file servers, extending these permissions across NFS mounts may make software distribution and maintenance a little easier. Again, the pitfalls await, but hopefully the community with networked root permissions is small and experienced enough to use these sharp instruments safely.

On the client side, you may want to protect the NFS client from foreign *setuid* executables of unknown origin. NFS-mounted *setuid* executables should not be trusted unless you control superuser access to the server from which they are mounted. If security on the NFS server is compromised, it's possible for the attacker to create *setuid* executables which will be found—and executed—by users who NFS mount the filesystem. The *setuid* process will have root permission on the host on which it is running, which means it can damage files on the local host. Execution of NFS-mounted *setuid* executables can be disabled with the **nosuid** mount option. This option may be specified as a command-line flag or in the **/etc/fstab** entry:

```
toolbox:/usr/local/bin  /usr/local/bin  nfs ro,nosuid 0 0
```

Unknown User Mapping

NFS handles requests that do not have valid credentials in them by mapping them to the *anonymous* user. There are several cases in which an NFS request has no credential structure in it:

- The NFS client and server are using Secure RPC, but the user on the client has not provided the proper authentication information to the Secure RPC system. Secure RPC will be discussed later in this chapter.

- The client is a PC running PC/NFS, but the PC user has not supplied a valid user name and password. The PC/NFS mechanisms used to establish user credentials are described in "Checking File Permissions," in Chapter 14, *PC/NFS*.

- The client is not a UNIX machine, and cannot produce UNIX-style credentials.

- The request was fabricated (not sent by a real NFS client), and is simply missing the credentials structure.

By default, the anonymous user is *nobody*, so unknown users (making the credential-less requests) are treated like root. Likewise, root is treated as an unknown

user. The **anon** export option allows a server to change the mapping of anonymous requests. By setting the anonymous user ID in **/etc/exports**, the unknown
user in an anonymous request is mapped to a well-known local user:

```
/home/engin      -anon=100
```

In this example, any request that arrives without user credentials will be executed
with UID 100. If **/home/engin** is owned by UID 100, this ensures that unknown
users can access the directory once it is mounted. The user ID mapping does not
affect the real or effective user ID of the process accessing the NFS-mounted file.
The anonymous user mapping just changes the user credentials used by the NFS
server for determining file access permissions.

The anonymous user mapping is valid only for the filesystem that is exported with
the **anon** option. It is possible to set up different mappings for each filesystem
exported by specifying a different anonymous user ID value in each line of the
/etc/exports file:

```
/home/engin      -anon=100
/home/admin      -anon=200
/home/marketing  -anon=300
```

Anonymous users should *never* be mapped to root, as this would grant superuser
access to filesystems to any user without a valid password file entry on the server.
Anonymous users should be thought of as transient or even unwanted users, and
should be given as few file access permissions as possible. RPC calls with missing UIDs in the credential structures are rejected out of hand on the server if the
server exports its filesystems with **anon=-1**. Rather than mapping anonymous
users to *nobody*, filesystems that specify **anon=-1** return authentication errors for
RPC calls with no credentials in them.

Normally, with the anonymous user mapped to *nobody*, anonymous requests are
accepted but have few, if any, permissions to access files on the server. Mapping
unknown users is a risky venture. Requests that are missing UIDs in their credentials may be appearing from outside the local network, or they may originate from
machines on which security has been compromised.

Access to Filesystems

In addition to being protected from root access, some filesystems require protection from certain hosts. A machine containing source code is a good example; the
source code may be made available only to a selected set of machines and not to

the network at large. The list of hosts to which access is restricted is included in the server's **/etc/exports** file with the **–access** option:

```
/export/root/noreast    -access=noreast,root=noreast
```

This specification is typical of that for the root filesystem of a diskless client. The client machine is given root access to the filesystem, and access is further restricted to host *noreast* only. No user can look at *noreast*'s root filesystem unless he or she can log into *noreast* and look locally. The hosts listed in an **access** list can be individual hostnames or netgroup names, separated by colons. Restricting host access in this manner ensures that NFS is not used to circumvent log-in restrictions. If a user cannot log into a host to restrict access to one or more filesystems, the user should not be able to recreate that host's environment by mounting all of its NFS-mounted filesystems on another system.

Read-only Access

A less severe instance of restricting access to NFS filesystems by host is to restrict write access by host. By default, NFS filesystems are exported with write access enabled for any host that mounts them. Using the **rw** option in the **/etc/exports** file, you can name the list of hosts that may mount the filesystem with write permissions:

```
/source         -rw=corvette:vacation,access=source-group
```

An important difference between the **rw** option and the **access** option is that the former only accepts hostnames, not netgroup names.

Any host not in the list must mount the filesystem using the **–ro** NFS option or the **–r** (read-only) option to **mount**. An attempt to mount a read-only filesystem writeable will succeed, but problems will appear when the NFS client writes to the filesystem. When an NFS client tries to write data to the filesystem, the RPC requests will be rejected with EROFS—a "read-only filesystem" error.

Port Checking

Port monitoring is used to prevent "spoofing"—hand-crafted imitations of valid NFS requests that are sent from unauthorized user processes. A clever user could build an NFS request and send it to the **nfsd** daemon port on a server, hoping to grab all or part of a file on the server. If the request came from a valid NFS client kernel, it would originate from a privileged UDP/IP port on the client. Because all UDP/IP packets contain both source and destination port numbers, the NFS server can check the originating port number to be sure it came from a privileged port.

NFS port monitoring may or may not be enabled by default. It is usually governed by a kernel variable that is modified at boot time using an **adb** script:

```
echo "nfs_portmon/W1" | adb -w /vmunix /dev/kmem
```

This script sets the value of *nfs_portmon* to 1 in the kernel's memory image, enabling port monitoring. Any request that is received from a non-privileged port is rejected.

The SunOS **rpc.mountd** daemons also performs port checking, to be sure that mount requests are coming from processes running with root privileges. It rejects requests that are received from non-privileged ports. To turn off port monitoring in the mount daemon, add the **-n** flag to its invocation in the boot scripts:

```
rpc.mountd -n
```

Not all NFS clients send requests from privileged ports; in particular, some PC implementations of the NFS client code will not work with port monitoring enabled. In addition, some older NFS implementations on UNIX workstations use non-privileged ports and require port monitoring to be disabled. Check your system's documentation and boot scripts to determine under what conditions, if any, port monitoring is enabled.

Secure RPC and Secure NFS

The security mechanisms described so far in this chapter are essentially refinements of the standard UNIX login/password and file permission constraints, extended to handle distributed environments. Some additional care is taken to restrict superuser access over the network, but nothing in the RPC protocol ensures that the user specified by the UID in the credential structure is permitted to use the RPC service, and nothing verifies that the user (or user running the application sending RPC requests) is really who the UID professes to be.

Simply checking user credentials is like giving out employee badges: the badge holder is given certain access rights. Someone who is not an employee could steal a badge and gain those same rights. Validating the user credentials in an NFS request is similar to making employees wear badges with their photographs on them: the badge grants certain access rights to its holder, and the photograph on the badge ensures that the badge holder is the "right" person. Sun's Secure RPC mechanism adds credential validation to the standard RPC system. When Secure RPC is used with NFS, the combination of systems is called Secure NFS. We'll start this discussion of Secure RPC by looking at some common encryption techniques.

Encryption Techniques

There are two encryption techniques that are used in Secure RPC: private key, or DES encryption, and public key encryption. In a DES encryption scheme, the user knows some secret value (such as a password), which is used to encrypt a value such as a timestamp. The secret value is known as a *secret key*. The problem with DES encryption is that to get another host to validate your DES-encrypted timestamp, you need to get your secret key (password) on that host. Think of this problem as a password checking exercise: normally your password is verified on the local machine. If you were required to get your password validated on an NFS server, you would somehow have to get your password on that machine for it to perform the validation.

Public key encryption helps solve the problem of getting a secret key on both hosts by letting each side choose its own secret key, and then defining a mechanism by which *combinations* of secret keys can be validated. A *public key* is merely some well-known, plain text value (such as a username known to both parties) encrypted using a secret key, such as a user's password. The public key is published so that it is available for authentication services. The encryption mechanism uses a variety of exponentiation and other arithmetic operators that have nice commutative properties. The encryption algorithm is complex enough, and the keys themselves are big enough (at least 50, and sometimes 100 bits) to guarantee that a public key cannot be decoded to discover the secret key used to encode it.

The public key encryption scheme used by Secure RPC is called *exponential key exchange*. Exponential key exchange schemes rely on the commutative properties used to generate keys. In this scheme, two agents, say a user and a server, generate a *conversation* key that uniquely identifies one to the other but cannot be reproduced by another agent, even if the conversation key is grabbed and analyzed by some attacker. The conversation key is a composition of each agent's private and public keys. The user creates a conversation key by encrypting the server's public key with his private key; the server generates the *same* key by taking the user's public key and encrypting it with his private key. Because the encryption algorithm uses commutative operations, the encryption order does not matter—both schemes generate the same key, but *only* those two agents can recreate the key because it requires knowing at least one private key. Figure 8-2 shows how an exponential key exchange is performed for agents A and B.

P(A) is A's public key and P(B) is B's public key. C(A,B) is a conversation key, formed by applying the encryption algorithm on each public key.

$$P(A) = \alpha^{K(A)}$$
$$P(B) = \alpha^{K(B)}$$
$$C(A,B) = \alpha^{K(A)K(B)} = P(A)^{K(B)} = P(B)^{K(A)}$$

Figure 8-2. Exponential Key Exchange

Using this encryption scheme, RPC can be made more secure by requiring each service user to establish a valid conversation key before making RPC requests.

How Secure RPC Works

Secure RPC uses a combination of DES encryption and exponential key exchange. User validation is performed by the server, based on information in the RPC request:

- The client and server decide on a conversation key. We'll see how the conversation key is formed and agreed upon soon.

- The client encrypts the current time (using DES encryption), using the conversation key as a secret key. It sends its RPC request to the server.

- The server decrypts the timestamp, using the same conversation key, and verifies that it is accurate. If the decrypted timestamp falls outside of a short time window, the server rejects the request.

To be able to perform the DES encryption and decryption, the client and server must first agree on a common conversation key. This key is created and shared using exponential key exchange and DES encryption:

- The client chooses the conversation key randomly. Using a large random number makes it difficult for an attacker to verify that he or she has correctly guessed the conversation key. If the conversation key was a timestamp, for example, then it could easily be compared against the current time to verify a successful decryption.

- The client needs to tell the server what conversation key it has chosen. It does this by encrypting the conversation key, and sending the encrypted key over the network.

- To encrypt the conversation key on the client, and decrypt it on the server, both machines use exponential key exchange to determine a *session key*. The session key is used as the secret key to encrypt the conversation key, which is sent to the server. This is the only time a key is sent over the network, limiting the times at which an encrypted key may be stolen.

• The server has generated the same session key as the client, and uses it to decrypt the conversation key. The client can now send RPC requests to the server that contain encrypted timestamps, serving the role of "badge photographs" for validation purposes.

We'll look at how Secure NFS works by first seeing how to add the security features to NFS, and then seeing how the public and secret (private) keys are managed within this system.

Enabling Secure NFS

Enabling secure NFS on a filesystem is quite simple: export and mount the filesystem with the **secure** option. On the NFS server, the **/etc/exports** entry looks like this:

```
/home/thud      -secure
```

When a filesystem is exported with the **secure** option, clients must mount it with the **secure** option if they are to enjoy normal user access privileges in the filesystem. On the NFS client, add the **secure** option in the **/etc/fstab** entry for the filesystem:

```
thud:/home/thud  /home/thud     nfs rw,secure,hard 0 0
```

If a user accessing the secure filesystem can generate a valid key with the NFS server, it is used to encrypt the timestamps sent with that user's NFS requests. If the server decrypts the timstamps successfully, the UNIX-style credentials presented by the user are trusted and are used to grant normal UNIX-style file permissions.

It's possible, though, that the user can't exchange a conversation key with the server. This will be the case if the user doesn't have a public key defined, or if the user cannot supply the proper secret key to generate a session key using exponential key exchange. When there is no valid conversation key, the NFS server remaps the user to *nobody*. Within the Secure NFS system, a user without a valid public/private key pair becomes an anonymous user on the NFS server and is subject to the same access restrictions (discussed earlier in this chapter) that apply to the anonymous user *nobody*. To utilize secure NFS without impairing user's ability to do work, you must define public and private key pairs for trusted users and trusted hosts.

Public and Private Keys

Public and private (secret) keys are maintained in the *publickey.byname* NIS map, which is built from **/etc/publickey** on the master NIS server. If you are not running NIS, you cannot create keys. The only key that is defined by default is one for *nobody*, which is required for the anonymous user mapping. Public and encrypted secrets keys are contained in the **/etc/publickey** file, along with a unique identifier for the machine or user owning these keys.

```
unix.10461@nesales publickey:secretkey
```

The keys are long strings of hexadecimal digits, representing the encrypted key values. Obviously, the NIS map cannot contain secret keys, or the entire encryption mechanism would be baseless. Instead, the **/etc/publickey** file's *secretkey* field contains the user's secret key, encrypted with the user's log-in password. For host entries, the secret key is encrypted using the root password. The secret keys themselves are large random numbers, just like the conversation key that is used by Secure RPC.

Identifiers in **/etc/publickey** take one of two forms:

```
unix.uid@NISdomain
unix.host@NISdomain
```

The first form is used for user keys; it defines a key valid in the current NIS domain. The host key is used to create a Secure RPC key for the superuser on the named host. No user key is required for *root*—only a host key.

The **/etc/publickey** is changed by the Secure RPC utilities that create and manage key values. Because it contains encrypted key strings, it is not easily edited by the superuser, just as the password fields in **/etc/passwd** cannot be hand-edited. The **publickey** file should exist *only* on the NIS master server, or else users' private keys will become out of date when they change their passwords (and therefore change the encryption key used to store their secret keys).

Creating Keys

The superuser can add user keys (on the NIS master server) using **newkey -u** *user*. Alternatively, users can create their own key pairs with the **chkey** command. In either case, the user's password must be supplied, so the superuser should only create keys if the user is available to be informed of his or her new password. As *root*, run **newkey** with the user's log-in name:

```
nismaster# newkey -u stern
Adding new key for unix.1461@nesales.East.Sun.COM.
New password:
```

If the *nobody* entry exists in the *publickey* NIS map, then users can create their own keys using **chkey**:

```
client% chkey
Generating new key for unix.11461@nesales.East.Sun.COM.
Password:
sending request to nismaster
```

If the user supplies an invalid password, the key will not be created. If the user's password is valid, and the NIS master server is receiving key updates, the key will be added to, or modified in, the NIS *publickey* map. Both the **chkey** and **newkey** utilities update the **/etc/publickey** file on the NIS master server. Note that creating a key does not make the public key available throughout the network immediately, since the *publickey* map will be out-of-date on slave NIS servers.

Keys can be created by any user on any NIS client machine, provided the *nobody* key exists. If this entry is removed from the *publickey* map, then users may use **chkey** only to change their private keys, but not to create new ones. Only the superuser can create new keys without a *publickey* map entry for *nobody*.

The only way to create host keys (for superuser verification) is to use **newkey –h** as root:

```
# newkey -h bitatron
Adding new key for unix.bitatron@nesales.East.Sun.COM.
New password:
```

After you've created keys, explicitly push the *publickey* NIS map to all NIS servers, so that you can start using Secure NFS before the next NIS map **ypxfr**.

To receive NIS map updates from **newkey** or **chkey**, the master NIS server must be able to run **rpc.ypupdated**. You can either start this daemon at boot time by uncommenting it in **/etc/rc.local**, or have it started on demand by allowing **inetd** to manage it. In **/etc/rc.local**, you can start **rpc.ypupdate** at boot time:

```
if [ -f /usr/etc/rpc.ypupdated -a -d /var/yp/`domainname` ]; then
        rpc.ypupdated;          echo -n ' ypupdated'
fi
```

To have **rpc.ypupdated** started on demand, uncomment its line in **/etc/inetd.conf**:

```
ypupdated/1     stream rpc/tcp wait root /usr/etc/rpc.ypupdated rpc.ypupdated
```

After editing **/etc/inetd.conf**, restart **inetd** to enable key updates:

```
nismaster# ps -agux | fgrep inetd
root        382 0.0 0.0   56    0 ? IW   Mar  5  0:04 inetd
root      29310 0.0 0.8  144  248 p2 S   00:16  0:00 fgrep inetd
nismaster# kill -1 382
```

On every machine that will be using Secure NFS, make sure you are running the **keyserv** daemon. This process is used to cache conversation keys, and is also started out of **/etc/rc.local** with lines of the form:

```
if [ -f /usr/etc/keyserv ]; then
        keyserv;                       echo -n ' keyserv'
fi
```

Make sure this clause is not commented out, or you will not be able to create conversation keys, even if you have a valid public and private key pair in the *publickey* NIS map.

Establishing a Conversation Key

When you log into a machine that is running secure NFS, the password you supply to **login** is used to decrypt your encrypted private key (in the *publickey* map). The secret key is given to the **keyserv** daemon, which caches it for generation of session keys. The session keys are used to exchange conversation keys with NFS servers, as described earlier in this section. Therefore, the entire conversation key generation procedure goes like this:

- You define a public and private key pair, using **chkey**. The private key is a large, random number; it is stored in the *publickey* map by encrypting it with your password.

- When you log into a machine, your password is used to decrypt your secret key. The secret key is given to the **keyserv** daemon, where it is cached until you log out.

- To access an NFS filesystem mounted with the *secure* option, you must establish a conversation key with the NFS server. You form a session key using your secret key and the public key for the NFS server. This is done automatically by the Secure RPC system.

- If your secret key was successfully decoded, you will be able to exchange a conversation key with the NFS server. All of your NFS requests to that server contain a timestamp encrypted with the conversation key. The server decrypts this timestamp to validate your NFS requests.

Note that you must supply your log-in password for the **keyserv** daemon to be given your secret key. If you don't supply a password when you log into a machine—for example, you **rlogin** to another machine—then there is no way for **keyserv** daemon to automatically receive your decrypted secret key. To establish a conversation key in this situation, use the **keylogin** utility, which accepts your log-in password and uses it to decrypt your secret key:

```
remote% keylogin
Password:
```

Keys that are decrypted via **keylogin** are also passed to **keyserv**, where they remain until the user executes a **keylogout**. If you are going to be logging into non-trusted hosts, use **keylogin** to decrypt your key, and add **keylogout** to your .logout file (in your home directory) so that your key is destroyed when you log out.

You must reference the NIS *passwd* map for the automatic secret key caching to occur. For proper operation of secure NFS, do not put users in the local /etc/passwd file, or their encrypted secret keys may become out-of-date when they change their local passwords but do not change the NIS-managed password used to encrypt the secret key in the *publickey* map. On the NIS master server, make sure you use an alternate password source file, instead of the default /etc/passwd.

There's one thing missing: how does the root, or host, secret key get decrypted? You establish a session key using the *host* key for the NFS server. In order for the server to exchange keys with you, it must be able to decrypt the host's secret key, and this requires the root password or a "hidden" copy of the root key. One obvious approach is to force someone to supply the root password when the machine boots, so that the host secret key in the *publickey* map can be decrypted and given to the **keyserv** daemon. However, this is often too restrictive: if an NFS server boots and no system administrator is present to supply the root password, no Secure NFS services will be available.

The **keyserv** daemon solves this dilemma by storing the host's secret key in the /etc/.rootkey file. Note that this is *not* the root password; it's the large, random number used as the host's secret key. When the **keyserv** daemon starts up, it reads the host's key out of this file so that clients of the host can exchange conversation keys with it.

Secure NFS Checklist

This list summarizes the various daemons and files that must be in place for proper operation of secure NFS:

- Create keys for users with **chkey** or **newkey −u**. Create a host key for each machine on which you need secure *root* access using **newkey −h**.

- Remove the *publickey* entry for *nobody* if users are not allowed to add their own keys.

- Make sure the NIS master server has **rpc.ypupdated** uncommented in **/etc/inetd.conf**.

- Push the *publickey* map to all NIS clients after making any changes to it, so that secure NFS is operating before the next NIS map transfer.

- If you are using secure NFS on trusted hosts, make sure that users perform a **keylogin** to produce a temporary private key. If users do not supply a password when they log into a host, the local **keyserv** process on that host must be given the user's secret key explicitly. Also have users add **keylogout** to their **.logout** files to remove the temporary keys given to **keyserv**.

- Ensure that each client that is using secure NFS is running the **keyserv** daemon.

- To export a filesystem using secure NFS, add the **secure** option to its entry in **/etc/exports**. On the client, mount the filesystem with the **secure** option in the **/etc/fstab** file.

Finally, make sure that your client and server clocks remain well synchronized (see "Time Synchronization," in Chapter 10, *Diagnostic and Administrative Tools*, for a simple scheme). Since Secure NFS uses encrypted timestamps for validation, drifting client clocks may cause the server to reject otherwise valid secure NFS requests because they appear to be replays of out-of-date requests. The NFS server code has a small window for checking client timestamps, and if the clock drift falls within this window the RPC call is executed.

The default window size is one hour (3600 seconds), although if you are serious about using secure NFS you will probably want to reduce the window to a few minutes. To shorten the authentication window to 5 minutes, use **adb** to patch the kernel:

```
# adb -k -w /vmunix /dev/mem
authdes_win/W 0t300
authdes_win:    3600  = 300
authdes_win?W 0t300
authdes_win:    3600  = 300
```

The shorter the window, the less time a would-be network spoofer has to attempt to replay any request.

Kerberos

The Kerberos system was developed at MIT's Project Athena. It is another mechanism for enforcing security within a service, but it differs from Secure RPC in several ways:

- Kerberos uses multiple levels of DES encryption to exchange keys and passwords. No public key encryption is used.

- A central server is required to maintain Kerberos service passwords; this server must be kept safe from attack to preserve the integrity of the Kerberos system. Secure RPC uses the *publickey* map, which is available to all NIS clients. The data in the *publickey* map is encrypted using user's log-in passwords, not an additional Secure RPC password.

- Kerberos authentication is built into the entire service, or application, not just into the session layer. For example, you can use Kerberos to make the **lpd** line printer spooling daemon secure. Doing so, however, requires the source code to **lpd**.

It is likely that most vendors will adopt Kerberos as another authentication scheme to be used at the RPC and NFS layers.

Viruses

A computer virus is a piece of code that modifies the operating system or system utilities with harmful or annoying side effects. Like human viruses, a computer virus reproduces itself and spreads through a vector, or carrier. Once one computer is infected, the virus attempts to copy itself onto floppies or other removable media that will be taken to other systems. When an infected disk is inserted into a healthy system, the virus loads itself into the uninfected system. Entire networks of computers may be infected from a single disk that infects a system that later infects a file server, for example.

Effects of viruses vary greatly. Some simply render the machine useless, echoing annoying messages back to the user but preventing any "real" command execution. Others are destructive in nature, scribbling on critical filesystem information on hard disks or removing key files.

Viruses are virtually unknown in time-sharing operating systems such as UNIX that enforce kernel protection. The operating system cannot be modified without superuser permission, so random user applications cannot inject viruses into the system. The DOS operating system, on the other hand, does not protect its kernel code or disk files, so an executable can overwrite parts of the kernel, the DOS image on disk, or various system utilities. Once the disk image is infected, the system remains infected, even through reboots or power cycles. Note that viruses are not the same as worms, rabbits, or other user-level processes that consume resources or reproduce rapidly enough to bring a system to a halt. A computer virus specifically damages the operating system.

Enforcing basic security around the root password and superuser access to machines should be sufficient to deter deliberate planting of viruses in the UNIX kernel. In addition to securing access from the local area network, verify that your systems are safe from attacks from external networks such as the Internet. If you can prevent unauthorized superuser access, then you must only worry about things that you or your system administrators do as root.

Watch what you put into **cron** entries. Any script that gets run by cron should be owned by root and either not writeable or writeable only by root. If a user asks for a shell script to be added to root's **crontab**, install the script so that the user cannot modify it once it has been added to the **crontab** file.

Similarly, avoid any package that requires an executable to be run as root as part of its installation process, unless you can vouch for the integrity of the package's provider. In general, vendors stand behind the safety of their software, and you should not worry about "branding" utilities that write serial number information into executable images. However, the same guidelines that apply to DOS users also apply to UNIX system administrators: if you don't know where an executable came from, don't run it as *root*. This is especially true for executables taken from public domain sources. If you can't get the source code, don't experiment with it unless you are willing to perform a post-installation check for damage. Above all else, use common sense. If you feel uncomfortable loaning your car keys to a complete stranger, you should feel equally queasy about installing strange software on your system as root.

9

Centralizing Mail Services with NFS and NIS

Creating a Shared Mail Spool
Name Hiding
NIS Alias Expansion
Wide-area Aliases
Merging NIS and Local Aliases
Forwarding

Electronic mail has become so much of an essential service in most computing environments that it merits the focused attention given to these other system administration tasks. In addition to its common uses as a replacement for memos, reports, and telephone calls, electronic mail is also used for archive search and retrieval, information distribution, automated user request handling, and scheduling functions. Reliance upon electronic mail is so great that nearly all users—regardless of their expertise—notice an interruption in mail service or an anomaly in its behavior.

Complexity of the mail system increases with many machines handling mail or multiple mail delivery mechanisms. Each increase in the complexity of the system multiplies the number of ways that the mail service can develop problems. Managing electronic mail on a large network is similar to managing user and host information: there are many places where configuration information is needed, making distributed management a difficult task.

However, NFS and NIS can solve these problems. Throughout this book, we've stressed how the appearance of desktop workstations has caused a corresponding distribution of configuration information and system administration duties. NFS and NIS refocus the administrative functions that should properly be under some single point of control, such as management of filesystems and user account information. Electronic mail is important enough to most organizations that it requires this same single point of administration.

Many sites simplify mail administration by setting up a single machine to handle all mail-related functions. Assigning all mail delivery and spooling functions to a single machine—the mail hub—eliminates most of the complexity of a distributed mail system. The mail hub is responsible for talking to the outside world via UUCP, Internet, CSNet, X.25, or DECnet, and it is the default handler for all mail that any other machine feels it cannot handle. Outbound and incoming mail delivery are consolidated into one place, so that only one machine needs a detailed set of mail delivery rules. Other hosts on the network get by with minimum knowledge of how to deliver their own mail.

Even with the mail hub, there are also the issues of how mail gets delivered on the local network, how aliases are created and managed, and how users find, forward, and manage their mail. These problems are candidates for NFS- and NIS-based solutions. This chapter describes mechanisms for creating a shared mail spool directory, managing aliases, and forwarding mail in an NFS environment.

Creating a Shared Mail Spool

It's not uncommon to find a network in which every machine has its own mail spool and users read their mail only on one machine. These networks usually have a mail hub machine for passing mail into and out of the company, but once mail is inside the hub machine it is forwarded to another host on the local network for delivery to the user. One of the major motivations for NFS—to eliminate duplicate filesystems and maintain only a single copy of a file—applies directly to the mail spool.

Problems With Distributed Spool Directories

A network with distributed spool directories has a separate and independent **/usr/spool/mail** directory on every host. This architecture creates several user and system administration headaches:

- Users must be on the machine that owns their mail spool to read mail. They should send mail from that machine to avoid having replies sent to another host where they will never be picked up. If you send mail from someone else's workstation, any replies to that mail will go back to that workstation, where you probably won't find them once you return to your "regular" machine.

- Assigning users to machines may be possible in an environment where every user has a workstation. However, in a computing lab where users (normally students) sit in front of machines as they become available, distributing the mail spool generally makes electronic mail more of a nuisance than a service.

- If every machine must be able to deliver mail, it must run the **sendmail** daemon to accept incoming mail at any time. Machines that are using all or most of their physical memory suffer a noticeable performance penalty when sendmail wakes up and processes a message, since interactive processes may get swapped out to make room for the sendmail daemon.

- Distributing the mail spool requires backing up the spool directory on every host. This may mean extending backups to include hosts that contain no other valuable, irreproducible files, just to get their **/usr/spool/mail** directories.

Allowing every machine to spool mail exposes the underlying network structure to mail recipients both inside and outside the local network. On the local network, sender addresses will always be of the form *user@host* instead of just *user*. Getting users to remember hostnames as well as usernames is not easy and requires more mnemonic aliases. Outside the company, recipients see hostnames that cloud the real source of the mail. Consider a UUCP host *polygon*, with hosts *grant* and *taylor* on its network. Without a centralized mail spool, recipients of mail from *polygon* see the mail originating from *grant* and *taylor* (see Table 9-1).

Table 9-1. Exposed Hostnames

Complete Address	Mail shows as
polygon!grant!peter	grant!peter
polygon!taylor!joeg	taylor!joeg

Name hiding refers to the process of fixing sender addresses so that all mail comes from a well-known host. If all incoming mail is handled by the mail hub instead of being distributed for delivery, the probability of dropping mail due to local changes decreases. As with many other system administration tasks, being a good neighbor means eliminating impacts of your changes local to your network. Moving a user from one host to another (or changing a hostname) should not break an alias created by that user's friend at another company. If local network names are hidden, then changes to the mail delivery scheme are hidden as well.

NFS Mounting the Mail Spool

With a shared mail spool, a single copy of the spool directory is maintained on one server and mounted on each host on the network. Users can read their mail from any host, and send mail to *user* instead of *user@host*. The mail spool server is charged with performing all local mail delivery. Typically, the host with the mail spool is the mail hub, placing all mail delivery duties—local or remote—on one host. This need not be the case. You can have the mail hub perform all remote delivery while another host holds the mail spool and does local network delivery. In this case, the mail hub forwards mail to the machine with the local spool.

From this point on, we'll call the host that performs mail delivery to the outside world the *mail hub*, assuming it has the most robust mail delivery mechanism. The machine that exports the mail spool directory via NFS is the *spool server*, and is usually the same machine as the *mail hub*. We'll point out particular cases where you need to adjust configurations if the spool server and mail hub are different hosts.

There is one disadvantage of using a shared mail spool: it can grow fairly large fairly quickly, since it contains mail for all users on the network. You may have to shuffle some disks to set up a shared mail spool. You'll need to leave plenty of free space on the spool filesystem to accommodate incoming mail.

To set up a shared mail spool, export the mail spool directory **/usr/spool/mail** or **/var/spool/mail** on the mail hub. The **exports** file entry looks like this:

```
/var/spool/mail
```

If you put **/usr/spool/mail** in the **exports** file, make sure it isn't a symbolic link to **/var/spool/mail**. If it is, you'll have to include the link's target in the **exports** file so that the directory containing mail files is exported, and not just the link pointing to them.

On each mail spool client, mount the mail spool using the **rw** and **hard** options. A typical **/etc/fstab** entry is:

```
wahoo:/var/spool/mail    /var/spool/mail nfs rw,hard 0 0
```

The **hard** option ensures that in-progress NFS operations will not corrupt a mail file if the mail hub crashes. Note that other NFS or NIS servers may be NFS clients of the mail spool machine, if users read their mail on these hosts.

You may disable the **sendmail** daemon on every mail client that will not have to accept and deliver mail. Note that **sendmail** is still run on demand when mail is *sent* from a client host, but there is usually no reason to have it run as a daemon waiting for incoming mail. A mail client may require a **sendmail** daemon if it has some mail delivery or forwarding responsibilities. For example, you may have a DECnet gateway running on a machine other than the mail hub, and mail going to DECnet hosts must be sent to this gateway and forwarded by its **sendmail** daemon.

On those hosts with no delivery duties, turn off the daemon by commenting it out of the boot scripts. **sendmail** is started by a line like this in **/etc/rc.local**:

```
/usr/lib/sendmail -bd -q15m -om
```

If the host doesn't have a mail queue to process (because it never receives messages), then the periodic scheduling of sendmail wastes CPU cycles and possibly causes paging or swapping activity that impacts performance.

Remote sendmail Execution

You now have to force all mail to be delivered on the mail hub. There are two ways of setting up local mail forwarding: using sendmail options or aliases. To use the sendmail option, first alias the name of the mail hub as *mailhost* in the **hosts** file or NIS map.

```
131.40.52.28    wahoo mailhost
```

sendmail looks for the *mailhost* when it is told to deliver mail in *remote mode*. Enabling remote mode simply tells the local sendmail process to forward the message to another host for address parsing and delivery. Turn on remote mode using the **OR** option in the **sendmail.cf** configuration file:

```
# forward all mail to mailhost for delivery
OR
# location of alias file
OA/etc/aliases
# default delivery mode (deliver in background)
Odbackground
# rebuild the alias file automagically
OD
# temporary file mode -- 0600 for secure mail, 0644 for permissive
OF0600
# default GID
Og1
```

```
# location of help file
OH/usr/lib/sendmail.hf
```

This option should be placed with the other definitions in the prologue of the sendmail configuration file, before the section labeled "Rewriting rules." Every mail client should have this option in its sendmail configuration file, so that all mail is passed to the mail spool server for delivery. Note that this works even if the mail hub and machine with the spool directory are different hosts. The mail hub accepts incoming mail, and its configuration forces **sendmail** to pass it to the spool server for delivery.

Mail Hub Forwarding Aliases

As an alternative to using sendmail for remote delivery, set up forwarding aliases for each local user. While this requires more per-user work, it is necessary if local variations in sendmail configuration files prohibit enabling remote mode, or if you aren't using sendmail at all for mail delivery. To perform the same function with aliases, create an alias for each user of the form:

```
stern:    stern@wahoo
johnc:    johnc@wahoo
```

where *wahoo* is the name of the mail hub. The mail delivery process finds the alias and sends the mail to the user on the mail hub. These aliases should go in the global NIS *aliases* map or in the /**etc**/**aliases** file on each machine.

When sendmail is run in remote mode, the local host's name never gets a chance to become part of the the sender address. However, when aliases are used, the local hostname does appear in the sender address, because sendmail runs on the sending host and inserts the local host's name. For example, when user *stern* sends mail to user *johnc* from mail client *bitatron*, the sender (and return) addresses seen by *johnc* depend upon how the mail was delivered. With sendmail in remote mode, **mail johnc** causes *bitatron*'s invocation of sendmail to forward the message to user *johnc* on host *wahoo*. *bitatron* never does any address parsing and doesn't add its name to the sender's address. When *johnc* reads his mail, he sees a message with the following sender and recipient addresses:

```
From: stern (Hal Stern)
To: johnc
```

If aliases are used to forward mail to the mail hub, then *bitatron*'s sendmail process looks up *johnc* in the aliases map and rewrites the recipient as *johnc@wahoo*. *bitatron* actually delivers the message to *wahoo* instead of simply passing it off to a remote instance of sendmail. When user *johnc* reads his mail, he sees the sender and recipients as:

```
From: stern@bitatron (Hal Stern)
To: johnc@wahoo
```

If *johnc* replies to the message, the reply is sent to host *bitatron*—thus requiring *bitatron* to be running a sendmail daemon to accept the message. When mail is picked up by the *bitatron* sendmail daemon, it tries to deliver it to user *stern*, who is aliased to *stern@wahoo*, and the actual delivery occurs on the mail hub. The mail client machine is an intermediate hop, picking up mail addressed to a user and forwarding it to the mail hub for delivery. Using aliases by themselves is useful to consolidate mail delivery onto a single host, but it does not offer all of the advantages of running sendmail in remote mode. Mail clients still have to run the sendmail daemon to accept incoming messages (addressed to them), and there is no name hiding.

Mail Notification

The **biff** mail notification mechanism does not work when all mail is delivered on the mail hub. Some users rely on **biff** to inform them of new mail, and want the same functionality in the shared mail spool environment. Normally, when mail is delivered to you, the **comsat** daemon checks to see if you have set **biff**, and notifies you of the new mail if desired. The **comsat** daemon only notifies users on the host on which the mail was delivered, but mounting the mail spool via NFS requires that users be notified on their NFS client machines.

Short of modifying the source code with the **comsat** daemon to perform remote notification, you have two choices to implement mail notification: use the C shell's **mail** variable, or pick up a networked copy of **xbiff** from an archive server such as *uunet.uu.net*. The **xbiff** utility is only useful if you are running the X Window System, so we'll look at the more general solution of using the shell to perform mail notification.

The C shell **mail** variable includes a list of files to check for new mail and a time interval at which to poll these files. If the first value in the variable is numeric, then it is taken as the polling time (in seconds). The default is five minutes. To have the shell check your default mail file every two minutes, add the following line to your **.login** or **.cshrc** file, substituting your username for *stern*:

```
set mail = "( 120 /usr/spool/mail/stern )"
```

When new mail arrives in **/usr/spool/mail/stern**, the C shell prints:

```
You have new mail.
```

before the next prompt.
You can specify a list of file names to check for new mail. This feature is useful if you use a mail sorting script that dumps your mail into your default spool file, and also into several folder files that you read at your leisure. For example:

```
set mail = "( /usr/spool/mail/stern /home/thud/stern/folders/noise )"
```

checks both the default spool directory and the "noise" folder for new mail. Some users prefer the C shell's mail notification mechanism to that of **biff**, because it is not as intrusive—mail notification won't interrupt an editing session, for example.

Name Hiding

Name hiding is performed implicitly when sendmail is run in remote mode, if the mail spool server and the mail hub are the same machine. Mail sent within the local network will not have any hostnames in sender addresses, and mail leaving the network will always be from *user@mailhost*. If aliases are used to forward mail to the mail hub, then explicit name hiding must be done to remove local hostnames from sender addresses in mail that leaves the local network.

One approach is to have sendmail on the mail hub clean up sender addresses before delivering the mail. Every mail delivery agent definition includes a send-mail rewriting rule applied to sender addresses and one for recipient addresses. By changing the rules used by the *local* mailer (the one that does delivery on the local machine), sender addresses of the form *user@host* can be rewritten as *user* if *host* is on the local network.

The following explanation is only useful if you have a basic understanding of **sendmail** mailer definitions and address rewriting rules. Feel free to skip over it if you are not a sendmail wizard. If you are going to venture into the depths of sendmail, start by finding the definition of the *local* mailer in the sendmail configuration file on the mail hub:

```
# Local and Program Mailer specification
Mlocal, P=/bin/mail, F=rlsDFMmnP, S=10, R=20, A=mail -d $u
Mprog,  P=/bin/sh,   F=lsDFMeuP,  S=10, R=20, A=sh -c $u

S10
# None needed.
S20
# None needed.
```

The **S=** and **R=** specifications name the sendmail ruleset used for sender and recipient address rewriting, respectively. In the previous example, these rulesets contain no actions. Notice that the *prog* mailer, used for sending a message to a program, uses the same rulesets for address rewriting.

To add the local hostname information, create a class that defines the names of hosts that should be hidden:

```
CCbitatron corvette poi lamachine
```

and add a line to set 10 of the form:

```
S10
R$+<@$=C>          $1              user@host -> user
```

The rewriting rule matches *user@host*, where the hostname is in the class *C*. The address simply becomes *user*. No other information is rewritten, because the delivery information (including the mailer and recipient name or names) has already been generated. If the spool server is not the mail hub, you need to make similar modifications to the wide-area or UUCP mailer specifications on the mail hub to hide the name of the spool server. The mail hub's name is normally the one by which the site is known to the outside world.

Other mail delivery agents enforce use rewriting schemes, and combining Internet domain name services and aliases can hide not only names but internal mail hosts and network structure as well. For example, as mail moves upward through hierarchies in the network, the sender address becomes more and more generic:

```
stern@wahoo.East.Sun.COM      Within East subdomain
stern@East.Sun.COM            Within Sun.COM
stern@Sun.COM                 Outside of Sun.COM domain
```

Each successive rewriting of the sender's address hides more of the delivery routing and internal structure of the *Sun.COM* domain.

These are only a few examples of name hiding mechanisms. Name hiding is not a requirement for a shared mail spool, but it may make user education about mail addressing an easier task. Consult your vendor's mail system documentation for details about other name hiding or address rewriting utilities.

NIS Alias Expansion

Aliases are used for creating mnemonic user naming systems, setting up automated mail handlers, and creating local- and wide-area mailing lists. Alias expansion under NIS or from the **/etc/aliases** file assumes that aliases are of the form:

```
user1:    user2@host
```

where *user1* and *user2* may be the same name. Note that not all vendors use **/etc/aliases** for the list of mail aliases; some place this file in **/usr/lib/aliases** or **/usr/lib/mail.aliases**. You can determine the location of your aliases file from the definition of the **OA** option in the early part of the **sendmail.cf** file:

```
# location of alias file
OA/etc/aliases
# default delivery mode (deliver in background)
Odbackground
# rebuild the alias file automatically
```

If an alias does not contain any hostname in its final expansion, then NIS appends the name of the NIS domain as a hostname. For example, in NIS domain *nesales*, the alias:

```
frederick:      fred
```

is expanded as *fred@nesales*. The addition of the domain name only occurs if the last expansion of the alias contains no hostname. If *fred* had another alias pointing him to the mail hub, the domain name would not be appended:

```
frederick:      fred
fred:           fred@wahoo
```

In this case, *frederick* expands to *fred*, which is expanded to *fred@wahoo*. Since the last expansion contains a hostname, the alias expansion is not modified. Without the additional alias, a hostname alias must be created for the domain name if the mail hub and the NIS domain do not share a common name. In the example above, the *nesales* domain mail hub is *wahoo*, so host-less aliases require an entry in the hosts file aliasing the mail hub and NIS domain name:

```
131.40.52.28    wahoo mailhost nesales
```

Appending the Domain Name Server domain name might be more appropriate for mail delivery, which is one motivation for qualifying the NIS domain name with the DNS domain name.

Wide-area Aliases

Wide-area mailing lists may contain enumerations of all users at all sites in the list, or they may be set up as a hierarchy of aliases. In this sense, wide-area simply means that the alias spans networks or NIS domains, but may not necessarily cross a wide-area network connection. Example of a wide-area aliases are "all employees at this site" and "all engineers in building 14." NIS eases the management of wide-area aliases by giving each NIS domain administrator the authority to add or remove users from a mailing list, if the list is maintained in a hierarchical fashion.

Setting Up A Distribution List

To set up a wide-area mailing list, one machine is chosen as the top of the hierarchy. The list manager should have superuser access to this machine to change the distribution and to handle delivery problems. The list is then given a name for distribution and a name for submissions. Two aliases are used to prevent feedback loops: separating inbound and outbound mail traffic reduces the probability that someone will use the alias name in the local distribution list. At each level in the hierarchy, the distribution alias is expanded to include NIS domains or the next lower levels in the distribution chain. At the lowest level—individual NIS domains—the distribution alias expands to individual users. Going the other way, each host handling the list sets up a submission alias pointing at the top of the hierarchy, so that all messages get routed to the top of the tree for distribution.

For example, a list of all ski-bums within a university could be distributed by department, and then by NIS domains within each department. The submission alias retains the well-known name *ski-bums*, and the distribution alias is called *ski-bums-dist*. On the host responsible for generating the list, *ski-lodge*, the alias expands to the top-level hosts doing the distribution:

```
ski-bums:        ski-bums-dist
ski-bums-dist:   ski-bums-dist@compsci,
                 ski-bums-dist@politics,
                 ski-bums-dist@history,
                 ski-bums-dist@english
```

The first alias passes submissions into the distribution chain. On the departmental hosts, the alias is further expanded into NIS domains. Aliases on *compsci* are:

```
ski-bums:        ski-bums@ski-lodge
ski-bums-dist:   ski-bums-dist@gradlab, ski-bums-dist@ugradlab,
                 ski-bums-dist@faculty
```

And finally on the NIS master server for domain *gradlab*, the NIS aliases map contains the names of skiers:

```
ski-bums:        ski-bums@ski-lodge
ski-bums-dist:   rich, pep, steve, vanessa
```

Usernames are not restricted to the lowest level of the distribution; if the system administrator of host *compsci* wants to join the list he or she can add his or her name to the distribution that fans out to other NIS domains.

The advantage to fully distributed alias expansion is that it gives local system administrators responsibility and control over the lists. The managers of central machines for each site do not have to deal with a (fairly) constant barrage of requests to be added or dropped from the list. Adding the submission alias on each host handling distribution makes it easier for users to send mail to lists, without having to remember the machine on which each list originates.

Handling Errors

Whenever a wide-area alias is created, it invites a variety of delivery problems. Users leave but are not removed from the list, users break their own mail forwarding, hosts are down and cannot accept list distributions, and (rarely) system administrators change the aliases so that they no longer distribute the list correctly. With normal mail delivery, errors are returned to the person sending the mail, so errors that occur on hosts all throughout the wide area network are dropped into the mailbox of the unsuspecting list member. In addition to confusing or aggravating the user, this does little to notify the list management authorities of the problem.

If an alias is named *owner-list*, then errors that occur while distributing mail to alias *list* are sent to the alias *owner-list*. The owner of a list should be a local system administrator who is familiar with the distribution scheme and is capable of fixing it at that level when it breaks. In the example of the skier's list, the owners of the list would be defined at each level in the hierarchy. In each department, the list owner is someone who can cut off individual NIS domains that are not well behaved:

```
ski-bums:          ski-bums@ski-lodge
ski-bums-dist:     ski-bums-dist@gradlab, ski-bums-dist@ugradlab,
                   ski-bums-dist@faculty
owner-ski-bums-dist:    root
```

At the level of individual NIS domains, the list owner may be the system administrator in charge of the domain, or someone from another domain who manages aliases across domain boundaries.

Archiving and Management

With any widely distributed list, people join the list after its inception and are interested in previous messages or the "culture" of the list. All messages sent to the list can be archived on any machine by adding a local filename to the distribution list:

```
ski-bums-dist:  ski-bums-dist@gradlab, ski-bums-dist@ugradlab,
                ski-bums-dist@faculty, /usr/spool/ski-bums/archive
owner-ski-bums-dist:   root
```

Every message sent to the list is appended to the archive file; the system manager should periodically rename the file and compress it to prevent overflowing the spool area. Instead of naming a file, a forwarding script can be used to sort out the submissions by week or month. Archiving is best left up to the lower level list managers, since they are the ones to service requests for archives of old messages.

Even with local management of the list, there may not be an obvious way to join or leave the list, or to report problems with it, other than sending a message to the list. In many cases, the managers who maintain list distributions do not read the lists themselves, so sending a message to the list may not produce any action. To separate the list management from its stream of submissions, define a request alias to be used for management issues:

```
ski-bums-request:  root
ski-bums-dist:  ski-bums-dist@gradlab, ski-bums-dist@ugradlab,
                ski-bums-dist@faculty
owner-ski-bums-dist:  root
```

The list owner and request handler are generally the same person or team of administrators.

Merging NIS and Local Aliases

Because the NIS aliases map augments the local **alias** file, a combination of NIS- and locally-managed aliases can be used to create host-specific alias expansions. If users want to be kept apprised of changes to the machines on their desks or in their labs, this mechanism allows a single alias to be used. Note that this only works if sendmail is run locally, and not in remote mode; with remote execution aliases are always expanded on the mail hub.

To set up globally named but locally expanded aliases, create the global name in the NIS *alias* map. Include users who always need this information independent of the host affected, as well as another alias to be expanded into the local portion of the list:

```
system-change: johnc, local-system-change
local-system-change:   /dev/null
```

The default local portion, *local-system-change*, is kept in the NIS alias file and throws away the mail. Remember that a local alias overrides an NIS alias of the same name, so defining *local-system-change* on a host adds users to the distribution list:

/etc/aliases excerpt on host bitatron:
```
local-system-change:   stern
+
```

When mail is sent to *system-change* from host *bitatron*, the NIS alias adds *johnc* to the list, and the local definition of *local-system-change* adds *stern*. On a host without a local definition of *local-system-change*, the mail goes only to *johnc*.

Forwarding

NFS and NIS are an excellent framework for centralizing mail services with a shared mail spool and mail delivery. With this simplification, mail forwarding becomes more complex. When mail is delivered to a user, the mailer looks for a file called **.forward** in the user's home directory. This forwarding file can be used to pass mail along to other users or pipe it into a shell script or executable. One popular use of forwarding files is for the **vacation** utility that replies to each new message with an electronic form letter.

The mail hub must be able to find every user's home directory in order to locate a **.forward** file, and any scripts or filters used to forward mail must be executable on the mail hub. Furthermore, any directories or files referenced must exist on the mail hub, which may have a configuration different from that of the user's desktop machine.

Mounting home directory trees with NFS on the mail hub ensures that the mailer can find each user's **.forward** file. To have your **.forward** file read by **sendmail**, you should make sure that your home directory is world-readable and world-executable and your **.forward** file is world-readable. Forwarding files are treated like aliases, and the same rules for shell script or filter execution apply:

- The script is run as user *daemon* in directory **/usr/spool/mqueue**. If the script needs to reference files in the user's home directory, it must do an explicit **cd $HOME** to get there. Full pathnames of directories and files should be used in scripts to avoid problems.

- Care must be taken that executables found via explicit pathnames are executable on the mail hub. If the user writes a private mail filtering utility, and compiles it a 68020-based machine, that executable cannot be used if the mail hub is a VAX or SPARC machine. Forwarding scripts should be flexible enough to find binary files for the proper architecture if required.

- Scripts should end with **exit 0**, and C programs should call **exit(0)**, to guarantee an exit status of 0. If the exit status is not set explicitly, it may be a random non-zero value and **sendmail** may think that delivery of the message failed.

10

Diagnostic and Administrative Tools
Broadcast Addresses
MAC and IP Layer Tools
Remote Procedure Call Tools
NIS Tools
NFS Tools
Time Synchronization

Distributed computing architectures rely on a well-conditioned network and properly configured servers for their promised performance and proper operation. NFS and NIS client performance degrades if your network is congested or your servers are unreliable. Retransmitted requests add to the noise level on the network or to the request backlog on the server, generally exacerbating any performance problems. Services underlying NFS and NIS, such as RPC, may break in abruptly changing networks.

Whenever you make a change, you run the risk of affecting more than just one machine. If you add a new NFS client, for example, you should consider all possible impacts on the computing environment: electrical implications of an additional network connection, network bandwidth consumed by traffic to and from this node, or the incremental workload imposed on any servers used by the client. Similarly, when upgrading server resources you must identify those areas that are the tightest constraints: CPU speed, disk speed, or aggregate disk space. Adding another server to a network may not be as economical or beneficial as upgrading to faster disks or offloading other tasks, such as terminal service to another server.

This portion of the book focuses on network analysis, debugging, and performance tuning. Its goal is to present the tools, procedures, and evaluation criteria used for analyzing network, NFS, or NIS problems. In addition to tuning and administration, these techniques can be used to evaluate proposals for expanding an existing network with additional clients, servers, or extended physical cabling. Symptoms and causes of common problems will be examined in detail, but the overall focus is on developing techniques to be used on complex problems peculiar to your specific combination of hardware, software, and physical cabling.

In this chapter, we present tools for examining the configuration and performance of individual network components, starting at the lowest level of basic point-to-point connectivity and working up to the RPC layer where the NFS- and NIS-specific issues come into play. The chapter includes examples relevant to problem diagnosis to define the methods for collecting and interpreting data about the network and its components. While network diagnostics and explanations of electrical phenomenon are not directly related to NFS and NIS, they are a necessary background for resolving problems that are apparent only at the application level. NFS may behave poorly because of a saturated network or due to an overloaded server; a thorough examination of the problem requires checking each component involved.

Chapter 11, *Debugging Network Problems*, integrates the theories and methodologies by walking through the resolution of several real-world crises. It is intended to be an overview of debugging processes common to many network-related crises, and to add life to the rather dry, fact-filled chapters on either side of it. Performance issues are covered last in Chapter 12, *Performance Analysis and Tuning*, since some performance bottlenecks may be traced to a lower-level constraint in the kernel or filesystem that manifests itself as an NFS problem. If you fail to understand the low-level operation of a facility, you are more likely to misinterpret performance or usage statistics provided for that facility. We cover the lower layers of the network protocols in detail so that you can see how they affect the performance and behavior of the application layer protocols like NFS and NIS.

Throughout the remainder of this book, we assume that NIS is running. In some cases, we refer to local files that are used without NIS. However, examples and discussions refer to the most common NIS maps, as shown in Table 10-1.

Table 10-1. Common NIS Maps and Their Nicknames

Map Name	Nickname	Local File
passwd.byname	*passwd*	/etc/passwd
group.byname	*group*	/etc/group
hosts.byname	*hosts*	/etc/hosts
rpc.bynumber	*rpc*	/etc/rpc
services.byname	*services*	/etc/services

Broadcast Addresses

Many network problems stem from confusion or inconsistency in the way hosts form their IP broadcast addresses. Broadcast addresses are used when a packet must be sent to all machines on the local area network. For example, if your host needs to send a packet to another machine, it must know the remote machine's IP address and Ethernet address. It can determine the remote IP address by looking up the remote hostname in the NIS *hosts* map, but it may not have the corresponding Ethernet address. If this is the first time your machine is talking to this particular remote host, it won't have had an opportunity to locate or save the remote Ethernet address. The way to determine the remote machine's Ethernet address is to ask all of the hosts on the network if they have the information, using the Address Resolution Protocol (ARP). To broadcast this request to all hosts on the network, your host uses a special kind of destination address called a broadcast address. A normal (or unicast) address identifies only one host; a broadcast address identifies all hosts on the network.

To be an effective broadcast, the packet must reach all nodes on the local area network and be recognized as a broadcast packet by them. An improperly formed broadcast address, or one which other systems do not recognize as such, can be responsible for failures ranging from NIS clients that cannot find servers to storms of broadcast packets initiated by a single packet sent with the wrong broadcast address.

Like host addresses, broadcast addresses exist in both the MAC and IP layers of the protocol stack. An IP broadcast address is converted into a MAC broadcast address, just as a host-specific IP address is converted into a 48-bit Ethernet address. At the MAC layer, there is exactly one broadcast address:

```
ff:ff:ff:ff:ff:ff
```

Every node on the local network receives a packet having this destination MAC address. A host may ignore a broadcast if the request is for a service that it does not provide. A host processes every broadcast packet, at the very least deciding to discard it. Therefore, a high level of broadcast traffic hurts the performance of each host on the network.

While the MAC layer broadcast address is very clearly defined, there is some variation in the form of IP broadcast addresses. There are two distinct popular forms, mostly due to evolution of the networking code in Berkeley-based UNIX systems.* Examples of broadcast addresses of each form are shown for each IP address class in Table 10-2. IP address classes are described in the section "IP Address Classes," in Chapter 1, *Networking Fundamentals*.

Table 10-2. Broadcast Address Forms

Address Class	Example	Ones Form	Zeros Form
Class A	89.	89.255.255.255	89.0.0.0
Class B	129.7.	129.7.255.255	129.7.0.0
Class C	192.6.4.	192.6.4.255	192.6.4.0

The ones form is the most widely accepted and is used in all examples in this handbook. Octets of the IP address that specify the host number are filled in with 1-valued bits. A variation on the ones form is the zeros form, in which the host number is expressed as zero-valued octets. The all-ones form:

```
255.255.255.255
```

is a variation of the proper ones form address where the 255-valued octets occupy only the host number portion of the address.

---

*The 4.2 BSD release of UNIX introduced TCP/IP, and required use of the zeros form of broadcast addresses. All derivatives of 4.2 BSD, including SunOS 3.x and early versions of Ultrix, retained this broadcast address requirement. In 4.3 BSD, the ones form of broadcast addresses was adopted, although the zeros form was still supported. UNIX operating systems that are descendants of 4.3 BSD—SunOS 4.x and current versions of Ultrix included—support both one- and zero-filled broadcast addresses.

Confusion regarding the "proper" broadcast address stems from the interpretation of octet values 0 and 255 in IP addresses. Zero-valued octets should be used as place holders when specifying a network number and imply "this" network, without any real implication for host numbers. For example, 129.7.0.0 means *network number* 129.7., but it does not necessarily name any hosts on the network.

Conversely, the one-filled octets are treated like wildcards and imply "any" host on the network. The network number is specified but the host number matches all hosts on that network. Using these connotations for octet values 0 and 255, the ones form of the broadcast address is "correct." There are cases in which the zeros form must be used for backwards compatibility with older operating system releases. Many systems were built using the zeros form of broadcast addresses.

The sole requirement in adopting a broadcast address form is to make the choice consistent across all machines on the network and compatible with your vendor's supported convention. Machines that expect a zeros-form broadcast address interpret a one-filled octet as part of a host number rather than a wildcard. Mixing broadcast address forms on the same network is the most common cause of broadcast storms, in which every confused node on the network transmits and retransmits replies to a broadcast address of a form complementary to the one it is using.

Broadcast addresses, IP addresses, and other characteristics of the Ethernet interface are set with the **ifconfig** utility. Because **ifconfig** governs the lowest level interface of a node to the network, it is the logical place to begin the discussion of network tools.

MAC and IP Layer Tools

The tools covered in this section operate at the MAC and IP layers of the network protocol stack. Problems that manifest themselves as NFS or NIS failures may be due to an improper host configuration or a break in the physical cabling. The tools described in this section are used to ascertain that the basic network connectivity is sound. Issues that will be covered include setting network addresses, testing connectivity, and burst traffic handling.

ifconfig: Interface Configuration

ifconfig sets or examines the characteristics of a network interface, such as its IP address or availability. At boot time, **ifconfig** is used to initialize network interfaces, possibly doing this in stages since some information may be available on the network itself through NIS. You can also use **ifconfig** to examine the current state of an interface and compare its address assignments with NIS map information.

Examining Interfaces

To examine a network interface, invoke **ifconfig** with its name as an argument:

```
% ifconfig le0
le0: flags=63<UP,BROADCAST,NOTRAILERS,RUNNING>
        inet 131.40.52.26 netmask ffffff00 broadcast 131.40.52.0

% ifconfig lo0
lo0: flags=49<UP,LOOPBACK,RUNNING>
        inet 127.0.0.1 netmask ff000000
```

The interface may be a physical device, such as an Ethernet interface or a packet driver stacked on top of a low-level synchronous line driver, or a pseudo-device like the loopback device. If the specified interface does not exist on the system or is not configured into the kernel, **ifconfig** reports the error "No such device."

The **flags** field is a bitmap that describes the state of the interface. Values for the flags may be found in **/usr/include/net/if.h**. The most common settings are:

UP
The network interface has been marked up, and is enabled to send or receive packets.

RUNNING
Kernel resources, such as device driver buffers, have been allocated to the interface to allow it to handle packets. An interface can be marked UP but not be running if the kernel is having trouble getting resources assigned to the interface. This is usually never a problem for Ethernet interfaces, but may surface when synchronous serial lines or fiber optic links are used.

BROADCAST
A valid broadcast address has been assigned to this interface. The interface reports its broadcast address when queried, and broadcast packets can now be sent from the interface.

LOOPBACK
The interface is a loopback device: packets sent out on the device are immediately placed on a receive queue for other processes on the local host. Although the loopback device is implemented entirely in software, you must configure it as though it were a physical network interface.

TRAILERS
Some implementations of the Ethernet protocols encapsulate information in the data link layer packet trailers. If the **NOTRAILERS** option is set, the host will never send data link trailers.

The second line of **ifconfig**'s output shows the Internet (IP) address assigned to this interface, the broadcast or destination IP address it uses, and the network mask that is applied to the IP address to derive the broadcast address. Some implementations of **ifconfig** also display the interface's Ethernet address where applicable. In this example, we see a zeros-form broadcast address, which is a potential problem if other hosts are configured using the ones-form.

The output of **ifconfig** resembles the first example for almost all Ethernet interfaces. **ifconfig** reports different state information if the interface is to a synchronous serial line, which is the underlying data link for a point-to-point IP network. Point-to-point links are one foundation of a wide-area network, since they allow IP packets to be run over long-haul serial lines. When configuring a point-to-point link, the broadcast address is replaced with a destination address for the other end of the point-to-point link, and the BROADCAST flag is replaced by the POINTTOPOINT flag:

```
this-side% ifconfig ptp0
ptp0: flags=8051<UP,POINTOPOINT,RUNNING,PRIVATE>
      inet 131.40.46.1 --> 131.40.1.12 netmask ffffff00
```

This interface is a serial line that connects networks 131.40.46.0 and 131.40.1.0; the machine on the other end of the line has a similar point-to-point interface configuration with the local and destination IP addresses reversed:

```
that-side% ifconfig ptp0
ptp0: flags=8051<UP,POINTOPOINT,RUNNING,PRIVATE>
      inet 131.40.1.12 --> 131.40.46.1 netmask ffffff00
```

Marking the line PRIVATE means that the host-to-host connection will not be advertised on the network.

Initializing an Interface

In addition to displaying the status of a network interface, **ifconfig** sets its configuration. During the boot process, **ifconfig** initializes each network interface, using the hostname assigned to the interface. Host names and their corresponding IP addresses may be managed through NIS, which requires a functioning network to retrieve map values. This chicken-and-egg problem is solved by invoking **ifconfig** twice during the four steps required to bring a host up on the network.

1. Early in the boot sequence, **/etc/rc.boot** executes **ifconfig** to set the IP address of the interface:

   ```
   ifconfig le0 wahoo
   ```

   or:

   ```
   ifconfig le0 `hostname`
   ```

   ypbind has not yet been started, so NIS is not running at this point. **ifconfig** matches the hostname in the local **/etc/hosts** file, and assigns the IP address found there to the interface. If NIS is going to be used on this host, this is the only time at which the local **/etc/hosts** file is consulted. The broadcast address is formed based on the class of the IP address, as shown in Table 10-3.

2. Critical network daemons, such as **ypbind** and the portmapper, are started next. The default broadcast address may include a wider audience than expected if subnetting is enabled, but it is sufficient for **ypbind**'s first broadcast to reach an NIS server.

3. **ifconfig** is invoked again, out of **/etc/rc.local**, to set the broadcast address and network mask. Now that NIS is running, maps that override the default values may be referenced, or you can hand-tailor broadcast addresses and masks:

   Using netmasks map:
   ```
   ifconfig le0 wahoo netmask + broadcast +
   ```

   Hand-crafted:
   ```
   ifconfig le0 wahoo netmask 255.255.255.0 broadcast 131.40.51.255
   ```

   The *netmask* argument tells **ifconfig** which parts of the IP address form the network number, and which form the host number. Any bit represented by a one in the *netmask* becomes part of the network number. The *broadcast* argument specifies the broadcast address to be used by this host. The plus signs in the first example cause **ifconfig** to read the appropriate NIS map for the required information. For the netmask, **ifconfig** reads the *netmasks* map, and for the broadcast address, it performs a logical AND of the netmask and host IP address read from the NIS hosts map. In this example, the ones-form of broadcast addresses is the default. Note that including the hostname in the **ifconfig** command line also sets the IP address again; although in this second case the NIS hosts map is used to determine the machine's IP address.

4. **inetd**-based services and RPC services such as NFS and the lock manager are started once the network interface is fully configured. Applications that require a fully functional network interface, such as network database servers, should be started after the last **ifconfig** is issued in the boot sequence.

Multiple interfaces

To put a machine on more than one network, it needs multiple network interfaces. A host may be part of several networks if it provides servers to hosts on each of them, or if it acts as a gateway between the networks. **ifconfig** sets up one interface at a time, assigning it an IP address and broadcast or destination addresses. If a host has several interfaces, they must be configured individually by using **ifconfig**:

```
...
ifconfig ie0 acadia netmask + broadcast +
...
ifconfig ie1 acadia-gw up broadcast 192.254.1.255 netmask +
```

As in the previous example, the plus signs (+) make **ifconfig** read the NIS maps for its data. In the second example, the interface is marked **up** and configured in a single command; this isn't done in the other example because the interface is marked **up** early in the boot process, and given a netmask later on (as described earlier).

Each network interface has a distinct hostname and IP address. One convention for two-network systems is to append *-gw* to the "primary" hostname. Each network interface must be on a separate IP network. Host *acadia* from the example above appears in the NIS **hosts** map on network 192.254.1.0 and 131.40.52.0:

```
192.254.1.1     acadia
131.40.52.20    acadia-gw
```

To hosts on the 131.40.52 network, the machine is *acadia-gw*, but on the 192.254.1 network, the same host is called *acadia*.

Systems with more than two network interfaces can use any convenient host naming scheme. For example, in a campus with four backbone Ethernet segments, machine names can reflect both the "given" name and the network name. A host sitting on all four IP networks is given four hostnames and four IP addresses:

```
Hosts file:
128.44.1.1      boris-bb1
128.44.2.1      boris-bb2
128.44.3.1      boris-bb3
128.44.4.1      boris-bb4
```

Excerpt from /etc/rc.local on boris:
```
ifconfig ie0 boris-bb1 netmask + broadcast +
...
ifconfig ie1 boris-bb2 up netmask + broadcast +
ifconfig ie2 boris-bb3 up netmask + broadcast +
ifconfig ie3 boris-bb4 up netmask + broadcast +
```

If the additional Ethernet interfaces are configured after NIS is started, then the NIS *hosts* map is relied upon to provide the IP address for each interface. To configure an interface early in the boot process—before NIS is started—the appropriate hostname and IP address must be in /etc/hosts on the local machine.

Mismatched host information

If you have inconsistent hostname and IP address information in the NIS *hosts* map, the local "runt" hosts file, and the host's boot scripts, major confusion will result. The host will not be able to start all of its services if its host IP address changes during the boot process, and other machines will not know how to map the host's name to an IP address that is represented on the network.

The most common symptom of a mismatched host entry is an error from the portmapper of the form:

```
portmap: Non-local attempt to unset prog 100105
```

or:

```
portmap: unset attempted from host 192.9.6.4
```

The portmapper notes the IP address of the local host when it is started; this is the IP address gleaned from /etc/hosts on the local machine. When RPC programs such as the **nfsd** daemons attempt to register themselves with the portmapper, the **portmap** process checks the IP address of the sending process against its recorded value. If they do not match, portmap refuses to register the program. This kind of failure indicates that the local host's IP address has changed between the early boot phase and the last **ifconfig**. You may find that the local /etc/hosts file disagrees with the NIS *hosts* map.

Subnetwork Masks

The second **ifconfig** in the boot process installs proper masks and broadcast addresses if subnetting is used to divide a larger IP address space. Default subnetwork masks and broadcast addresses are assigned based on IP address class, as shown in Table 10-3.

Table 10-3. Default Broadcast Addresses

Address Class		Network Mask	Broadcast Address
Class A	x.0.0.0	255.0.0.0	x.255.255.255
Class B	x.y.0.0	255.255.0.0	x.y.255.255
Class C	x.y.z.0	255.255.255.0	x.y.z.255

The NIS *netmasks* map contains an association of network numbers and subnetwork masks and is used to override the default network masks corresponding to each class of IP address. A simple example is the division of a Class B network into Class C-like subnetworks, so that each subnetwork number can be assigned to a distinct physical network. To effect such a scheme, the *netmasks* NIS map contains a single entry for the Class B address:

```
131.40. 255.255.255.0
```

Broadcast addresses are derived from the network mask and host IP address by performing a logical AND of the two. Any bits that are *not* masked out by the netmask become part of the broadcast address, while those that are masked out are set to either all zeros or all ones (depending upon your system's choice of a default broadcast address).

Network numbers are matched based on the number of octets normally used for an address of that class. IP address 131.40.52.28 has a Class B network number, so the first two octets in the IP address are used as an index into the **netmasks** map. Similarly, IP address 89.4.1.3 is a Class A address; therefore, only the first octet is used as a key into **netmasks**. This scheme simplifies the management of **netmasks**. By listing the network number to be partitioned, you do not have to itemize all subnetworks in the **netmasks** file.

Continuing the previous example, consider this **ifconfig**:

hosts excerpt:
```
131.40.52.28    mahimahi
```

netmasks map:
```
131.40. 255.255.255.0
```

ifconfig line:
```
ifconfig le0 mahimahi netmask +
```

Resulting interface configuration:
```
% ifconfig le0
le0: flags=63<UP,BROADCAST,NOTRAILERS,RUNNING>
        inet 131.40.52.28 netmask ffffff00 broadcast 131.40.52.0
```

Using a plus sign (+) as the netmask instead of an explicit network mask forces the second **ifconfig** to read the NIS *netmasks* map for the correct mask. The four-octet mask is logically AND-ed with the IP address, producing the broadcast network number. In the example above, the broadcast address is in the zeros form; a more proper broadcast is 131.40.52.255. Note that the *network* mask is actually displayed as a hexadecimal mask value, and not as an IP address.

A more complex example involves dividing the Class C network 192.6.4 into four subnetworks. To get four subnetworks, we need an additional two bits of network number, which are taken from the two most significant bits of the host number. The netmask is therefore extended into the next two bits, making it 26 bits instead of the default 24-bit Class C netmask:

```
Partitioning requires:
24 bits of Class C network number
2 additional bits of subnetwork number
6 bits left for host number

Last octet has 2 bits of netmask, 6 of host number:
11000000 binary = 192 decimal

Resulting netmasks file entry:
192.6.4          255.255.255.192
```

Again, only one entry in **netmasks** is needed, and the key for the entry matches the Class C network number that is being divided.

ifconfig only governs the local machine's interface to the network. If a host cannot exchange packets with a peer host on the same network, then it is necessary to verify that a datagram circuit to the remote host exists and that the remote node is properly advertising itself on the network. Tools that perform these tests are **arp** and **ping**.

IP to MAC Address Mappings

Applications use IP addresses and hostnames to identify remote nodes, but packets sent on the Ethernet identify their destinations via a 48-bit MAC-layer address. The Ethernet interface on each host only receives packets that have its MAC address of a broadcast address in the destination field. IP addresses are completely independent of the 48-bit MAC-level address; several disjoint networks may use the same sets of IP addresses although the 48-bit addresses to which they map are unique world-wide.

You can tell who makes an Ethernet interface by looking at the first three octets of its address. The most popular prefixes are shown in Table 10-4.

Table 10-4. Ethernet Address Prefixes

Prefix	Vendor	Prefix	Vendor
00:00:0C	Cisco	08:00:10	AT&T
00:00:0F	NeXT	08:00:1A	Data General
00:00:10	Sytek	08:00:1B	Data General
00:00:6B	MIPS	08:00:1E	Apollo
00:00:77	MIPS	08:00:20	Sun Microsystems
00:00:89	Cayman Systems	08:00:2B	DEC
00:00:93	Proteon	08:00:69	Silicon Graphics
00:00:A2	Wellfleet	08:00:89	Kinetics
00:80:2D	Xylogics	AA:00:03	DEC
02:60:8C	3Com (IBM PCs)	AA:00:04	DEC
08:00:09	Hewlett-Packard		

ARP, the Address Resolution Protocol, is used to maintain tables of 32- to 48-bit address translations. The *ARP table* is a dynamic collection of MAC-to-IP address mappings. To fill in the MAC-level Ethernet packet headers, the sending host must resolve the destination IP address into a 48-bit address. It first checks its ARP table for an entry keyed by the IP address, and if none is found, the host broadcasts an ARP request containing the recipient's IP address. Any machine supporting ARP address resolution responds to an ARP request with a packet containing its MAC address. The requester updates its ARP table, fills in the MAC address in the Ethernet packet header, and transmits the packet.

If no reply is received for the ARP request, the transmitting host sends the request again. Typically, a delay of a second or more is inserted between consecutive ARP requests to prevent a series of ARP packets from saturating the network. Flurries of ARP requests sometimes occur when a malformed packet is sent on the network; some hosts interpret it as a broadcast packet and attempt to get the Ethernet address of the sender via an ARP request. If many machines are affected, the ensuing flood of network activity can consume all of the available bandwidth. This behavior is referred to as an *ARP storm*, and is most frequently caused by an electrical problem in a transceiver that damages packets after the host has cleanly written them over its network interface.

To examine the current ARP table entries, use **arp –a**:

```
% arp -a
nantasket (131.40.52.83) at 8:0:20:1:9f:a4
hoby (131.40.52.25) at 8:0:20:6:b3:59
fenwick (131.40.52.44) at 8:0:20:0:46:c8
cape (131.40.52.79) at 8:0:20:0:9:4d
relax (131.40.52.87) at (incomplete)
```

The **arp −a** output listing shows the hostname, IP address, and the Ethernet address reported by the host. The **(incomplete)** entry is for a host that did not respond to an ARP request; after several minutes the entry is removed from the table. Complete entries in the ARP table may be *dynamic* or *permanent*, indicating how the address mappings were added and the length of their expected lifetimes.

When you display the ARP table, you'll see some entries tagged with the keywords *temporary* or *permanent* and some that are unqualified. In general, vendors implement **arp -a** so that their notion of a "default" ARP entry—dynamic or permanent—is left untagged, and the other type is marked with a keyword:

```
nantasket (131.40.52.83) at 8:0:20:1:9f:a4 (temporary)
```

In this example, the entry *nantasket* was added dynamically, and we can infer that this system assumes that permanent ARP table entries are the default.

Dynamic entries are added on demand during the course of normal IP traffic handling. Infrequently used mappings added in this fashion have a short lifetime; after five minutes without a reference to the entry, the ARP table management routines remove it. This ongoing table pruning is necessary to minimize the overhead of ARP table lookups. The ARP table is accessed using a hash table; a smaller, sparser table has fewer hash key collisions. A host that communicates regularly with many other hosts may have an ARP table that is fairly large, while a host that is quiescent or exchanging packets with only a few peers has a small ARP table. "Large" and "small" refer only to the number of slots occupied in the table; the actual size of the table in the kernel is fixed.

The difference between dynamic and permanent entries is how they are added to the ARP table. Dynamic entries are added on the fly, as a result of replies to ARP requests. Permanent entries are loaded into the ARP table once at boot time, and are useful if a host must communicate with a node that cannot respond to an ARP request during some part of its startup procedure. For example, a diskless client may not have ARP support embedded in the boot PROM, requiring its boot server to have a permanent ARP table entry for it. Once the diskless node is running the UNIX kernel, it should be able to respond to ARP requests to complete dynamic ARP table entries on other hosts.

A variation of the permanent ARP table entry is a *published* mapping. Published mappings are marked as such in the dump of the ARP table:

```
% arp -a
fenwick (131.40.52.44) at 8:0:20:0:46:c8
relax (131.40.52.87) at 8:0:20:0:94:a1 (published)
```

Publishing ARP table entries turns a host into an ARP server. Normally, a host replies only to requests for its own IP address, but if it has published entries then it replies for multiple IP addresses. If an ARP request is broadcast containing the IP address of a published entry, the host publishing that entry returns an ARP reply to the sender, even though the IP address in the ARP request does not match its own.

This mechanism is used to cope with machines that cannot respond to ARP requests due to lack of ARP support or because they are isolated from broadcast packets by a piece of network partitioning hardware that filters out broadcast packets. When either of these situations exist, a machine is designated as an ARP server and is loaded with ARP entries from a file containing host names, Ethernet addresses, and the *pub* qualifier. For example, to publish an ARP entry for host *relax* on server *irie*, we put the ARP information into the configuration file /etc/arptable and then load it using **arp –f**:

```
irie# cat /etc/arptable
relax  8:0:20:0:94:a1 pub
irie# arp -f /etc/arptable
```

The **–f** option forces **arp** to read the named file for entries.

As a diagnostic tool, **arp** is useful for resolving esoteric point-to-point connectivity problems. If a host's ARP table contains an incorrect entry, the machine using it will not be reachable, since outgoing packets will contain the wrong Ethernet address. ARP table entries may contain incorrect Ethernet addresses for several reasons:

• Another host on the network is answering ARP requests for the same IP address, or all IP addresses, emulating a duplicate IP address on the network.

• A host with a published ARP entry contains the wrong Ethernet address in its ARP table.

• Either of the above situations exist, and the incorrect ARP reply arrives at the requesting host after the correct reply. When ARP table entries are updated dynamically, the last response received is the one that "wins." If the correct ARP response is received from a host that is physically close to the requester, and a duplicate ARP response arrives from a host that is located across several Ethernet bridges, then the later—and probably incorrect—response is the one that the machine uses for future packet transmissions.

Inspection of the ARP table can reveal some obvious problems; for example, the three-octet prefix of the machine's Ethernet address does not agree with the vendor's label on the front of the machine. If you believe you are suffering from intermittent ARP failures, you can delete specific ARP table entries and monitor the table as it is repopulated dynamically. ARP table entries are deleted with **arp –d**, and only the superuser can delete entries. In the following example, we delete the ARP table entry for *fenwick*, then force the local host to send an ARP request for *fenwick* by attempting to connect to it using **telnet**. By examining the ARP table after the connection attempt, we can see if some other host has responded incorrectly to the ARP request:

```
# arp -d fenwick
fenwick (131.40.52.44) deleted
# telnet fenwick
...Telnet times out...
# arp -a
fenwick (131.40.52.44) at 8:0:20:2:3:ff
```

An example involving intermittent ARP failures is presented in Chapter 11, *Debugging Network Problems*.

Using ping to Check Network Connectivity

ping is similar to **arp** in that it provides information about hosts on a network rather than information about data that is sent on the network. **arp** provides a low-level look at the MAC addressing used by a host, but it is not that powerful for diagnosing connectivity problems. **ping** is a more general purpose tool for investigating point-to-point connectivity problems and areas of questionable physical network topology.

ping relies on the Internetwork Control Message Protocol (ICMP), another component of the network protocol stack that is a peer of IP and ARP. **ping** uses the ICMP echo facility to ask a remote machine for a reply. The returned packet contains a timestamp added by the remote host; the timestamp is used to compute the round trip packet transit time. In its simplest form, **ping** is given a hostname or IP address and returns a verdict on connectivity to that host:

```
% ping shamrock
shamrock is alive

% ping 131.40.1.15
131.40.1.15 is alive
```

The –s option puts **ping** into continuous-send mode, and displays the sequence numbers and transit times for packets as they are returned. Optionally, the packet size and packet count may be specified on the command line:

```
ping [-s] host [packet-size] [packet-count]
```

For example:

```
% ping -s mahimahi
PING mahimahi: 56 data bytes
64 bytes from mahimahi (131.40.52.28): icmp_seq=0. time=3. ms
64 bytes from mahimahi (131.40.52.28): icmp_seq=1. time=2. ms
64 bytes from mahimahi (131.40.52.28): icmp_seq=2. time=2. ms
```

```
64 bytes from mahimahi (131.40.52.28): icmp_seq=3. time=3. ms
64 bytes from mahimahi (131.40.52.28): icmp_seq=4. time=2. ms
^C
----mahimahi PING Statistics----
5 packets transmitted, 5 packets received, 0% packet loss
round-trip (ms)  min/avg/max = 2/2/3
```

and:

```
% ping -s mahimahi 100 3
PING mahimahi: 100 data bytes
108 bytes from mahimahi (131.40.52.28): icmp_seq=0. time=3. ms
108 bytes from mahimahi (131.40.52.28): icmp_seq=1. time=3. ms
108 bytes from mahimahi (131.40.52.28): icmp_seq=2. time=3. ms

----mahimahi PING Statistics----
3 packets transmitted, 3 packets received; 0% packet loss
round-trip (ms)  min/avg/max = 3/3/3
```

The eight bytes added to each ICMP echo request in the corresponding reply are the timestamp information added by the remote host. If no explicit count on the number of packets is specified, then **ping** continues transmitting until interrupted. By default, **ping** uses a 56-byte packet, which is the smallest IP packet, complete with headers and checksums, that will be transmitted on the Ethernet.

The **ping** utility is good for answering questions about whether the remote host is attached to the network and whether the network between the hosts is reliable. Additionally, **ping** can indicate that a host name and IP address are not consistent across several machines. The replies received when the host is specified by name may contain an incorrect IP address. Conversely, if **ping**ing the remote host by name does not produce a reply, try the IP address of the host. If a reply is received when the host is specified by address, but not by name, then the local machine has an incorrect view of the remote host's IP address. These kinds of problems are generally machine specific, so intermittent **ping** failures can be a hint of IP address confusion: machines that do not agree on the IP addresses they have been assigned.

If NIS is used, this could indicate that the NIS *hosts* map was corrupted or changed (incorrectly) since the remote host last booted. The NIS *hosts* map supercedes the local /etc/hosts file, so a disparity between the two for a remote machine is ignored; the NIS *hosts* map takes precedence. However, in the absence of NIS, the failure of a remote node to answer a **ping** to its hostname indicates the /etc/hosts files are out of synchronization.

Larger packet sizes may be used to test connectivity through network components that are suspected of damaging large packets or trains of packets. **ping** only sends one packet at a time, so it won't test the capacity of a network interface. However, it tells you whether packets close to the network's MTU can make it from point to point intact, through all of the network hardware between the two hosts.

Using the packet count indicators and transit times, **ping** can be used to examine connectivity, network segment length, and potential termination problems. Electrical problems, including poor or missing cable termination, are the among most difficult problems to diagnose and pinpoint without repeatedly splitting the network in half and testing the smaller segments. If **ping** shows that packets are dropped out of sequence, or that return packets are received in bursts, it is likely that either a network cable segment has an electrical fault or that the network is not terminated properly.

For example, the following output from **ping** indicates that the network is intermittently dropping packets; this behavior is usually caused by improper termination and is quite random in nature:

```
% ping -s mahimahi
PING mahimahi: 56 data bytes
64 bytes from mahimahi (131.40.52.28): icmp_seq=0. time=3. ms
64 bytes from mahimahi (131.40.52.28): icmp_seq=1. time=2. ms
64 bytes from mahimahi (131.40.52.28): icmp_seq=16. time=1295. ms
64 bytes from mahimahi (131.40.52.28): icmp_seq=17. time=3. ms
64 bytes from mahimahi (131.40.52.28): icmp_seq=18. time=2. ms
```

The gap between packets 1 and 16, along with the exceptionally long packet delay, indicates that a low-level network problem is consuming packets. A scenario involving termination problems like the one shown in the previous example is covered in "Improper Network Termination," in Chapter 11, *Debugging Network Problems*; a detailed examination of termination is included there as well.

Gauging Ethernet Interface Capacity

Even with a well-conditioned network and proper host configuration information, a server may have trouble communicating with its clients because its network interface is overloaded. If an NFS server is hit with more packets than it can receive through its network interface, some client requests will be lost and eventually retransmitted. To the NFS clients, the server appears painfully slow, when it's really the server's network interface that is the problem.

The **spray** utility provides a very coarse estimate of network interface capacity, both on individual hosts and through network hardware between hosts. **spray** showers a target host with consecutive packets of a fixed length by making remote procedure calls to the **rpc.sprayd** daemon on the remote host. After the last packet is sent, the **rpc.sprayd** daemon is queried for a count of the packets received; this value is compared to the number of packets sent to determine the percentage dropped between client and server.

By itself, **spray** is of limited usefulness as a measure of the packet handling capability of a machine. The packet containing the RPC call may be lost by the client, due to other activity on its network interface; it may be consumed by a collision on the network; or it may be incident to the server but not copied from the network by the server's network interface due to a lack of buffer space or excessive server CPU loading. Many packets are lost on the sending host, and **spray** has no knowledge of where the packets vanish once they pass out of the application layer. Due to these factors, **spray** is best used to gauge the relative packet-handling speeds of two or more machines.

Here are some examples of using **spray** to test various network constraints. **spray** requires a hostname and takes a packet count and packet length as optional arguments:

```
spray host [-c count] [-l length] [-d delay]
```

For example:

```
% spray wahoo
sending 1162 packets of lnth 86 to wahoo ...
        in 0.8 seconds elapsed time,
        347 packets (29.86%) dropped by wahoo
Sent:   1382 packets/sec, 116.1K bytes/sec
Rcvd:   969 packets/sec, 81.4K bytes/sec
```

spray reports the number of packets sent, the total wall clock time required to send the packets, and statistics on the survival rate of the packets. The packet drop rates are only meaningful when used to compare the relative network input and output rates of the two machines under test.

It's important to note that network interface speed depends upon much more than CPU speed. A faster CPU helps a host process network protocols faster, but the network interface and bus hardware usually determine how quickly the host can pull packets from the network. A fast network interface may be separated from the CPU by a bus that has a high latency. Even a high-throughput I/O system may exhibit poor network performance if there is a large time overhead required to set up each packet transfer from the network interface to the CPU. Similar hosts stress each other fairly, since their network interfaces have the same input capacity.

Even on a well-conditioned, little-used network, a client machine that has a significantly faster CPU than its server may perform worse under the stress of **spray** than the same two machines with the client and server roles reversed. With increased CPU speed comes increased packet handling speed, so a faster machine can transmit packets quickly enough to outpace a slower server. If the disparity between client and server is great, then the client is forced to retransmit requests and the server is additionally burdened with the duplicate requests. Use **spray** to exercise combinations of client and server with varying packet sizes to identify cases in which a client may race ahead of its server. When a fast NFS client is teamed with a slower server, the NFS mount parameters require tuning as described in "Slow Server Compensation," in Chapter 12, *Performance Analysis and Tuning*.

Send various sized packets to an NFS server to see how it handles "large" and "small" NFS requests. Disk write operations are "large," usually filling several full-size IP packets. Other operations, such as getting the attributes of a file, fit into a packet of 150 bytes or less. Small packets are more easily handled by all hosts, since there is less data to move around, but NFS servers may be subject to bursts of large packets during intense periods of client write operations. If no explicit arguments are given, **spray** sends 1162 packets of 86 bytes. In most implementations of **spray**, if either a packet count or packet length are given, the other argument is chosen so that 100 kbytes of data are transferred between client and server. Try using **spray** with packet sizes of 1500 bytes to judge how well an NFS server or the network handle write requests.

Normally, no delay is inserted between packets send by **spray**, although the –d option may be used to specify a delay in microseconds. Insert delays between the packets to simulate realistic packet arrival rates, under "normal" conditions. Client requests may be separated by several tens of microseconds, so including a delay between packets may give you a more accurate picture of packet handling rates.

In Figure 10-1, *baxter* and *arches* are identical machines and *acadia* is a faster machine with a faster network interface. **spray** produces the following output:

Fast machine to slow machine:
```
[acadia]% spray baxter -c 100 -l 1160
sending 100 packets of lnth 1162 to baxter ...
        39 packets (39.000%) dropped by baxter
        520 packets/sec, 605037 bytes/sec
```

Fast machine to slow machine, with delay:
```
[acadia]% spray baxter -c 100 -l 1160 -d 1
sending 100 packets of lnth 1162 to baxter ...
        no packets dropped by baxter
        99 packets/sec, 115680 bytes/sec
```

Slow machine to fast machine:
```
[baxter]% spray acadia -c 100 -l 1160
sending 100 packets of lnth 1162 to acadia ...
        no packets dropped by acadia
        769 packets/sec, 893846 bytes/sec
```

Slow machine to identical machine:
```
[baxter]% spray arches -c 100 -l 1160
sending 100 packets of lnth 1162 to arches ...
        no packets dropped by arches
        769 packets/sec, 893846 bytes/sec
```

When the fast machine sprays the slower one, a significant number of packets are dropped; but adding a one-microsecond delay between the packets allows the slow machine to keep pace and receive all incident packets. The slow machine to fast machine test produces the same packet handling rate as the slow machine showering an identical peer; if the slow machine sprays the fast one, the network bandwidth used is more than 30% greater than when the fast machine hammers the slow one. Note that you couldn't get NFS to insert delays like this, but performing the test with delays may indicate the location of a bottleneck. Knowing your constraints, you can change other configuration parameters, such as NFS client behavior, to avoid the bottleneck. We'll look at these tuning procedures more in Chapter 12, *Performance Analysis and Tuning*.

The four tools discussed to this point—**ifconfig, arp, ping,** and **spray**— focus on the issues of packet addressing and routing. If they indicate a problem, all network services, such as **telnet** and **rlogin,** will be affected. We now move up through the network and transport layers in the network protocol stack, leaving the MAC and IP layers for the session and application layers.

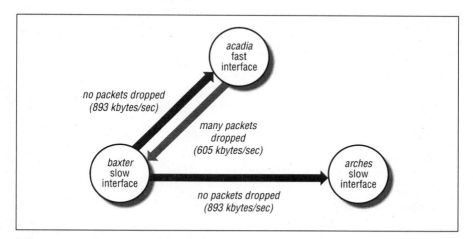

Figure 10-1. Testing relative packet handling rates

Remote Procedure Call Tools

Network failures on a grand scale are generally caused by problems at the MAC or IP level, and are immediately noticed by users. Problems involving higher layers of the network protocol stack manifest themselves in more subtle ways, affecting only a few machines or particular pairs of clients and servers. The utilities discussed in the following sections analyze functionality from the remote procedure call (RPC) layer up through the NFS or NIS application layer. The next section contains a detailed examination of the RPC mechanism at the heart of NFS and NIS.

RPC Mechanics

The Remote Procedure Call (RPC) mechanism imposes a client/server relationship on machines in a network. A server is a host that physically owns some shared resource, such as a disk exported for NFS service or an NIS map. Clients operate on resources owned by servers by making RPC requests; these operations appear (to the client) to have been executed locally. For example, when performing a read RPC on an NFS-mounted disk, the reading application has no knowledge of where the read is actually executed. Many client-server relationships may be defined for each machine on a network; a server for one resource is often a client for many others in the same network.

Identifying RPC Services

Services available through RPC are identified by four values:

- Program number.

- Version number.

- Procedure number.

- Protocol (UDP or TCP).

The program number uniquely identifies the RPC service. Each RPC service, such as the **mountd** or NIS server daemons, is assigned a program number. The file **/etc/rpc** and the *rpc* NIS map contain an enumeration of RPC program numbers, formal names, and nicknames for each service:

```
Excerpt from /etc/rpc
nfs     100003  nfsprog
ypserv  100004  ypprog
mountd  100005  mount showmount
ypbind  100007
```

Note that program 100005, **mountd**, has two names, reflecting the fact that the **mountd** daemon services both **mount** requests and the **showmount** utility.

Program numbers are expressed in hexadecimal. Well-known RPC services such as NFS and NIS are assigned reserved program numbers in the range 0x0 to 0x199999. Numbers above this range may be assigned to local applications such as license servers.

The program number is used to tag an RPC service; the service itself may be composed of many procedures. The NFS service, program number 100003, consists of several procedures, each of which is assigned a procedure number. These procedures perform client requests on the NFS server. For example: read a directory, create a file, read a block from a file, write to a file, get the file's attributes, or get statistics about a filesystem. The procedure number is passed in an RPC request as an "op code" for the RPC server. Procedure numbers start with 1, since procedure 0 is reserved for a "null" function. While RPC program numbers are well advertised, procedure numbers are particular to the service, and often are contained in a header file that gets compiled into the client program. NFS procedure numbers, for example, are defined in the header file **/usr/include/nfs/nfs.h**.

RPC clients and servers deal exclusively with RPC program numbers. At the session layer in the protocol stack, the code doesn't really care what protocols are used to provide the session services. The UDP and TCP transport protocols need port numbers to identify the local and remote ends of a connection. The portmapper is used to perform translation between the RPC program number-based view of the world and the TCP/UDP port numbers.

RPC Portmapper

The portmapper daemon, **portmap**, exists to register RPC services and to provide their IP port numbers when given an RPC program number. The portmapper itself is an RPC service, but it resides at a well-known IP port (port 111) so that it may be contacted directly by remote hosts. For example, if host *fred* needs to mount a filesystem from host *barney*, it must send an RPC request to the **mountd** daemon on *barney*. The mechanics of making the RPC request are as follows:

- *fred* gets the IP address for the *barney*, using the the **hosts** NIS map. *fred* also looks up the RPC program number for **mountd** in the **rpc** NIS map. The RPC program number is 0x100005.

- Knowing that the portmapper lives at port 111, *fred* sends an RPC request to the portmapper on *barney*, asking for the IP port (on *barney*) of RPC program 0x100005. *fred* may also specify a particular protocol or version number for the RPC service. *barney*'s portmapper responds to the request with port 704, the IP port at which **mountd** is listening for incoming mount RPC requests. Note that it is possible for the portmapper to return an error, if the specified program does not exist or if it hasn't been registered on the remote host. *barney*, for example, might not be an NFS server and would therefore have no reason to run the **mountd** daemon.

- *fred* sends a **mount** RPC request to *barney*, using the IP port number returned by the portmapper. This RPC request contains an RPC procedure number, which tells the **mountd** daemon what to do with the request. The RPC request also contains the parameters for the procedure; in this case, the name of the filesystem *fred* needs to mount and the NFS mount options that were specified in the command line.

The portmapper is also used to handle an *RPC broadcast*. Recall that a network broadcast is a packet that is sent to all hosts on the network; an RPC broadcast is a request that is sent to all servers for a particular RPC service. For example, the NIS client **ypbind** daemon uses an RPC broadcast to locate an NIS server for its domain. There's one small problem with RPC broadcasts: to send a broadcast packet, a host must fill in the remote port number, so all hosts receiving the packet know where to deliver the broadcast packet. RPC doesn't have any knowledge of port numbers, and the RPC server daemons on some hosts may be registered at different port numbers. This problem is resolved by sending RPC broadcasts to the portmapper, and asking the portmapper to make the RPC call indirectly on behalf of the sender. In the case of the **ypbind** daemon, it sends a broadcast to all **portmap** daemons; they in turn call the **ypserv** RPC server on each host.

RPC Version Numbers

We've seen how the program numbers, procedure numbers, and TCP/UDP port numbers fit together, but haven't touched on version numbers yet. Each new implementation of an RPC server has its own version number. Different version numbers are used to coordinate multiple implementations of the same service, each of which may have a different interface. As an RPC service matures, the service's author may find it necessary to add new procedures or add arguments to existing procedures. Changing the interface in this way requires incrementing the version number. The first (and earliest) version of an RPC program is version 1; subsequent releases of the server should use consecutive version numbers. For example, the mount service has several versions, each one supporting more options than its predecessors.

Multiple versions are implemented in a single server process; there is not an instance of the RPC server daemon for each version supported. Each RPC server daemon registers its RPC program number and all versions it supports with the portmapper. It is helpful to think of dispatching a request through an RPC server as a two-level switch: the first level discriminates on the version number, and chooses a set of procedure routines comprising that version of the RPC service. The second level dispatch invokes one of the routines in that set based on the program number in the RPC request.

When contacting the portmapper on a remote host, the local and remote sides must agree on the version number of the RPC service that will be used. The rule of thumb is to use the highest-numbered version that both parties understand. In cases where version numbers are not consecutively numbered, or no mutually agreeable version number can be found, the portmapper returns a *version mismatch* error looking like:

```
mount: RPC: Program version mismatch
```

An RPC service may use either the TCP or UDP transport protocol. Servers may register themselves for one or both protocols, depending upon the varieties of connections they need to support. UDP packets are unreliable and unsequenced and are often used for broadcast or stateless services (such as NFS). The RPC server for the **spray** utility, which "catches" packets thrown at the remote host, uses the UDP protocol to accept as many requests as it can without requiring retransmission of any missed packets. In contrast to UDP, TCP packets are reliably delivered and are presented in the order in which they were transmitted, making them a requirement when requests must be processed by the server in the order in which they were transmitted by the client.

RPC servers listen on their own behalf on the ports registered with the port mapper, and are used repeatedly for short-lived sessions. Each connection to an RPC server exists for the duration of the RPC call only. They do not fork new processes for each request, since the overhead of doing so would significantly impair the performance of RPC-intensive services such as NFS. RPC servers are single-threaded and complete processing of one request before accepting the next. If there is sufficient demand for a particular RPC service, or if the host can process simultaneous RPC requests more efficiently, the host can run multiple copies of the server; this approach is used with the **nfsd** NFS server daemons. Running eight instances of the **nfsd** daemon allows the host to have eight NFS requests being processed in parallel. With only one NFS server daemon, advantages of multiple disks and disk controllers would be lost, and "fast" NFS requests such as attribute or name lookups would get trapped behind slower disk requests.

RPC Registration

Making RPC calls is a reasonably complex affair because there are several places for the procedure to break down. The **rpcinfo** utility is an analog of **ping** that queries RPC servers and their registration with the portmapper. Like **ping**, **rpcinfo** provides a measure of basic connectivity, albeit at the session layer in the network protocol stack. Pinging a remote machine ensures that the underlying physical network and IP address handling are correct; using **rpcinfo** to perform a similar test verifies that the remote machine is capable of accepting and replying to an RPC request.

rpcinfo can be used to detect and debug a variety of failures:

- "Dead" or hung servers caused by improper configuration or a failed daemon.

- RPC program version number mismatches between client and server.

- Bogus or renegade RPC servers, such as an NIS server that does not have valid maps for the domain it pretends to serve.

- Broadcast-related problems.

In its simplest usage, **rpcinfo –p** takes a remote hostname (or uses the local hostname if none is specified) and queries the portmapper on that host for all registered RPC services:

```
% rpcinfo -p corvette
   program vers proto   port
    100000    2   tcp    111  portmapper
    100000    2   udp    111  portmapper
    100007    2   tcp   1024  ypbind
    100007    2   udp   1027  ypbind
    100007    1   tcp   1024  ypbind
    100007    1   udp   1027  ypbind
    100029    1   udp    653  keyserv
    100024    1   udp    692  status
    100024    1   tcp    694  status
    100001    2   udp   1039  rstatd
    100001    3   udp   1039  rstatd
    100001    4   udp   1039  rstatd
    100002    1   udp   1040  rusersd
    100002    2   udp   1040  rusersd
    100012    1   udp   1041  sprayd
    100008    1   udp   1042  walld
```

The output from **rpcinfo** shows the RPC program and version numbers, the protocols supported, the IP port used by the RPC server, and the name of the RPC service. Service names come from the *rpc.bynumber* NIS map; if no name is printed next to the registration information then the RPC program number does not appear in the map. This may be expected for third-party packages that run RPC server daemons, since the hardware vendor creating the **/etc/rpc** file doesn't necessarily list all of the software vendors' RPC numbers. However, a well-known RPC service should be listed properly. Missing RPC service names could indicate a corrupted or incomplete *rpc.bynumber* NIS map.

If the portmapper on the remote machine has died or is not accepting connections for any reason, **rpcinfo** times out attempting to reach it and reports the error. This is a good first step toward diagnosing any RPC-related problem: verify that the remote portmapper is alive and returning valid RPC service registrations.

rpcinfo can also be used like *ping* for a particular RPC server:

```
rpcinfo -u host program version        UDP-based services
rpcinfo -t host program version        TCP-based services
```

The **–u** or **–t** parameter specifies the transport protocol to be used—UDP or TCP respectively. The hostname must be specified, even if the local host is being queried. Finally, the RPC program and version number are given; the program may be supplied by name (one reported by **rpcinfo –p**) or by explicit numerical value.

As a practical example, consider trying to mount an NFS filesystem from server *mahimahi*. You can mount it successfully, but attempts to operate on its files hang the client. You can use **rpcinfo** to check on the status of the NFS RPC daemons on *mahimahi*:

```
% rpcinfo -u mahimahi nfs 2
program 100003 version 2 ready and waiting
```

In this examples, the NFS RPC service is queried on remote host *mahimahi*. Since the service is specified by name, **rpcinfo** looks it up in the *rpc* NIS map. The **–u** flag tells **rpcinfo** to use the UDP protocol, since NFS is built on UDP. If the **–t** option was given instead, **rpcinfo** would report that it could not find a registration for the service using that protocol.

rpcinfo –u and **rpcinfo –t** call the null procedure (procedure 0) of the RPC server. The null procedure normally does nothing more than return a zero-length reply. If you cannot contact the null procedure of a server, then the health of the server daemon process is suspect. If the daemon never started running, **rpcinfo** would have reported that it couldn't find the server daemon at all. If **rpcinfo** finds the RPC server daemon but can't get a null procedure reply from it, then the daemon is probably hung.

Debugging RPC Problems

In the previous examples, we used **rpcinfo** to see if a particular service was registered or not. If the RPC service is not registered, or if you can't reach the RPC server daemon, there's a low-level problem in the network. However, sometimes you reach an RPC server, but you find the wrong one or it gives you the wrong answer. If you have a heterogeneous environment and are running multiple versions of each RPC service, it's possible to get RPC version number mismatch errors.

These problems affect NIS and diskless client booting; they are best sorted out by using **rpcinfo** to emulate an RPC call and by observing server responses. Networks with multiple, heterogeneous servers may produce multiple, conflicting responses to the same broadcast request. Debugging problems that arise from this behavior often requires knowing the order in which the responses are received.

Here's an example: we'll perform a broadcast and then watch the order in which responses are received. When a diskless client boots, it may receive several replies to a request for boot parameters. The boot fails if the first reply contains incorrect or invalid boot parameter information. **rpcinfo –b** sends a broadcast request to the specified RPC program and version number:

```
% ypcat rpc.bynumber | fgrep bootparam
bootparam       100026

% rpcinfo -b 100026 1
131.40.52.13 thud
131.40.52.27 onaga
131.40.52.26 wahoo
131.40.52.28 mahimahi
Next broadcast

% rpcinfo -b bootparam 1
131.40.52.26 wahoo
131.40.52.28 mahimahi
131.40.52.27 onaga
131.40.52.13 thud
Next broadcast
```

In this example, a broadcast packet is sent to RPC program 1000026, which is the registered program number for the boot parameter server (the RPC program number was found by dumping the **rpc** NIS map and looking for the appropriate name). Any host that is running the boot parameter server replies to the broadcast with the standard null procedure "empty" reply. Host names and IP addresses are printed by the requesting host in the order in which replies are received from these hosts. After a short interval, another broadcast is sent.

Server loading may cause the order of replies between successive broadcasts to vary significantly. A busy server takes longer to schedule the RPC server and process the request. Differing reply sequences from RPC servers are not themselves indicative of a problem, if the servers all return the correct information. If one or more servers has incorrect information, though, you will see irregular failures. A machine returning correct information may not always be the first to deliver a response to a client broadcast, so sometimes the client gets the wrong response.

In the last example (diskless client booting), a client that gets the wrong response won't boot. The boot failures may be very intermittent due to variations in server loading: when the server returning an invalid reply is heavily loaded, the client will boot without problem. However, when the servers with the correct information are loaded, then the client gets an invalid set of boot parameters, and cannot start booting a kernel.

Binding to the wrong NIS server causes another kind of problem. A renegade NIS server may be the first to answer a **ypbind** broadcast for NIS service, and its lack of information about the domain makes the client machine unusable. Sometimes, just looking at the list of servers that respond to a request may flag a problem, if you notice that one of the servers should not be answering the broadcast:

```
% rpcinfo -b ypserv 1
131.40.52.138 poi
131.40.52.27 onaga
131.40.52.28 mahimahi
```

In this example, all NIS servers on the local network answer the **rpcinfo** broadcast request to the null procedure of the *ypserv* daemon. If *poi* should not be an NIS server, then the network will be prone to periods of intermittent failure if clients bind to it. Failure to fully decommission a host as an NIS server—leaving empty NIS map directories, for example—may cause this problem.

There's another possibility for NIS failure that **rpcinfo** cannot detect: there may be NIS servers on the network, but no servers for the client's NIS domain. In the previous example, *poi* may be a valid NIS server in another domain, in which case it is operating properly by responding to the **rpcinfo** broadcast. You might not be able to get **ypbind** started on an NIS client because all of the servers are in the wrong domain, and therefore the client's broadcasts are not answered. The **rpcinfo –b** test is a little misleading because it doesn't ask the NIS RPC daemons what domains they are serving, although the client's requests will be domain-specific. Check the servers that reply to an **rpcinfo –b** and ensure that they serve the NIS domain used by the clients experiencing NIS failures.

If a client cannot find an NIS server, **ypbind** hangs the boot sequence with errors of the form:

```
ypbind: cannot find server for domain polygon
```

Using **rpcinfo** as shown helps to determine why a particular client cannot start the NIS service: if no host replies to the **rpcinfo** request, then the broadcast packet is failing to reach any NIS servers. If the NIS domain name and the broadcast address are correct, then it may be necessary to override the broadcast-based search and hand **ypbind** the name and address of a valid NIS server. Tools for examining and altering NIS bindings are the subject of the next section.

NIS Tools

Tools discussed to this point help to dissect the session and transport layers under an application such as NIS. The application and the utilities that analyze its behavior and performance all rely on a well behaved network. Assuming that the lower layers are in place, NIS-oriented tools fine-tune the NIS system and to resolve problems that are caused by information in the NIS maps, rather than the way in which the maps are accessed. The tools described below alter client-server bindings, locate NIS servers and information for a particular map, and look-up keys in maps.

Key Lookup

ypmatch is a **grep** command for NIS maps. **ypmatch** finds a single key in an NIS map and prints the data associated with that key:

```
% ypmatch root aliases
       postmaster

% ypmatch onaga hosts
131.40.52.27    onaga
```

This procedure differs from using **grep** on the ASCII source file that produced the map in two ways:

- The client may be bound to an NIS server with a corrupted map set or one that is out-of-date with the NIS master server. In this case, the output of **ypmatch** will not agree with the output of **grep** run on the ASCII source file.

- **ypmatch** can be run from any client, while the NIS map source files may only exist on a server with limited user access. Therefore, users who need to parse maps such as the password or hosts files must use NIS-oriented tools to gather their data.

Associated with **ypmatch** is **ypcat**, which is the equivalent for **cat** for NIS files. It writes the entire map file to the standard output:

```
% ypcat hosts
131.40.52.121  vineyard
131.40.52.54   hannah
131.40.52.132  positive
```

NIS maps are stored as DBM databases, indexed files with fast access provided through a hash table. Standard utilities such as **grep** do not produce meaningful results when used on DBM data files. To peer into the contents of an NIS map, you must use **ypmatch** or **ypcat**. Output from NIS tools is colored by the underlying DBM index file organization, and presents several avenues of confusion:

- By default, only the value paired with the key in the map is displayed, and not the key itself. Some maps retain the key as part of the data value because it is needed by applications that retrieve the map entry. Library routines that locate a password file entry based on UID, for example, return the user's log-in name as part of the password file structure. Other maps such as **aliases** simply store the value associated with the key, when applications (such as mail) that reference the NIS map already have the key value. The following excerpt from **ypcat aliases** is of little value because there are no alias names associated with the alias expansions:

```
% ypcat aliases
            dan, lauri, paul, harry, bob
            dave, michael
            michael, jan, stewart, tom
```

Both **ypcat** and **ypmatch** use the **–k** option to print the data value with its associated key:

```
% ypcat -k aliases
south-sales     dan, lauri, paul, harry, bob
engin-managers  dave, michael
north-engin     michael, jan, stewart, tom
```

- Some maps do not associate a data value with a key. The most common map of this variety is the *ypservers* map, which simply contains hostnames of NIS servers without any additional information. When using **ypcat** or **ypmatch** with value-less maps, blank lines are produced as output:

  ```
  % ypcat ypservers
  ```

  unless the –**k** option is specified:

  ```
  % ypcat -k ypservers
  mahimahi
  wahoo
  thud
  ```

- An NIS server implements separate procedures to get the "first" key in a map and to get each successive key. **ypcat** uses the "get first key" and "get next key" procedures to locate the first key in the DBM file and to walk through all keys. The ordering of the keys is determined by a linear scan through the DBM index file, rather than the order in which the records appear in the plain text file. Because keys are encountered in the order in which they are hash chained together, **ypcat** produces a seemingly random ordering of the keys. In the hosts file example above, the original /etc/hosts file was sorted by increasing host number in the IP addresses; but the process of hashing the keys into the DBM file produced the ordering seen with **ypcat**.

As a diagnostic tool, **ypmatch** can be used to identify NIS maps that are out of synchronization even after a map transfer has been requested or scheduled. It is often used to see if a change has "taken." Generally, building a new map pushes it to other servers, using **yppush**. However, NIS map changes may not propagate as quickly as desired. A slave server may be down when a map transfer occurs, in which case it will not get an updated map until the next **ypxfr** transfer. If you are not running the **rpc.yppasswd** daemon so that it rebuilds the NIS password map after a user's password update, you will have a window in which the NIS master's ASCII source file is out-of-date with the NIS servers' data.

Displaying and Analyzing Client Bindings

ypwhich provides information about a client's NIS domain binding, and the availability of master servers for various maps in the domain. With no arguments, it returns the name of the NIS server to which the client is currently bound by **ypbind**:

```
% ypwhich
mahimahi
```

If a hostname is passed as a parameter, then **ypwhich** queries the named host for its current binding. If **ypwhich** cannot resolve the hostname into an IP address, it reports an error:

```
% ypwhich gonzo
ypwhich: can't find gonzo
```

An IP address may be used in place of a hostname if you are debugging NIS problems, since NIS itself is used to map the hostname into an IP address. If NIS operation is not reliable, then explicit IP addresses should be used with all of the NIS-oriented debugging tools. For example:

```
% ypwhich 131.40.52.34
wahoo
```

Querying client bindings individually is useful for debugging client problems, but it doesn't provide much useful information about the use of NIS on the network. **ypwhich** is better suited for answering questions about NIS servers: Are there enough servers? Are the clients evenly distributed among the NIS servers? There is no client binding information kept by an NIS server—the binding is something created by the client and known only to the client. The server simply answers requests that are sent to it. To determine the distribution of NIS clients to servers, you must poll the clients.

ypwhich, embedded in a shell script, collects NIS client demographics to perform a "census" of server usage:

```
#! /bin/sh
#         ypcensus - poll for ypservers

( for h in `ypcat hosts | awk '{print $2}'`
  do
        ypwhich $h
  done ) | grep -v 'not bound' | sort | uniq -c
```

The **for** expression dumps the **hosts** NIS file, and **awk** extracts the second field— the hostname—from each entry. The loop then queries each host for its NIS server, and then the output from the loop is sorted. The entire loop is executed in a subshell so that its output is treated as a single stream by the next stage of the command pipeline. The **grep** command filters out error from **ypwhich**, produced when an NIS client has not found a server for its domain. At the end of the pipe, **uniq -c** counts the occurrences of each line, producing the census of NIS servers. Sample output from the script is:

```
% ypcensus
26 onaga
 7 mahimahi
 8 thud
```

You may find that the total number of bindings recorded is less than the number of clients—some clients may not have formed a server binding when the script was run. Executing **ypwhich** causes the client to bind to a server, so if you "miss" some hosts on the first attempt, execute the script again after all clients have been forced to find servers.

What does the output indicate? With multiple NIS servers, it is possible for the client distribution to load one server more heavily than the others. In the previous example, the large number of clients bound to server *onaga* could be caused by several things:

• NIS server *onaga* is significantly faster than the other NIS servers, so it always replies to **ypbind** requests before other servers.

• The servers have about the same CPU speed, so the lopsided binding indicates that *onaga* has the lightest CPU load. It generates replies faster than the other servers.

• *onaga* may be "closer" to more NIS clients on the network, counting delays in network hardware. Network topology favors NIS servers that are physically close to the client if bridges or repeaters separate clients and potential NIS servers, adding packet transmission delays that can overshadow CPU scheduling delays on loaded servers.

The few clients bound to *mahimahi* and *thud* may experience NIS timeouts if these NIS servers are heavily loaded. The relatively small number of clients bound to these servers may indicate that they aren't the best candidates for NIS service because they have a higher CPU load.

Results of the binding poll should be compared to desired goals for balancing NIS server usage. If one NIS server is much faster than the others, you may improve the NIS binding distribution by shifting the fast machine's NIS service to one or two machines that are more similar to the other NIS servers.

To see if you have enough NIS servers, or if your choice of servers provides adequate NIS service, watch for broadcasts from NIS clients to the **yserv** port. You can observe network broadcasts using a tool like Sun's **etherfind**, which watches every packet on the network and prints those that meet certain criteria. To find all RPC broadcasts, use the following **etherfind** command line:

```
# etherfind -r -broadcast -dstport sunrpc
Using interface le0
                                        icmp type
  lnth proto        source      destination   src port    dst port
  UDP from vacation.1065 to 129.151.52.0.sunrpc  120 bytes
   RPC Call portmapper  PMAPPROC_CALLIT  V2 [280c8fa9]
  UDP from vacation.1066 to 129.151.52.0.sunrpc  120 bytes
   RPC Call portmapper  PMAPPROC_CALLIT  V2 [280f0949]
```

ypbind sends its RPC broadcast to the portmapper on the *sunrpc* port (port 111), and the portmapper calls the **ypserv** process indirectly. If you see a large number of broadcast calls being made to the portmapper, then your NIS clients are rebinding frequently and you should add more NIS servers or choose servers that have a lighter load.

Other NIS Map Information

In addition to providing NIS server binding information, **ypwhich** examines the NIS map information: the master server for a map, the list of all maps, and map nickname translations. Map nicknames are more mnemonic forms of map names used in place of the actual DBM file names in NIS-related utilities; the nickname usually has the **.byaddr** or **.byname** suffix removed. Nicknames exist only within the **ypmatch**, **ypcat**, and **ypwhich** utilities; they are not part of the maps and are not part of the NIS servers. No application will ever perform a key lookup in map *passwd*; it has to use *passwd.byname* or *passwd.byuid*.

ypwhich -x prints the table of nicknames:

```
% ypwhich -x
Use "passwd" for map "passwd.byname"
Use "group" for map "group.byname"
Use "networks" for map "networks.byaddr"
Use "hosts" for map "hosts.byaddr"
Use "protocols" for map "protocols.bynumber"
Use "services" for map "services.byname"
Use "aliases" for map "mail.aliases"
Use "ethers" for map "ethers.byname"
```

While map nicknames provide a shorter command-line option for tools that take a map name as a parameter, they can also create name conflicts with non-standard maps that share commonly used map names. For example, a daemon that maps popular internal resource server names to IP ports might create an NIS map called *services* advertising its default mappings. This map name will not conflict with the NIS map created from **/etc/services** because the latter is converted into the map *services.byname*. Users of **ypcat** and **ypmatch** may be surprised by output that appears to confuse the map names.

The example below doesn't work at first because the **ypmatch** utility turns the map name *services* into *services.byname*, using the standard nickname translation. NIS completely ignores the map you want. If you use **ypmatch -t**, nickname translation is suppressed and you locate the desired map:

```
% ypmatch cullinet services
Can't match key cullinet in map services.byname.  Reason: no such key in map.
% ypmatch -t cullinet services
cullinet        6667
```

If you create your own maps, it's best to pick names that do not conflict with the standard map nicknames. Finally, **ypwhich** finds the master server for a map, or prints the list of all known maps if passed the **–m** option:

```
% ypwhich -m passwd
mahimahi

% ypwhich -m
excerpt follows
protocols.bynumber mahimahi
protocols.byname mahimahi
hosts.byname mahimahi
hosts.byaddr mahimahi
ethers.byaddr mahimahi
ethers.byname mahimahi
netgroup mahimahi
netgroup.byuser mahimahi
ypservers mahimahi
mail.aliases mahimahi
netmasks.byaddr mahimahi
```

ypwhich –m examines the NIS master server name embedded in the NIS map DBM file.

You can also explode an NIS map using **makedbm –u**, which "undoes" a DBM file. You see the data records as well as the two additional records added by DBM containing the NIS master name and the map's timestamp. If you have concerns about data disappearing from NIS maps, dump the entire map (including keys) using **makedbm –u**:

```
[wahoo]% cd /var/yp/nesales
[wahoo]% /usr/etc/yp/makedbm -u  ypservers
YP_LAST_MODIFIED 0649548751
YP_MASTER_NAME wahoo
wahoo wahoo
redsox redsox
thud thud
```

The map master information is useful if you have changed NIS master servers and need to verify that client maps are built correctly and synchronized with the new master server.

Modifying Client Bindings

The **ypset** utility forcefully changes the server binding. Its sole applications are for dissecting tangles of intertwined NIS servers, and for pointing a client at a server that is not hearing its broadcasts. The normal NIS server search is conducted by **ypbind** through a broadcast request. The first server answering the request is bound to the domain, and is probably the most lightly loaded or is closest to the requesting host. As shown in the previous **rpcinfo** examples, a server's response time, relative to other NIS servers, varies over time as its load fluctuates.

If the server's load increases so that NIS requests are not serviced before the RPC call times out on the client machine, then the client's **ypbind** daemon dissolves the current binding and rebroadcasts a request for NIS service. With varying server loads and local network traffic conditions, the timeout/rebroadcast system effects a dynamic load balancing scheme between NIS clients and servers.

ypset should not be used to implement a static load balancing scheme for two reasons:

- The initial **ypset** may implement your chosen server allocation, but poor response time from this server causes the client to break the binding and perform a broadcast-based search. This dynamic rebinding will undo the attempts to effect a preferred binding.

- Extreme disparity in NIS server usage is indicative of other network problems or of excessive server loading imposed by NFS service, interactive use, or print spooling.

There are three valid uses of **ypset**:

- Point a client at an NIS server that is isolated from it by a router or gateway that does not forward broadcast packets.

- Test the services provided by a particular server, if you have recently installed or rebuilt the maps on that server.

- Force servers to rebind to themselves instead of cross-binding.

In any of these cases, **ypset** must be used to make **ypbind** find an explicitly named server. Once **ypbind** is started, the local **/etc/hosts** file is supplanted by the NIS *hosts* map, so the server cannot be specified by hostname: **ypbind** attempts to use the very NIS service that it is having trouble starting. Instead, use an IP address as the argument to **ypset**, so that **ypbind** will not have to make any references to the *hosts* map:

```
# ypset 131.40.52.28
# ypwhich
mahimahi
```

Excerpt from /etc/rc.local
```
ypbind;     (echo -n 'ypbind') > /dev/console
/usr/etc/yp/ypset 131.40.52.28;
```

In the excerpt from **/etc/rc.local**, **ypset** is invoked with a full pathname, since the default command path setting inside of **/etc/rc.local** does not contain the /usr/etc/yp utility directory.

In some NIS implementations (SunOS 4.0 and others), **ypbind** has been made less tolerant of changing its binding via **ypset**. If the **–ypset** option is used when ypbind is started from **/etc/rc.local**, then it accepts requests to rebind to a specificed server:

```
ypbind -ypset
```

Without the **-ypset** parameter, attempts to change the server binding fail:

```
wahoo# ypset thud
ypset: Sorry, ypbind on host wahoo has rejected your request.
```

A more restrictive form is:

```
ypbind -ypsetme
```

which only allows local invocations of **ypset** to alter the binding.

NFS Tools

The tools discussed so far examine the fairly dynamic world of NIS and network configuration. NFS is a little more static in its operation: you either do or do not mount a filesystem. NFS either runs fairly well or it doesn't run at all. If NFS isn't working, it can be subject to export problems, permission problems, missing or out-of-date information, or severe performance constraints. The output of these NFS tools will serve as inputs for the performance analysis and tuning procedures in Chapter 12, *Performance Analysis and Tuning*.

Displaying Mount Information

Mount information is maintained in three files, as shown in Table 10-5.

Table 10-5. Mount Information Files

File	Host	Contents
/etc/xtab	server	Currently exported filesystems.
/etc/rmtab	server	host:directory name pairs for clients of this server.
/etc/mtab	client	Currently mounted filesystems.

An NFS server is interested in what filesystems (and directories within those filesystems) it has exported, and what clients have mounted filesystems from it. The /etc/xtab contains a list of the current exported file systems and under normal conditions, it reflects the contents of the /etc/exports file line-for-line.

The existence of /etc/exports usually determines whether or not a machine becomes an NFS server and runs the **mountd** daemon. During the boot process, it checks for this file and starts **rpc.mountd** if it is found:

```
if [ -f /etc/exports ]; then
        > /etc/xtab
        exportfs -a
        nfsd 8 &                    echo -n ' nfsd'
        rpc.mountd -n
fi
```

/etc/xtab, the dynamically managed file of exported filesystems, is truncated to zero length inside the **then** clause. Once **rpc.mountd** is running, the contents of /etc/xtab determine the mount operations that will be permitted by **mountd**.

/etc/xtab is maintained by the **exportfs** utility, so the modification time of /etc/xtab indicates the last time filesystem export information was updated. If a client is unable to mount a filesystem even though the filesystem is named in the server's /etc/exports file, verify that the filesystem appears in the server's /etc/xtab file by using **exportfs** with no arguments:

```
server% exportfs
/usr
/home/wahoo                 -root=mahimahi:thud:onaga
/var/spool/mail
```

If the **xtab** is out-of-date, then re-running **exportfs** on the server should make the filesystem available. Note that there's really no difference between **cat /etc/xtab** and **exportfs** with no arguments. Except for formatting differences, the output is the same.

When **mountd** accepts a mount request from a client, it notes the directory name passed in the mount request and the client hostname in /etc/rmtab. Entries in **rmtab** are long-lived; they remain in the file until the client performs an explicit

umount of the filesystem. This file is not purged when a server reboots because the NFS mounts themselves are persistent across server failures.

Before an NFS client shuts down, it should try to unmount its remote filesystems. Clients that mount NFS filesystems but never unmount them leave stale information in the server's **rmtab** file. When a machine boots, it usually clears out old remote mount information by performing a **umount –a** during the boot sequence, but this command only broadcasts unmount requests to servers on the local network. If you have mounted filesystems from servers on other IP networks, **umount -a** will not notify them.

In an extreme case, changing a hostname without performing a **umount –a** before taking the host down makes permanent entries in the server's **rmtab** file. Old information in **/etc/rmtab** has an annoying effect on **shutdown**, which uses the remote mount table to warn clients of the host that it is about to be rebooted. **shutdown** actually asks the **rpc.mountd** daemon for the current version of the remote mount table, but **rpc.mountd** loads its initial version of the table from the **/etc/rmtab** file. If the **rmtab** file is not accurate, then uninterested clients may be notified, or **shutdown** may attempt to find hosts which are no longer on the network. The out-of-date **rmtab** file won't cause the shut down procedure to hang, but it will produce confusing messages.

showmount is used to review server-side mount information. It has two invocations:

```
showmount -a [server]   Prints client:directory pairs for server's clients.
showmount -d [server]   Just prints directory names mounted by server's clients.
```

For example:

```
% showmount -a
bears:/var/spool/mail
bears:/home/wahoo
honeymoon:/home/wahoo
honeymoon:/var/spool/mail
131.40.52.44:/home/wahoo
131.40.52.44:/var/spool/mail

% showmount -d mahimahi
/usr
/home/mahimahi
/tools/mahimahi
```

In the first example, an unknown host, indicated by the presence of an IP address instead of a hostname, has mounted filesystems from the local host. If the IP address is valid on the local network, then the host's name and IP address are mismatched in the NIS hosts file or in the client's **/etc/hosts** file. However, this could also indicate a breach of security, particularly if the host is on another network or the host number is known to be unallocated.

Finally, the client can review its currently mounted filesystems using **df**, getting a brief look at the mount points and corresponding remote file system information:

```
df                   Shows current mount information.
df -t fstype         Looks at filesystems of type fstype only.
df directory         Locates mount point for directory.
```

For example:

```
% df -t nfs
Filesystem              kbytes      used    avail capacity  Mounted on
onaga:/home/onaga       585325    483295    43497     92%   /home/onaga
thud:/home/thud         427520    364635    20133     95%   /home/thud
mahimahi:/home/mahimahi
                        371967    265490    69280     79%   /home/mahimahi
```

When **df** is used to locate the mount point for a directory, it resolves symbolic links and determines the filesystem mounted at the link's target:

```
% ls -l /usr/local/bin
lrwxrwxrwx  1 root            16 Jun  8 14:51 /usr/local/bin -> /tools/local/bin
% df /usr/local/bin
Filesystem              kbytes      used    avail capacity  Mounted on
mahimahi:/tools/local   217871    153022    43061     78%   /tools/local
```

df may produce confusing or conflicting results in heterogeneous environments. Not all systems agree on what the bytes used and bytes available fields should represent; in most cases they are the number of user-usable bytes left on the filesystem. Other systems may include the 10% space buffer included in the filesystem, and overstate the amount of free space on the filesystem.

Detailed mount information is maintained in the **/etc/mtab** file on the local host. Along with host (or device) names and mount points, **mtab** lists the mount options used on the filesystem. **mtab** shows the current state of the system, while **/etc/fstab** only shows the filesystems to be mounted "by default." Invoking **mount** with no options prints the contents of **mtab**; supplying the **-p** option produces a listing that is suitable for inclusion in the **/etc/fstab** file:

```
% mount
/dev/id000a on / type 4.2 (rw)
/dev/id000g on /usr type 4.2 (rw)
/dev/id000h on /var type 4.2 (rw)
/dev/id001h on /home/wahoo type 4.2 (rw)
onaga:/home/onaga on /home/onaga type nfs (rw,bg,hard)
thud:/home/thud on /home/thud type nfs (rw,bg,hard)
mahimahi:/home/mahimahi on /home/mahimahi type nfs (rw,bg,hard)
```

```
% mount -p
/dev/id000a          /                  4.2 rw         1 1
/dev/id000g          /usr               4.2 rw         1 2
/dev/id000h          /var               4.2 rw         1 3
/dev/id001h          /home/wahoo        4.2 rw         1 4
onaga:/home/onaga    /home/onaga        nfs rw,bg,hard 0 0
thud:/home/thud      /home/thud         nfs rw,bg,hard 0 0
mahimahi:/home/mahimahi  /home/mahimahi nfs rw,bg,hard 0 0
```

If you have been experimenting with combinations of NFS mounts on a client, use
mount −p to "freeze" the NFS configuration. Take the output of this command
and add it to the client's **/etc/fstab** file, so that the client will perform this same
set of NFS mounts each time it boots.

NFS Statistics

The client- and server-side implementations of NFS compile per-call statistics of
NFS service usage at both the RPC and application layers. **nfsstat −c** displays the
client-side statistics while **nfsstat −s** shows the server tallies. With no arguments,
nfsstat prints out both sets of statistics.

```
% nfsstat -s
Server rpc:
calls       badcalls    nullrecv    badlen      xdrcall
13910643    0           0           0           0


Server nfs:
calls       badcalls
13910643    0
null        getattr     setattr    root        lookup       readlink    read
7774  0%    2140751 15% 38289  0%  0   0%      2303449 16%  503057  3%  4743967 34%
wrcache     write       create     remove      rename       link        symlink
0   0%      3569183 25% 191783  1% 100826  0%  19419   0%   797  0%     379  0%
mkdir       rmdir       readdir    fsstat
4960  0%    4940  0%    258096  1% 22973   0%
```

The server-side RPC fields indicate if the server is receiving packets that are damaged in transit, or if there are problems removing the packets from the NFS service socket. The fields detail each kind of problem:

calls   Total number of NFS RPC calls made to this server, from all cli-
              ents. RPC calls made for other services, such as NIS, are not
              included in this count.

badcalls   RPC requests that were rejected out of hand by the server's RPC
              mechanism, before the request was passed to the NFS service
              routines in the kernel. An RPC call will be rejected if there is an
              authentication failure, where the calling client does not present
              valid credentials. Similarly, badcalls is incremented if *root* on a

client attempts to perform write or modification operations on a filesystem that is not exported with *root* permissions enabled.

nullrecv   The nullrecv field is incremented whenever an **nfsd** daemon is scheduled to run but finds that there is no packet on the NFS service socket queue. If the server is running an excessive number of **nfsd** daemons, it is possible that there will be more runnable daemons than requests to drain from the NFS socket, so some daemons wake up but do not receive any data.

badlen/xdrcall   The RPC request received by the server was too short (badlen) or the XDR headers in the packet are malformed (xdrcall). It is possible that the packet was truncated or damaged by a network problem. On a local area network, it's rare to have XDR headers damaged, but running NFS over a wide-area network could result in malformed requests. We'll look at ways of detecting and correcting packet damage on wide-area networks in "NFS Over Wide-area Networks," in Chapter 12, *Performance Analysis and Tuning.*

The NFS statistics show the total number of NFS calls made to this server, and they show a breakdown by procedure of those calls handled. Each of the call types corresponds to a procedure within the NFS RPC service; mappings between UNIX system calls and utilities and the NFS RPC requests they generate are presented in Appendix D, *NFS Benchmarks.*

The null procedure is included in every RPC program for **ping**ing the RPC server. The null procedure returns no value, but a successful return from a call to *null* ensures that the network is operational and that the server host is alive. **rpcinfo** calls the null procedure to check RPC server health, and the automounter (see Chapter 13, *The Automounter*) calls the null procedure of all NFS servers in parallel when multiple machines are listed for a single mount point. The automounter or **rpcinfo** should account for the total *null* calls reported by **nfsstat.**

Client-side NFS statistics include the number of calls of each type made to all servers, while the client RPC statistics indicate how successful the client machine is in reaching NFS servers:

```
% nfsstat -c
Client rpc:
calls       badcalls    retrans     badxid      timeout     wait      newcred
2534514     304         1109        49          1410        0         0

Client nfs:
calls       badcalls    nclget      nclsleep
2533982     0           2533982     0
null        getattr     setattr     root        lookup      readlink   read
0   0%      1197622 47% 222   0%    0   0%      64115   2%  28280   1%  60533   2%
```

wrcache	write	create	remove	rename	link	symlink
0 0%	596932 23%	568178 22%	5407 0%	138 0%	199 0%	13 0%

mkdir	rmdir	readdir	fsstat
2 0%	1 0%	11905 0%	435 0%

In addition to the total number of NFS calls made and the number of rejected NFS calls (badcalls), the client-side statistics indicate if NFS calls are being delayed due to a lack of client RPC handles. Client handles are opaque pointers used by the kernel to hold server connection information. The kernel creates a fixed number of client handles and uses them for each NFS operation. The *nclget* count shows how many times the client had to request a new client handle for an NFS call, and *nclsleep* is the number of times an NFS call was blocked because no client handle was available.

Ideally, *nclsleep* should always be zero. In early implementations of NFS, the number of client handles was fixed; in more recent implementations the client handles are allocated on demand. If client-side calls are blocked on a shortage of client RPC handles, increase the number of client handles (usually a kernel parameter in the **param.c** file).

Included in the client RPC statistics are counts for various failures experienced while trying to send NFS requests to a server:

calls   Total number of calls made to all NFS servers.

badcalls   Number of RPC calls that returned an error. The two most common RPC failures are timeouts and interruptions, both of which increment the *badcalls* counter. If a server reply is not received within the RPC timeout period, an RPC error occurs. If the RPC call is interrupted, as it may be if a filesystem is mounted with the **intr** option, then an RPC interrupt code is returned to the caller. **nfsstat** also reports the *badcalls* count in the NFS statistics. NFS call failures do not include RPC timeouts or interruptions, but do include other RPC failures such as authentication errors (which will be counted in both the NFS and RPC level statistics).

retrans   Number of calls that were retransmitted because no response was received from the NFS server within the timeout period. An NFS client that is experiencing poor server response will have a large number of retransmitted calls.

timeout   Number of calls that timed out waiting for a server response. For hard-mounted filesystems, calls that time out are retransmitted, with a new timeout period that is longer than the previous one. Calculation of timeout periods is explained in detail in "Timeout Calculations." However, calls made on soft-mounted filesystems may eventually fail if the retransmission count is exceeded, so that the call counts obey the relationship:

```
timeout + badcalls >= retrans
```

The final retransmission of a request on a soft-mounted filesystem increments *badcalls* (as previously explained). For example, if a filesystem is mounted with **retrans=5**, the client re-issues the same request five times before noting an RPC failure. All five requests are counted in *timeout*, since no replies are received. Of the failed attempts, four are counted in the *retrans* statistic and the last shows up in *badcalls*.

badxid   The XID in an NFS request is a monotonically increasing serial number that uniquely identifies the request. When a request is retransmitted, it retains the same XID through the entire timeout and retransmission cycle. With multiple **biod** processes, it is possible for the NFS client to have several RPC requests outstanding at any time, to any number of NFS servers. When a response is received from an NFS server, the client matches the XID in the response to an RPC call in progress. If an XID is seen for which there is no active RPC call—because the client already received a response for that XID—then the client increments badxid. A high badxid count, therefore, indicates that the server is receiving some retransmitted requests, but is taking a long time to reply to all NFS requests. This scenario is explored in "Slow Server Compensation," in Chapter 12, *Performance Analysis and Tuning*.

wait   Number of calls that had to wait on a busy client handle.

newcred   Number of times client authentication information had to be refreshed. This statistic only applies if a secure RPC mechanism has been integrated with the NFS service. If your vendor does not support Secure RPC, then the *newcred* field will always be zero or may not appear in the output of **nfsstat**.

NFS server implementations that utilize a duplicate request cache for requests do not reflect the total number of retransmitted calls handled by the server. This duplicate request cache notes the XID of transactions currently being serviced by the **nfsd** daemons. If a request arrives with an XID matching one in the cache, it is ignored. The client will have counted the retransmission in its statistics, but it does not receive a reply that would increment the *badxid* as well. Note that the duplicate request cache only condenses duplicates of calls currently in progress; if the reply is already on its way back to the client when a duplicate request arrives, the server actually performs the same operation twice. The net effect of the duplicate request cache is that the client's *badxid* count is smaller.* The statistics shown by **nfsstat** are cumulative from the time the machine was booted, or the last time they were zeroed using **nfsstat –z**:

nfsstat –cz	*Zeros client-side RPC and NFS statistics.*
nfsstat –sz	*Zeros server-side RPC and NFS statistics.*
nfsstat –z	*Resets all counters.*
nfsstat –crz	*Zeros client-side RPC statistics only.*

Only the superuser can reset the counters.

nfsstat provides a very coarse look at NFS activity, and it is limited in its usefulness for resolving performance problems. Server statistics are collected for all clients, while in many cases it is important to know the distribution of calls from each client to determine which client is imposing the greatest load on the server. Similarly, client-side statistics are aggregated for all NFS servers.

However, you can still glean useful information from **nfsstat**. Consider the client-side example above. From the relative call counts and RPC statistics, there are several noteworthy observations to be made about the client's activity during the period measured:

- *write* and *create* are nearly equal, and together they account for a significant percentage of all NFS calls. The client machine was creating large numbers of small files; the small difference between *write* and *create* implies that each file creation was followed by one file write, making the total size of each file less than 8 kbytes (the default NFS packet write size).

- *remove* is much smaller than *create*, so the files created either still exist (and are filling up the filesystem), or were short-lived temporary files that were continually overwritten.

---

*SunOS 4.1 also has dynamic NFS buffer resizing that affects the **rsize** and **wsize** used for NFS mounts that traverse gateways. The dynamic resizing code only comes into play when the client and server are on different networks, and a gateway or router forwarding the NFS packets is dropping some number of the fragments. To effect the dynamic resizing, an RPC call that times out is divided into two RPC calls of a smaller size, each with new XIDs. Because of this tacit retransmission scheme, the **retrans** count in the client-side statistics is much less accurate when NFS mounts occur through gateways.

- The RPC timeouts and retransmissions could have been caused by the large number of write operations, if the server was unable to complete the writes during the RPC timeout period.

Because there is no time history associated with the counts, it is hard to pinpoint the client machine activity that caused this burst of file creation. If the files were indeed temporary files, moving them out of the NFS-mounted directory and into /tmp would greatly decrease the load on the NFS server handling these requests if /tmp is on a local filesystem. Similarly, if the writes are in fact the cause of the retransmissions, using a local filesystem will improve performance even more. Analysis of situations such as this one will be the focus of Chapter 12, *Performance Analysis and Tuning*.

Time Synchronization

Distributing files across several servers introduces a dependency on synchronized time of day clocks on these machines and their clients. Consider the following sequence of events:

```
barney % date
Fri Jun 15 10:02:58 1990
barney % pwd
/home/stern
barney % touch foo
barney % ls -l foo
-rw-rw-r--  1 stern          0 Jun 15 10:03 foo

fred % date
Fri Jun 15 09:00:00 EDT 1990
fred % pwd
/home/stern
fred % ls -l foo
-rw-rw-r--  1 stern          0 Jun 15  1990 foo

fred % su
fred # rdate barney
Fri Jun 15 10:04:28 1990
fred % ls -l foo
-rw-rw-r--  1 stern          0 Jun 15 10:03 foo
```

On host *fred*, a file is created that is stamped with the current time. Over on host *barney*, the time of day clock is over an hour behind, and file *foo* is listed with the month-day-year date format normally reserved for files that are more than six months old. The problem stems from the time skew between *barney* and *fred*: when the ls process on *barney* tries to determine the age of file *foo*, it subtracts the file modification time from the current time. Under normal circumstances, this produces a positive integer, but with *fred*'s clock an hour ahead of the local clock, the difference between modification time and current time is a negative number. This makes file *foo* a veritable UNIX artifact, created before the dawn of UNIX time. As such, its modification time is shown with the "old file" format.*

Time of day clock drift can be caused by repeated bursts of high priority interrupts that interfere with the system's hardware clock or by powering off (and subsequently booting) a system that does not have a battery-operated time of day clock.†

In addition to confusing users, time skew wreaks havoc with the timestamps used by **make**, jobs run out of **cron** that depend on **cron**-started processes on other hosts, and the transfer of NIS maps to slave servers, which fail if the slave server's time is far enough ahead of the master server. It is essential to keep all hosts sharing filesystems or NIS maps synchronized to within a few seconds.

rdate synchronizes the time of day clocks on two hosts to within a one-second granularity. Because it changes the local time and date, **rdate** can only be used by the superuser, just as the **date** utility can only be used by **root** to explicitly set the local time. **rdate** takes the name of the remote time source as an argument:

```
% rdate mahimahi
couldn't set time of day: Not owner
% su
# rdate mahimahi
Sun Jul 15 11:57:22 1990
```

One host is usually selected as the master timekeeper, and all other hosts synchronize to its time at regular intervals. The ideal choice for a timekeeping host is one that has the minimum amount of time drift, or that is connected to a network providing time services. If the time host's clock loses a few seconds each day, the entire network will fall behind the real wall clock time. All hosts agree on the current time, but this time slowly drifts further and further behind the real time.

---

*Some UNIX utilities were modified to handle small time skews in a graceful manner. ls tolerates clock drifts of a few minutes, and correctly displays file modification times that are slightly in the future. Similarly, **ranlib** parses a library file with a post-dated table of contents.

† The hardware clock, or "hardclock" is a regular, crystal-driven timer that provides the system heartbeat. In kernel parlance, the hardclock timer interval is a "tick," a basic unit of time-slicing that governs CPU scheduling, process priority calculation, and software timers. The software time of day clock is driven by the hardclock. If the hardclock interrupts at 100 Hz, then every 100 hardclock interrupts bump the current time of day clock by one second. When a hardclock interrupt is missed, the software clock begins to lose time. If there is a hardware time of day clock available, the kernel can compensate for missed hardclock interrupts by checking the system time against the hardware time of day clock and adjusting for any drift. If there is no time of day clock, missed hardware clock interrupts translate into a tardy system clock.

While the remote host may be explicitly specified, it is more convenient to create the hostname alias *timehost* in the NIS hosts file and to use the alias in all invocations of **rdate**:

```
131.40.52.28    mahimahi timehost
131.40.52.26    wahoo
131.40.52.150   kfir
```

Some systems check for the existence of the hostname *timehost* during the boot sequence, and perform an **rdate timehost** if *timehost* is found.

This convention is particularly useful if you are establishing a new timekeeping host and you need to change its definition if your initial choice proves to be a poor time standard. It is far simpler to change the definition of *timehost* in the NIS hosts map than it is to modify the invocations of **rdate** on all hosts.

Time synchronization may be performed during the boot sequence, in **/etc/rc.local**, and at regular intervals using **cron**. The interval chosen for time synchronization depends on how badly each system's clock drifts: once-a-day updates may be sufficient if the drift is only a few seconds a day, but hourly synchronization is required if a system loses time each hour. To run **rdate** from **cron**, add a line like the following to each host's **crontab** file:

Hourly update:
```
52 * * * * rdate timehost > /dev/null 2>&1
```

Daily update:
```
52 1 * * * rdate timehost > /dev/null 2>&1
```

The redirection of the standard output and standard error forces **rdate**'s output to **/dev/null**, suppressing the normal echo of the updated time. If a **cron**-driven command writes to standard output or standard error, **cron** will mail the output to **root**.

To avoid swamping the *timehost* with dozens of simultaneous **rdate** requests, the previous example performs its **rdate** at a random offset into the hour. A common convention is to use the last octet of the machine's IP address (mod 60) as the offset into the hour, effectively scattering the **rdate** requests throughout each hour.

The use of **rdate** ensures a gross synchronization accurate to within a second or two on the network. The resolution of this approach is limited by the **rdate** and **cron** utilities, both of which are accurate to one second. This is sufficient for many activities, but finer synchronization—with a resolution in the millisecond range—may be needed. The Network Time Protocol (NTP) provides fine-grain time synchronization, and also keeps wide-area networks in lock step. On a local area network, the Berkeley **timed** daemon can be used to replace regular calls to **rdate**. Both time synchronization methods are outside the scope of this book.

11

Debugging Network Problems

Duplicate ARP Replies
Renegade NIS Server
Boot Parameter Confusion
Interpreting NFS Error Messages

This chapter consists of case studies in network problem analysis and debugging, ranging from physical cabling problems to a machine posing as an NIS server in the wrong domain. This chapter is a bridge between the formal discussion of NFS and NIS tools and their use in performance analysis and tuning. The case studies presented here walk through debugging scenarios, but should give you an idea of how the various tools work together.

When debugging a network problem, it's important to think about the potential cause of a problem, and use that to start ruling out other factors. For example, if your attempts to bind to an NIS server are failing, you should know that you could try testing the network using **ping**; the health of **ypserv** processes using **rpcinfo**, and finally the binding itself with **ypset**. Working your way through the protocol layers ensures that you don't miss a low-level problem that is posing as a higher-level failure. Keeping with that advice, we'll start by looking at a network layer problem.

Improper Network Termination

In the network configuration shown in Figure 11-1, the PCs on the Novell LAN can telnet to the workstation on the far end of the thinnet Ethernet, but not to the workstation that is physically closest to the Novell TCP/IP gateway machine.

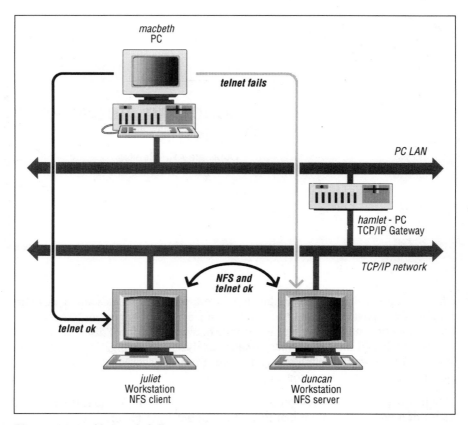

Figure 11-1. Network failures across a gateway

Selective connectivity, or connectivity that is intermittent on a per-machine basis, usually indicates a problem with the physical cabling or termination of the network. As confirmation, we used **ping** on *juliet* to note the packet transit times to *duncan*. The machines were adjacent to each other on the network so we expected to see times in the zero millisecond range.

Instead, ICMP replies were received with delays ranging up to 20 milliseconds, and some packets never made it back to *juliet*:

```
juliet% ping -s duncan
PING duncan: 56 data bytes
64 bytes from vacation (192.9.200.2): icmp_seq=0. time=10. ms
64 bytes from vacation (192.9.200.2): icmp_seq=1. time=20. ms
64 bytes from vacation (192.9.200.2): icmp_seq=4. time=53. ms
64 bytes from vacation (192.9.200.2): icmp_seq=5. time=8. ms
^C
----duncan PING Statistics----
5 packets transmitted, 4 packets received, 20% packet loss
round-trip (ms)  min/avg/max = 10/18/53
```

To isolate the fault, we replaced the thinnet segment joining *duncan* and *hamlet* with a terminating resistor, creating a smaller, disjoint network with just the two workstations on it. Again using **ping** to test the network's health, packet transit times between the two hosts dropped to zero milliseconds. The fault was somewhere in the cabling and transceivers joining the Novell gateway and *duncan*. Following the cable back to the Novell server lead us to an unterminated segment; the thinnet cable joining *duncan* and *hamlet* had been connected directly to the latter's BNC connector without a T-connector and a terminating resistor.

Why then, with an electrical fault on the thinnet network, were PCs on the Novell side able to reach *juliet*, and how were the two workstations able to run NFS between them? Signals propagating from the unterminated end toward *juliet* did not suffer too badly from the missing termination, since they saw a fairly long thinnet segment with proper termination in front of them. The issue lies with signals going from the terminated end of the thinnet segment toward the Novell gateway, which were being reflected back along the thinnet segment toward the transmitter, creating electrical interference on the network.

A proper explanation of signal reflection requires differential equations and a large dose of electrical engineering theory. The body of knowledge concerning the behavior of electrical signals over long paths is *transmission line theory*, and a fairly detailed explanation of this phenomenon is in Appendix A, "Transmission Line Theory." The following real world model illustrates the salient points sufficiently.

Imagine you are throwing a rubber ball to a friend who is standing in front of a brick wall. Your friend plays the role of a terminating resistor: his or her job is to catch the ball and keep it from bouncing back to you. Terminating resistors "catch" the electrical signals on the network, preventing them from traveling back down the signal path from which they originated. If your friend doesn't catch the ball, it bounces off of the wall, the same way an electrical signal bounces off of the unterminated endpoint of a network segment.

If you are close to the wall, the ball may return to you at knee or waist height. The further you get from the wall, the less likely it is that the ball bounces back to you; you also hear less of a sound from the ball's rebound. At some sufficiently long distance, the ball never comes back to you, and you cannot tell (from sound alone) whether it was caught. In the network problem, *juliet* was sufficiently far from the point of reflection to not be bothered by it, although the interference on the network did impact its connectivity with an adjacent machine. *duncan*, on the other hand, was close to the point of signal reflection and was unable to have its packets cleanly received by the gateway.

Had we looked at the network with an analyzer or oscilloscope, we would have seen "ringing" before the extra terminator was added. The network configurations are shown in Figure 11-2 in a "before" and "after" state.

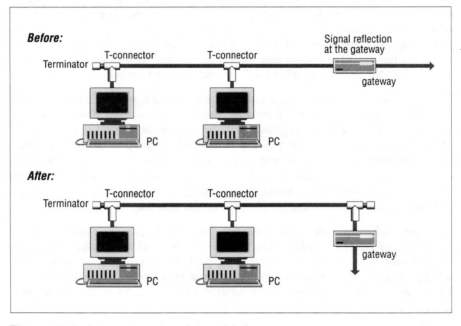

Figure 11-2. Improper network termination

A similar problem exhibited much stranger symptoms. In this case, several PCs were joined to a thinnet backbone through a multiport transceiver, and on the backbone segment were two UNIX machines, as shown in Figure 11-3.

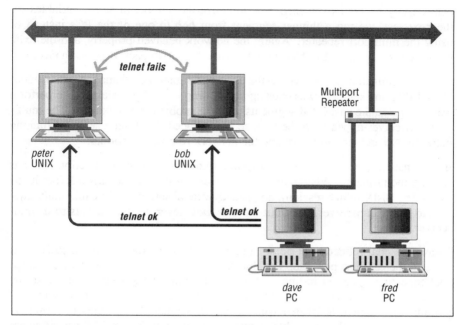

Figure 11-3. Network failures across a repeater

Either PC could **telnet** to either UNIX node without any problems but the UNIX nodes could not exchange packets regularly. Occasionally, **telnet** sessions between *peter* and *bob* would be closed with notification that the connection had been terminated by the remote host. After examining situations in which a tenuous connection could be made versus those in which the UNIX machines would not communicate at all, it was found that the *peter-bob* connection was possible only when a PC user had used **telnet** to reach one of the UNIX machines.

Things appeared to function properly when the PC users were working; they never reported any problems. When there was no PC activity, the network broke. When debugging a problem that is activity dependent, it's helpful to identify actions or loads that make the problem noticeably better or worse. Noticing that the level of PC activity seemed to affect the problem, we researched combinations of machines that made the problem worst.

On *peter*, **ping –s bob** returned a few packets, followed by a long period during which no ICMP echo replies were received. When the next burst of packets was received, the sequence numbers indicated that about 100 packets had been lost. The next step in resolving this problem was again to split the network near the suspected point of failure, and to isolate the machines exhibiting the connectivity failures. We put *peter* and *bob* on their own thinnet segment, and their connectivity problems vanished. To minimize the number of added variables for the next test, we ran a thinnet segment from *bob* to one of the PCs instead of using the multiport repeater. Again, the network behaved properly, and the existence or absence of a PC-UNIX **telnet** session had no impact on performance.

We had eliminated places where the Ethernet signal was damaged, so we concluded that one segment was causing signal drop out. The easiest test to perform was to replace the suspected segments until the problem was resolved. The multiport transceiver appeared to be fine, so we replaced the thinnet segment running between *bob* and the multiport, and the network returned to normal.

In this instance, it was a signal absorption, rather than a signal reflection that was causing the problem. When many packets were present on the network (produced by the PC-UNIX **telnet** session), no packets were absorbed at the cable fault adjacent to *bob*'s transceiver. Without the bias, *bob* never got the packets to its transceiver.

To avoid signal reflection at points along the Ethernet coax, keep transceivers as close to the cable as possible. For thicknet, the transceiver either screws into the backbone or is inserted in-line with the cable; thinnet transceivers attach to the network via a T-connector that accomplishes the same goal. A different kind of termination problem is created when a thinnet segment is extended to form a T- or Y-shape. The following cable arrangement shown in Figure 11-4 causes signal reflection at the T-connector and is an invalid configuration.

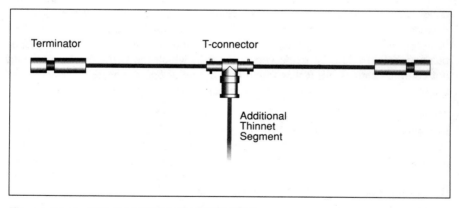

Figure 11-4. Improper thinnet termination

Instead of seeing something like a flat brick wall, the electrical signals on the coax see this configuration as the corner of a building. There is still some reflection, although the amplitude of the reflected signal and of the signals split along the two paths will be determined by the relative lengths and loads on the cable segments. The symptoms of this problem are similar to those of other termination problems.

Some general cabling rules when using thinnet:

- Thinnet Ethernet segments should not exceed 185 meters in length, and should have less than 30 nodes on them.

- Ensure that there is exactly one linear signal path from termination point to termination point. No T- or Y-shaped circuits with more than two termination points are permitted.

- Attach T-connectors on the thinnet directly to the BNC connectors on hosts; don't insert a thinnet segment as a "drop cable." The extension of the T-connector appears as a T-shaped circuit on the thinnet and causes signal reflection at this point.

- Always terminate the endpoint of a thinnet segment with a T-connector and terminating resistor. The exception to this rule is a multiport thinnet repeater/fanout unit, which is internally terminated. When running cables from a fanout, the thinnet segment attaches directly to the BNC connector without a T-connector and terminator.

Similar guidelines exist for thicknet cabling:

- Constrain thicknet backbones to 500 meters or 100 nodes.

- Ensure that both ends of the backbone are terminated with the proper value resistor.

- Keep transceiver taps spaced at multiples of 2.5 meters to minimize signal reflection from taps. Look for the black marks on the cable, which properly space out the transceivers. The 2.5 meter spacing is a product of various Ethernet electrical properties.

- Watch out for multiple grounds on the network. If you are using vampire taps with metal cases, and the cases rest against a metal ceiling support, it's possible that you will ground the network in two places through the ceiling framework.

Duplicate ARP Replies

ARP misinformation was briefly mentioned in "IP to MAC Address Mappings," in Chapter 10, *Diagnostic and Administrative Tools*, and this story showcases some of the baffling effects it creates. A network of two servers and ten clients suddenly began to run very slowly, with the following symptoms:

- Some users attempting to start Interleaf, a document processing application, were waiting 10 to 30 *minutes* for the application's window to appear, while those on well behaved machines waited a few seconds. The Interleaf executables resided on a file server and were NFS mounted on each client. Every machine in the group experienced these delays over a period of a few days, although not all at the same time.

- Machines would suddenly "go away" for several minutes. Clients would stop seeing their NFS and NIS servers, producing streams of messages like:

      NFS server muskrat not responding, still trying

  or:

      ypbind: no server for domain techpubs

The local area network with the problems was joined to the campus-wide backbone via a bridge. An identical network of machines, running the same applications with nearly the same configuration, was operating without problems on the far side of the bridge. We were assured of the health of the physical network by two engineers who had verified all termination and cable routing.

The very sporadic nature of the problem—and the fact that it resolved itself over time—pointed toward a problem with ARP request and reply mismatches. This hypothesis neatly explained the extraordinarily slow loading of Interleaf: a client machine trying to read the Interleaf executable would issue an NFS request. To send the UDP packet, the client would ARP the server, randomly get the wrong reply, and then be unable to use that entry for several minutes. When the ARP table entry had aged and was deleted, the client would again ARP the server; if the correct ARP response was received then the client could continue reading pages of the executable. Every wrong reply received by the client would add a few minutes to the loading time.

There were several possible sources of the ARP confusion, so to isolate the problem, we forced a client to ARP the server and watched what happened to the ARP table:

```
# arp -d muskrat
muskrat (139.50.2.1) deleted
# ping -s muskrat
PING muskrat: 56 data bytes
No further output from ping
```

By deleting the ARP table entry and then directing the client to send packets to *muskrat*, we forced an ARP of *muskrat* from the client. **ping** timed out without receiving any ICMP echo replies, so we examined the ARP table and found a surprise:

```
# arp -a | fgrep muskrat
muskrat (139.50.2.1) at 8:0:49:5:2:a9
```

Since *muskrat* was a Sun workstation, we expected its Ethernet address to begin with 8:0:20 (the prefix assigned to Sun Microsystems), not the 8:0:49 prefix used by Kinetics gateway boxes. The next step was to figure out how the wrong Ethernet address was ending up in the ARP table: was *muskrat* lying in its ARP replies, or had we found a network imposter?

Using a network analyzer, we repeated the ARP experiment and watched ARP replies returned. We saw two distinct replies: the correct one from *muskrat*, followed by an invalid reply from the Kinetics FastPath gateway. The root of this problem was that the Kinetics box had been configured using the IP broadcast address **0.0.0.0**, allowing it to answer all ARP requests. Reconfiguring the Kinetics box with a non-broadcast IP address solved the problem.

The last update to the ARP table is the one that "sticks," so the wrong Ethernet address was overwriting the correct ARP table entry. The Kinetics FastPath was located on the other side of the bridge, virtually guaranteeing that its replies would be the last to arrive, delayed by their transit over the bridge. When *muskrat* was heavily loaded, it was slow to reply to the ARP request and its ARP response would be the last to arrive. Reconfiguring the Kinetics FastPath to use a proper IP address and network mask cured the problem.

ARP servers that have out-of-date information create similar problems. This situation arises if an IP address is changed without a corresponding update of the server's published ARP table initialization, or if the IP address in question is re-assigned to a machine that implements the ARP protocol. If an ARP server was employed because *muskrat* could not answer ARP requests, then we should have seen exactly one ARP reply, coming from the ARP server. However, an ARP server with a published ARP table entry for a machine capable of answering its own ARP requests produces exactly the same duplicate response symptoms described above. With both machines on the same local network, the failures tend to be more intermittent, since there is no obvious time-ordering of the replies.

There's a moral to this story: you should rarely need to know the Ethernet address of a workstation, but it does help to have them recorded in a file or NIS map. This problem was solved with a bit of luck, because the machine generating incorrect replies had a different manufacturer, and therefore a different Ethernet address prefix. If the incorrectly configured machine had been from the same vendor, we would have had to compare the Ethernet addresses in the ARP table with what we believed to the correct addresses for the machine in question.

Renegade NIS Server

A user on our network reported that he could not log into his workstation. He supplied his username and the same password he'd been using for the past six months, and he consistently was told "Login incorrect." Out of frustration, he rebooted his machine. When attempting to mount NFS filesystems, the workstation was not able to find any of the NFS server hosts in the *hosts* NIS map, producing errors of the form:

```
mount: wahoo:/home/wahoo: RPC: Unknown host
mount: giving up on:
       /home/wahoo
```

There were no error messages from **ypbind**, so it appeared that the workstation had found an NIS server. The culprit looked like the NIS server itself: our guess was that it was a machine masquerading as a valid NIS server, or that it was an NIS server whose maps had been destroyed. Because nobody could log into the machine, we rebooted it in single-user mode, and manually started NIS to see where it bound:

```
Single-user boot
# domainname nesales
# ypbind
# ypwhich
131.40.52.25
```

ypwhich was not able to match the IP address of the NIS server in the **hosts** NIS map, so it printed the IP address. The IP address belonged to a gateway machine that was not supposed to be a slave (or master) NIS server. It made sense that clients were binding to it, if it was posing as an NIS server, since the gateway was very lightly loaded and was probably the first NIS server to respond to **ypbind** requests.

We logged into that machine, and verified that it was running **ypserv**. The domain name used by the gateway was *nesales*—it had been brought up in the wrong domain. Removing the **/var/yp/nesales** subdirectory containing the NIS maps took the machine out of service:

```
# cd /var/yp
# rm -rf nesales
```
Kill and restart ypserv

We contacted the person responsible for the gateway and had him put the gateway in its own NIS domain (his original intention). Machines in *nesales* that had bound to the renegade server eventually noticed that their NIS server had gone away, and they rebound to valid servers.

As a variation on this problem, consider an NIS server that has damaged or incomplete maps. Symptoms of this problem are nearly identical to those previously described, but the IP address printed by **ypwhich** will be that of a familiar NIS server. There may be just a few maps that are damaged, possibly corrupted during an NIS transfer operation, or all of the server's maps may be corrupted or lost. The latter is most probable when someone accidentally removes directories in **/var/yp**.

To check the consistency of various maps, use **ypcat** to dump all of the keys known to the server. A few damaged maps can be replaced with explicit **yppush** operations on the master server. If all of the server's maps are damaged, it is easiest to re-initialize the server. Slave servers are easily rebuilt from a valid master server, but if the master server has lost the DBM files containing the maps, initializing the machine as an NIS master server regenerates only the default set of maps. Before rebuilding the NIS master, save the NIS **Makefile**, in **/var/yp** or **/etc/yp**, if you have made local changes to it. The initialization process builds the default maps, after which you can replace your hand-crafted **Makefile** and build all site-specific NIS maps.

Boot Parameter Confusion

Different vendors do not always agree on the format of responses to various broadcast requests. Great variation exists in the **bootparam** RPC service, which supplies diskless nodes with the name of their boot server, and pathnames for their root and swap partitions. If a diskless client's request for boot parameters returns a packet that it cannot understand, the client produces a rather cryptic error message and then aborts the boot process.

As an example, we saw the following strange behavior when a diskless Sun 3/50 attempted to boot. The machine would request its Internet address using RARP, and receive the correct reply from its boot server. It then downloaded the boot code using **tftp**, and sent out a request for boot parameters. At this point, the boot sequence would abort with one of the errors:

```
null domain name
invalid reply
```

Emulating the request for boot parameters using **rpcinfo** located the source of the invalid reply quickly. Using a machine close to the diskless node, we sent out a request similar to that broadcast during the boot sequence, looking for **boot-param** servers:

```
% rpcinfo -b bootparam 1
192.9.200.14 clover
192.9.200.1 lucy
192.9.200.4 bugs
```

lucy and *bugs* were boot and root/swap servers for diskless clients, but *clover* was a machine from a different vendor. It should not have been interested in the request for boot parameters. However, *clover* was running **rpc.bootparamd**, which made it listen for boot parameter requests, and it used the NIS *bootparams* map to glean the boot information. Unfortunately, the format of its reply was not digestible by the diskless Sun node, but its reply was the first to arrive. In this case, the solution merely involved turning off **rpc.bootparamd** by commenting it out of the startup script on *clover*.

If *clover* supported diskless clients of its own, turning off **rpc.bootparamd** would not have been an acceptable solution. To continue running **rpc.bootparamd** on *clover*, we would have had to ensure that it never sent a reply to diskless clients other than its own. The easiest way to do this is to give *clover* a short list of clients to serve, and to keep *clover* from using the *bootparams* NIS map. Removing the plus sign from the **/etc/bootparams** file on *clover* would solve the problem.

Interpreting NFS Error Messages

This final section provides an in-depth look at how an NFS client does write-behind, and what happens if one of the write operations fails on the remote server. It is intended as an introduction to the more complex issues of performance analysis and tuning, many of which revolve around similar subtleties in the implementation of NFS.

When an application calls *read()* or *write()* on a local, or UNIX file system (UFS) file, the kernel uses inode and indirect block pointers to translate the offset in the file into a physical block number on the disk. A low-level physical I/O operation, such as "write this buffer of 1024 bytes to physical blocks 5678 and 5679" is then passed to the disk device driver. The actual disk operation is scheduled, and when the disk interrupts, the driver interrupt routine notes the completion of the current operation and schedules the next. The block device driver queues the requests for the disk, possibly re-ordering them to minimize disk head movement.

Once the disk device driver has a read or write request, only a media failure causes the operation to return an error status. Any other failures, such as a permission problem, or the filesystem running out of space, are detected by the filesystem management routines before the disk driver gets the request. From the point of view of the *read()* and *write()* system calls, everything from the filesystem write routine down is a black box: the application isn't necessarily concerned with how the data makes it onto or from the disk, as long as it does so reliably. The actual write operation occurs asynchronously to the application calling *write()*. If a media error occurs—for example, the disk has a bad sector brewing—then the media-level error will be reported back to the application during the next *write()* call or during the *close()* of the file containing the bad block. When the driver notices the error returned by the disk controller, it prints a media failure message on the console.

A similar mechanism is used by NFS to report errors on the "virtual media" of the remote file server. When *write()* is called on an NFS-mounted file, the data buffer and offset into the file are handed to the NFS write routine, just as a UFS write calls the lower-level disk driver write routine. Like the disk device driver, NFS has a driver routine for scheduling write requests: each new request is put into the local buffer or page cache. When a full buffer or page has been written, it is handed to a block I/O daemon, or **biod** daemon, that performs the RPC call to the remote server and returns a result code. Once the request has been written into the local cache, though, the *write()* system call returns to the application—just as if the application was writing to a local disk. The actual NFS write is synchronous to the **biod** process, allowing the block I/O daemons to perform write-behind. A similar process occurs for reads, where **biod** performs some read-ahead by fetching NFS buffers in anticipation of future *read()* system calls. See "Server nfsd Daemons," in Chapter 6, *Network Filesystem Design and Operation*, for details on the operation of the block I/O daemon.

Occasionally, a **biod** daemon detects an error when attempting to write to a remote server, and the error is printed (by **biod**) on the client's console. The scenario is identical to that of a failing disk: the *write()* system call has already returned, so the error must be reported on the console and in the next similar system call.

The format of these error messages is:

```
NFS write error 13 on host mahimahi fh 27b26ff7
```

The error number reported is what is found in **errno**, the error return variable set by system calls. To decipher the error number, refer to **/usr/include/sys/errno.h**. Error numbers in the messages and in the header file are in decimal; the file handle is in hexadecimal.

The number of potential failures when writing to an NFS-mounted disk exceed the few media-related errors that would cause a UFS write to fail. Table 11-1 gives some examples.

Table 11-1. NFS-related Errno Values

errno	Error	Typical Cause
13	Permission Denied	Superuser cannot write to remote filesystem.
28	No Space	Remote disk is full.
70	Stale File Handle	Open file or directory destroyed and recreated.

Both the "Permission Denied" and the "No Space" errors would have been detected on a local filesystem, but the NFS client has no way to determine if a write operation will succeed at some future time (when the **biod** process eventually sends it to the server). For example, if a client writes out 1-kbyte buffers, then its NFS **biod** daemons write out 8-kbyte buffers to the server on every eighth call to *write()*. Several seconds may go by between the time the first *write()* system call returns to the application and the time that the eighth call forces **biod** to perform an RPC to the NFS server. In this interval, another process may have filled up the server's disk with some huge write requests, so **biod**'s attempt to write its 8-kbyte buffer will fail.

If you are consistently seeing NFS writes fail due to full filesystems or permission problems, you can usually chase down the user or process that is performing the writes by identifying the file being written. In SunOS 4.1, the **showfh** utility correlates the file handles printed by **biod** with the pathname of the file on the remote server.

To use **showfh**, you must start the RPC server daemon **rpc.showfhd** on the server:

```
mahimahi# rpc.showfhd
```

On the client showing the NFS write errors, use **showfh** with the remote server's name and the file handle from the error message to see the full pathname of the file on the server:

```
client% showfh mahimahi 2 7 b 2 6 7 7 f
/home/mahimahi/stern/foo
```

The eight values on the command line are the eight hex digits in the file handle reported in the NFS error message.

You can avoid delayed client write problems by having a good idea of what your clients are doing and how heavily loaded your NFS servers are. Determining your NFS workload and optimizing your clients and servers to make the best use of available resources requires tuning the network, the clients and the servers. The next chapter presents NFS tuning and benchmarking techniques.

12

Performance Analysis and Tuning

Characterization of NFS Behavior
Measuring Performance
Benchmarking
Identifying NFS Performance Bottlenecks
Network Congestion and Network
    Interfaces
Network Partitioning Hardware
Server Tuning
Client Tuning

Performance analysis and tuning, particularly when it involves NFS and NIS, is a topic subject to heated debate. The focus of this chapter is on the analysis techniques and configuration options used to identify performance bottlenecks and improve overall system response time. Tuning a network and its servers is similar to optimizing a piece of user-written code. Finding the obvious flaws and correcting poor programming habits generally leads to marked improvements in performance. Similarly, there is a definite and noticeable difference between networked systems with abysmal performance and those that run reasonably well; those with poor response generally suffer from "poor habits" in network resource use or configuration. It's easy to justify spending the time to eliminate major flaws when the return on your time investment is so large.

However, all tuning processes are subject to a law of diminishing returns. Getting the last 5-10% out of an application usually means hand-rolling loops or reading assembly language listings. Fine-tuning a network server to an "optimum" configuration may yield that last bit of performance, but the next network change or new client added to the system may make performance of the finely tuned system worse than that of an untuned system. If other aspects of the computing environment are neglected as a result of the incremental server tuning, then the benefits of fine-tuning certainly do not justify its costs.

Our approach will be to make things "close enough for jazz." Folklore (learned from a high school music teacher) has it that jazz musicians take their instruments from their cases, and if all of the keys, strings, and valves look functional, they start playing music. Fine-tuning instruments is frowned upon, especially when the ambient street noise masks its effects. Simply ensuring that network and server performance are acceptable—and remain consistently acceptable in the face of network changes—is often a realistic goal for the tuning process.

As a network manager, you are also faced with the task of balancing the demands of individual users against the global constraints of the network and its resources. Users have a local view: they always want their machines to run faster, but the global view of the system administrator must be to tune the network to meet the aggregate demands of all users. There are no constraints in NFS or NIS that keep a client from using more than its fair share of network resources, so NFS and NIS tuning requires that you optimize both the servers and the ways in which the clients use these servers.

Finally, some people may argue that tuning NFS is not worth the effort in the first place. Consider the differences between the following:

```
# mount bluenote:/home/stern /home/stern
% cp jazz.ms /home/stern/jazz.ms
% rcp jazz.ms bluenote:/home/stern/jazz.ms
```

In general, doing **rcp** of a large file to an NFS server is faster than a functionally similar **cp** over an NFS mount point. There are two possible explanations:

- NFS writes are synchronous on the server. All data must be flushed to disk before the *write* RPC request returns to the **biod** daeman that made it. However, **rcp** enjoys the benefits of completely asynchronous disk activity on server *bluenote*.

- **rcp** is a TCP/IP application while NFS uses UDP packets. TCP/IP has a lower overhead for multiple packet transmissions, and writing a large file is similar to sending a sequence of packets in a connection-oriented stream. If the network is overloaded or the remote server cannot keep up with incoming NFS requests, the local client ends up retransmitting entire NFS requests, whereas TCP has inherent congestion detection logic. **rcp** doesn't experience timeouts at the RPC level, as does NFS, when talking to a slow server.

If **rcp** is always faster, why bother tuning NFS? The motivation for using NFS is transparency in accessing files: **rcp** requires that you know the remote server name, the remote pathname, and that host equivalencies be set up properly. In a well-designed NFS configuration, boundaries between servers and filesystems are hidden and users see a consistent naming scheme imposed on all files. The goal of performance analysis and tuning, therefore, is to affect this tradeoff between transparency and speed, minimizing the costs of the transparency and consistency features provided by NFS and NIS.

Characterization of NFS Behavior

You must be able to characterize the demands placed on your servers as well as available configuration options before starting the tuning process. You'll need to know the quantities that you adjust, and the mechanisms used to measure the success of any particular change. Above all else, it helps to understand the general behavior of a facility before you begin to measure it. In the first part of this book, we have examined individual NFS and NIS requests, but haven't really looked at how they are generated in "live" environments.

NFS requests exhibit randomness in two ways: they are typically generated in bursts, and the types of requests in each burst usually don't have anything to do with each other. It is very rare to have a steady, equally spaced stream of requests arriving at any server. The typical NFS request generation pattern involves a burst of requests as a user loads an application from an NFS server into memory or when the application reads or writes a file. These bursts are followed by quiet periods when the user is editing, thinking, or eating lunch. In addition, the requests from one client are rarely coordinated with those from another; one user may be reading mail while another is building software. Consecutive NFS requests received by a server are likely to perform different functions on different parts of one or more disks.

NFS traffic volumes also vary somewhat predictably over the course of a day. In the early morning, many users read their mail, placing a heavier load on a central mail server; at the end of the day most file servers will be loaded as users wrap up their work for the day and write out modified files. Perhaps the most obvious case of time-dependent server usage is a student lab. The hours after class and after dinner are likely to be the busiest for the lab servers, since that's when most people gravitate toward the lab.

Simply knowing the sheer volume of requests won't help you characterize your NFS work load. It's easy to provide "tremendous" NFS performance if only a few requests require disk accesses. Requests vary greatly in the server resources they need to be completed. "Big" RPC requests force the server to read or write from disk. In addition to the obvious NFS read and write requests, some symbolic link resolutions require reading information from disk. "Small" NFS RPC requests simply touch file attribute information, or the directory name look-up cache, and can usually be satisfied without a disk access.

The average percentage of all RPC calls of each type is the "NFS RPC mixture," and it defines the *kind* of work the server is being asked to do, as opposed to simply the volume of work presented to it. The RPC mixture indicates possible areas of improvement, or flags obvious bottlenecks. For example, clients producing an RPC distribution that is heavily weighted in disk write operations will experience abysmal performance if the server is disk-bound. Similarly, a high percentage of symbolic link resolutions might indicate an inefficient client mount point naming scheme. Knowing how to characterize your NFS workload, you now need to know how to measure server performance as seen by NFS clients.

Measuring Performance

The NFS RPC mixture is useful for tuning the server to handle the load placed on it, but the real measure of success is whether the clients see a faster server or not. Users may still get "server not responding" messages after some bottlenecks are eliminated because you haven't removed all of the constraints, or because something other than the server is causing performance problems.

Measuring the success of a tuning effort requires you to measure the average response time as seen by an average client. There are two schools of thought on how to determine this threshold for this value:

- Use an absolute value for the "threshold of pain" in average server response time. Usually, these thresholds are set at 25-50 milliseconds for diskless clients and 50-70 milliseconds for other NFS clients.

- Base the threshold on the performance of the server with a minimal load, such as only one client. When the server's performance exceeds twice this "ideal" response time, the server has become loaded.

It's easy to measure the average server response time on a client by dividing the number of NFS RPC calls made by the time in which they were completed. Use the **nfsstat** utility to track the number of NFS calls, and a clock or the UNIX **time** command to measure the elapsed time in a benchmark or network observation. Obviously, this must be done over a short, well-monitored period of time when the client is generating NFS requests nearly continuously. Any gap in the NFS requests will increase the average server response time. You can also use the NFS benchmark traffic generators described in Appendix D, "NFS Benchmarks," or review the smoothed response times recorded by some versions of **nfsstat –m**.

You'll get different average response times for different RPC mixtures, since disk-intensive client activity is likely to raise the average response time. However, it is the *average* response that matters most. The first request may always take a little longer, as caches get flushed and the server begins fetching data from a new part of the disk. Over time, these initial bumps may be smoothed out, although applications with very poor locality of reference may suffer more of them. You must take the average over the full range of RPC operations, and measure response over a long enough period of time to iron out any short-term fluctuations.

Users are most sensitive to the sum of response times for all requests in an operation. One or two slow responses may not be noticed in the sequence of an operation with several hundred NFS requests, but a train of requests with long response times will produce complaints of system sluggishness.

An NFS server must be able to handle the traffic bursts without a prolonged increase in response time. The randomness of the NFS requests modulates the server's response time curve, subject to various constraints on the server. Disk bandwidth and CPU scheduling constraints can increase the time required for the server's response time to return to its average value. Figure 12-1 shows a typical relationship between the number of NFS requests and server response time.

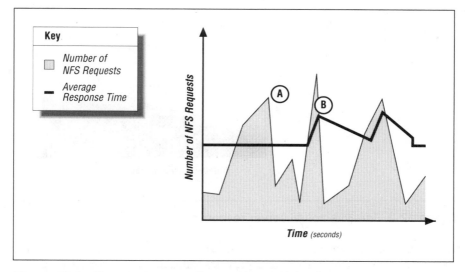

Figure 12-1. Server response time under peak load

Ideally, the average response time curve should remain relatively "flat" as the number of NFS requests increases. During bursts of NFS activity, the server's response time may increase, but it should return to the average level quickly (point A in Figure 12-1). If a server requires a relatively long time to recover from the burst, then its average response time will remain inflated even when the level of activity subsides. During this period of increased response time, some clients may experience RPC timeouts, and retransmit their requests. This additional load increases the server's response time again, increasing the total burst recovery time.

NFS performance does not scale linearly above the point at which a system constraint is hit. The NFS retransmission algorithm introduces positive feedback when the server just can't keep up with the request arrival rate. As the average response time increases, the server becomes even more loaded from retransmitted requests. A slow server removes some of the random elements from the network: the server's clients that are retransmitting requests generate them with a fairly uniform distribution; the clients fall into lock step waiting for the server, and the server itself becomes saturated. Tuning a server and its clients should move the "knee" of the performance curve out as far as possible, as shown in Figure 12-2.

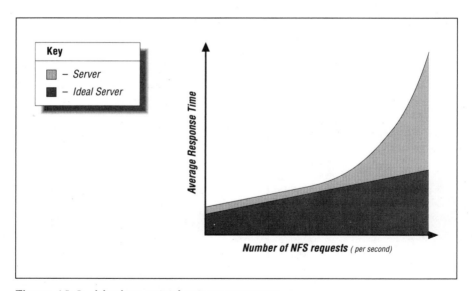

Figure 12-2. Ideal vs actual server response

Knowing what to measure and how to measure it lets you evaluate the relative success of your tuning efforts, and provides valuable data for evaluating NFS server benchmarks.

Benchmarking

Benchmarks of NFS performance should be judged in terms of their realistic reproduction of the NFS call arrival rates and RPC distribution. A benchmark that sends out a steady, regularly spaced stream of NFS requests tests only how well a server operates under ideal conditions. If you can't run actual client workloads on a network, there are a few conditions to be aware of:

- Ensure that the RPC mixture of the benchmark matches that of your NFS clients. Running a benchmark that does a large percentage of write operations tells you little about how NFS servers perform if your clients mostly read files. Conversely, if you have a large percentage of write operations, the wrong benchmark RPC mixture overstates expected server performance. Use the **nfsstat** tool to determine accurate RPC mixtures for your servers. You may want to run several benchmarks, testing performance with client loads simulating normal and heavy conditions. Appendix D, *NFS Benchmarking*, contains information about the **nhfsstone** RPC-generating benchmark and hints for constructing your own traffic generator using UNIX utilities.

- Watch out for cache effects. Clients cache parts of files that have been recently read and not modified. Repeatedly reading the same file may only generate a fraction of the desired number of *read* RPC requests.

- When gauging a particular limit, such as the maximum number of short RPCs or the maximum NFS disk transfer rate, try to isolate the quantity under test as much as possible. Stress testing is often useful for determining a server's behavior under severe loads, but it helps to stress only one component at a time.

The last point rings of Heisenberg's Uncertainty Principle. In short, Heisenberg stated that the process of observing something changes it. A goal of NFS performance measurement should be to change the actual performance being measured as little as possible. Using networked measurement tools that add to the traffic level on a congested network, or running suites of utilities that drain the server's CPU, color the results of any benchmarks.

When benchmarking a network router or gateway, ensure that you are measuring the desired capacity and not another constraint. To determine maximum IP packet forwarding rates, for example, you should put a packet generator on one side of the router and a packet counting device such as a LAN analyzer on the other. Timing **rcp** transfers of large files through the router gives a fair indication of maximum disk transfer rates or maximum network data transfer rates, but tells you little about the router's network interface because the packets forwarded are not "typical" in size.

The goal of the next section is to indicate the common areas in which performance bottlenecks are created. The remainder of this chapter covers techniques for relaxing these constraints as much as possible. The majority of the following discussion concerns NFS, although NIS-specific topics will be introduced where applicable.

Identifying NFS Performance Bottlenecks

The stateless design of NFS makes crash recovery simple, but it also makes it impossible for a client to distinguish between a server that is slow and one that has crashed. In either case, the client does not receive an RPC reply before the RPC timeout period expires. Clients can't tell why a server appears slow, either: packets could be dropped by the network and never reach the server, or the server could simply be overloaded. Using NFS performance figures alone, it is hard to distinguish a slow server from an unreliable network. Users complain that "the system is slow," but there are several areas that contribute to system sluggishness.

An overloaded server responds to all packets that it enqueues for its **nfsd** daemons, perhaps dropping some incoming packets due to the high load. Those requests that are received generate a response, albeit a response that arrives sometime after the client has retransmitted the request. If the network itself is to blame, then packets may not make it from the client or server onto the wire, or they may vanish in transit between the two hosts.

Problem Areas

The potential bottlenecks in the client-server relationship are:

Client Network Interface
> The client may not be able to transmit or receive packets due to electrical problems at its network interface.

Network Bandwidth
> An overly congested network slows down both client transmissions and server replies. Network partitioning hardware installed to reduce network saturation adds delays to round-trip times, increasing the effective time required to complete an RPC call. If the delays caused by network congestion are serious, they contribute to RPC timeouts.

Server Network Interface

A busy server may be so flooded with packets that it cannot receive all of them, or it cannot queue the incoming requests in a protocol-specific structure once the network interface receives the packet. Interrupt handling limitations can also impact the ability of the server to pull packets in from the network.

Server CPU Loading

NFS is rarely CPU constrained. Once a server has an NFS request, it has to schedule an **nfsd** daemon to have the appropriate operation performed. If the server has adequate CPU cycles, then the CPU does not affect server performance. However, if the server has few free CPU cycles then scheduling latencies may limit NFS performance; conversely a system that is providing its maximum NFS service will not make a good CPU server. CPU loading also affects NIS performance, since a heavily loaded system is slower to perform NIS map lookups in response to client requests.

Server Memory Usage

NFS performance is somewhat related to the size of the server's memory, if the server is doing nothing but NFS. NFS will use either the local disk buffer cache (in systems that do not have a page-mapped VM system) or free memory to cache disk pages that have recently been read from disk. Running large processes on an NFS server hurts NFS performance. As a server runs out of memory and begins paging, its performance as either an NIS or NFS server suffers. Disk bandwidth is wasted in a system that is paging local applications, consumed by page fault handling rather than NFS requests.

Server Disk Bandwidth

This area is the most common bottleneck: the server simply cannot get data to or from the disks quickly enough. NFS requests tend to be random in nature, exhibiting little locality of reference for a particular disk. Many clients mounting filesystems from a server increase the degree of randomness in the system. Furthermore, NFS is stateless, so write operations on the server must be committed to disk before the client is notified that the RPC call completed. This synchronous nature of NFS write operations further impairs performance, since caching and operation disk controller ordering will not be utilized to their fullest extent.

Configuration Effects

Loosely grouped in this category are constrictive server kernel configurations, poor disk balancing, and inefficient mount point naming schemes. With poor configurations, all services operate properly but inefficiently.

Locating Bottlenecks

Given all of the areas in which NFS can break down, it's hard to pick a starting point for performance analysis. Inspecting server behavior, for example, may not tell you anything if the network is overly congested or dropping packets. One approach is to start with a typical NFS client, and evaluate its view of the network's services. Tools that examine the local network interface, the network load perceived by the client, and NFS timeout and retransmission statistics indicate whether the bulk of your performance problems are due to the network or the NFS servers.

This chapter looks at performance problems from network congestion to excessive server loading, and offers suggestions for easing constraints at each of the problem areas outlined above. However, you may want to get a rough idea of whether your NFS servers or your network is the biggest contributor to performance problems before walking through all diagnostic steps. On a typical NFS client, use the **nfsstat** tool to compare the retransmission and duplicate reply rates:

```
% nfsstat -rc
Client rpc:
calls       badcalls    retrans     badxid      timeout     wait        newcred
2534514     304         1109        49          1410        0           0
```

The *timeout* value indicates the number of NFS RPC calls that did not complete within the RPC timeout period. Divide *timeout* by *calls* to determine the *retransmission rate* for this client. We'll look at an equation for calculating the maximum allowable retransmission rate on each client later in this section, in "Retransmission Rate Thresholds."

If the client-side RPC counts for *timeout* and *badxid* are close in value, the network is healthy. Requests are making it to the server but the server cannot handle them and generate replies before the client's RPC call times out. The server eventually works its way through the backlog of requests, generating duplicate replies that increment the *badxid* count. In this case, the emphasis should be on improving server response time.

Alternatively, **nfsstat** may show that *timeout* is large while *badxid* is zero or negligible. In this case, packets are never making it to the server, and the network interfaces of client and server, as well as the network itself, should be examined. NFS does not query the lower protocol layers to determine where packets are being consumed; to NFS the entire RPC and transport mechanisms are a black box. Note that NFS is like **spray** in this regard—it doesn't matter whether it's the local host's interface, network congestion, or the remote host's interface that dropped the packet—the packets are simply lost. To eliminate all network-related effects, you must examine each of these areas.

The next section explores network diagnostics and partitioning schemes aimed at reducing congestion and improving the local host's interface to the network.

Network Congestion and Network Interfaces

A network that was designed to ensure transparent access to filesystems and to provide "plug-and-play" services for new clients is a prime candidate for regular expansion. Limitations on physical cable lengths sometimes require that a single cable be divided into segments to accommodate a new host or hosts. Joining several independent networks with bridges or repeaters may add to the traffic level on one or more of the networks. Finally, repeated shuffling of desktop hardware and network equipment can introduce electrical problems due to component failures or improper cabling. However, a network cannot grow indefinitely without eventually experiencing congestion problems. Therefore, don't grow a network without planning its physical topology (cable routing and limitations) as well as its logical design. After several spurts of growth, performance on the network may suffer due to excessive loading or to damaged host network interfaces.

The problems discussed in this section affect NIS as well as NFS service. Adding network partitioning hardware affects the transmission of broadcast packets, and poorly placed bridges or routers can create new bottlenecks in frequently used network "virtual circuits." Throughout this section, the emphasis will be on planning and capacity evaluation, rather than on low-level electrical details.

Local Network Interface

Chapter 11, *Debugging Network Problems*, introduced some common problems with Ethernet cabling that disrupt or prevent point-to-point connections on the network. Improper termination and other cable-specific problems affect all of the machines on the network, while a local interface problem is only visible to the machine suffering from it. Examples of local interface problems include a faulty transceiver, intermittent drop cable failures (in thicknet configurations), or an Ethernet interface device driver that cannot handle the packet traffic.

The **netstat** tool gives a good indication of the reliability of the local network interface:

```
% netstat -i
Name Mtu  Net/Dest     Address    Ipkts  Ierrs Opkts   Oerrs Collis Queue
ie0  1500 131.40.52.0  wahoo      139478 11    102155  0     3055   0
lo0  1536 loopback     localhost  7188   0     7188    0     0      0
```

The first three columns show the network interface, the maximum transmission unit (MTU) for that interface, and the network to which the interface is connected. The *Address* column shows the local host's name or IP address. The last five columns contain counts of the total number of packets sent and received, as well as errors encountered while handling packets. The collision count indicates the number of times a collision occurred when this host was transmitting.

Input errors can be caused by:

- Malformed or runt packets, damaged on the network by electrical problems.

- Bad CRC checksums, which may indicate that another host has a network interface problem and is sending corrupted packets. Alternatively, the cable connecting this workstation to the network may be damaged, and corrupting frames as they are received.

- The device driver's inability to receive the packet due to insufficient buffer space.

A high output error rate indicates a fault in the local host's connection to the network or prolonged periods of collisions (a jammed network). Errors included in this count are exclusive of packet collisions.

Ideally, both the input and output error rates should be as close to zero as possible, although some short bursts of errors may occur as cables are unplugged and reconnected, or during periods of intense network traffic. After a power failure, for example, the flood of packets from every diskless client that automatically reboots may generate input errors on the servers that attempt to boot all of them in parallel. During normal operation, an error rate of more than a fraction of 1% deserves investigation. This rate seems incredibly small, but consider the data rates on an Ethernet: at 10 Mbit/sec, the maximum bandwidth of a network is about 15,000 minimum-sized packets each second. An error rate of 0.01% means that at least one of those 15,000 packets gets damaged each second. Diagnosis and resolution of low-level electrical problems such as CRC errors is beyond the scope of this book, although such an effort should be undertaken if high error rates are persistent.

Collisions and Network Saturation

Ethernet is similar to an old party-line telephone: everybody listens at once, everybody talks at once, and sometimes two talkers start at the same time. In a well-conditioned network, with only two hosts on it, it's possible to use 90% of the network's bandwidth. However, NFS clients and servers live in a burst-filled environment, where many machines try to use the network at the same time. When you remove the well behaved conditions, usable network bandwidth decreases rapidly.

On the Ethernet, a host first checks for a transmission in progress on the network before attempting one of its own. This process is known as *carrier sense*. When two or more hosts transmit packets at exactly the same time, neither can sense a carrier, and a collision results. Each host recognizes that a collision has occurred, and backs off for a period of time *t* before attempting to transmit again. For each successive retransmission attempt that results in a collision, *t* is increased exponentially, with a small random variation. The variation in back-off periods ensures that machines generating collisions do not fall into lock step and seize the network.

As machines are added to the network, the probability of a collision increases. Network utilization is measured as a percentage of the ideal bandwidth consumed by the traffic on the cable at the point of measurement. Various levels of utilization are usually compared on a logarithmic scale. The relative decrease in usable bandwidth going from 5% utilization to 10% utilization, is about the same as going from 10% all the way to 30% utilization.

Measuring network utilization requires a LAN analyzer or similar device. Instead of measuring the traffic load directly, you can use the average collision rate as seen by all hosts on the network as a good indication of whether the network is overloaded or not. The collision rate, as a percentage of output packets, is one of the best measures of network utilization. The *Collis* field in the output of **netstat -i** shows the number of collisions:

```
% netstat -i
Name Mtu  Net/Dest     Address     Ipkts  Ierrs Opkts  Oerrs Collis Queue
ie0  1500 131.40.52.0  wahoo       139478 11    102155 0     3055   0
lo0  1536 loopback     localhost   7188   0     7188   0     0      0
```

The collision rate for a host is the number of collisions seen by that host divided by the number of packets it writes, as shown in Figure 12-3.

$$\text{collision rate} = \frac{\text{number of collisions}}{\text{output packets}}$$

Figure 12-3. Collision rate calculation

Collisions are only counted when the local host is transmitting; the collision rate experienced by the host is dependent on its network usage. Because network transmissions are random events, it's possible to see small numbers of collisions even on the most lightly loaded networks. Any collision rate over 5%, though, is an indication of high network utilization and a signal that you should consider reorganizing your network.

To understand the exponential decrease in usable network bandwidth, consider a model in which random packet transmissions are represented by people throwing dice. A "six" will mean the host (person) transmits a packet. This example is incomplete in that it does not accurately model non-random transmission patterns (packets tend to be sent in groups), nor does it account for collision avoidance through carrier sensing. However, it is a fair representation of collision generation in a busy network in which any two hosts are not functionally related. If you are reading mail and the person in the next cube is building software, your actions are not functionally related: you are probably using different servers, different filesystems, and you submit different sequences of NFS requests to the servers. The packet generation rate of one workstation does not depend at all on the activities on one of its peers.

With only two dice thrown, there are 6^2 possible outcomes, and only one of them—a pair of sixes—results in a collision. The probability of a collision, therefore, is 1/36, or about 3%. If the number of dice thrown is increased to five, the only requirement for a collision is that any two of the dice show a six. In this situation, the number of possible outcomes is $6^5 = 7776$. The number of outcomes in which two or more dice show a six is computed by finding the number of states in which *exactly* two, three, four or all five dice have sixes up, while the other dice have any of the other five numbers showing. Because the dice showing sixes may be any of the five, we compute the number of combinations of five things taken i at a time to find the number of ways i sixes can show up; the $(5 - i)$ other dice can fall in $6^{(5-i)}$ other ways. There are 1526 outcomes in which two or more sixes are showing, as shown in Figure 12-4.

$$P_{\text{collision}} = P_{2 \text{ or more 6s}} = \frac{\sum_{i=2}^{5} C \begin{bmatrix} 5 \\ i \end{bmatrix} \cdot 6^{(5-i)}}{6^5} = \frac{1526}{7776} \approx 19\%$$

Figure 12-4. Probability of two or more dice showing a six

The probability of a collision jumps to 19% with just five dice. The number of players (or hosts) was increased by a factor of 2.5, and the probability of a collision increased by more than six-fold.

Due to this exponential decay in usable bandwidth, minor increases in network utilization have increasingly noticeable effects on performance. Once more than 35-40% of the available bandwidth is consumed, the Ethernet itself becomes a bottleneck. Above 55% utilization, the network becomes loaded with packet fragments from collisions, and the probability of a "clean" packet being transmitted goes to zero. It is rare for the *average* traffic volume to exceed these thresholds, since NFS traffic tends to be burst oriented. The average network utilization is often fairly low, with spikes during traffic bursts. To avoid being a bottleneck, peaks above the 55% meltdown point should be avoided, and the average traffic volume should be low enough to prevent frequent packet collisions.

When computing the average collision rate for the entire network, add the individual output packet and collision counts together first, so that busy machines weights the average more heavily than fairly quiescent nodes with abnormally low (or high) collision rates. Use the left hand equation shown in Figure 12-5.

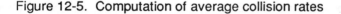

$$\frac{\sum_{i=1}^{N} \text{collisions}_i}{\sum_{i=1}^{N} \text{output pkts}_i} \neq \sum_{i=1}^{N} \left(\frac{\frac{\text{collisions}_i}{\text{output pkts}_i}}{N} \right)$$

Figure 12-5. Computation of average collision rates

A non-uniform distribution of collisions—a few hosts experiencing significantly more collisions than other hosts with similar network usage—may indicate an electrical problem rather than network saturation. If the average collision rate exceeds 10% after all electrical problems have been resolved, then the network is a prime candidate for partitioning. See Table 12-1 for a summary.

Table 12-1. Network Loading Thresholds

Statistic	Threshold
Average network utilization	35%
Peak network utilization	55%
Average collision rate	10%

Of course, opinions vary as to the exact collision rate threshold that corresponds to a network utilization in the 35-40% range. If nodes on the network transmit packets independently of each other, then the collision rate may be lower for the same network load than if the hosts have a tendency to fall into lock step. A collision rate upwards of 5% is the first sign of network loading, but the actual point at which partitioning will be required depends on your usage patterns and future growth requirements.

Network Partitioning Hardware

Network partitioning involves dividing a single backbone into multiple segments, joined by some piece of hardware that forwards packets. There are four types of these devices: repeaters, bridges, routers, and gateways. These terms are sometimes used interchangeably although each device has a specific set of policies regarding packet forwarding, protocol filtering, and transparency on the network.

Repeaters   A repeater joins two segments at the physical layer. It is a purely electrical connection, providing signal amplification and pulse "clean up" functions without regard for the semantics of the signals. Repeaters are primarily used to exceed the single-cable length limitation. No more than four repeaters can exist between any two nodes on the same network, keeping the minimum end-to-end transit time for a packet well within the Ethernet specified maximum time-to-live. Because repeaters do not look at the contents of packets (or packet fragments), they pass collisions on one segment through to the other, making them of little use to relieve network congestion.

Bridges   Bridges function at the data link layer, and perform selective forwarding of packets based on their destination MAC addresses. Some delay is introduced into the network by the bridge, as it must receive entire packets and decipher their MAC-layer headers. Broadcast packets are always passed through, although some bridge hardware can be configured to forward only ARP broadcasts and to suppress IP broadcasts such as those emanating from **ypbind**.

Intelligent or learning bridges glean the MAC addresses of machines through observation of traffic on each interface. "Dumb" bridges must be loaded with the Ethernet addresses of machines on each network and impose an administrative burden each time the network topology is modified. With either type of bridge, each new segment is likely to be less heavily loaded than the original network, provided that the most popular inter-host virtual circuits do not run through the bridge.

Routers

Both repeaters and bridges divide the network into two or more distinct physical pieces, but the collection of backbones is still a single *logical* network. That is, the IP network number of all hosts on all segments will be the same. It is often necessary to divide a network logically into multiple IP networks, either due to physical constraints (i.e. two offices that are separated by several miles) or because a single IP network has run out of host numbers for new machines.

Multiple IP networks are joined by routers that forward packets based on their source and destination IP addresses rather than 48-bit Ethernet addresses. One interface of the router is considered "inside" the network, and the router forwards packets to the "outside" interface. A router usually corrals broadcast traffic to the inside network, although some can be configured to forward broadcast packets to the "outside" network. The networks joined by a router need not be of the same type or physical media, and routers are commonly used to join local area networks to point-to-point long-haul internetwork connections. You can purchase a dedicated router, or install multiple network interfaces in a host and allow it to route packets in addition to its other duties. Appendix B, *IP Packet Routing*, contains a detailed description of how IP packets are forwarded and how routes are defined to UNIX systems.

Gateways

At the top-most level in the network protocol stack, a gateway performs forwarding functions at the application level, and frequently must perform protocol conversion to forward the traffic. A gateway need not be on more than one network; for example, a host that forwards SMTP mail on a TCP/IP network to the VAX/VMS VAX-11 mailer might be on only one network (if TCP/IP and DECnet are co-existent on the wire). However, gateways are most commonly used to join multiple networks with different sets of native protocols, and to enforce tighter control over access to and from each of the networks.

The remainder of this section discusses the impacts of each type of partitioning device on NFS and NIS.

Protocol Filtering

If you have a large volume of non-IP traffic on your network, isolating it from your NFS and NIS traffic may improve overall system performance by reducing the load on your network and servers. You can determine the relative percentages of IP and non-IP packets on your network using a LAN analyzer or a traffic filtering program such as Sun's **traffic** utility. The best way to isolate your NFS and NIS network from non-IP traffic is to install a bridge or other device that performs selective filtering based on protocol. Any packet that does not meet the selection criteria is not forwarded across the bridge.

Devices that monitor traffic at the IP protocol level, such as routers, filter any non-IP traffic such as XNS and DECnet packets. If two segments of a local area network must exchange IP and non-IP traffic, a bridge or router capable of selective forwarding must be installed. The converse is also an important network planning factor: to insulate a network using only TCP/IP-based protocols from volumes of irrelevant traffic—XNS packets generated by a PC network, for example—a routing device filtering at the IP level is the simplest solution.

Partitioning With Bridges

LAN bridges are useful for separating independent streams of client-server traffic. Not all NFS clients talk to all servers, or they get very few files from some servers, so it's possible to separate clients and servers into related groups. Bridges reduce congestion by keeping "uninteresting" packets away from the other network segment.

Bridges don't affect NIS operation, since they usually do not filter broadcast traffic. The point-to-point traffic between an NIS server and its clients is small enough compared to NFS traffic to be ignored in this discussion. We'll just talk about partitioning with bridges here, and leave issues of running NFS through IP routers for later when we cover NFS over wide-area networks.

To determine the ideal separation of nodes in the network, draw the network as a graph, with one graph node for each host. Join the nodes with edges representing a client-server usage, and assign weights to each edge based on the level of service that the client gets from the server. Each NFS mount is therefore represented by an edge in the graph, with the value assigned to the edge proportional to the usage of the NFS-mounted filesystem. A simple value allocation scheme is shown in Table 12-2.

Table 12-2. NFS Mount Weight Allocations

Weight	NFS Filesystem
8	Diskless client swap and root.
4	Home directories, diskless client /**usr**.
2	Source code or tools directories.
1	Infrequently used filesystems.

Adjust these weights to best reflect the relative traffic for each class of filesystem. The edge joining a client and server should be assigned the total weight for all NFS mounts from that server. For example, the diskless client *suds* sits on the desk of a user with home directory /**home/wahoo/stern**. It uses the following mount points and corresponding weights, as shown in Table 12-3.

Table 12-3. NFS Server Weights for Client suds

Filesystem	Weight
wahoo:/export/root/suds	8
wahoo:/export/swap/suds	(Counted with root)
wahoo:/home/wahoo	4
thud:/home/thud	1
mahimahi:/tools/mahimahi	2
Server	**Total Weight**
wahoo	12
mahimahi	2
thud	1

/**home/thud** isn't all that interesting to the workstation's user, so it is assigned a weight of 1. Add all the weights for every mount from each server, producing the totals shown in the lower half of the table. Continue this process for all the nodes in the network to produce a graph showing all clients and servers, and the "weight" of the NFS mounts used by each client. The weights are assigned to the edges in the graph that join the client to each server: *suds* assigns the weight 12 to the edge that joins it to server *wahoo*; weight 2 to the edge to *mahimahi*, and a weight of 1 to the edge joining *suds* and *thud*.

To evaluate a partitioning, enclose the nodes on each side of the bridge with a loop, and add the values of graph edges that intersect the loops. Two sample partitions for the previous diskless client example are shown in Figure 12-6. These numbers indicate the relative traffic flow through the bridge in each direction, and should be made as small as possible to avoid creating a bottleneck at the bridge itself.

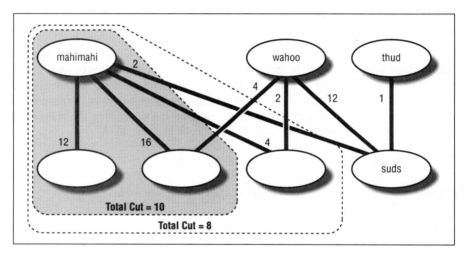

Figure 12-6. Network partitioning with a bridge

Dividing the network in this manner ensures that traffic that is of interest to pairs of hosts on one side of the bridge will not be seen by the other side of the bridge. If there is an imbalance in the traffic flows through the bridge, moving just one client or server across the bridge may eliminate a large portion of the cross-bridge traffic.

These network partitioning metrics are based loosely on the Ford and Fulkerson max-flow min-cut theorem. The work done by L. R. Ford and D. R. Fulkerson proves that in any flow network, its maximum capacity is gated by one or more bottleneck points. The max-flow min-cut theorem really applies to networks with a single source and sink node, while the NFS network has multiple sources at each client and multiple sinks at each server node. The same flow analysis determines the optimum location of a bridge if you tie all of the sources (NFS clients) to an "infinite source" and all of the sinks (NFS servers) to an "infinite sink," both with infinite capacity to generate or accept NFS requests. The actual flow through the network will then be determined by the weights assigned to each client-server edge in the graph of nodes. The ideal "cut" between sets of nodes determines the smallest total capacity crossing the boundaries between the node sets.

Joining two network segments with a bridge introduces a single point of failure into the network, so it is tempting to join the networks at more than one point with multiple bridges. However, this is a mistake. Introducing a loop into a network with bridges, where two networks are redundantly joined, hopelessly confuses the bridges as they see the same MAC addresses appearing as packet transmitters on both interfaces. See Figure 12-7 for an example.

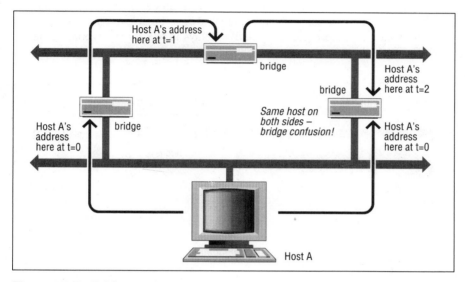

Figure 12-7. Bridge cycle

If redundant routing is required, a spanning-tree bridge must be employed. Spanning-tree bridges eliminate cycles from the network topology by turning off packet forwarding when the same MAC address appears on both interfaces. A spanning tree bridge provides redundant segment connectivity in the event of a failure, but it does not typically improve performance. In a network topology containing loops, one of the spanning tree bridges stops forwarding packets, putting all of the load onto the other bridge. The bridge that shuts itself off stands by as a "hot spare" if the primary bridge fails.

NIS in a Partitioned Network

NIS is a point-to-point protocol once a server binding has been established. However, when **ypbind** searches for a server, it broadcasts an RPC request. Bridges do not affect **ypbind**, because the bridge forwards broadcast packets to the other *physical* network. Routers don't forward broadcast packets to other IP networks, so you must make configuration exceptions if you have NIS clients but no NIS server on one side of a router.

Unequal distribution of NIS servers on opposite sides of a bridge can lead to server victimization. The typical bridge adds a small delay to the transit time of each packet, so **ypbind** requests will almost always be answered by a server on the client's side of the bridge. The relative delays in NIS server response time are shown in Figure 12-8.

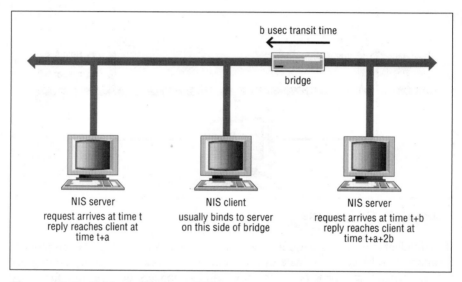

Figure 12-8. Bridge effects on NIS

If there is only one server on bridge network A, but several on bridge network B, then the "A" network server handles all NIS requests on its network segment until it becomes so heavily loaded that servers on the "B" network reply to **ypbind** faster, including the bridge-related packet delay. An equitable distribution of NIS servers across bridge boundaries eliminates this excessive loading problem.

Routers and gateways present a more serious problem for NIS. NIS servers and clients must be on the same IP network because a router or gateway will not forward the client's **ypbind** broadcast outside the local IP network. If there are no

NIS servers on the "inside" of a router, use **ypset** at boot time as discussed in "Modifying Client Bindings," in Chapter 10, *Diagnostic and Administrative Tools.*

Effects on Diskless Nodes

Diskless nodes should be kept on the same physical and logical network as their servers unless tight constraints require their separation. If a bridge is placed between a diskless client and its server, every disk operation on the client, including swap device operations, has to go through the bridge. The volume of traffic generated by a diskless client is usually much larger—sometimes twice as much—than that of an NFS client getting user files from a server, so it greatly reduces the load on a bridge if clients and servers are kept on the same side of the bridge device.

If bridges are adversely affected by diskless client traffic, routers and gateways suffer even worse consequences. The traffic generated by a diskless client can easily overload a router or gateway, adversely affecting other internetwork functions relying on that link. Booting a client through a gateway is not recommended, since the diskless client's root and swap partition traffic would be sufficient to consume the entire packet forwarding bandwidth of the router. However, if necessary, a diskless client can be booted through a router or from a gateway as follows:

- Some machine on the client's local network must be able to answer Reverse ARP (RARP) requests from the machine. This can be accomplished by publishing an ARP entry for the client and running:

  ```
  rarpd ie0 ono
  ```

  on some host on the same network (in this case, host *ono*), or by running **rarp** on the second network interface of the gateway host:

  ```
  rarpd ie1 acadia-gw
  ```

  rarpd takes the name of the host, as it is known on that network, as an argument.

- A host on the local network must be able to **tftp** the boot code to the client, so that it can start the boot sequence. This usually involves adding client information to **/tftpboot** on another diskless client server on the local network.

- Once the client has loaded the boot code, it looks for boot parameters. Some NIS server on the client's network must be able to answer the **bootparams** request for the client. This entails adding the client's root and swap partition information to the local **bootparams** file or NIS map. The machine that supplies the **bootparam** information may not have anything to do with actually booting the system, but it must give the diskless client enough information for it to reach its root and swap filesystem servers through IP routing. Therefore, if the proxy **bootparam** server has a default route defined, that route must point to the network with the client's NFS server on it.

- In the diskless client's boot scripts, it may need to perform an explicit **ypset** if its NIS server is located across the router.

Partitioning a network should ease the constraints imposed by the network, and spur an increase in NFS performance. However, the network itself is not always the sole or primary cause of poor performance. The next two sections cover server- and client-side tuning that should be performed in concert with changes in network topology.

Server Tuning

NFS and NIS performance can still be unacceptable even with a lightly loaded network. If the NFS server is not able to field new requests or efficiently schedule and handle those that it does receive, then overall performance suffers. Clients that do not receive prompt replies from NIS servers regularly try to locate faster servers, delaying execution of user processes while the NIS server is handling the RPC request. In some cases, the only way to rectify the problem is to add a new server or upgrade existing hardware. However, identification of the problem areas should be a prerequisite for any hardware changes, and some analyses may point to software configuration changes that provide sufficient relief. The first area to examine is the server's CPU utilization.

CPU Loading

The CPU speed of a pure NFS server is rarely a constraining factor. Once the **nfsd** daemon is running, and has read and decoded an RPC request, it doesn't do much more within the NFS protocol that requires CPU cycles. Other parts of the system, such as the UNIX filesystem and cache management code, may use CPU cycles to perform work given to them by NFS requests. NFS usually poses a light load on a server that is providing pure NFS service. However, very few servers are used solely for NFS service. More common is a central server that performs mail spool and delivery functions, serves terminal users, and provides NFS file service.

There are two aspects to CPU loading: increased NFS daemon scheduling latency, and decreased performance of server-resident, CPU-bound processes. Normally, the **nfsd** daemons will run as soon as a request arrives, because they are running with a kernel process priority that is higher than that of all user processes. However, if there are other processes doing I/O, or running in the kernel (doing system calls) the latency to schedule the **nfsd** daemons is increased. Instead of getting the CPU as soon as a request arrives, the **nfsd** daemon must wait until the next context switch, when the process with the CPU uses up its time slice or goes to sleep. Running several interactive processes on an NFS server will generate enough I/O activity to impact NFS performance. These loads affect a server's ability to schedule its **nfsd** daemons; latency in scheduling the daemons translates into decreased NFS request handling capacity since the **nfsd** daemons cannot accept incoming requests as quickly.

All of the **nfsd** daemons read requests from the same UDP socket. In order to remove data from a socket, the process reading from it must be scheduled and currently running. This implies that an **nfsd** daemon cannot drain incoming requests until it is run; if each daemon must contend for the CPU with other runnable processes, then there will be an increase in the server's response time. In extreme cases, the socket structure itself can overflow with requests. If this happens, the lower level network driver drops incident packets because there is no room to enqueue them on the socket.

The other aspect of CPU loading is the effect of NFS daemons on other user-level processes. The **nfsd** daemons are processes that run entirely in the kernel, and therefore they run at a higher priority than other user-level processes. NFS daemons take priority over other user-level processes, so CPU cycles spent on NFS activity are taken away from user processes. If you are running CPU-bound (computational) processes on your NFS servers, they will not impact NFS performance. Instead, handling NFS requests cripples the performance of the CPU-bound processes, since the NFS daemons always get the CPU before they do.

CPU loading is easy to gauge using any number of utilities that read the CPU utilization figures from the kernel. **vmstat** is the simplest Berkeley tool that breaks CPU usage into user, system, and idle time components:

```
% vmstat 10
procs     memory              page                  disk        faults      cpu
 r b w   avm   fre  re at  pi  po  fr  de  sr i0 i1 s0 d3   in  sy  cs us sy id
...Ignore first line of output...
 0 0 0     0  2672   0 32   0   0   1   0   0  4  1  0  0   60  87  60  1  5 94
```

The last three columns show where the CPU cycles are expended. If the server is CPU bound, the *idle* time decreases to zero. When **nfsd** daemons are waiting for disk operations to complete, and there is no other system activity, the CPU is idle, not accumulating cycles in *system* mode. The *system* column shows the amount of time spent executing system call code, exclusive of time waiting for disks or other devices. If the NFS server has very little (less than 10%) CPU idle time, consider upgrading to a faster server, or moving some CPU-bound processes off of the NFS server.

The "pureness" of NFS service provided by a machine and the type of other work done by the CPU determines how much of an impact CPU loading has on its NFS response time. A machine used for print spooling or hardwired terminal service, for example, is forced to handle large numbers of high priority interrupts from the serial line controllers. If there is a sufficient level of high-priority activity, the server may miss incoming network traffic. Use **iostat, vmstat,** or similar tools to watch for large numbers of interrupts. Every interrupt requires CPU time to service it, and takes away from the CPU availability for NFS.

If an NFS server must be used as a home for terminals, consider using a networked terminal server instead of hardwired terminals.* The largest advantage of terminal servers is that they can accept terminal output in large buffers. Instead of writing a screenful of output a character at a time over a serial line, a host writing to a terminal on a terminal server sends it one or two packets containing all of the output. Streamlining the terminal and NFS input and output sources places an additional load on the server's network interface and on the network itself. These factors must be considered when planning or expanding the base of terminal service.

Along these lines, NFS servers make terrible gateway hosts. Each fraction of its network bandwidth that is devoted to forwarding packets or converting protocols is taken away from NFS service. If an NFS server is used as a router between two or more networks, it is possible that the non-NFS traffic occludes the NFS packets. The actual performance effects, if any, will be determined by the bandwidth of the server's network interfaces and other CPU loading factors.

---

*A terminal server has RS-232 ports for terminal connections, and runs a simple ROM monitor that connects terminal ports to servers over **telnet** sessions. Terminal servers vary tremendously: some use RS-232 DB-25 connectors, others have RJ-11 phone jacks; the number of ports ranges from 8 to 32; some use XNS or DECnet services instead of **telnet** over TCP/IP.

NFS Server Daemons

The default number of **nfsd** daemons is chosen empirically by the system vendor, and provides average performance under average conditions. The number of daemons is specified as an argument to **nfsd** when it is started from the boot scripts:

```
nfsd 8 &                echo -n ' nfsd'
```

The example above starts eight instances of **nfsd**.

In many cases, varying the number of daemons provides better performance. In theory, the number of **nfsd** daemons could be increased until process table limits were hit, although in practice the problem of scheduling too many **nfsd** daemons decreases performance before the theoretical process limit of the server is reached.

The **nfsd** daemon is nothing more than a process container for the kernel subroutines that perform the filesystem operations. It exists as a separate process to provide a scheduling handle for the kernel, allowing a server to accept more NFS requests while other **nfsd** daemons are waiting for a disk operation to complete. Intuitively, it seems that increasing the number of server-side daemons improves NFS performance by allowing the server to grab incoming requests more quickly. However, running more processes loads the system in other ways, making the optimal choice an exercise in observation and tuning.

Server Socket Overflows

All **nfsd** daemons read requests from the same socket; this socket is created on the server when the first daemon starts and registers the NFS service with the portmapper. Because all daemons are reading from the same socket, all daemons are marked as runnable when packets are enqueued on the NFS service socket. Daemon processes are scheduled to run in the order in which they arrived on the sleep queue after completing their previous operations.

If there are too few **nfsd** daemons, the volume of client requests exceeds the server's ability to drain them from the UDP socket queue. A real-world model is the single line for tellers in a bank: all customers arriving at the bank file into a single queue, and each teller accepts a customer from the front of the queue when the previous transaction has been completed. If all of the tellers are busy, the line grows longer. By opening new teller windows, the bank can decrease the average queue length. The single-queue system is the most efficient queueing structure because it minimizes the average waiting time. If there are multiple queues, and customers choose one freely, then some tellers will be sitting idle while line variations even out. With the single queue model, every teller is kept busy as long as there are customers in the queue.

Similarly, when all of the **nfsd** daemons are waiting for disk requests to complete, none of them can read a new request from the UDP socket. Incoming requests are queued until the socket structure fills up, and then no new requests can be received. These UDP socket overflows are reported by **netstat –s**:

```
% netstat -s
udp:
        0 incomplete headers
        0 bad data length fields
        0 bad checksums
        1375 socket overflows
...TCP and IP information follows...
```

UDP socket overflows can be caused by other input events, such as a server being subjected to repeated instances of **spray**, but regular socket overflows on an NFS server indicate that there are too few **nfsd** daemons.

In many UNIX implementations, it's possible to increase the kernel space used for buffering data in UDP sockets. In SunOS 4.1, for example, the default UDP buffer size is set in the C source file **/sys/netinet/in_proto.c**:

```
int     udp_recvspace = 2*(9000+sizeof(struct sockaddr)); /* 2 8K dgrams */
```

Increasing this buffer size may only mask the symptom of the problem and make actual server performance worse. Go back to the bank teller example for a moment: if the bank's teller line is already too long, very few bank managers "fix" the problem by extending the queue. The preferred solution, from the customer's view, is to add tellers until the queue is drained. Take the same approach with NFS daemons and add them on the server until the NFS UDP socket is always drained.

Context Switching Overhead

You can't increase the number of **nfsd** daemons to an arbitrarily large value. As the number of NFS daemons increases, context switching and scheduling overhead becomes more of a factor, as the daemons "bump into" each other and other processes in their rush to get scheduled on the CPU. Running too many **nfsd** processes may degrade NFS performance, and it is likely to adversely affect the scheduling of other processes on the server.

The two major costs associated with a context switch are loading the address translation cache and resuming the newly scheduled task on the CPU. In the case of NFS server daemons, both of these costs are near zero. All of the NFS server code lives in the kernel, and therefore has no user-level address translations loaded in the memory management unit. In addition, the task-to-task switch code in most kernels is on the order of a few hundred instructions. Systems can context switch much faster than the network can deliver NFS requests.

NFS server daemons don't impose the "usual" context switching load on a system because all of the NFS server code is in the kernel. Instead of using a per-process context descriptor or a user-level process "slot" in the memory management unit, the **nfsd** daemons use the kernel's address space mappings. This eliminates the address translation loading cost of a context switch.

So where's the problem with context switching? When an NFS request arrives, the kernel wakes up *all* of the **nfsd** daemons waiting on that event. All of the daemons get moved onto the queue for the CPU. Even though the NFS server daemons have no user-level code, scheduling them still adds to the kernel's process management overhead—this translates into CPU cycles spent shuffling processes rather than running them.

Simply measuring the number of context switches doesn't provide enough information to gauge **nfsd** allocation, since each new NFS request is received by a different **nfsd** daemon and causes a context switch. A more useful observation is the additional operating system overhead incurred by the increase in context switching. Unfortunately, few tools are available to measure the impact of context switching. A consistently high load average, close or equal to the number of **nfsd** daemons, indicates that processes are runnable but cannot get scheduled on the CPU.

An excess of NFS server daemons can have unexpected side effects as well. **sendmail**, for example, can be configured not to run if the load average on the host reaches a certain value. If there are too many **nfsd** daemons, the load average may be raised above this threshold, halting mail delivery during periods of intense NFS activity.

A graph of average response time as a function of the number of **nfsd** daemons has a local minimum between the points at which socket overflows and context switching or processor contention limit performance, as shown in Figure 12-9.

When the number of NFS server daemons is increased, NFS requests may not be arriving fast enough to keep all of the daemons occupied. If the number of arriving requests exceeds the number of server daemons that can be made runnable, then each daemon reads at least one request from the socket. On the other hand, if only four requests arrive and eight **nfsd** processes are sleeping, the last four **nfsd** daemons to run will find the UDP socket empty. In this case, the *nullrecv* count (as shown by **nfsstat**) is incremented. When *nullrecv* is incremented, it indicates that the **nfsd** daemons are input-starved. In this situation, running fewer daemons will free server CPU cycles, because daemons that can't do any work won't be scheduled.

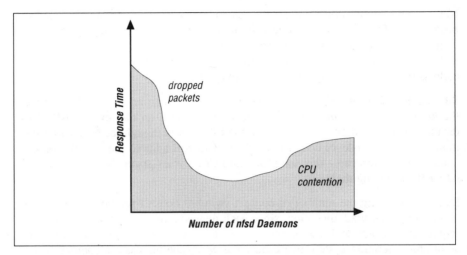

Figure 12-9. NFS response time as a function of nfsd daemons

In general, though, it's very hard to wake up daemons to read from an empty socket because NFS requests arrive in bursts. Between the time the kernel makes all of the NFS daemons runnable and the time each actually gets the CPU, it's probable that more NFS requests have arrived in the socket. You're much more likely to see the effects of context switching and CPU contention caused by too many **nfsd** daemons before you have *nullrecv* become nonzero.

Choosing the Number of Server Daemons

The explanations of **nfsd** scheduling and CPU contention provide many questions but few real guidelines for choosing the best number of **nfsd** daemons for an NFS server. If you decide to vary the number of **nfsd** daemons, a fair baseline is to start with two **nfsd** daemons for each simultaneous disk operation that can be performed. This allows a request to be received while another is awaiting disk service. On a system with two disks on a controller that can schedule two disk operations at once (an interleaving controller), four **nfsd** daemons are probably what the vendor has recommended as a minimum.

From this baseline, add daemons until you are not seeing UDP socket overflows. At some point, CPU contention levels off the response time improvements achieved by adding daemons. Two good upper limits are to never use more than 3/4 the number of hardware context descriptors for **nfsd** processes, and to stop adding daemons when the server's load average increases without a corresponding performance increase. If you see a steadily increasing load average (using **uptime**), it implies that the server is making processes runnable but they are not actually running to completion (or blocking) right away. An increase in load average is a hint that you are experiencing some CPU contention from an excess of **nfsd** daemons.

Memory Usage

NFS uses the server's buffer cache or page cache (in SunOS 4.x and System V Release 4) for file blocks read in NFS *read* requests. On systems that use the traditional buffer cache, you may want to increase the number of pages allocated for the cache. The default buffer cache uses 10% of the server's memory. The size of the cache is determined by the kernel variable **bufpages** (if it is non-zero when the system is booted). To change the size of the buffer cache to 100 pages, for example, use **adb** on the kernel image **/vmunix**:

```
server# echo "bufpages?W 0t100" | adb -w /vmunix
```

You must reboot the system for this change to take effect, since the buffer cache is allocated at boot time. On systems that implement page mapping, the NFS server will use any available page frames to cache file pages.

If the server is used for non-NFS purposes, ensure that it has enough memory to run all of its processes without paging. Problems caused by server swapping will be particularly acute if users log into the servers. Interactive processes contend with NFS service for CPU cycles, and any disk accesses required, in addition to paging caused by memory shortfalls, further reduce the effective bandwidth of the server's disks. In addition, interactive processes generate high-priority I/O interrupts, which will be serviced ahead of NFS requests.

Disk and Filesystem Throughput

The problems discussed to this point have focused on getting NFS requests to the server as efficiently as possible and ensuring that the server's replies reach the client. For NFS requests requiring disk access, the constraining performance factor is often the server's ability to turn around disk requests. A well-conditioned network feels sluggish if the file server is not capable of handling the load placed on it. While there are both network and client-side NFS parameters that may be tuned, optimizing the server's use of its disks and filesystems may deliver the largest benefit. Efficiency in accessing the disks, adequate kernel table sizes, and an equitable distribution of requests over all disks providing NFS service determine the round-trip filesystem delay.

A basic argument about NFS performance centers on the overhead imposed by the network when reading or writing to a remote disk. If identical disks are available on a remote server and on the local host, total disk throughput will be better with the local disk. This is not grounds for an out-of-hand rejection of NFS for two reasons: NFS provides a measure of transparency and ease of system administration that is lost with multiple local disks, and centralized disk resources on a server take advantage of economies of scale. A large, fast disk on a server provides better throughput, with the network overhead, than a slower local disk if the decrease in disk access time outweighs the cost of the network data transfer.

UNIX Filesystem Effects

NFS read and write operations are rarely able to take advantage of disk controller optimizations or caching. A synchronous write from one client must be completed and acknowledged by the server before the next write request from the same client is handled. The situation is exacerbated if multiple clients are writing to different areas on the same disk. Many controllers use an elevator-seek algorithm to schedule disk operations according to the disk track number accessed, minimizing seek time. These optimizations are of little value if the disk request queue is never more than one or two operations deep. Read operations suffer from similar problems because read-ahead caching done by the controller is wasted if consecutive read operations are from different clients using different parts of the disk.

Filesystem fragmentation can further impair performance. Large files that have grown slowly over time may be badly allocated on disk, and require several disk head movements to satisfy a request that spans non-consecutive disk block boundaries. For example, if the last block in a file contains one filesystem block fragment, and then a write operation extends the file into another filesystem block that cannot be optimally placed, any read operation that crosses this same boundary requires two head seek operations. Unfortunately, the only way to repair fragmentation is to dump the filesystem to tape and rebuild it.

Writing large files multiplies the number of NFS write operations that must be performed. As a file grows beyond the number of blocks described in its inode, indirect and double indirect blocks are used to point to additional arrays of data blocks. A file that has grown to several megabytes, for example, requires three write operations to update its indirect, double indirect, and data blocks on each write operation. The design of the UNIX filesystem is ideal for small files, but imposes a penalty on large files.

Large directories also adversely impact NFS performance. Directories are searched linearly during an NFS *lookup* operation; the time to locate a named directory component is directly proportional to the size of the directory and the position of a name in the directory. Doubling the number of entries in a directory will, on average, double the time required to locate any given entry. Furthermore, reading a large directory from a remote host may require the server to respond with several packets instead of a single packet containing the entire directory structure.

Disk Transfer Rates

Sequential disk transfer rates affect NFS performance less than you might believe. Because NFS requests may be scattered all over a disk, and because they only deal with 8 kbytes of data at a time, disk seek time is usually more important than the time spent moving data to or from the disk head. If you are using NFS to access large files, higher sequential transfer rates may improve performance if multiple NFS requests are strung together by the disk driver. But in general, NFS performance is gated by how quickly you can get the head to the right spot on the disk platter.

If you have one or more "hot" disks that receive an unequal share of requests, your NFS performance suffers. To keep requests in fairly even queues, you must balance your NFS load across your disks.

Disk Load Balancing

Server response time is improved by balancing the load among all disks and minimizing the average waiting time for disk service. Disk balancing entails putting heavily used filesystems on separate disks so that requests for them may be serviced in parallel. This division of labor is particularly important for diskless client servers. If all clients have their root and swap filesystems on a single disk, requests using that disk may far outnumber those using any other on the server. Performance of each diskless client is degraded, as the single path to the target disk is a bottleneck. Dividing client partitions among several disks improves the overall throughput of the client root and swap filesystem requests.

The average waiting time endured by each request is a function of the random disk transfer rate and of the backlog of requests for that disk. Use the **iostat –D** utility to check the utilization of each disk, and look for imbalance in the disk queues. The **rps** and **wps** values are the number of read and write operations, per second, performed on each disk device, and the **util** column shows the utilization of the disk's bandwidth:

```
% iostat -D 5
      id000          id001
  rps wps util   rps wps util
    1   3  7.9     1   1  2.4
   17   6 50.2     0   0  0.4
    9   1 21.0     0   0  0.0
```

If the disk queues are grossly uneven, consider shuffling data on the filesystems to spread the load across more disks.

If all of your disks are more than 75-80% utilized, you are disk bound and either need faster disks, more disks, or an environment that makes fewer disk requests. Tuning kernel and client configurations usually helps to reduce the number of disk requests made by NFS clients.

Kernel Configuration

Many NFS requests require only information in the underlying inode for a file, rather than access to the data blocks composing the file. A bottleneck can be introduced in the inode table, which serves as a cache for recently opened files. If file references from NFS clients frequently require reloading entries in the inode table, then the file server is forced to perform expensive linear searches through disk-based directory structures for the new file pathname requiring an inode table entry.

In Berkeley-derived operating systems, the size of the inode table is governed by the **MAXUSERS** parameter, which is typically defined in the system configuration file. **MAXUSERS** is passed as a compile-time parameter to, or defined as a constant in, various modules using it to compute table sizes. The simplistic definition of **MAXUSERS** is the number of simultaneous users, plus a small margin for daemons. However, each NFS client places a load on the server similar to that of an interactive user. On any NFS server, the default value for **MAXUSERS** is probably insufficient. A good method for determining a value is:

- Start with the vendor's default value (typically 4 or 8).

- Add 1.0 for each diskless client supported by the server.

- For rough calculations, add 0.5 for each NFS client. A more refined approach is to add a fraction equal to the proportion of filesystems mounted on the NFS client from this server. For example, if a client mounts eight filesystems, with three of them from this server, the client should contribute 0.375 to the server's **MAXUSERS** computation. This is a tedious calculation for each combination of client and server, but it should impact the weight assigned to NFS clients when one server provides a majority of the filesystems exported in the network.

In System V, increase the size of the inode table using the **INODE** or **NINODE** parameters in the kernel configuration file.

In addition to governing the size of the inode table, increasing **MAXUSERS** also increases the size of the directory name look-up cache. Recently read directory entries are cached on the NFS server, and a sufficiently large cache speeds NFS *lookup* operations by eliminating the need to read directories from disk. Taking a directory cache miss is a fairly expensive operation, since the directory must be read from disk and searched linearly for the named component. You can check your directory name look up cache hit rate by running **vmstat –s** on your NFS servers:

```
% vmstat -s
...Page and swap info...
  5263691 total name lookups (cache hits 72%  per-process)
```

If you are hitting the cache less than 70% of the time, increase **MAXUSERS** on the NFS servers.

Cross-mounting Filesystems

An NFS client may find many of its processes in a high-priority wait state when an NFS server on which it relies stops responding for any reason. If two servers mount filesystems from each other, and the filesystems are hard-mounted, it is possible for processes on each server to wait on NFS responses from the other. To avoid a deadlock, in which processes on two NFS servers go to sleep waiting on each other, cross-mounting of servers should be avoided. This is of particular import in a network that uses hard-mounted NFS filesystems with fairly large timeout and retransmission count parameters, making it hard to interrupt the processes that are waiting on the NFS server.

If filesystem access requires cross-mounted filesystems, they should be mounted with the background (**bg**) option. This ensures that servers will not go into a deadly embrace after a power failure or other reboot. During the boot process, a machine attempts to mount its NFS filesystems before it accepts any incoming NFS requests. If two fileservers request each other's services, and boot at about the same time, it is likely that they will attempt to cross-mount their filesystems before either server is ready to provide NFS service. With the **bg** option, each NFS mount will time out and be put into the background. The background option only needs to be included in one server's **/etc/fstab**, making it the one to give up and break the deadlock. Eventually the servers will complete their boot processes, and when the network services are started the backgrounded mounts complete.

Multi-homed Servers

When a server exports NFS filesystems on more than one network interface, it may expend a measurable number of CPU cycles forwarding packets between interfaces. Consider host *boris* on four networks:

```
138.1.148.1     boris-bb4
138.1.147.1     boris-bb3
138.1.146.1     boris-bb2
138.1.145.1     boris-bb1 boris
```

Hosts on network 138.1.148.0 are able to "see" *boris* because *boris* forwards packets from any one of its network interfaces to the other. Hosts on the 138.1.148.0 network may mount filesystems from either hostname:

```
boris:/home/boris
boris-bb4:/home/boris
```

The second form is preferable on network 138.1.148.0 because it does not require *boris* to forward packets to its other interface's input queue. Likewise, on network 138.1.145.0, the **boris:/home/boris** form is preferable. Even though the requests are going to the same physical machine, requests that are addressed to the "wrong" server must be forwarded, as shown in Figure 12-10. This adds to to the IP protocol processing overhead. If the packet forwarding must be done for every NFS RPC request, then *boris* uses more CPU cycles to provide NFS service.

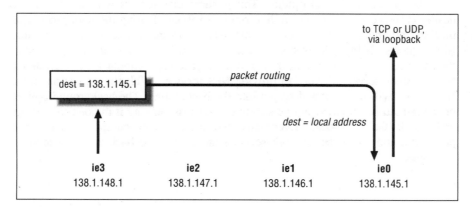

Figure 12-10. A multi-homed host

Client Tuning

The performance measurement and tuning techniques we've discussed so far have only dealt with making the NFS server go faster. Part of tuning an NFS network is ensuring that clients are well behaved so that they do not flood the servers with requests and upset any tuning you may have performed. Server performance is usually limited by disk or network bandwidth, but there is no throttle on the rate at which clients generate requests unless you put one in place. If you can't make your servers or network any faster, you have to tune the clients to handle the network "as is."

Slow Server Compensation

The RPC retransmission algorithm cannot distinguish between a slow server and a congested network. If a reply is not received from the server within the RPC timeout period, the request is retransmitted subject to the timeout and retransmission parameters for that mount point. It is immaterial to the RPC mechanism whether the original request is still enqueued on the server or if it was lost on the network. Excessive RPC retransmissions place an additional strain on the server, further degrading response time.

Identifying NFS Retransmissions

Inspection of the load average and disk activity on the servers may indicate that the servers are heavily loaded and imposing the tightest constraint. The NFS client-side statistics provide the most concrete evidence that one or more slow servers are to blame:

```
% nfsstat -rc
Client rpc:
calls   badcalls retrans badxid   timeout  wait  newcred
430660  2242     718     1566     2941     0     0
```

The –rc option is given to **nfsstat** to look at the RPC statistics only, for client-side NFS operations. The call type demographics contained in the NFS-specific statistics are not of value in this analysis. The test for a slow server is having *badxid* and timeout of the same magnitude. In the example above, *badxid* is nearly half the value of *timeout*. The high *badxid* count implies that requests are reaching the various NFS servers, but the servers are too loaded to send replies before the local host's RPC calls time out and are retransmitted. *badxid* is incremented each time a duplicate reply is received for a retransmitted request (an RPC request retains its XID through all retransmission cycles). In this case, the server is replying to all requests, including the retransmitted ones. The client is simply not patient enough to wait for replies from the slow server. If there is more than one NFS server, the client may be outpacing all of them or just one particularly sluggish node.

If the server has a duplicate request cache, retransmitted requests that match an NFS call currently in progress are ignored. Only those requests in progress are recognized and filtered, so it is still possible for a sufficiently loaded server to generate duplicate replies that show up in the *badxid* counts of its clients. Without a duplicate request cache, *badxid* and *timeout* may be nearly equal, while the cache may reduce the number of duplicate replies by half. With or without a duplicate request cache, if the *baxid* and *timeout* statistics reported by **nfsstat** (on the client) are of the same magnitude, then server performance is an issue deserving further investigation.

A mixture of network and server-related problems can make interpretation of the **nfsstat** figures difficult. A client served by four hosts may find that two of the hosts are particularly slow while a third is located across a network router that is digesting streams of large write packets. One slow server can be masked by other, faster servers: a retransmission rate of 10% (calculated as *timeout/calls*) would indicate short periods of server sluggishness or network congestion if the retransmissions were evenly distributed among all servers. However, if all timeouts occurred while talking to just one server, the retransmission rate *for that server* could be 50% or higher.

A simple method for finding the distribution of retransmitted requests is to perform the same set of disk operation on each server, measuring the incremental number of RPC timeouts that occur when loading each server in turn. This experiment may point to a server that is noticeably slower than its peers, if a large percentage of the RPC timeouts are attributed to that host. Alternatively, you may shift your focus away from server performance if timeouts are fairly evenly distributed or if no timeouts occur during the server loading experiment. Fluctuations in server performance may vary by the time of day, so that more timeouts occur during periods of peak server usage in the morning and after lunch, for example.

Server response time may be clamped at some minimum value due to fixed-cost delays of sending packets through bridges and routers, or due to static configurations which cannot be changed for political or historical reasons. If server response cannot be improved, then the clients of that server must adjust their mount parameters to avoid further loading it with retransmitted requests. The relative patience of the client is determined by the timeout, retransmission count, and hard-mount variables.

Timeout Period Calculation

The timeout period is specified by the mount parameter **timeo**, and is expressed in tenths of a second. The default value is vendor-specific, ranging from 5 to 11 (0.5 seconds to 1.1 seconds). If a reply is not received by the client within the **timeo** period, a *minor timeout* has occurred for this RPC call. The timeout period is doubled, and the RPC request is sent again. The process is repeated until the retransmission count specified by the **retrans** mount parameter is reached; if no reply has been received then a *major timeout* has occurred. The retransmission count has a default value that ranges from 3 to 5, and is also vendor-specific.

After a major timeout, the message:

```
NFS server host not responding, still trying
```

is printed on the client's console. If a reply is eventually received, the "not responding" message is followed with the message:

```
NFS server host OK
```

Hard-mounting a file system guarantees that the sequence of retransmissions continues until the server replies. After a major timeout on a hard-mounted filesystem, the *initial* timeout period is doubled, and the count of retransmission attempts is reset to zero, beginning a new major cycle. Hard mounts are the default option. For example, a filesystem mounted via:

```
# mount -o retrans=3,timeo=5 wahoo:/home/wahoo /mnt
```

has the retranssmision sequence shown in Table 12-4.

Table 12-4. NFS Timeout Sequence

Absolute Time	Current Timeout	New Timeout	Event
0.5	0.5	1.0	Minor.
1.5	1.0	2.0	Minor.
3.5	2.0	1.0	Major, double initial timeout.
	...NFS server *wahoo* not responding...		
4.5	1.0	2.0	Minor.
6.5	2.0	4.0	Minor.
10.5	4.0	2.0	Major, double initial timeout.
	...NFS server *wahoo* not responding...		

Timeout periods are not increased without bound. The initial timeout period never exceeds 30 seconds (**timeo=300**) and the maximum timeout for any call is 60 seconds.

To accommodate slower servers, increase the **timeo** parameter used in /etc/fstab. Increasing **retrans** increases the length of a minor timeout period, but it does so at the expense of sending more requests to the NFS server. These duplicate requests further load the server, particularly when they require repeating disk operations. In many cases, the client receives a reply after sending the second or third retransmission, so doubling the initial timeout period eliminates about half of the NFS calls sent to the slow server.

Adjusting the Timeout Period

In general, increasing the NFS RPC timeout is more helpful than increasing the retransmission count for hard-mounted filesystems. If the server doesn't respond to the first few RPC requests, it's likely that it won't respond for a "long" time, compared to the RPC timeout period. It's best to let the client sit back, double its timeout period on major timeouts, and wait for the server to recover. Increasing the retransmission count simply increases the noise level on the network while the client is waiting for the server to respond.

In SunOS 4.1, you can use **nfsstat -m** on an NFS client to review the kernel's observed NFS server response times:

```
% nfsstat -m
/home/wahoo from wahoo:/home/wahoo (Addr 130.1.14.13)
 Flags: hard  read size=8192, write size=8192,  count = 5
 Lookups: srtt=13 (32ms), dev=7 (35ms), cur=5 (100ms)
  Reads: srtt=21 (52ms), dev=11 (55ms), cur=8 (160ms)
  Writes: srtt=79 (197ms), dev=14 (70ms), cur=16 (320ms)
  All: srtt=28 (70ms), dev=18 (90ms), cur=12 (240ms)
```

The smoothed, average round-trip (*srtt*) times are reported in milliseconds, as well as the average deviation (*dev*) and the current "expected" response time (*cur*). The numbers in parentheses are the actual times in milliseconds; the other values are unscaled values kept by the kernel and can be ignored. Response times are shown for read and write operations, which are "big" RPCs, and for lookups, which typify "small" RPC requests. If you see an average or current response time for writes of, say, 900 ms, increase the timeout value to **timeo=9**.

Without the kernel's values as a baseline, choosing a new timeout value is best done empirically. Doubling the initial value is a good baseline; after changing the timeout value observe the RPC timeout rate and *badxid* rate using **nfsstat**. At first glance, it does not appear that there is any harm in immediately going to **timeo=300**, the maximum initial timeout value used in the retransmission algorithm. If server performance is the sole constraint, then this is a fair assumption. However, even a well-tuned network endures bursts of traffic that can cause packets to be lost at congested network hardware interfaces or dropped by the server. In this case, the excessively long timeout will have a dramatic impact on client performance. With **timeo=300**, RPC retransmissions "avoid" network congestion by waiting for *minutes* while the actual traffic peak may have been only a few milliseconds in duration.

Adjusting the timeout parameter to eliminate regular "NFS server not responding" messages improves the user community's subjective evaluation of server performance. For example, a user who regularly gets NFS server messages after firing off a **make** will always feel that the system is slow. Removing the visual cue by increasing the length of a major timeout cycle may reduce the strength of the user's negative opinions while simultaneously reducing the load on the server.

Retransmission Rate Thresholds

There is little agreement among system administrators about acceptable retransmission rate thresholds. Some people claim that *any* request retransmission indicates a performance problem, while others chose an arbitrary percentage as a "goal." Determining the retransmission rate threshold for your NFS clients depends upon your choice of the **timeo** mount parameter and your expected response time variations. The equation in Figure 12-11 expresses the expected retransmission rate as a function of the allowable response time variation and the **timeo** parameter.*

$$\text{retransmission rate threshhold} = \frac{\text{response time variation (millisecond/call)}}{\text{timeo value (millisecond/retransmission)}}$$

$$= \text{X\% (millisecond/call)}$$

Figure 12-11. NFS retransmission threshold

If you allow a response time fluctuation of ten milliseconds, or about 20% of a 50 millisecond average response time, and use the default 0.7 second (700 millisecond) timeout period, then your expected retransmission rate is (10/700) = 1.4%.

If you increase your timeout value, this equation dictates that you should *decrease* your retransmission rate threshold. This makes sense: if you make the clients more tolerant of a slow NFS server, they shouldn't be sending as many NFS

---

*This retransmission threshold equation is presented in the *Prestoserve User's Manual*, March 1991 edition. This manual and the Prestoserve NFS write accelerator are produced by Legato Systems.

RPC retransmissions. Similarly, if you want less variation in NFS client performance, and decide to reduce your allowable response time variation, you also
need to reduce your retransmission threshold.

Soft Mount Issues

Repeated retransmission cycles only occur for hard-mounted file systems. When
the **soft** option is supplied in a mount, the RPC retransmission sequence ends at
the first major timeout, producing messages like:

```
NFS write failed for server wahoo: Timed out
```

The NFS operation that failed is indicated, as well as the server that failed to
respond before the major timeout. RPC timeouts may be caused by extremely
slow servers, or they can occur if a server crashes and is down or rebooting while
an RPC retransmission cycle is in progress.

With soft-mounted filesystems, you have to worry about damaging data due to
incomplete writes, losing access to the text segment of a swapped process (in
SunOS 4.0 and System V Release 4), and making soft-mounted filesystems more
tolerant of variances in server response time. If a client does not give the server
enough latitude in its response time, the first two problems impair both the performance and correct operation of the client. If *write* operations fail, data consistency on the server cannot be guaranteed. The write error is reported to the application during some later call to *write()* or *close()*, which is consistent with the
behavior of a local filesystem residing on a failing or overflowing disk. When the
actual write to disk is attempted by the kernel device driver, the failure is reported
to the application as an error during the next similar or related system call.

A well-conditioned application should exit abnormally after a failed write, or
retry the write if possible. If the application ignores the return code from *write()*,
then it is possible to corrupt data on a soft-mounted filesystem. Some write
operations may fail and never be retried, leaving holes in the open file.

To guarantee data integrity, *all* filesystems mounted read-write should be hard-
mounted. Server performance as well as server reliability determine whether a
request eventually succeeds on a soft-mounted filesystem, and neither can be
guaranteed. Furthermore, any operating system that maps executable images
directly into memory (SunOS 4.x and System V Release 4) should hard-mount
filesystems containing executables. If the filesystem is soft-mounted, and the NFS
server crashes while the client is paging in an executable (during the initial load
of the text segment or to refill a page frame that was paged out), an RPC timeout
will cause the page daemon to fail. What happens next is system-dependent; the
application may be terminated or the system may panic with unrecoverable swap
errors.

Make NFS clients more tolerant of soft-mounted NFS fileservers by increasing the **retrans** mount option. Increasing the number of attempts to reach the server makes the client less likely to produce an RPC error during brief periods of server loading. In the next section, we'll look at timeout patterns and use of the **intr** option to replace soft mounts.

Timeout Calculations

A common objection to hard-mounting filesystems is that NFS clients remain catatonic until a crashed server recovers, due to the infinite loop of RPC retransmissions and timeouts. A compromise is to mount the filesystem *hard*, and to specify the **intr** option allowing an interrupt to break the retransmission loop.

Older implementations of NFS do not process keyboard interrupts until a major timeout has occurred: with even a small timeout period and retransmission count, the time required to recognize an interrupt can be quite large.

The timeout values used by the NFS retransmission algorithm range from the initial *timeo* to a maximum value expressed by the equation in Figure 12-12.

$$t_{max} = \min \begin{pmatrix} 600 \\ \text{timeout} \cdot 2^{\text{retrans} - 1} \end{pmatrix}$$

Figure 12-12. Maximum NFS RPC timeout period

Expressed as a sum of a geometric progression, the delay between major timeouts is shown in Figure 12-13 and Figure 12-14.

$$t_{major} = \min \begin{pmatrix} 300 + 600 \cdot (\text{retrans} - 1) \\ \text{timeout} \cdot (2^{\text{retrans}} - 1) \end{pmatrix}$$

Figure 12-13. NFS major timeout period

$$t_{\text{major}} = \sum_{i=1}^{\text{retrans}} \text{timeout} \cdot 2^{i-1} = \text{timeout} \cdot (2^{\text{retrans}} - 1)$$

Figure 12-14. NFS major timeout period, with RPC timeout limit

Using the default values of 0.7 second timeouts and four retransmissions, the first major timeout occurs after 10.5 seconds. If the timeout value is increased to 1.5 seconds and the retransmission count increased to six, the major timeout delay explodes to over a minute and a half. Even with the **intr** option, it may appear that mounts are uninterruptible if major timeouts present the only window for terminating the system call.

Adjusting for Network Reliability Problems

NFS client mount parameters must be adjusted to handle problems with network reliability just as they are tuned to accommodate a slow server. Even a lightly loaded network can suffer from reliability problems if bridges, routers, or gateways joining the network segments routinely drop parts of long packet trains. Bridges and routers are most likely to affect NFS performance if their network interfaces cannot keep up with the packet arrival rates generated by the NFS clients and servers on each side.

Determining the impact of a bridge or router or the effect of network unreliability requires another look at the client-side RPC statistics:

```
% nfsstat -rc
Client rpc:
calls    badcalls retrans  badxid   timeout  wait  newcred
432760   2242     718      3        2941     0     0
```

When *badxid* is close to zero, it implies that the network or one of the network interfaces on the client, server, or any intermediate routing hardware is dropping packets. Some host Ethernet interfaces are tuned to handle page-sized packets and do not reliably handle larger packets; similarly, many older Ethernet bridges cannot forward long bursts of packets. A router or host acting as an IP router may have limited forwarding capacity, so reducing the number of packets sent for any request reduces the probability that the router drops packets that build up behind its network interface.

The NFS buffer size determines how many packets are required to send a single, large *read* or *write* request. The default buffer size is 8 kbytes, and is determined by the client at boot time. The server doesn't enter into the calculation of buffer size; it just has to be able to handle the trains of packets generated to send each buffer.

Compensating for unreliable networks involves changing the NFS buffer size, controlled by the **rsize** and **wsize** mount options. **rsize** determines how many bytes are requested in each NFS read, and **wsize** gauges the number of bytes sent in each NFS write operation. Reducing **rsize** and **wsize** eases the peak loads on the network by sending shorter packet trains for each NFS request. By spacing the requests out, and increasing the probability that the entire request reaches the server or client intact on the first transmission, the overall load on the network and server is smoothed out over time.

The read and write buffer sizes are specified in bytes. They are generally made multiples of 512 bytes, based on the size of a disk block. There is no requirement that either size be an integer multiple of 512, although using an arbitrary size can make the disk operations on the remote host less efficient. Write operations performed on non-disk block aligned buffers require the NFS server to read the block, modify the block, and rewrite it. The read-modify-write cycle is invisible to the client, but adds to the overhead of each *write()* performed on the server.

These values are of interest to the **biod** process, and are completely independent of buffer sizes internal to any client-side processes. An application that writes 400-byte buffers, writing to a filesystem mounted with **wsize=4096**, does not cause an NFS *write* request to be sent to the server until the 11th write is performed.

Here is an example of mounting an NFS filesystme with the read and write buffer sizes reduced to 2048 bytes:

```
# mount -o rsize=2048,wsize=2048 wahoo:/home/wahoo /mnt
```

It is not necessary to change both the read and write buffer sizes. When a piece of network hardware or general network loading requires changing buffer size, the same change is usually applied to requests going to and from the server. Read and write sizes can be made asymmetric if the server's interface to the network has a greater effect than the network hardware. On a server that can send larger packets than it can receive, for example, there is no need to reduce **rsize** on the client, but decreasing *wsize* prevents the server from dropping parts of large NFS write buffers. Hosts that cannot accept bursts of IP packets usually do not suffer from the same constraint when writing packets, so one convention is to have the client machine read using its page size and write using the server's page size. This approach attempts to capitalize on page-size-oriented optimizations in the kernel. Any machine should be able to receive a series of packets that fills an entire page.

For example, a machine with an 8-kbyte page mounting a filesystem from a server with a 2-kbyte page could explicitly set **wsize=2048** in its **/etc/fstab** entry, using the default 8-kbyte value for **rsize**:

```
slick:/home/projects    /home/projects  nfs rw,bg,wsize=2048 0 0
```

Decreasing the NFS buffer size has the undesirable effect of increasing the load on the server *and* sending more packets on the network to read or write a given buffer. The size of the actual packets on the network does not change, but the number of IP packets composing a single NFS buffer decreases as the **rsize** and **wsize** are decreased. For example, an 8-kbyte NFS buffer is divided into five IP packets of about 1500 bytes, and a sixth packet with the remaining data bytes. If the write size is set to 2048 bytes, only two IP packets are needed.

The problem lies in the number of packets required to transfer the same amount of data. Table 12-5 shows the number of IP packets required to copy a file for various NFS read buffer sizes.

Table 12-5. IP Packets, RPC Requests as Function of NFS Buffer Size

File Size	IP Packets/RPC Calls			
	rsize	rsize	rsize	rsize
(kbytes)	1024	2048	4096	8192
1	1/1	1/1	1/1	1/1
2	2/2	2/1	2/1	2/1
4	4/4	4/2	3/1	3/1
8	8/8	8/4	6/2	6/1

As the file size increases, transfers with smaller NFS buffer sizes send more IP packets to the server. The number of packets will be the same for 4096- and 8192-byte buffers, but for file sizes over 4k, setting **rsize=4096** always requires twice as many RPC calls to the server. The increased network traffic adds to the very problem for which the buffer size change was compensating, and the additional RPC calls further load the server.

Due to the increased server load, it is sometimes necessary to increase the RPC timeout parameter when decreasing NFS buffer sizes. Reducing **rsize** and **wsize** eases one performance bottleneck but may further constrain another by placing an additional load on the server and causing client-side timeouts. If a change in either **rsize** or **wsize** produces a corresponding increase in the **badxid** count shown by **nfsstat**, adjust the client's mount parameters to the server's response time under the new load. The composition of the two tuning processes should yield the best performance.

NFS Over Wide-area Networks

It is possible to run NFS over wide-area networks (WANs), but you must adjust the buffer sizes and timeouts to account for the differences between the wide-area and an Ethernet. Decrease the **rsize** and **wsize** to match the MTU of the slowest wide-area link you traverse with the mount; if you are running over an X.25 network then consider decreasing the NFS buffer size down to 128 bytes. While this greatly increases the number of RPC requests that are needed to move a given part of a file, it is the most social approach to running NFS over a WAN.

If you use the default 8-kbyte NFS buffer, you send long trains of maximum sized packets over the wide-area link. Your NFS requests will be competing for bandwidth with other, interactive users' packets, and the NFS packet trains are likely to crowd the **rlogin** and **telnet** packets. Sending an 8-kbyte buffer over a 56 kbaud line takes almost one second. Writing a small file ties up the WAN link for several seconds and infuriates interactive users who do not get keyboard echo during that time. Reducing the NFS buffer size forces your NFS client to wait for replies after each short burst of packets, giving bandwidth back to other WAN users.

In addition to decreasing the buffer size, increase the RPC timeout values to account for the significant increase in packet transmission time. Over a wide-area network, the network transmission delay will be comparable to the RPC service time on the NFS server, so set your timeout values based on the average time required to send or receive a complete NFS buffer. On a 56-kbaud line, with a buffer size of 128 bytes, the time required for a request and reply to cross the wide-area network is significant compared to the server's response time:

```
RPC request (~100 bytes) to server:    15 msec
Server response time:                  20 msec
Data (128 bytes) to client:            15 msec
```

Contention for bandwidth on the 56 kbaud line, caused by someone else using **ftp**, for example, could increase the network component of the response time into the full-second range. Increase your NFS RPC timeout to at least several seconds to avoid retransmitting requests and further loading the wide-area network link.

Over a long-haul network, particularly one that is run over modem lines, you may want to enable UDP checksum calculations. Normally, no UDP checksums are used, because they add significantly to the cost of sending and receiving a packet. However, if packets are damaged in transit over the modem line, UDP checksums allow you to reject bad data in NFS requests. NFS requests containing UDP checksum errors are rejected on the server, and will be retransmitted by the client. Without the checksums, it's possible to read or write corrupted data.

Turn on UDP checksums by changing the **udp_cksum** variable in the kernel, using **adb**:

```
client# echo "udp_cksum/W 1" | adb -k -w /vmunix /dev/mem
server# echo "udp_cksum/W 1" | adb -k -w /vmunix /dev/mem
```

You need to enable the checksums on both the client and server, so that the client generates the checksums and the server verifies them. Check your vendor's documentation to be sure that UDP checksums are supported; the checksum generation is not always available and may not work in older releases of the operating system.

biod Tuning

If server performance is a problem, adding **biod** daemons to the client machines usually makes it worse. The **biod** processes impose an implicit limit on the number of NFS requests requiring disk I/O that may be outstanding from any client at any time. Each **biod** process has at most one NFS request outstanding at any time, and if you increase the number of **biod** daemons, you allow each client to send more disk-bound requests at once, further loading the network and the servers. If you have n processes performing file I/O, and m **biod** daemons, then you can have $n+m$ RPC requests outstanding on the client at one time: one from each of the client **biod** daemons, and one from each of the processes.

Decreasing the number of **biod** daemons doesn't improve performance, and usually reduces NFS filesystem throughput. You must have some small degree of NFS request multi-threading on the NFS client to maintain the illusion of having filesystems on local disks. Eliminating or reducing the number of **biod** daemons effectively throttles the filesystem throughput of the NFS client—no read-ahead and write-behind will be done.

In some cases, you want to eliminate write-behind client requests because the network interface of the NFS server cannot handle multiple NFS write requests at once. In these radical cases, adequate performance can only be achieved by turning off **biod** and forcing each *write()* system call to complete synchronously to the calling process. Normally, **biod** does write-behind caching to improve NFS performance, and running multiple copies of **biod** allows a single process to have several write requests outstanding at once. If you are running four copies of **biod** on an NFS client, then the client will generate five NFS *write* requests at once when it is performing a sequential write to a large file: the first four write operations will be handled by **biod** daemons, and the fifth will be done by the writing process itself (since all of the daemons are busy). At this point, the writing process is blocked, waiting for its RPC to complete, so the client cannot generate any more write requests. When writing process's RPC call completes, it will again fill the buffer (or page) cache, and send another burst of NFS *write* operations to the server.

If the server handling these requests cannot keep pace with the incoming NFS *write* requests, even with a 512-byte packet size, then it may be necessary to force NFS requests to be single-threaded with respect to *all* processes on the client host. Turning off the **biod** daemons accomplishes this; the kernel RPC mechanism continues to work without the daemons, albeit less efficiently. Each process is forced to make its own *write* RPC calls, and the writing processes wait for these calls to complete. No write-behind is performed.

biod daemons are started at boot time with a command line like:

```
biod 4;        echo -n 'biod'
```

Commenting this line out of the appropriate boot script eliminates all NFS read-ahead and write-behind. The argument passed to **biod** is the number of instances of the daemon to be started. Decreasing the number of daemons may produce an effect similar to that of eliminating them completely. Increasing the number of **biod** processes above the default only allows an NFS client to send more RPC requests at one time. This will not improve performance at all, and often makes it worse, if server request handling bandwidth is a constraint.

Attribute Caching

NFS clients cache file attributes such as the modification time and owner to avoid having to go to the NFS server for information that does not change frequently. The motivations for an attribute caching scheme are explained in "File Attribute Caching," in Chapter 6, *Network File System Design and Operation*. Once a *getattr* for a file handle has been completed, the information is cached for use by other requests. Cached data is updated in subsequent write operations; the cache is flushed when the lifetime of the data expires. Repeated attribute changes caused by write operations can be handled entirely on the client side, with the net result written back to the server in a single *setattr*. Note that explicit *setattr* operations, generated by a **chmod** command on the client, are not cached at all on the client. Only file size and modification time changes are cached.

The lifetime of the cached data is determined by four mount parameters shown in Table 12-6.

Table 12-6. Attribute Cache Parameters

Parameter	Default(seconds)	Cache Limit
acregmin	3	Minimum lifetime for file attributes.
acregmax	60	Maximum lifetime for file attributes.
acdirmin	30	Minimum lifetime for directory attributes.
acdirmax	60	Maximum lifetime for directory attributes.

The default values again vary by vendor, as does the accessibility of the attribute cache parameters. The minimum lifetimes set the time period for which a size/modification time update will be cached locally on the client. If another update occurs within this period, then the attributes are held for another minimum period. Attribute changes are written out at the end of the maximum period to avoid having the client and server views of the files drift too far apart. In addition, changing the file attributes on the server makes those changes visible to other clients referencing the same file (when their attribute caches time out).

Attribute caching can be turned off with the **noac** mount option:

```
mahimahi:/tools/mahimahi          /tools/mahimahi nfs noac,hard   0 0
```

Without caching enabled, every operation requiring access to the file attributes must make a call to the server. This won't disable read caching (in either **biod** or the VM system), but it adds to the cost of maintaining cache consistency. The **biod** daemons and the VM system still perform regular cache consistency checks by requesting file attributes, but each consistency check now requires a *getattr* RPC on the NFS server. When many clients have attribute caching disabled, the server's *getattr* count skyrockets:

```
% nfsstat -ns
Server nfs:
calls       badcalls
1896085     0
null        getattr     setattr     root        lookup      readlink    read
3724  0%    795111 41%  10199  0%   0   0%      349126 18%  14883   0%  467247 24%
wrcache     write       create      remove      rename      link        symlink
0  0%       65860  3%   30896  1%   2731  0%    1938  0%    94  0%      439  0%
mkdir       rmdir       readdir     fsstat
355  0%     95  0%      149916  7%  3471  0%
```

Upwards of 60% of the NFS calls handled by the server may be requests to return file or directory attributes.

If changes made by one client need to be reflected on other clients with finer granularity, the attribute cache lifetime can be reduced to one second using the **actime** option, which sets both the regular file and directory minimum and maximum lifetimes to the same value:

```
mahimahi:/tools/mahimahi   /tools/mahimahi  nfs actime=1,hard      0 0
```

This has the same effect as:

```
mahimahi:/tools/mahimahi   /tools/mahimahi  nfs acregmin=1,acregmax=1,\
   acdirmin=1,acdirmax=1,hard 0 0
```

Mount Point Constructions

The choice of a mount point naming scheme can have a significant impact on NFS server usage. Two common but inefficient constructions are stepping-stone mounts and server-resident symbolic links. In each case, the client must first query the NFS server owning the intermediate mount point (or symbolic link) before directing a request to the correct target server.

A stepping-stone mount exists when you mount one NFS filesystem on top of another directory which is itself part of an NFS-mounted filesystem from a different server. For example:

```
# mount mahimahi:/usr          /usr
# mount wahoo:/usr/local       /usr/local
# mount poi:/usr/local/bin     /usr/local/bin
```

To perform a name lookup on **/usr/local/bin/emacs**, the NFS client performs directory searches and file attribute queries on all three NFS servers, when the only "interesting" server is *poi*. It's best to mount all of the subdirectories of /usr and /usr/local from a single fileserver, so that you don't send RPC requests to other fileservers simply because they own the intermediate components in the pathname. Stepping-stone mounts are frequently created for consistent naming schemes, but they add to the load of "small" RPC calls handled by all NFS servers.

Symbolic links are also useful for imposing symmetric naming conventions across multiple filesystems but they impose an unnecessary load on an NFS server that is regularly called upon to resolve the links. NFS pathnames are resolved a component at a time, so any symbolic links encountered in a pathname must be resolved by the host owning them.

For example, consider a **/usr/local** that is composed of links to various subdirectories on other servers:

```
# mount wahoo:/usr/local /usr/local
# cd /usr/local
# ls -l
lrwxrwxrwx 1 root 16 May 17 19:12 bin -> /tools/poi/bin
lrwxrwxrwx 1 root 16 May 17 19:12 lib -> /tools/mahimahi/lib
lrwxrwxrwx 1 root 16 May 17 19:12 man -> /tools/irie/man
```

Each reference to any file in **/usr/local** must first go through the server *wahoo* to get the appropriate symbolic link resolved. Once the link is read, the client machine can then look up the directory entry in the correct subdirectory of **/tools**. Every request that requires looking up a pathname now requires two server requests instead of just one.

Use **nfsstat -s** to examine the number of symbolic link resolutions performed on each server:

```
% nfsstat -s
Server rpc:
calls         badcalls      nullrecv      badlen        xdrcall
92207         0             0             0             0

Server nfs:
calls         badcalls
92207         0
null          getattr       setattr       root          lookup        readlink      read
0   0%        18423 19%     0   0%        0   0%        23344 25%     300100 32%    3614   3%
wrcache       write         create        remove        rename        link          symlink
0   0%        0   0%        0   0%        0   0%        0   0%        0   0%        8   0%
mkdir         rmdir         readdir       fsstat
0   0%        0   0%        16760 18%     18   0%
```

If the total percentage of *readlink* calls is more than 10% of the total number of *lookup* calls on all NFS servers, there is a symbolic link fairly high up in a frequently traversed path component. You should look at the total number of *lookup* and *readlink* calls on all servers, since the *readlink* is counted by the server that owns the link while the *lookup* is directed to the target of the symbolic link.

If you have one or more symbolic links that are creating a pathname lookup bottleneck on the server, remove the links (on the server) and replace them with a client-side NFS mount of the link's target. In the example above, mounting the **/tools** subdirectories directly in **/usr/local** would cut the number of **/usr/local**-related operations in half. The performance improvement derived from this change may be substantial, since symbolic links are not cached: every *readlink* call requires the server to read the link from disk. Stepping-stone mounts, although far from ideal, are faster than an equivalent configuration built from symbolic links.

Most filesystem naming problems can be resolved more easily and with far fewer performance penalties by using the automounter, as described in the next chapter.

Routing Information

In a small network, or one in which there is only one router connecting it to other networks, static routing is preferable to the dynamic routing requiring **routed**. Gateway and router hosts broadcast route information every 30 seconds, and each client running **routed** receives these packets and runs the **routed** daemon to update its kernel routing tables. In a single-outlet network, every route goes through the solitary router, so the entire routing table can be compressed into a default route entry:

```
route add default 131.40.52.14 1
```

The destination is given as *default*, and the gateway address is the IP address or hostname of the router. This command can be added to the boot scripts where **routed** gets commented out:

```
#if [ -f /usr/etc/in.routed ]; then
#       in.routed;       echo -n ' routed'
#fi
route add default acadia-gw 1
```

Under SunOS 4.1.1 and later, the presence of an **/etc/defaultroute** file accomplishes the same goal. Create **/etc/defaultroute** on each machine, and put the name of the default router or gateway in this file. If this file exists, the **/etc/rc.local** script will read the router name from it and set up a default route, as shown in the excerpt below:

```
if [ ! -f /sbin/route -a -f /etc/defaultrouter ]; then
    route -f add default 'cat /etc/defaultrouter' 1
fi
```

Furthermore, if a default route has been established, the SunOS 4.1.1 **/etc/rc.local** skips the invocation of **in.routed**:

```
defroute="'netstat -n -r | grep default'"
if [ -z "$defroute" ]; then
    if [ -f /usr/etc/in.routed ]; then
        in.routed;       echo 'running routing daemon.'
    fi
fi
```

The **-n** option is passed to **netstat** so that IP addresses are used in its output, rather than host names, because NIS or DNS may not be available at this point to provide the IP address-to-hostname conversion.

In networks with multiple routers or gateways, take care to define non-redundant routes explicitly if static routing is used. When one router is listed as the default, it may receive packets that it cannot forward, so it sends the packets to another router on the same local area network. On some routers (and routing hosts), sending a packet out on the same interface on which it arrived also causes an ICMP redirect message to be sent to the transmitting host, although the host may ignore the redirect request. In this case, using default routes adds to the noise level on the network, because the default routers will be sending routing "hints" on every packet.

Stale File Handles

A file handle becomes stale whenever the file or directory represented by the handle is removed by one client while another client still has it open. For example, the following sequence of operations produces a stale file handle error for the current directory of the process running on *client1*:

```
client1                 client2
% cd /src/mod1
                        % cd /src
                        % rm -rf mod1
% ls
.: Stale File Handle
```

If you consistently suffer from stale file handle errors, you should look at the way in which users share files using NFS. Even though users see the same set of files, they do not necessarily have to do their work in the same directories. Watch out for users who share directories or copies of code. Use a source code control system that lets them make private copies of source files in their own directories. NFS provides an excellent mechanism for allowing all users to see the common source tree, but nobody should be doing development in it. Similarly, users who share scratch space may decide to clean it out periodically. Any user who had a scratch file open when another user on another NFS client purged the scratch directory will receive stale file handle errors on the next reference to the (now removed) scratch file.

As with most things, it helps to have an understanding of how your users are using the filesystems presented to them by NFS. In many cases, users want access to a wide variety of filesystems, but they do not want all of them mounted at all times (for fear of server crashes), nor do they want to keep track of where all filesystems are exported from and where they should be mounted. The NFS automounter solves all of these problems by applying NIS management to NFS mount information. As part of your client tuning, consider using the automounter to make client NFS administration easier.

13

The Automounter

Automounter Maps
Invocation and the Master Map
Integration with NIS
Key and Variable Substitutions
Advanced Map Tricks
Side Effects

The automounter is a tool that automatically mounts NFS filesystems when they are referenced and unmounts them when they are no longer needed. It applies NIS management to NFS configuration files so that you can edit a single NIS map and have it affect client mount information throughout the network. Using the automounter, you don't have to keep **/etc/fstab** files up to date by hand.* Mount information including the server's name, filesystem pathname on the server, local mount point and mount options, is contained in automounter *maps*, which are usually maintained in NIS maps.

---

*The automounter is included in the most recent releases of Sun's SunOS and its derivatives, DEC's Ultrix, and IBM's AIX. A public domain version called **amd** is available on *uunet.uu.net* and **amd** runs on almost any UNIX system. Because it is kernel- and server-independent, the automounter is easily migrated to other NFS client platforms.

Why would you want to bother with another administrative tool? What's wrong with putting all of the remote filesystem information in each hosts' /etc/fstab files? There are many motivations for using the automounter:

- /etc/fstab files on every host become much less complex as the automounter handles the common entries in this file.

- The automounter maps may be maintained using NIS, streamlining the administration of mount tables for all hosts in the network the same way NIS streamlines user account information.

- Your exposure to hanging a process when an NFS server crashes is greatly reduced. The automounter unmounts all filesystems that are not in use, removing dependencies on file servers that are not currently referenced by the client.

- The automounter extends the basic NFS mount protocol to find the "nearest server" for replicated, read-only filesystems. The NFS server that is closest to the client—going through the fewest number of bridges and routers—will handle the mount request. Distributing client load in this manner reduces the load on the more heavily used network hardware.

In a large and dynamic NFS environment, it is difficult to keep the **fstab** file on each machine up-to-date. Doing so requires creating mount points and usually hand-editing configuration files; automatic distribution of **fstab** files is made difficult by the large number of host-specific entries in each. As you add new software packages or filesystems on the network, you usually have to edit every **fstab** file. Using the automounter, you change one NIS map and allow the automounter to provide the new mount point information on all NIS clients.

Adding NFS servers is usually accompanied by a juggling of directories. It is likely that every client will be required to mount filesystems from the new server. As new NFS servers add filesystems to the network, the clients develop new dependencies on these servers, and their **fstab** files grow in complexity.

Users cannot simply mount filesystems at their whim without **root** privileges. The automounter handles this problem by performing the mount as the filesystems are referenced, which is usually the point at which users decide they need to perform the mount themselves. Some users request that their machines mount only those filesystems of interest to them to eliminate the possibility that their machines will hang if a server containing "uninteresting" files hangs. The automounter eliminates dependencies on these unrelated NFS servers by imposing a working-set notion on the set of mounted filesystems. When a filesystem is first referenced, the automounter mounts it at the appropriate place in the local filesystem. After several minutes (five by default), the automounter attempts to unmount all filesystems that it previously mounted. If the filesystem is quiescent, and therefore probably uninteresting to the client, then the automounter's *umount( )* system call succeeds and the client is relieved of the server dependency. If the filesystem is busy, the automounter ignores the error returned by *umount( )*.

Using the automounter also adds another level of transparency to the network. Once a client's **/etc/fstab** file is created, the client has a static idea of *where* each remote filesystem is located. It becomes difficult for the system administrator to move tools, users, or any other directory without going to each host and changing the **/etc/fstab** files to reflect the change. The automounter make the location of NFS filesystems even more transparent to NFS clients by removing hard-coded server and pathnames from the clients' **/etc/fstab** files.

Placing NFS filesystems in automounter maps greatly simplifies the administrative overhead of adding or reconfiguring NFS servers. Because the maps may be maintained using NIS, a single file is propagated to all NFS clients. Editing of individual **/etc/fstab** files is not required. The automounter is also conducive to simpler mounting schemes. For example, mounting 50 directories of tools and utilities under **/tools** produces an unwieldy **fstab** file. In addition, the **tools** mount point becomes a bottleneck, since any directory *stat()* or *getwd()* call that touches it also touches all NFS servers with filesystems mounted in **/tools**. More frequently, tools and utilities are mounted haphazardly, creating administrative problems. Simply remembering where things are is difficult, as users become confused by irregular naming schemes.

Managing **/tools** with the automounter offers several advantages. All of the individual mount points are replaced by a single map that creates the appropriate mount points as needed. The automounter mount point only contains the handful of entries corresponding to the working set of tools that the user employs at any one time. It's also much simpler to add a new tool: instead of having to create the mount point and edit **/etc/fstab** on every host in the network, you simply update the NIS-managed automounter map.

Finally, the automounter looks for a filesystem on one of several servers. Manual pages, read-only libraries, and other replicated filesystems will be mounted from the first server in a set to respond to the mount request. In addition to providing a simple load balancing scheme similar to that of NIS, the automounter removes single-host dependencies that would make a diskless or dataless workstation unusable in the event of a server crash. The automounter does not provide fault tolerance in the form of fail-over to another NFS server if the server from which the directory is mounted crashes. However, it allows NFS clients to boot completely even if a preferred server is off-line.

Automounter Maps

The behavior of the automounter is governed by its maps. An *indirect map* is useful when you are mounting several filesystems with common pathname prefixes (as seen on the client, not necessarily on the servers). A good example is the /tools directory described previously, although home directories also fit the indirect map model well. A *direct map* is used for irregularly named filesystems, where each mount point does not have a common prefix with other mount points. Some good examples of mounts requiring direct maps are **/usr/local** and **/usr/man**.

Direct and indirect maps vary in how the automounter emulates the underlying mount point. For a direct map, the automounter looks like a symbolic link at each mount point in the map. With an indirect map, the automounter emulates a directory of symbolic links, where the directory is the common pathname prefix shared by all of the automounter-managed mount points. This is confusing, and is best explained by the examples that follow.

The *master map* is a meta-map (a map describing other maps). It contains a list of indirect maps and direct mount points and tells the automounter where to look for all of its map information. We'll look at a typical master map after seeing how the indirect and direct maps are used to mount NFS filesystems.

Indirect Maps

Indirect maps are the simplest and most useful automounter convention. They correspond directly to regularly named filesystems, such as home directories, desktop tools, and system utility software. While tools directories may not be consistently named across fileservers, for example, you can use NFS mounts to make them appear consistent on a client machine. The automounter replaces all of the **/etc/fstab** entries that would be required to effect this naming scheme on the clients.

Each indirect map has a directory associated with it that is specified on the command line or in the master map (see "The Master Map"). The map itself contains a *key*, which is the name of the mount point/link in the directory, optional NFS mount options, and the server:pathname pair identifying the source of the filesystem. Automounter maps are usually named **auto.***contents*, where *contents* describes the map. The map name does not have to correspond to its mount point—it can be anything that indicates the map's function. Maps are placed in /etc or maintained via NIS.

The best way to understand how an indirect map works is to look at an example. We'll look at an automounter map and equivalent **fstab** file for a directory structure like this:

```
/tools/deskset
/tools/sting
/tools/news
/tools/bugview
```

Here is an indirect automounter map for the **/tools** directory, called **auto.tools**:

```
deskset          -ro,intr mahimahi:/tools2/deskset
sting                     mahimahi:/tools2/sting
news                      thud:/tools3/news
bugview                   jetstar:/usr/bugview
```

The map name suffix and the mount point do not have to share the same name, but adopting this convention makes it easy to associate map names and mount points. This four-entry map is functionally equivalent to the **/etc/fstab** excerpt:

```
mahimahi:/tools2/desket  /tools/deskset  nfs ro,intr 0 0
mahimahi:/tools2/string  /tools/sting    nfs         0 0
thud:/tools3/news        /tools/news     nfs         0 0
jetstar:/usr/bugview     /tools/bugview  nfs         0 0
```

Notice that the server-side mount points have no common pathname prefixes, but that the client's **fstab** and automounter map establish a regularly named view of filesystems.

Using the *auto.tools* map above, the automounter emulates **tools** as a directory of symbolic links. When any process on the client makes a reference to something in **/tools**, the automounter completes the appropriate NFS mount and makes a symbolic link in **/tools** pointing to the actual mount point for the filesystem. Suppose you go to execute **/tools/news/bin/rn**. Using the automounter effectively breaks this pathname up into three components:

- The prefix **/tools** picks an automounter map. In this case, the map for the **/tools** directory is *auto.tools* map.

- The next pathname component is the key within this map. **news** selects the server filesystem **thud:/tools3/news**; the automounter mounts this filesystem and makes a link to it in **/tools** on the client.

- The remainder of the path, **bin/rn**, is passed to the NFS server *thud* since it is relative to the directory from which the **news** toolset is mounted.

Note that the automounter map doesn't contain any information about the **/tools** directory itself, only about the subdirectories in it that are used for mount points. This makes it extremely easy to relocate a set of mount points—you simply change the master map that associates the directory **/tools** with the map *auto.tools*. We'll come back to the master map later on.

Inside the Automounter

At this point, it's useful to take a look under the hood of the automounter to see just how it emulates symbolic links. This background makes the operation of indirect maps a little clearer and will make direct maps much easier to understand.

Before walking through the sequence of automounter operations in detail, some knowledge of mount information is necessary. The *mount()* system call takes the filesystem type (4.2, nfs, sys5, etc.) and mount point from the **/etc/fstab** table, and a packet of parameters that are type-specific. For NFS mounts, the argument vector passed to *mount()* includes the server's hostname and a socket address (IP host address and port number pair) to be used for sending requests to that server. For normal NFS mounts, the remote server's hostname and IP address are used, and the IP port number is well-known NFS port number 2049. The kernel uses this information to put together an RPC client handle for calling the remote NFS server.

The automounter capitalizes on this architecture by creating a set of mount arguments that point to itself, a process on the local host. In effect, a system running the automounter has mounted a *daemon* on each mount point, instead of a remote filesystem. NFS requests for these mount points are intercepted by the automounter, since it appears to be a regular, remote NFS server to the kernel. No kernel modifications are necessary to run the automounter, and the automounter's functions are transparent to user processes.

We'll take a look at how the automounter works using the indirect *auto.tools* map above. The NFS client host is named *wahoo*. From boot time, the complete sequence of events is:

1. The automounter advertises the **/tools** mount point in **/etc/mtab**, making it look like any other NFS-mounted filesystem except for the more verbose information about the server's IP address and port:

    /etc/mtab excerpt
    ```
    thud:/home/thud /home/thud nfs rw,bg,hard,dev=8201 0 0
    wahoo:(pid124) /tools ignore ro,intr,port=724,map=/etc/auto.tools,
    indirect,dev=8204 0 0
    ```

    The first **mtab** entry is for a normal NFS mount point listed in the **fstab** file. The second is for an indirect map and was added when the automounter was started. Instead of a server:directory pair, the automounter entry contains its process ID and the local host's name. The device numbers for NFS-mounted filesystems are assigned by the kernel on each **mount** operation; the automounter's device ID just indicates the relative order in which the automounter's entry was added to the mount table. *port=724* indicates the local IP port on which the automounter is accepting connections. This entry is added to **mtab** when the automounter starts up and reads its maps.

2. A user goes to execute **/tools/news/bin/rn**. The kernel performs a look up of the executable's pathname, and finds that the **tools** component is a mount point. An NFS *lookup* request for the next component, **news**, is sent to the listed process—the automounter— via a loopback RPC mechanism.

3. The automounter emulates a directory of symbolic links under the indirect map mount point. The *lookup* request on the **news** component is received by the automounter daemon, and it returns returns information identical to that received when performing a *lookup* on a symbolic link on a remote NFS server. The automounter looks up the appropriate filesystem in **/etc/auto.tools**, and mounts it in its staging area, **/tmp_mnt**. This operation uses the *mount()* system call, which places a new entry in the **mtab** file.

4. Now that the automounted filesystem has been referenced, the automounter adds a symbolic link to its emulated directory. The new link in **/tools** points to the newly mounted filesystem. The equivalent command-line operations are:

```
# mount thud:/tools3/news /tmp_mnt/tools/news
# ln -s /tmp_mnt/tools/news /tools/news
```

5. The client-side process receives the reply from its *lookup* request and goes to read the link. This time, the automounter returns the contents of the symbolic link, which points to the automounter staging area. Note that the automounter fabricates a response to the client's *readlink* request; it looks like there's a symbolic link on the disk but it's really an artifact of the automounter. The client process follows the link's target pathname to the appropriate subdirectory of **/tmp_mnt**.

6. The client process can now trace every pathname in **/tools/news** to a subdirectory of **/tmp_mnt/tools/news**, through the new entry in **/etc/mtab** and the symbolic link emulation provided by the automounter. A client process pathname lookup finds **/tools** in the mount table, and sends its query to the automounter. The automounter's link points to **/tmp_mnt/news**, which is also listed in the mount table. To the client, the automounter looks exactly like a directory and a symbolic link.

If this seems to be a convoluted mechanism for mounting a single filesystem, it is. However, this approach is taken to minimize the number of NFS mounts performed, and to thereby improve performance by keeping **/etc/mtab** as small as possible. When you mount several subdirectories of the same remote filesystem, only one NFS mount is required. The various subdirectories of this common mount point are referenced by symbolic links, not by individual mounts. In the sample indirect map above, **mahimahi:/tools2** contains several utilities. **/tools2** will be mounted on the NFS client when the first utility in it is referenced, and references to other subdirectories of **/tools2** simply contain links back to the existing mount in **/tmp_mnt**.

The staging area **/tmp_mnt** is a key to the indirect map mechanism. If the staging area concept is eliminated, then the indirect map mount point becomes another directory filled with direct mounts. The primary advantage of indirect maps is that they allow the mount points in a directory to be managed independently—the mounts occur when a process references the mount point, and not the parent directory itself. We'll look at some problems with direct mounts shortly.

There are some side-effects of the automounter that may catch the user off-guard. The automounter creates and controls the indirect map mount point. It emulates the entire directory, so that no user, even the superuser, can create entries in it. This has an important implication for creating indirect maps: they cannot be mounted over an existing directory, because the automounter hides the underlying files. If a directory must contain a mixture of automounter mount points and "normal" directory entries, a direct map must be used.

This is an important but subtle point: when you poke at an automounter mount point with **ls**, it appears that there is a directory filled with symbolic links. In reality, this directory and the links in it do not exist on any disk. If this hurts to think about, it's really no different than the way NFS itself works: there may be no filesystem called **/tools/news** on your local disk, but NFS makes it *look* like it's there. The automounter speaks the NFS protocol, allowing it to fabricate replies to NFS RPC calls that are indistinguishable from the real thing.

Because the automounter controls the contents of a *readdir* NFS RPC reply, **ls** behaves strangely. The automounter displays only currently-mounted links in the directory it emulates. If no reference is made to a subdirectory of the indirect map directory, it appears empty:

```
% cd /tools
% ls
% ls /tools/news
bin lib spool
% cd /tools
% ls -l
total 1
lrwxrwxrwx  1 root             19 Aug 31 12:59 news -> /tmp_mnt/tools/news
```

Why not display potential mounts as well? Doing so could result in a great deal of unintended mounting activity—a *mount storm*—when **ls –l** is executed in this directory.

Direct Maps

Direct maps define point-specific, non-uniform mount points. The best example of the need for a direct map entry is **/usr/man**. The **/usr** directory contains numerous other entries, so it cannot be an indirect mount point. Building an indirect map for **/usr/man** that uses **/usr** as a mount point will "cover up" **/usr/bin** and **/usr/etc**. A direct map allows the automounter to complete mounts on a single directory entry, appearing as a link with the name of the direct mount point.

The key in a direct map is a full pathname, instead of the last component found in the indirect map. Direct maps also follow the **/etc/auto.***contents* naming scheme. Here is a sample **/etc/auto.direct**:

```
/usr/man          wahoo:/usr/share/man
/usr/local/bin    mahimahi:/usr/local/bin.sun4
```

The automounter registers the entire direct mount point pathname in the **mtab** file, instead of the parent directory of all of the mount points:

```
wahoo:(pid124) /usr/local/bin ignore intr,port=724,direct,dev=8204 0 0
```

The **mtab** entry does not have a map name, like the indirect mount point, and the map type is listed as *direct*. Operation of the automounter on a direct mount point is similar to the handling of an indirect mount. The automounter is passed the entire direct mount point pathname in the first RPC, since that is what is matched as a mount point. It answers *getattr* RPC requests with the symbolic link information, and completes the appropriate NFS mount. If the calling process is referencing a file through the direct mount point, the *getattr* will be followed by a *readlink*, as is the case with indirect mount points.

A major difference in behavior is that direct mount points are always visible to **ls** and other tools that read directory structures. The automounter treats direct mounts as individual directory entries, not as a complete directory, so the automounter gets queried whenever the directory containing the mount point is read. Client performance is affected in a marked fashion if direct mount points are used in several well-traveled directories. When a user reads a directory containing a number of direct mounts, the automounter initiates a flurry of mounting activity in response to the directory read requests. "Conversion of Direct Maps" describes a trick that lets you use indirect maps instead of direct maps. By using this trick, you can avoid mount storms caused by multiple direct mount points.

Invocation and the Master Map

Now that we've seen how the automounter manages NFS mount information in various maps, we'll look at how it chooses which maps to use and how it gets started. The key file that tells the automounter about map files and mount points is the master map, which is the default map read by the automounter if no other command-line options are specified. This covers the format and use of the master map, some command-line options, and some timeout tuning techniques.

The Master Map

When the automounter is started, it reads the master map from the NIS map *auto.master*. The master map lists all direct and indirect maps and their associated directories. It consists of triplets of directory name, map name, and mount options to be used with that map:

```
# Directory        Map                  NFS Mount Options
/tools             /etc/auto.tools          -ro
/-                 /etc/auto.direct
```

The first entry is for the indirect map **/etc/auto.tools**; entries in this map are mounted read-only (due to the –ro option) under the **/tools** directory. The second line of the master file is for a direct map; because there is no directory for the automounter to manage, the placeholder **/-** is used. The master map file above could be described entirely on the **automount** command line:

```
automount /- /etc/auto.direct /tools /etc/auto.tools -ro
```

A map that is maintained using NIS may be specified by map name rather than by a local pathname:

```
automount /- auto.direct /tools auto.tools -ro
```

In this example, two NIS maps—*auto.direct* and *auto.tools*—are used in place of the files pulled from **/etc** in the example above it. The **-ro** option specifies that the entries in the *auto.tools* map should be mounted read-only.

Automounter Map Formats

indirect map:
key	*mount options*	*server:directory pair*
deskset	-intr	mahimahi:/tools2/deskset

direct map:
pathname	*mount options*	*server:directory pair*
/usr/man	-ro	thud:/usr/man

command line:
automount directory _map
automount /tools auto.tools /src auto.src

A complete master map keeps the command line as short as possible and allows new maps to be added without having to change the automounter command line on every NFS client.

Command-line Options

The automounter is started during the boot sequence from **/etc/rc.local**. It has a variety of options that control its use of the master map and its timeout values:

–m   Ignore the NIS master map, a useful option for testing new indirect mount point and map combinations. You can run multiple automounters on each system, as long as they do not attempt to manage the same mount points. This option allows you to start up test instances of the automounter without interfering with the automounter process handling entries in the NIS master map.

–T   Turns on NFS call tracing, so the user sees the expansion of NFS calls handled by the automounter. If this option is used for debugging, then the standard output and standard error of the automounter daemon should be redirected to a file from its invocation in **/etc/rc.local**:

```
automount -T /- auto.direct >& /tmp/auto.nfscalls
```

Excerpt from /tmp/auto.nfscalls
```
LOOKUP call(fh=[147, 672910649, 4], name=news)
LOOKUP return(stat=NFS_OK, fh=[147, 672910649, 18],
type=5, mode=120777, nlink=1, uid=0, gid=0,size=32,
blocksize=512, rdev=0, blocks=1, fsid=0, fileid=18,
atime=Mon Apr 29 03:38:47 1991, mtime=Mon Apr 29 03:38:47 1991,
ctime=Mon Apr 29 03:38:47 1991)
READLINK call(fh=[147, 672910649, 18])
READLINK return(stat=NFS_OK, data=/tmp_mnt/tools/news)
```

In this example, the automounter was asked to look up the file **news**; it returned a symbolic link status structure. The client then asked the automounter to resolve the link, and the automounter returned the link it was emulating for that mount point.

–f *initfile*   Reads the file *initfile* before reading the master map. This allows each machine to have a unique master map when the NIS-managed master map is empty or ignored:

```
automount -m -f /etc/auto.mymaster
```

–D var=*value* Assigns the *value* to the variable *var* within the automounter's environment. The Variable Substitutions section contains more information on variable substitutions within automounter maps.

–M *dirname*   Use *dirname* instead of **/tmp_mnt** as the automounter staging area.

–tl *time*   Time, in seconds, to wait before attempting to unmount a quiescent filesystem. The default is 300 seconds, but this value may need to be adjusted to accommodate various client usage patterns as described in the next section.

The automounter also has a map "white-out" feature, invoked with the **-null** command-line option. The **-null** option is really a special map; it used after a directory to effectively delete any map entry affecting that directory from the automounter's set of maps:

```
automount /tools -null
```

This feature is used to override *auto.master* or direct map entries that may have been inherited from an NIS map. If you need to make per-machine changes to the automounter maps, or if need local control over a mount point managed by the automounter, white-out the conflicting map entry with the *null* map.

Tuning Timeout Values

Every RPC request that is used to locate an automounted file or filesystem is intercepted by the automounter, but once the calling process has a handle for the remote file, calls such as *read* and *write* are sent directly to the remote server. Because the automounter intercedes in each opening reference to a remote file, it can easily track the time of the last reference to the filesystem. When a filesystem has remained quiescent for more than five minutes (or the period specified with the **–tl** flag), it is a candidate for unmounting. If the filesystem is busy, the attempts to unmount it fail until the last open files and directories are closed. If an unmount attempt fails, the automounter tries it again later.

There are two situations in which increasing the default unmount timeout period improve performance of the automounter:

- Client processes keep files open for more than five minutes.

- One or more processes requiring automounted filesystems run regularly, with periods greater than the default timeout.

The first *lookup* needed to locate a file is seen by the automounter, but subsequent read and write operations bypass it completely. After five minutes, the automounter believes the filesystem is no longer being accessed, so it attempts to unmount it. The open file causes the *umount()* call to return EBUSY. If there are several filesystems used by processes that behave in this fashion, then the automounter wastes numerous *umount()* system calls. Increasing the default unmount timeout period (using the −tl option) to match the average file handle lifetime reduces the overhead of using the automounter:

```
automount -tl 600 /- auto.direct /tools auto.tools
```

The timeout period is specified in seconds. The reduced number of mount operations comes at a cost of a longer binding to the NFS server. If the filesystem is mounted when the NFS server crashes, you will have lost the "working set" advantage of using the automounter—your system hangs until the server recovers.

As mentioned above, regularly scheduled processes may require longer automounter timeout periods. Regularly scheduled processes include those run by **cron** and repetitive operations performed by interactive users, such as **make** runs done several times an hour during bug-fixing cycles. Each regularly scheduled process begins by causing a filesystem mount; a corresponding unmount is done sometime before its next invocation if the default timeout period is shorter than the time between invocations.

If the time between process instances is long, the overhead of these repetitive mount operations is negligible. However, a job that is run every 10 minutes initiates a sequence of mount and unmount operations, adding to the overhead incurred by running the automounter. For interactive processes that run to completion in a minute or less, the time to complete the mount increases the response time of the system, and is sure to elicit complaints. In both cases, system performance is improved by reducing the overhead of the automounter through a longer default unmount timeout period.

You may not want to use the automounter for filesystems that are mounted or accessed nearly constantly through the day. The mail spool, for example, might be better placed in each client's **/etc/fstab** file because it will be in near-constant use on the client. Most other filesystems benefit from the streamlined NFS administration provided by the automounter. Using the automounter is simplified even further by managing the maps themselves with NIS.

Integration with NIS

If maps are maintained on each client machine, then the administrative benefits of using the automounter are lost; the burden of maintenance is shifted away from the **fstab** file to the new map files. To solve the administrative problem, all three types of maps may be distributed using NIS.

To add an automounter map to the NIS database, insert a set of clauses for it in the NIS master server's **Makefile**:

In definition of target all:
```
all:    passwd hosts ..... auto.tools

auto.tools:    auto.tools.time

auto.tools.time: $(DIR)/auto.tools
       -@if [ -f $(DIR)/auto.tools ]; then \
              sed -e "/^#/d" -e s/#.*$$// $(DIR)/auto.tools | \
                     /usr/etc/yp/makedbm - /var/yp/$(DOM)/auto.tools;\
              touch auto.tools.time; \
              echo "updated auto.tools"; \
              if [ ! $(NOPUSH) ]; then \
                     /usr/etc/yp/yppush auto.tools; \
                     echo "pushed auto.tools"; \
              fi \
       else \
              echo "couldn't find $(DIR)/auto.tools"; \
       fi
```

The new map name must be added to the list of targets built by default when **make** is issued with no arguments. A dependency linking the map name *auto.tools* to the timestamp file **auto.tools.time** is added, and the large section defines how to rebuild the map and the timestamp file from the map source file. The makefile actions strip out all lines beginning with comment (#), and strip comments from the ends of lines. The **makedbm** program builds a NIS map from the input file. The input file should not have blank lines in it.

The key in an automounter map becomes the NIS map key, and the mount options and server and directory names are the data values. Dumping a map with **ypcat** requires the **–k** option to match up map keys and server information:

```
% ypcat auto.tools
-ro,intr thud:/epubs/deskset
jetstar:/usr/Bugview
-ro,intr mahimahi:/tools2/deskset1.0

% ypcat -k auto.tools
sundesk -ro,intr thud:/epubs/deskset
bugview jetstar:/usr/Bugview
deskset -ro,intr mahimahi:/tools2/deskset1.0
```

NIS-managed maps are specified by map name rather than by absolute pathname, in either the automounter command line or the master map:

Command line
```
automount /- auto.direct /tools auto.tools
```

Master map
```
/tools          auto.tools        -ro
/source         auto.source       -rw
```

As with the password NIS map, it is sometimes necessary to have variations in the configuration on a per-machine basis. Using the notation **+mapname** it is possible to include a NIS map in a local automounter map. For example, if client machines share a common set of source trees, but some clients are allowed to access operating system source code as well, the automounter may be started using absolute map pathnames on each host:

```
automount /source /etc/auto.source
```

On those machines without source code rights, the **/etc/auto.source** map contains a single reference to the NIS map:

```
+auto.source
```

However, on clients that have more privileges, the operating system source code mount points can be included with the NIS map:

```
sunos3.5        -ro       srcserv:/source/sunos3.5
sunos4.0        -ro       srcserv:/source/sunos4.0
nfs             -ro       bigguy:/source/nfs_internals
+auto.source
```

Updating NIS-managed Automount Maps

The automounter reads indirect NIS maps for each mount request it must handle. A change in one of these maps is reflected as soon as the map is built and pushed to the NIS servers. New tools get installed in **/tools** by inserting a new map entry in **auto.tools** rather than editing the **/etc/fstab** files on each client machine. The automounter sees map updates the next time it has to perform a mount.

The only way to change the mount parameters for a currently mounted filesystem is to unmount the filesystem manually in **/tmp_mnt,** and send the automounter daemon a SIGHUP (kill -1). When the automounter receives this signal, it parses the **mtab** file and notices that some of its mounted filesystems were unmounted by someone else. It invalidates the links for those mount points; the next reference through the same entry remounts the filesystem with the new parameters.

Direct maps are subject to an update restriction. While the maps may be updated with the automounter running, changes are not made visible through the automounter until it is restarted. The automounter creates a mount table entry for each direct mount point, so they cannot be added or removed without the automounter's intervention. If a direct mount point is removed from a direct map maintained by NIS, attempts to reference the mount point return "file not found" errors: the mount point is still listed in the **mtab** file but the automounter's direct map no longer has a corresponding entry for it.

Using NIS to manage the automounter maps makes administration of a large number of NFS clients much simpler: all of the work that formerly went into **/etc/fstab** file maintenance is eliminated. In a large environment with hundreds of users, the task of map management can become quite complex as well. If new users are added to the system, or filesystems are shuffled to meet performance goals, then the automounter maps must be modified to reflect the new configurations. The benefits of using the automounter are significantly increased when the maps are simplified using key and variable substitutions.

Key and Variable Substitutions

There are two forms of substitutions that are performed in automounter maps: *variable substitution* and *key substitution*. Variables are useful for hiding architecture or operating system dependencies when maintaining a uniform naming scheme, while key substitutions impress a degree of regularity on the automounter maps.

Key Substitutions

The ampersand (&) expands to the matched key value in a map; it is used in the server:directory path pair to copy key values into directory path component names. The home directory map *auto.home* as shown here:

```
thud           -rw      thud:/home/thud
wahoo          -rw      wahoo:/home/wahoo
mahimahi       -rw      mahimahi:/home/mahimahi
```

is rewritten using key substitution:

```
thud           -rw      &:/home/&
wahoo          -rw      &:/home/&
mahimahi       -rw      &:/home/&
```

With the right-hand side rewritten, the map's regular form can be further condensed using the asterisk (*) wildcard:

```
*          -rw      &:/home/&
```

The asterisk is a default case. Nothing after it will ever be matched, so it should be the last (or only) entry in the map. It matches all keys, providing a value for the & substitutions that fill in the right-hand side of the map information.

For example, assume that the clients are using the *auto.home* map for the **/home** mount point. Every reference through **/home** matches the wildcard map entry. When a look up of **/home/thud/jan** is performed, the automounter gets an NFS RPC request to look up **thud** in the **/home** directory. Referring to the indirect map, the automounter finds the wildcard, which matches the key **thud**. The automounter makes **thud** the default key, and expands the server:directory component as:

```
thud:/home/thud
```

This entry is equivalent to a **thud**-specific entry:

```
thud  -rw    thud:/home/thud
```

Special case mappings may be added ahead of the wildcard map entry:

```
mahimahi2         -rw      mahimahi:/home/mahimahi2
*                 -rw      &:/home/&
```

Of course, wildcards can get you into trouble as well. Assume that you are using the following simple indirect map for **/home**:

```
*          -rw      &:/home/&
```

and a user tries to access **/home/foo**. The automounter then tries to mount **foo:/home/foo**, but it's probable that no host named **foo** exists. In this case, the user will get a somewhat puzzling "No such host" error message when the auto-mounter cannot find the server's name in the NIS *hosts* map.

The concise wildcard-based naming scheme is useful for machines exporting a single home directory, but when multiple home directories are exported from several disks on a server, the one-to-one mapping of home directory names to server names breaks down. If naming conventions permit, you can create hostname aliases in the NIS *hosts* map that match the additional home directory names, allowing the wildcard map to be used.

To see how this works, let's simplify the following *auto.homemap* for the three servers *mahimahi*, *thud*, and *wahoo*:

```
mahimahi        -rw     mahimahi:/home/mahimahi
mahimahi2       -rw     mahimahi:/home/mahimahi2
thud            -rw     thud:/home/thud
thud2           -rw     thud:/home/thud2
thud3           -rw     thud:/home/thud3
wahoo           -rw     wahoo:/home/wahoo
```

Applying wildcard key matching substitution to the regularly named directories shortens the *auto.home* map so that only the secondary and tertiary home directories are listed:

```
mahimahi2       -rw     mahimahi:/home/mahimahi2
thud2           -rw     thud:/home/thud2
thud3           -rw     thud:/home/thud3
*               -rw     &:/home/&
```

Adding hostname aliases for *mahimahi* and *thud* to the hosts file condenses the *auto.home* map even further:

```
hosts file
192.9.201.5     mahimahi mahimahi2
192.9.201.6     thud thud2 thud3
192.9.201.7     wahoo

auto.home map
*       -rw     &:/home/&
```

When a reference to **/home/thud2/jan** is seen by the automounter, the wildcard map turns it into the server:directory pair:

```
thud2:/home/thud2
```

Because **thud2** is a *hosts* database alias for **thud**, the mount request is sent to the right server.

This trick simply perpetuates the existing naming scheme but it does not help subsume all home directories under a single mount point. Users tend to like the C shell's tilde expansion mechanism, which locates a user's home directory from the NIS or local password files. Using a tilde reference such as ˜jan causes the correct mount to be completed, but there is no obvious, consistent absolute path to every user's home directory. You have to be prepared to look in several sub-directories of **/home** because home directories are mounted from several places. Furthermore, not everything understands tilde expansions: the Bourne shell doesn't; the automounter itself doesn't, and most user applications don't. You still have to know the server's exported directory if you are using absolute path-names.

To make a completely uniform naming scheme, you need to build a fairly verbose map that hides the hostname dependencies in the home directory paths. Given the set of home directories:

```
/home/thud/stern
/home/thud2/jan
/home/mahimahi/johnc
/home/wahoo/kenney
```

an indirect *auto.home* map that mounts all users' home directories under **/h** looks like this:

```
stern    -rw     thud:/home/thud/stern
jan      -rw     thud:/home/thud2/jan
johnc    -rw     mahimahi:/home/mahimahi/johnc
kenney   -rw     wahoo:/home/wahoo/kenney
```

Automounter invocation
```
automount /h auto.home
```

Users can find any user through the **/h** switchboard, without having to know their home directory server. This scheme is useful where hardcoded, absolute path-names are required, or where ˜**user** is not expanded, such as in Bourne shell scripts. You can juggle user's home directories to distribute free disk space without having to search for all occurrences of absolute pathnames; changing the automounter map effects the change.

Variable Substitutions

If you are managing automounter maps through NIS, you may end up using the same map on machines running different releases of the operation system or having different CPU architectures. Directories with utilities or source code frequently need to be discriminated based on operating system release and machine architecture. Presenting these directories with a uniform naming scheme eliminates ugly pathnames, user confusion, and potentially dangerous actions, for example, a user building an object tree in the wrong subdirectory for that operating system release.

The automounter allows variables to be substituted into the right-hand components of map entries. The following example shows how to mount **/usr/local/bin** from a set of architecture-specific directories:

Automounter invocation
```
automount -D ARCH='/bin/arch' /- auto.direct
```

auto.direct map
```
/usr/local/bin  -ro     mahimahi:/local/bin.$ARCH
```

Variable substitutions apply equally well to indirect maps. The following example shows how source code for a project is mapped out based on operating system release:

```
automount -D OS="sunos4.1"

notes    -rw     srcserv:/source/notes.$OS
news     -rw     srcserv:/source/news.$OS
chem     -rw     srcserv:/source/chem.$OS
```

Variable and key substitution combine to collapse the map in the previous example to another one-liner:

```
*         -rw     srcserv:/source/&.$OS
```

A source code automounter map is useful when there are one or more levels of dependencies in the source tree, or when the source trees themselves live on several different servers. The automounter ensures that the developers mount only those servers containing source code that they are currently using.

Advanced Map Tricks

The automounter has several features that complement the "normal" NFS mount options. It can mount replicated filesystems from one of several potential servers, and it can perform hierarchical mounts of all of a server's directories when any one of them is referenced. This section starts with a discussion of these advanced autmounter features, then explains how to get better performance out of the automounter by converting direct map entries into indirect maps and by using the automounter's subdirectory mount feature.

Replicated Servers

Multiple location support in the automounter implements a simple network load balancing scheme for replicated filesystems. At first glance, this seems to be a bit of overkill; after all, you don't need or want replication for read-write filesystems. However, serving large, read-only filesystems such as the manual pages may add to an NFS server's request load. Having multiple servers share this load improves performance by reducing the total load placed on the most heavily used servers. Ideally, you want clients that are "close" to each server to mount its filesystems, reducing the amount of traffic that must go through bridges or routers.

For example, if you have four NFS servers that each export the manual pages, the best client mounting scheme is probably not to have one-quarter of the clients mount /usr/man from each server. Instead, clients should mount the manual pages from the server that is closest to them. Replicated filesystems are included in automounter maps simply by listing all possible servers in the map:

```
/usr/man        -ro      wahoo:/usr/man mahimahi:/usr/man \
                         thud:/usr/man onaga:/usr/man
```

The backslash at the end of the first line continues this indirect map entry onto the next line. If more than one server:directory pair is listed in an automounter map, the automounter pings all servers by sending a request to the *null* procedure of all NFS servers; the first server in the list to respond is selected by the automounter to serve that mount point. If the servers are on different networks, machines on the local network generally receive their pings before those on remote networks.

There is also an element of load balancing at work here: if one of the **/usr/man** servers is so heavily loaded with other NFS traffic that it cannot reply to the ping before another server on the same net, then the client will choose the other server to handle its mount request. Note that there is no dynamic load balancing. Once a client performs a mount from a server, it continues to use that server until it unmounts the filesystem. It cannot choose a different server before unmounting its first choice.

You can use the first-answer feature of replicated map entries to solve the multi-homed host problem presented in "Multi-homed Servers," in Chapter 12, *Performance Analysis and Tuning*. Let's say that you have an NFS server on four networks, with hostnames *boris*, *boris-bb2*, *boris-bb3*, and *boris-bb4* on those networks. Mounting all filesystems from *boris* makes the multi-homed host perform loopback packet routing, but using the "right" hostname requires knowing which name is on your network. Building an automounter map with replicated entries solves this problem by letting the automounter find the fastest route to *boris*:

```
/home/boris     -rw,hard        boris:/home/boris \
                                boris-bb2:/home/boris \
                                boris-bb3:/home/boris \
                                boris-bb4:/home/boris
```

Since the server pathnames are the same, you can use a shorter form of the replicated map entry, putting all of the server names in a comma-separated list:

```
/home/boris   -rw,hard    boris,boris-bb2,boris-bb3,boris-bb4:/home/boris
```

The network interface on *boris* that is closest to the client will respond first, and each NFS client of *boris* will mount **/home/boris** from the best network interface. Note that the replicated mount points don't refer to multiple filesystems, but rather multiple names for the same filesystem. The automounter just provides a neat way of managing all of them in a single place.

When the automounter pings the remote servers, it is performing the equivalent of:

```
rpcinfo -u hostname nfs 1
```

for each listed server. No other NFS utilities (save **rpcinfo**) use the *null* NFS procedure, so *null* server calls reported by **nfsstat** may be attributed to the automounter daemons handling replicated filesystems. If you see a large number of *null* procedure calls in the output of **nfsstat** on the NFS server, it means that your automounter mounts of replicated filesystems are being performed repeatedly. The *null* calls do not require any disk accesses to service, but they can consume network bandwidth on the server; if the number of *null* calls becomes excessive it may be due to client machines continually mounting and unmounting replicated filesystems. Changing the unmount timeout parameter, as discussed previously, reduces the number of *null* calls.

You can also examine the **/etc/rmtab** file on the server to see how frequently its clients are mounting and unmounting automounted filesystems. When a filesystem is mounted, an entry is added to the **/etc/rmtab** file. When it gets unmounted, the entry isn't deleted from the file—it is commented out by making the first character in the line a pound sign (**#**):

```
#epeche:/usr/share/man
#haos:/usr/share/man
#epeche:/usr/share/man
depeche:/usr/share/man
chaos:/usr/share/man
```

In this example, client *depeche* has mounted **/usr/share/man** three times, and client *chaos* has mounted that filesystem twice. This gives you client information to go along with the *null* NFS RPC counts provided by **nfsstat**—you can tell which clients have been repeatedly mounting and unmounting a filesystem. Watch the size of the **/etc/rmtab** file over time; if it grows regularly and contains multiple entries for the same clients and filesystems, then you may want to change the automounter timeout on those clients.

Once a server is chosen for a replicated filesystem, the selection is static. The automounter does not include support for retrying mounts from failed servers because that would require adding some heuristic for identifying server failure to the automounter. Within the NFS protocol, a very slow server and a dead server cannot be distinguished by clients, so there is no inherent NFS support for deciding when to switch to another server for a replicated filesystem.

Hierarchical Mounts

In addition to handling multiple servers for the same filesystem, the automounter can mount multiple trees from the same server in a hierarchy of mount points. The most widely-used hierarchical mount is the built-in *–hosts* map, which mounts all exported filesystems from a named host.

The *–hosts* map references only the hosts database; the map semantics are built into the automounter. It is usually mounted on **/net** or **/machine** indicating that it contains filesystems from the entire network:

```
automount /net -hosts
```

A user can then force mounts of all filesystems from a server by referencing the server's name as a subdirectory of **/net**:

```
% rsh wahoo exportfs
/usr
/home/wahoo
/export/root/honeymoon   -access=honeymoon
/export/swap/honeymoon   -access=honeymoon

% cd /net/wahoo
% ls
export  home    usr
% ls /net/wahoo/export
root    swap
```

When the automounter has to mount a filesystem on **/net**, it sends a request to the server asking for all exported filesystems. The automounter sorts the filesystems by pathname length, ensuring that subdirectories of exported filesystems appear later in the list than their parents.* The automounter then mounts each item in the

---

*If a directory pathname has a length of x characters, then any of its subdirectory's pathnames have length $> x$. Sorting by pathname length puts a parent directory ahead of all paths to its subdirectories.

sorted list. All exported filesystems are mounted; the automounter does not parse the list of mount points to eliminate hierarchical mounts.

There are a number of caveats for using the *–hosts* map. First of all, by including the entire *hosts* database, it references servers that are both local and on remote networks; a casual reference to a remote server causes an NFS mount to occur through a router or gateway. If the server itself is slow, or has a large number of filesystems (diskless client servers), then the *–hosts* map has a definite performance impact. Finally, unmounts of the filesystems are done from the bottom up, in the reverse order of the mounts. If a higher-level mount point is busy, then an unmount of the entire hierarchy fails. When the automounter fails to unmount a higher-level mount point, it must remount the filesystems it just unmounted. It walks back down the hierarchy from the busy mount point, mounting each filesystem. The remote server's filesystems are mounted on an all-or-nothing basis.

Conversion of Direct Maps

Direct mounts are useful for handling non-uniform naming schemes, but they may cause a number of performance problems if several direct mount points are included in a directory that is frequently searched. You can usually get better performance out of the automounter by converting direct maps into indirect maps. Instead of putting direct map mount points in the client filesystem, create symbolic links that point to a staging area managed by an indirect map.

Again, an example helps to explain the conversion process. Consider replacing a direct map for **/usr/local** with an indirect map *auto.stage*. To convert the direct map into an indirect map, we first create a symbolic link **/usr/local** that points to a staging area that we'll let the automounter manage:

```
Original direct map
/usr/local      mahimahi:/local/$ARCH

# ln -s /stage/local /usr/local
# automount /stage auto.stage

New indirect map auto.stage
local    -ro    mahimahi:/local/$ARCH
```

Note that **/usr/local** didn't exist before we made the link, since it was managed by the automounter. Also, we don't have to create the **/stage** staging directory, since it is an indirect map mount point.

The symbolic link points to a subdirectory of the mount point managed by the indirect map *auto.stage*. With the direct map, any reference to **/usr/local** is directed to the **/stage** mount point, which causes the automounter to mount the appropriate architecture-specific directory. This makes **/usr/local** look like a link to the mount.

Let's say a user now accesses **/usr/local/bin/emacs**. The client kernel follows **/usr/local** down to the symbolic link, which points to the **/stage/local** automounter mount point. The automounter picks up the reference to **/stage** as a reference to the *auto.stage* map, and it uses the next component—**local**—as a key in the map. This causes **mahimahi:/local/$ARCH** to be automounted. If you have several direct mount points, they can all be converted into links and share a single *auto.stage* map.

Subdirectory Fields

While indirect maps are easy to maintain, maps for popular mount points such as **/tools** or **/home** can become large and may contain multiple references to the same parent directory. The automounter treats each indirect map entry as a separate entity, so multiple mounts from the same parent directory are performed for each of its subdirectories listed in the indirect map. The *auto.home* map in the next example has two users—*stern* and *howard*—with home directories under a common parent. This map is mounted on **/h**:

```
stern    -rw    thud:/home/thud/stern
howard   -rw    thud:/home/thud/howard
kenney   -rw    wahoo:/home/wahoo/kenney
```

If a reference is made to ˜**stern**, followed by a reference to ˜**howard**, the automounter mounts both **/home/thud/stern** and **/home/thud/howard**. The second mount can be avoided using subdirectory fields in the indirect map.

A subdirectory field specifies that the parent directory should be mounted only if needed; if the parent directory is already mounted then the automounter simply makes a link to the new subdirectory of the common parent. The subdirectory field is separated from the server:directory pair by another colon:

```
stern    -rw    thud:/home/thud:stern
howard   -rw    thud:/home/thud:howard
kenney   -rw    wahoo:/home/wahoo:kenney
```

When a reference to **/h/stern** is made, the automounter mounts **/home/thud** in **/tmp_mnt/home**, and makes a link to it in the **/h** directory. However, the automounter needs to make a unique name for this mount point, so it appends the key that caused the mount to the server path. This produces some strange-looking symbolic links. If *stern* is the key that causes **/home/thud** to be mounted, the mount point will be:

```
/tmp_mnt/home/thud/stern
```

The directory name is the server's pathname and the key that caused the mount. The automounter then makes a link to a subdirectory of this mount point for the key *stern*:

```
ln -s /tmp_mnt/home/thud/stern/stern /h/stern
```

When **/h/howard** is referenced, there is no need to mount **/home/thud** again. Instead, the symbolic link **/h/howard** is made in **/h**, pointing to *howard*'s subdirectory under the existing mount point for **/home/thud**. The mount point for **/home/thud** is **/home/thud/stern**—the pathname created when a reference to key *stern* caused the mount to be performed. The link made for key *howard*, then, looks like this:

```
ln -s /tmp_mnt/home/thud/stern/howard /h/howard
```

Using the subdirectory field reduces the number of mount operations and their associated overhead. However, if you find the link pathnames confusing or difficult to manage, you should skip subdirectory mounts and perform indirect mounts. You will perform more mount operations, which means that users may see slightly slower response time if the NFS servers are heavily loaded. However, this cost is incurred only under peak load periods, and is often worth the simpler pathnames produced by the automounter.

Side Effects

The automounter has several side effects that cause confusion in both processes and users that encounter its emulated directories. This section uncovers some utilities that are disturbed by the automounter.

Long Search Paths

If you have many directories listed in your search path, logging into a system using the automounter for some of these directories increases your log-in time significantly. Instead of listing the directories in your search path, create "wrappers" for the utilities of interest and put them in **/usr/local/bin**. The wrappers can set environment variables and execute the appropriate utility, causing the automounter to mount the necessary filesystem when you use it instead of when you log in.

For example, you can include Frame 2.0 in your search path in your .cshrc file:

```
set path = ( /tools/frame2.0/bin $path )
```

If **/tools** is managed by the automounter, your shell causes **/tools/frame2.0** to be mounted when it builds the command hash table after setting your search path. Instead of listing all directories in **/tools**, create a wrapper for the **maker** utility in **/tools/frame2.0/bin** so that you don't have to list any subdirectory of **/tools** in your search path:

Wrapper for maker
```
#! /bin/sh
setenv path ( /tools/frame2.0/bin $path )
exec /tools/frame2.0/bin/maker
```

This wrapper sets the search path as well, so that any executables invoked by **maker** will be able to find related utilities in its executable directory. By putting this wrapper in **/usr/local/bin**, you avoid having to automount **/tools/frame2.0** when you log in. For just a few directories, the automounter overhead isn't that large, but with ten or more software packages loaded, logging in becomes a slow process. Furthermore, not mounting all of these filesystems when you log in shields you from server crashes: your workstation will only hang if one of the servers you're using crashes.

Local Mounts

If the filesystem to be mounted is on the local host, the automounter makes a symbolic link to the UNIX file system mount point instead of remounting the filesystem on the local host using an NFS mount. When descending into a directory automounted from the local machine, the pathname shown by **pwd** will vary depending upon whether you arrived in the directory using the local host's path to the file or the automounter-managed one:

Automounter indirect map entry for /h:
```
stern    thud:/home/thud/stern
```

On thud:
```
% cd /home/thud/stern
% pwd
/home/thud/stern
% cd /h/stern
% pwd
/h/stern
```

To avoid confusion due to symbolic link names, use the **pwd** alias described in the section "Pathname Cleanup."

Avoiding Automounted Filesystems

Utilities run out of **cron**, such as nightly **find** jobs or the calendar, are easily overworked by the automounter. Calendar reminders are usually generated by **calendar -** in root's **crontab** file:

```
0 0 * * * calendar -
```

With the automounter, the **calendar** daemon finds all users whose home directories are accessible through it; if **calendar** is invoked on many machines then a good portion of the network's resources are spent processing calendar reminders each night. Furthermore, users get multiple copies of reminders, one from each machine that mounts their home directory.

The solution is to limit the invocations of **calendar** to servers not running the automounter, or to have it run on a per-user, per-machine basis.

Pathname Cleanup

The **pwd** command expands symbolic links by walking up the directory tree from the current directory. When used with automounted directories, it produces pathnames prefixed withe the automounter staging area:

```
/tmp_mnt/thud/home/stern
```

To eliminate the extra pathname component, use a shell alias to replace **pwd**. The shell's **cwd** variable contains the pathname used to *get* to the current directory, so it leaves symbolic link names alone. Adding an alias of the form:

```
alias pwd        (echo $cwd)
```

to each user's shell initialization suppresses the confusing pathnames produced by the automounter.

Shutting Down the Automounter

When a user process is waiting for an NFS server, it sits in a high-priority disk wait until the remote server recovers. The automounter appears to be an NFS server to all processes that mount filesystems through it, so killing the auto-mounter with **kill -9** hangs these processes. To halt the automounter, send it SIGTERM, which shuts it down gracefully:

```
% ps -agux | fgrep auto | fgrep -v fgrep
root      124  0.0  1.4  360 440 ?  S    Aug 24  6:54 automount -D
% kill -TERM 124
```

Restart the automounter from the command line to incorporate new maps or com-mand-line options.

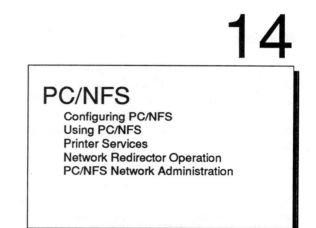

14

PC/NFS

Configuring PC/NFS
Using PC/NFS
Printer Services
Network Redirector Operation
PC/NFS Network Administration

PC/NFS is a client-only implementation of the NFS protocol for IBM-compatible personal computers running the DOS operating system. Using PC/NFS, DOS machines can mount NFS filesystems as logical disks, and use them as large virtual DOS disks. Note that a client-only implementation does not limit the direction or types of file transfer operations that are possible within PC/NFS. It simply means that the PC is always the active entity in the DOS-UNIX relationship; the user must mount a UNIX filesystem on the PC and then copy files between it and the DOS disk. In this chapter we'll look at setting up PC/NFS, and the integration of PC/NFS services and the DOS I/O system.

Configuring PC/NFS

PC/NFS comes with several pieces: an RPC and XDR library, DOS utilities to mount disks and create UNIX-style user credentials, an NIS implementation, a set of TCP, UDP, and IP protocol network drivers, and an optional network interface card. Follow the PC/NFS installation instructions to get the drivers into **CONFIG.SYS**, **AUTOEXEC.BAT**, and **NETWORK.BAT**, the batch file that starts up the PC network connection. It is possible to run PC/NFS over a serial connection to a UNIX host, but that is outside the scope of this book.

To get PC/NFS up and running, you must install all of the PC components such as drivers and startup scripts, and then install a new RPC server daemon on an NFS server to handle PC print requests. We'll start by looking at the PC configuration utilities used to get PC/NFS up and running.

PC Configuration

PC/NFS has a robust configuration program, **nfsconf**, that walks you through the initial installation and subsequent changes with a fairly simple menu-driven interface. For most installations, you should use the **nfsconf** screen-oriented configuration management tool. Refer to this section for information about commands added to startup files or before changing a line added by the PC/NFS configuration utility.

PC/NFS includes an NIS client implementation, so that it can use the NIS *passwd*, *hosts*, *rpc*, *services*, *netgroup*, *ethers*, and *networks* maps. If you are not running NIS on your UNIX machines, or choose not to use NIS on your PC clients, you have to edit the equivalent local configuration files on the PC. They normally live in the directory /NFS.

Most of the PC/NFS configuration occurs in the file **NETWORK.BAT**, which is started from **AUTOEXEC.BAT** at boot time. The **DRIVES.BAT** file contains commands to mount NFS filesystems on the PC, similar to the way the /etc/fstab file directs a UNIX host to mount filesystems at boot time. You will find almost all of the following commands in these three files.

Starting PC/NFS

Using NIS on a PC client presents configuration problems similar to those encountered booting a UNIX system that uses NIS maps for host information. NIS must be configured and running before it can be used to initialize other services, so it's usually the first thing started in **NETWORK.BAT**. The first step is defining an NIS domain name, which is done with the **net ypdomain** command:

```
net ypdomain nesales
```

This is the equivalent of performing a **domainname** on a UNIX NIS client. If your NIS domain name is longer than 14 characters, older versions of PC/NFS will not be able to bind to it. Create an alias for the NIS domain on the NIS servers, using the procedure described in the section "Domain Aliases," in Chapter 3, *System Management Using NIS*.

Use the shorter alias name *demonet* in PC commands that set the NIS domain name.

Using PC/NFS

Once the PC redirector and server daemons are running, you can use PC/NFS to mount NFS filesystems as virtual disks. To a UNIX user, the PC view of the UNIX filesystem is somewhat foreign, because disks are organized as named volumes, instead of in a tree of path names. In addition, filename conventions, file permissions and file structures are different between the two operating systems. This section covers the way in which PC clients mount filesystems, and the necessary conversions that occur when going from UNIX to the PC world.

Mounting Filesystems

The **net use** command assigns a logical disk name to a remote filesystem:

```
C> net use s: \\wahoo\home\stern
C> net use f: \\mahimahi\tools\dos
```

The server name is given after a leading double-backslash, and the pathname to the filesystem on the server follows in the normal DOS naming convention. The first example mounts directory **/home/stern** on server *wahoo* as the S: drive, while the second mounts **/tools/dos** from *mahimahi* on drive F:. Be careful not to attempt an NFS mount of a filesystem on top of an existing logical drive. After an NFS filesystem is mounted, you can treat it like a normal DOS disk, copying files to and from the drive or opening files as if they were local to the PC.

net use mounts a filesystem read-only if the **/ro** option is given on the command line:

```
C> net use s: \\wahoo\home\stern /ro
```

If your NFS fileserver exports the file system read-only, you must use the **/ro** option when mounting on the PC.

Checking File Permissions

DOS and UNIX have very different filenaming and permissions conventions. We'll cover filename mapping shortly, but first it's worth looking at how PC/NFS enforces user, group, and world access in a system that does not have file permissions. PC/NFS uses a user authentication server—the UNIX server running the

pcnfsd daemon—to perform UNIX-style file permission checking. By default, users on PCs are given the permissions of the anonymous user *nobody*, which generally means that PC users can access files with the appropriate world permissions. As discussed in "Superuser Mapping," in Chapter 8, *Network Security*, being mapped to *nobody* is very restrictive, and may prevent users from accessing their home directories on UNIX file servers.

To use UNIX authentication for less restrictive privileges, a PC user "logs in" to the authentication server using the **net name** command like this:

```
C> net name stern *
Password:
```

or:

```
C> net name *
Username: stern
Password:
```

In the first example, the username *stern* is used, and **net name** prompts for a password. In the second example, the user is prompted for both a username and password. PC/NFS performs UNIX login-like password and username verification on the authentication server, using user information retrieved from the PC/NFS NIS server. PC/NFS grants the PC user the same permissions accorded to this UNIX user if the authentication succeeds. You can change the mapping of PC user to UNIX user credentials at any time by issuing a new **net name** command.

Even with UNIX-style credentials, there is no mechanism in DOS to perform file permission checking—file permissions only exist on the UNIX server side, not on the PC/NFS side. This problem is solved by calling on the authentication server to perform checking of the user's credentials against the file's attributes. Any file access that does permission checking, such as opening a file, uses the authentication server.

Filename Mapping

Now we've seen how PC/NFS accesses remote files, and verifies that the PC user has permission to operate on these files. We still haven't looked at the problem of naming UNIX files in the DOS world. UNIX filenames may be up to 14 characters long, and in some UNIX systems, the maximum filename length is 256 characters. UNIX filenames also may contain a variety of mixed case and punctuation marks. DOS filenames, on the other hand, are eight characters with an optional three character extension, are uppercase only, and can't include punctuation such as leading dots. All DOS filenames are legal UNIX filenames, so no conversion is required for DOS-generated filenames. PC/NFS maps the DOS filename into lowercase when talking to a UNIX NFS server. If you create a file named

AUTOEXEC.BAT (from the PC) on an NFS-mounted filesystem, for example, the file will have the name **autoexec.bat** on the NFS server.

PC/NFS adopts a few simple filename mapping conventions for converting UNIX filenames into valid DOS filenames. Note that the mapping occurs on the PC, and that the UNIX filenames are not modified in any way. PC/NFS simply imposes its rules for handling the file server's name space on the client's view of these files. Recent name mappings are cached on the PC so that the client does not have to continuously perform conversions.

All files are visible to the PC/NFS client, including those "hidden" files whose names begin with a dot. NFS server filenames with any of the following characteristics are mapped to unique DOS filenames:

- Leading dots.

- Illegal DOS extensions.

- Prefixes longer than eight characters.

- Multiple dots.

- Names that are not unique in the first eight characters.

- Uppercase characters.

The mapping algorithm uses any lowercase or valid DOS characters such as the underscore (_) to construct five or more characters of the DOS filename. Lowercase letters are mapped to uppercase. If any of the first five characters are not valid DOS filename characters, they are replaced with tildes (~). If the filename is invalid under DOS for any reason, the last three characters of the name will be a tilde and a unique two-character identifier. Using the two-character name suffix trivially solves the problem of long filenames that are not unique in the first eight characters. Some examples make these rules clearer, as shown in Table 14-1.

Table 14-1. UNIX-to-DOS Filename Mapping

UNIX Name	DOS Name	Reason for Mapping
xy_svc.c	XY_SVC.C	None performed.
testfile	TESTFILE	None performed.
testfile2	TESTF~AC	Prefix longer than eight characters.
.login	~LOGI~AA	Leading dot.
Utils.obj	~TILS~AB	Uppercase.

In the first and second examples, no mapping is performed because lowercase filenames in UNIX are mapped to uppercase names in DOS, and the filenames contained no illegal DOS filename characters. The filename in the third example is mapped because it exceeds the eight-character limit on prefixes. The fourth example requires mapping because of the leading dot. DOS interprets this as a file with a null name and a 5-character extension, which is illegal. In the last example, the uppercase character is remapped. To preserve UNIX filename case sensitivity, PC/NFS maps lowercase letters (which are more common) to uppercase and therefore must map uppercase letters to something else that is unique. A filename with uppercase letters in it is treated as an illegal filename, and is remapped.

It's worth noting that you only need to worry about remapping files that were created under UNIX. Since DOS can't create a file with an illegal name, no file created on the PC client will ever require a name mapping. PC users who create files on the PC will not be confused by the PC/NFS filename mapping, because it will never apply to well-conditioned filenames.

The assignment of the unique 2-character suffixes depends upon the order of directory entries read from the server and the number of names requiring mapping. If you list a directory with **DIR** on the PC, add illegally named files to it, then list it again, the name mappings may be different in the second listing. Again, the UNIX to DOS name mappings are a PC convention and are imposed when the PC views the files, so no data on the server is changed as a result of new filename mappings.

The filename mapping character is configurable in PC/NFS 3.5. Some DOS applications, such as Microsoft Windows, use the tilde in temporary filenames. The default PC/NFS filename mapping may make UNIX files look like DOS temporary files, and cause unexpected side effects if DOS applications try to remove them as part of a cleanup operation. To avoid this confusion, change the default mapping character by editing the PC/NFS definition in **CONFIG.SYS**:

```
DEVICE=C:\NFS\PCNFS.SYS /C_
```

This example changes the default mapping character to an underscore (_). There are a variety of other PC/NFS options that may be defined in **CONFIG.SYS**, as discussed at the end of this chapter.

Symbolic Links

Symbolic links are used in UNIX filesystems to create an alternate pathname to a file or directory. The symbolic link is a directory entry that is nothing more than another pathname. Symbolic links can cross filesystem boundaries, and may point to directories or files that do not exist. Here is an example of creating a symbolic link to a directory:

```
server# ln -s /home/src.jun91 /usr/src
```

The link—**/usr/src**—contains the pathname **/home/src.jun91** as its target. Any utility that follows the pathname **/usr/src** will end up in the directory **/home/src.jun91**. Symbolic links are a useful UNIX filesystem convention for creating "shorthand" pathnames in place of longer, unwieldly file or directory pathnames.

An NFS client follows pathnames one component at a time. When an NFS client encounters a symbolic link in a pathname, it asks the server for the link's target. The client then continues resolving the pathname at the link's target. The server is responsible for reading the contents of the link and returning its target to the client, so symbolic links can be used by NFS clients that don't understand symbolic links in their native operating systems. DOS does not have support for symbolic links, but PC/NFS clients can follow symbolic links with some limitations.

UNIX-to-DOS filename mapping imposes the limitations on symbolic links used with PC/NFS. If any component in the symbolic link's target pathname requires UNIX-to-DOS filename mapping, then a PC/NFS client will not be able to follow the link. After the mapping is performed, the client's view of the pathname and the actual pathname on the server will not agree. The link created in the previous example cannot be followed by a PC/NFS client, because one component in the link's target—**src.jun91**—requires filename mapping. Symbolic links can be followed by a PC/NFS client only if the link's target pathnames follow DOS naming conventions. Many of the awkward pathnames that would be hidden by links do not meet DOS filename conventions, and would require mapping. This restriction makes symbolic links less useful in a PC/NFS environment.

UNIX to DOS file conversion

In addition to variations in names and permissions, DOS and UNIX also differ in their end-of-line and end-of-file conventions. PC/NFS includes the *dos2unix* and *unix2dos* utilities to convert between the two formats. When converting to DOS format, UNIX end of line characters (\n) are converted to newlines and carriage returns, and a DOS end-of-file character (CTRL-Z) is added. Going the other way, extra carriage returns and the DOS end-of-file marker are stripped out of the file.

If you look at a UNIX file on a PC without doing the end-of-line conversion, you'll find that consecutive lines of text fall into a stepped arrangement instead of starting on the left margin:

```
C> type h:\test
This is a line
                of text without carriage returns
```

In this example, you need to convert file **test** to DOS format before reading it on the DOS NFS client. The conversion entails the addition of carriage returns (CTRL-M characters) to the end of each line, and adding a DOS end-of-file marker (CTRL-Z) to the end of the file.

You can put DOS files of any sort—executable, binary, or text—on a UNIX fileserver and access them using normal DOS mechanisms. PC/NFS doesn't care about the content of the files. The file format conversion problem only exists for text files that were created on one system that must be read on another. If you put a DOS binary on a UNIX NFS server, it will not require any format conversion to be read and executed by the PC/NFS client.

Printer Services

PC/NFS lets you access a printer attached to a UNIX host, from the PC, by redirecting DOS printer output to a PC/NFS print host. It's up to the server to spool the file to the printer, using the standard UNIX **lpr** mechanism. There's no requirement that the UNIX printer be directly attached to the print host; if the server has to print remotely it does so transparently to the PC/NFS client. Printing from PC/NFS is not much different than copying print files to the print host and printing them from there.

Choosing a Printer

The **net use** command (used to define remote disks) also defines remote printers. The print host name is preceded with a double backslash, and the UNIX printer name is used as the server pathname:

```
C> net use lpt1: \\wahoo\lw1
```

Server *wahoo* must be running **pcnfsd**, and it must have a definition for printer *lw1* in its **/etc/printcap** file.

The PC/NFS print and authentication functions are performed by the same machine: both services are handled by the **pcnfsd** daemon that runs on the authentication server. You may choose to run **pcnfsd** daemons on several NFS servers to separate authentication and printing services. PC/NFS clients will send requests to **pcnfsd** daemons used for printing if the PC printer definitions explicitly name the print host.

For example, server *wahoo* provides authentication and NIS services to the PC/NFS clients, but server *ono* may be a better choice for print spooling because printers are attached to it, or because it handles less NFS traffic. The following commands define *wahoo* as the authentication and NIS host, but direct print requests to server *ono*:

```
net ypset wahoo
net use lpt1: \\ono\lw1
```

Put these commands in your **NETWORK.BAT** file so that the **LPT1:** printer will be defined once when you boot the PC.

Redirecting Printer Output

There are two classes of printer output from PC/NFS: complete files, and output from applications that write to the DOS printer devices. To send a file to the printer, you can use the normal DOS printing mechanism, and let PC/NFS redirect output to **LPT1:** to the UNIX printer. Alternatively, you can use the **net print** command:

```
C> net print foo.txt lpt1:
```

If you don't specify a printer name, **net print** uses **LPT1:**.

Redirecting printer output from an application is a little more difficult. The DOS printing mechanism simply sends an output stream to a device, without any spooling. DOS only executes one task at a time, so there's no chance of two tasks trying to print at the same time. The UNIX line printer system, though, spools output from multiple users on multiple hosts. It enforces one-at-a-time access to a printer by queuing jobs if the printer is in use. To be able to queue a job, the UNIX line printer daemon must be able to detect the beginning and end of the print file. This presents a problem when a UNIX daemon attempts to collect printer output from a DOS application: there is no clear indication of where the print file ends.

PC/NFS solves this problem by spooling print files on the PC until the application driving the printer does not access the printer device for five minutes or until the application doing the printing exits. You can change the inactivity timer using the PC/NFS configuration utility.

Any files in the print spool can be flushed to the print host using **net print** with an asterisk (*****) in place of a filename:

```
C> net print * lpt1:
```

All DOS application output that had been collected for printer **LPT1:** would be sent to the UNIX printer by this command.

How PC/NFS Printing Works

When the PC/NFS client prints, it asks the print host (named in the definition of the PC printer) to create a spool file for it in the **pcnfsd** temporary directory. The **pcnfsd** daemon returns the name of a temporary file, which the PC client can access via NFS. The client then writes data to the spool file using normal NFS operations, and finally asks **pcnfsd** to close the file and submit it to the associated UNIX printer device. There are several ways for this printing mechanism to break down:

- If you get the message "cannot connect to printer" from DOS when trying to define a remote printer with **net use**, it is because the PC cannot create its first spool file in the **pcnfsd** daemon temporary area. The most common cause of this problem is that the **pcnfsd** server host has not exported this directory. If you are using **/usr/tmp** as the **pcnfsd** temporary directory, be sure it is included in the server's **/etc/exports** file.

- Normally, a PC user's printer output has the username specified in a **net name** command on the banner page. If you see banner pages with a seemingly random username (or your own) on them, it's possible that the **pcnfsd** daemon was started by someone who did not log in as *root*. If you log in as a normal user and **su** to root, then start **pcnfsd** manually, print jobs sent from PC/NFS clients will have your username on the banner page. Older versions of **pcnfsd** can confuse the mechanism used by the Berkeley line printer daemon to decide who actually submitted the job. PC/NFS 3.5 does not have this problem.

- Your normal UNIX print filters may not digest output from a PC application because it contains DOS end-of-line and end-of-file characters or other non-printable characters. To preprocess PC/NFS print files before passing them on to the UNIX print queue, define a new printer in the print host's **/etc/printcap** that performs the input filtering before passing the file off to the "real" printer.

For example, consider defining printer *lw-pc* as a front-end for printer *lw*. In the server's **/etc/printcap** file, create a simple definition for the preprocessor:

```
lw-pc|PC/NFS preprocessor:\
        :sd=/usr/spool/lw-pc:\
        :sh:sb:sf:rw:\
        :of=/usr/local/share/pcfilter:
```

A simple **pcfilter** pre-processor that strips out carriage returns and $\boxed{\text{CTRL-Z}}$ end-of-file markers looks like this:

```
#! /bin/sh
sed -e 's/^Z//' -e 's/^M$//' -
```

The **sed** script does file format conversion and removes the $\boxed{\text{CTRL-Z}}$ characters that most printer drivers won't digest. If you are sending PostScript files to a printer, you may need to add a PostScript header to the file so that the printer driver recognizes the output as PostScript. A variation of the script above will strip out end-of-line and end-of-file control characters and prepend a PostScript header:

```
#! /bin/sh
( echo "%!" ; sed -e 's/^Z//' -e 's/^M$//' - )
```

The **sed** script is executed in a subshell so that the output of **echo** and the **sed** output will be merged in the filter's output stream.

We've now gone through all of the basic PC/NFS services and configuration options. The rest of this chapter discusses implementation and administrative details of PC/NFS as compared to NFS under UNIX.

Network Redirector Operation

PC/NFS is a client-side only implementation of NFS. You cannot mount a PC's disk on a UNIX workstation; PC/NFS only allows you to mount the UNIX machine's disks as logical disks on the PC. This restriction is primarily due to the architecture of the DOS operating system, which can only execute one task at a time. Because DOS is single-threaded, it cannot have NFS daemons waiting for client requests while it is performing other functions. DOS is either in a user application or in the DOS kernel, but it can't time-slice between multiple contexts like the UNIX kernel.

The *network redirector* is the heart of PC/NFS operation. It intercepts requests that would normally go to the DOS I/O system and packages them up in RPC requests to the appropriate NFS server. The redirector is similar to the **biod** daemons on a UNIX NFS client, but it handles all file operations, not just those requiring block data transfers.

Remember that the **biod** daemons ensure reasonable NFS performance by doing read-ahead and write-behind of 8-kbyte buffers. There are no client-side daemons in PC/NFS—only the redirector interposed between user code and the DOS kernel. PC/NFS gains a similar performance boost by employing a cache of 1-kbyte buffers. All of the read and write operations done by PC/NFS occur in 1-kbyte chunks, and data read from NFS servers is saved in the buffer cache. In addition, some **biod**-like write-behind is done. DOS applications writing to NFS-mounted files do not cause an NFS write request to be sent to the server until a full 1-kbyte buffer has been filled.

A PC/NFS client waits for an RPC acknowledgement just like a UNIX client. If no response is received, the call is retried until the utility timeout period is exceeded or until the retry count is exhausted. When either failure condition is met, the RPC call returns an error and DOS reports a disk access error. Tuning PC/NFS timeout and retry values is discussed in the next section on PC/NFS network administration.

PC/NFS Network Administration

There is usually a large difference between installing a network product and using it successfully. The diagnostic and administrative tools discussed in Chapter 10, *Diagnostic and Administrative Tools*, allow you debug problems with UNIX clients, and PC/NFS includes its own set of DOS tools to perform similar functions. The PC/NFS network administration toolset allows you to define routes to remote UNIX fileservers, review PC/NFS statistics, and configure the network drivers to optimize PC client performance on your network.

Routing

UNIX clients that run the **in.routed** daemon dynamically build roadmaps of the various networks that can be reached through routers and gateways. Being a single-threaded operating system, DOS cannot run a routing protocol daemon; storing the routing table in the DOS kernel would also consume memory which is usually at a premium. PC/NFS solves the DOS routing problem by defining a single, default route to other networks.

Define the default route in the **NETWORK.BAT** file using the **net route** command:

```
net route gatehost
```

If you give the **net route** command with no arguments, it displays the current default router:

```
C> net route
Non-local routing via gateway gatehost (130.1.14.8)
```

Add the route definition if your PC/NFS clients need to access filesystems that are on servers on other networks, or if you need to connect to non-local hosts via **telnet**. If you aren't sure of router's name, check out the routing tables on a PC/NFS file server using **netstat –r**, and choose either the *default* route or the most popular router:

```
[wahoo]% netstat -r
Routing tables
Destination      Gateway      Flags    Refcnt    Use      Interface
130.1.14.0       lincgate     UG       0         47       le0
130.1.15.0       lincgate     UG       0         0        le0
default          lexgate      UG       0         0        le0
```

You could use *lincgate* or *lexgate* as the PC/NFS router, although **lexgate** might be a better choice if you know that you will not be using the networks connected through *lincgate*.

When adding the route, make sure that the named host is really a router or a gateway, and not just a single-interface host on the local network. If you send packets that require routing to a single-interface host, it forwards them (along the same network on which they were received) to a better router on the network. Whenever a UNIX host forwards a packet back on the network from which it was received, it sends a routing hint to the packet's originator called an *ICMP redirect* (see Appendix B, *IP Packet Routing*). It's up to the sender to patch its routing tables based on the hint information, but again, PC/NFS doesn't have a mechanism for maintaining large routing tables, so it chooses to ignore ICMP redirection hints. If PC/NFS clients attempt to route through hosts that aren't really routers, you will see large numbers of ICMP packets on your network, serving no purpose and consuming bandwidth.

Network Tools

When you run into trouble accessing filesystems via PC/NFS, you should follow the debugging procedures used for UNIX NFS clients. PC/NFS includes several network diagnostic tools that are similar in use and function to their UNIX counterparts. These are described in the following list:

netstat [-s] [-i]   Shows statistics about the network interface (**netstat -i**) and about the number of packets of each protocol handled by the host (**netstat -s**). The **-s** option is the default.

arp   The PC/NFS **arp** function displays the PC's ARP table. This function is identical to that on UNIX hosts. If you are having trouble communicating with NFS servers, ensure that you at least have valid ARP table entries for them using this command.

nfsstat   Like its UNIX equivalent, **nfsstat** prints client-side RPC and NFS statistics showing the number of calls to each RPC procedure and the number of errors recorded. PC/NFS uses a buffer cache instead of **biod** daemons, and **nfsstat** reports the buffer cache hit rates.

nfsping *host*   **nfsping** performs an **rpcinfo** to the named host, and verifies that it is running NFS server daemons. **nfsping** can be used in batch files to test whether a file server is available before issuing a **net use** command to mount a filesystem from it.

The smaller NFS buffer size and restricted buffer and cache management in PC/NFS place a different set of demands on NFS servers. Use the tools and techniques described in Chapter 10, *Diagnostic and Administrative Tools*, and Chapter 12, *Performance Analysis and Tuning*, to monitor the behavior of servers and the network when they are loaded with PC/NFS clients. With many PC/NFS clients, you will probably have to tune the NFS server and its network interfaces:

- Make sure that your NFS server is running enough **nfsd** daemons to match the NFS request arrival rate. PC/NFS requests come in smaller buffers than most UNIX system NFS requests, so more read and write operations are needed to move the same file between a client and its server.

- Watch the directory name look-up cache hit rate on the NFS server. PC clients may generate more name look-up requests than UNIX clients. Having a larger name look-up cache will result in fewer server disk operations. Increase the kernel's **MAXUSERS** parameter to increase the size of the cache.

- Check the networks containing PC/NFS clients and the network interfaces on their NFS servers to be sure that network loading is not a problem. Again, a PC/NFS client needs to send more packets than a UNIX client. Even though the packets are smaller (1024 bytes versus a full-sized 1518-byte packet), there are more of them, which could lead to network bottlenecks.

PC/NFS Network and Mount Parameters

Even with a well-tuned server, you may need to modify the PC/NFS configuration to your network configuration and utilization. Fine-tune the PC/NFS network and mount parameters by specifying options in the CONFIG.SYS file, on the line that loads the PC/NFS driver:

```
DEVICE=C:\NFS\PCNFS.SYS [options]
```

There are many options; we'll cover the most popular ones here.

The PC/NFS package includes a full TCP/IP implementation. The network layer (IP) driver will perform datagram re-assembly if required (see "Datagrams and Packets," in Chapter 1, *Networking Fundamentals*, for an explanation of fragmentation). When you route datagrams over something other than an Ethernet, it's likely that they will be broken up into smaller packets. On the other hand, if your PC/NFS clients and servers are all on Ethernets, without any non-Ethernet links between them, there is no chance that datagrams will be fragmented.

In an all-Ethernet configuration, remove the re-assembly code from the network driver. To do so, specify the /i0 option in the device configuration:

```
DEVICE=C:\NFS\PCNFS.SYS /i0
```

Removing this feature frees about 4 kbytes of memory used by the PC/NFS driver.

You may also need to explicitly set the PC's broadcast address to the 1-filled octet form; for example, 130.1.14.255 instead of 130.1.14.0. The /b option controls the format of broadcast addresses:

/b0   *Use x.y.z.0*
/b1   *Use x.y.z.255*

At the NFS level, you can modify the timeout and retry counts used by the PC/NFS driver to accommodate slow servers. These NFS mount options are similar to those used on UNIX hosts. However, their functions are slightly different because PC/NFS does not support the notions of hard and soft mounts. By default, PC/NFS clients retry requests up to four times. If no response is received from the server before the retries are exhausted, then the operation in progress fails. The user is asked to resolve the failure with the popular message:

```
Not ready error reading drive
Abort, Retry, Ignore?
```

You can increase both the number of retries and the timeout between retries. Increase the retransmission count using the /r option:

```
DEVICE=C:\NFS\PCNFS.SYS /r8
```

This example increases the retry count to eight. If you make the retry count zero, PC/NFS behaves as if the filesystem is hard-mounted and retries the request until the server responds (or the PC is rebooted). The default timeout period is one second. You can increase the timeout with the /t option, specifying the new value in seconds:

```
DEVICE=C:\NFS\PCNFS.SYS /t3
```

This configuration line increases the PC/NFS timeout to three seconds.

A second is a long time for an NFS timeout, considering that server response time is usually measured in tens of milliseconds. Because of this long initial timeout period, most PC/NFS failures will be caused by server crashes or by requests that are lost on the network. If frequent server crashes are causing PC/NFS client failures, try changing the retry count to zero to emulate a hard mount and force the PC client to wait for the server to reboot.

If you are seeing frequent PC/NFS "Not ready" errors without any server crashes, it's probable that requests are being lost on the network between the NFS server and the PC client. Handle these PC/NFS request failures by increasing the retry count before experimenting with the request timeout period. This is similar to the tuning methodology suggested for soft-mounted filesystems on UNIX clients, as discussed in "Soft Mount Issues," in Chapter 12, *Performance Analysis and Tuning*. PC/NFS treats its remote filesystems as though they were soft-mounted: it's possible to get failures on a remote filesystem if the number of operation retries is exhausted. To accommodate an unreliable network, increase the retry count to make the PC client more persistent in its attempts to reach the server.

If you increase the timeout period first, you are likely to degrade PC client performance by inserting large, multiple-second delays between request retransmissions. If the network is really the problem, increasing the time between requests won't improve the probability that a request makes it to the server; it simply makes the client slower.

A

Transmission Line Theory

Chapter 1, *Networking Fundamentals*, discussed the different layers in the network protocol stack, starting with the physical layer and working up to the application layer where NIS and NFS are implemented. Since then, we have treated the physical layer as something of a black box. We looked at a few instances where network-wide failures were caused by breakdowns in the physical layer but have not seen why network wiring behaves in the strange ways that it does.

The electrical characteristics of the media used to send network datagrams partly define the physical layer: they determine the maximum transmission rate, the longest straight run of cable, and other constraints of the network. Nearly all of these properties of the physical layer are a product of transmission line theory, a branch of electrical engineering that studies how signals behave when they are transmitted over long distances. While this extremely low-level theory doesn't have any direct implications for top-level protocols like NFS, violating the constraints imposed by transmission line theory can lead to intermittent and puzzling network failures that appear to be high-level protocol breakdowns.

A transmission line is any signal path that is long compared to the wavelength of the signal traveling the path. Signals of higher frequencies have shorter wavelengths, so higher frequency signals require transmission line analysis over much shorter path lengths. For example, AC line voltage going from a power company generator to a substation or transformer is affected by transmission line problems over a distance of several miles. On the other end of the spectrum, high-speed integrated circuits that produce pulses in the nanosecond range require transmission line treatment for signal paths that are a few centimeters long. Signals on the Ethernet have wavelengths of about one meter, so transmission line theory applies to every network with at least two stations on it, assuming the machines aren't located on top of each other.

Every signal conductor has some inherent capacitance and inductance. The inductance comes from the fact that any conductor must have a real, non-zero thickness; the capacitance is due to coupling with the ground plane and other nearby wires. Ethernet backbones are limited in length partly because of these *capacitive loading* effects: the longer the cable is, the greater its capacitance. As the capacitance increases, each signal must "charge up" the line for a longer time, and after some critical value, the time required to charge the line's capacitance is significant compared to the time required to send the packet's preamble.

At low frequencies, the non-ideal characteristics of the wire may be ignored, but at the Ethernet data transmission frequency of 10 Mhz, they become important. A real-world Ethernet cable looks like the drawing in Figure A-1.

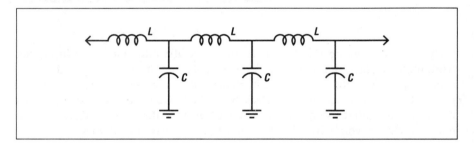

Figure A-1. Electrical model of Ethernet cable

The series of inductor/capacitor pairs define an AC impedance for the cable. Impendence is usually a function of the frequency of the signal encountering the L/C pairs. Ethernet packets are sent with a constant frequency—not the frequency of the packets themselves, but the frequency of the modulated signal representing the packet—fixing the AC impedance of the cable. This fixed impedance is why you can put a fixed-value resistor on the Ethernet as a terminator; the rest of this discussion explores the transmission line theory underpinnings that determine the value of that terminator.

On a non-ideal wire, the voltage at an endpoint cannot change instantaneously, due to the capacitive and inductive effects described earlier. When a signal is impressed on a line—for example, when a host sends a packet on the Ethernet— the voltage at the end of the wire must go from 0 volts to -2.5 volts. A packet rolling down the Ethernet cable is represented as a series of voltage changes, each with a corresponding change in current as defined by Ohm's law. The endpoint of the wire appears to be a signal load; for this discussion assume that the load has an arbitrary value, as shown in Figure A-2.

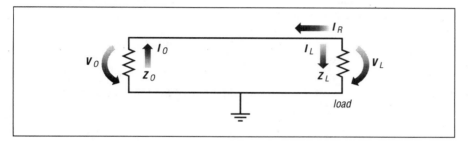

Figure A-2. Signal on an Ethernet

The endpoint of the wire, represented as the "load" above, is initially at 0 volts. In order to satisfy Ohm's and Kirkhoff's laws, a reflected signal must be created. Kirkhoff's law dictates that the current flowing into a node must equal the current leaving it. The incident, load, and reflected currents obey the following equation:

$$I_O = I_L - I_R$$

Expressed another way, Kirkhoff's law states that the loop voltage around a circuit must add up to zero. We can use this form of Kirkhoff's law to express the relationship of the voltages in the circuit:

$$V_L = V_O + V_R$$

Ohm's law is used to describe the relationship of the line impedance, Z, and the current:

$$V_L = I_L \cdot Z_L$$

Substituting for V_L and I_L, we get:

$$V_O + V_R = Z_L[I_O - I_R]$$

Apply Ohm's law again, with $V_R = I_R Z_0$, since the reflected signal sees the same impedance as the incident signal:

$$V_O + V_R = \left[\frac{Z_L}{Z_O}\right][V_O - V_R]$$

Rearranging terms, we can express the amplitude of the reflected signal as a function of the original signal:

$$\frac{V_R}{V_O} = \frac{Z_L - Z_O}{Z_L + Z_O}$$

Now let's revisit our assumption that the load impedance, Z_L, is some arbitrary value. An unterminated cable endpoint has an infinite load impedance, so with Z_L infinite, the fraction's value is approximately unity and $V_O = V_R$. The reflected current becomes a signal that looks electrically similar to the incident packet, traveling in the opposite direction.

Again, the non-ideal physical characteristics of the wire prevent the reflected signal from being a mirror image of the incident signal. At the same time, the end point of the line starts to "charge" to -2.5 volts, so the voltage V at the endpoint of the wire isn't precisely 0 volts. The combination of these two effects makes the reflected signal a slightly attenuated version of the original. After several trips down the length of the cable, the reflected signal is damped out completely. During the voltage rise time, however, reflected signals are making the line "ring."

The fairly obvious solution is to make the reflection coefficient—the numerator in the fraction above—equal to zero, so that there is no signal reflection. By placing a terminating resistor between the cable and ground, the incident signal is "caught" and any reflection is suppressed.

Ethernet cabling has a characteristic impedance of 50 ohms, which is precisely the value used for termination. Note that the line impedance is seen by AC signals only, and that DC testing of the line itself (without the terminators) should show a DC resistance of a fraction of an ohm. However, this fact can be exploited to perform a simple cable test: with a multimeter set on "ohms," measure the DC resistance between the center conductor of the Ethernet and the ground shield on a network with no traffic*.

The multimeter should read 25 ohms—half of the terminating resistor value—for a properly terminated Ethernet. The resistance of the entire cable is 25 ohms because it is the effective resistance of the two 50 ohm terminators wired in parallel, joined by the two conductors of the Ethernet cable:

$$R_{\text{effective}} = \frac{R \cdot R}{R + R} = \frac{R}{2} = 25 \text{ ohms}$$

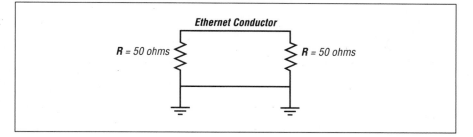

WARNING

Do not measure resistance on a live network. The network activity will cause the ohmmeter to give an inexact reading. You may inadvertently create a short on the network, possibly damaging some transceiver equipment.

Sometimes the most perplexing network problems stem from a failure in the physical layer. This theoretical discussion may not help you debug open circuits or locate bad transceivers by watching waveforms, but it should help you build a mental checklist of potential problems to be used when examining network cabling.

---

*For thinnet cabling, this is fairly easy; for thicknet cabling it requires removing a transceiver and inserting one multimeter probe into the hole normally occupied by the transceiver pin. Of course, you have to be careful not to short the center tap probe against the exposed ground shield, which brings back vivid memories of playing the Milton-Bradley board game *Operation!*.

B

IP Packet Routing

Routers and gateways join multiple IP networks, forwarding packets between the networks. A single organization may have multiple IP networks because it has multiple buildings, multiple sites, or multiple subgroups that require their own networks. For example, the history and math departments at a university are likely to have their own IP networks, just as an engineering and manufacturing facility separated by several miles will have independent networks. "Network Partitioning Hardware," in Chapter 12, *Performance Analysis and Tuning*, discussed network partitioning using routers, and some of the performance considerations when running NFS and NIS in an internetworked environment. This appendix explores the mechanics of IP packet routing in greater detail.

A router has a unique IP address on each network interface; associated with each IP address is also a unique hostname. A common convention is to add a –gw suffix to the name of the host used on the second network interface:

```
#
# local network hosts
#
192.9.200.1     fred
192.9.200.2     barney
192.9.200.3     wilma
```

```
#
# remote network gateway
192.9.201.1    fred-gw
```

Host *fred* is on both the 192.9.200.0 and 192.9.201.0 networks, and has a distinct name and address on each. **netstat -i** shows both interfaces and their associated networks and hostnames:

```
% netstat -i
Name  Mtu   Net/Dest      Address      Ipkts   Ierrs Opkts   Oerrs Collis Queue
ie0   1500  192.9.200.0   fred         349175  104   542039  363   816    0
ie1   1500  192.9.201.0   fred-gw      108635  1     4020    22    301    0
lo0   1536  loopback      localhost    74347   0     74347   0     0      0
```

To send a packet to another network, the local host needs some picture of the network and its connections to other networks. Ideally, this picture presents other networks as a "black box" outside of some local gateway, rather than an itemization of a route to every host on every attached network. This paradigm is how we view the US Post Office. Once you drop a letter in the mailbox, the route it takes may involve trucks, planes, or people, and the decisions about routing vehicles are left up to the people doing the delivery.

A host's picture of the local network's connections to other IP networks is contained in the kernel's routing table. This table may be modified in three ways:

1. Dynamic routing information is sent periodically by hosts that have multiple network connections. These routers advertise themselves using some well-known protocols, and daemons such as **in.routed** send and interpret route announcements and update the routing table.*

2. Static routing involves hand-crafting a route table. Static routing is typically used when there is only one router on a network, so a single default route suffices for all outbound traffic. Client machines often set up static routing to avoid having to listen to the regular route information broadcasts (see "Routing Information," in Chapter 12, *Performance Analysis and Tuning*).

3. Route redirection requests are sent by routers that are asked to forward packets to networks for which the chosen router is not the best choice. These route table updates are sent in *ICMP redirect* messages.

---

*The protocol used by **in.routed** is called RIP, for Routing Information Protocol. There are other routing protocols that send less information or that allow hosts to perform preferential routing when multiple gateways are present, but a discussion of these protocols is beyond the scope of this handbook.

The routing table determines how to get to foreign IP networks. You can examine the current routing table using **netstat -r**:

```
% netstat -r
Routing tables
Destination         Gateway           Flags    Refcnt Use      Interface
131.40.191.1        gatehost          UGH      0      0        ie0
131.40.56.0         gatehost          UG       0      0        ie0
131.40.208.0        gatehost2         UGD      0      0        ie0
131.40.52.0         wahoo             U        60     80770    ie0
127.0.0.1           127.0.0.1         UH       4      4767     lo0
default             gatehost          UG       0      0        ie0
```

The term "gateway" is used somewhat improperly in **netstat -r** and the following discussion. A gateway performs services at the application layer in the protocol stack, while a router is concerned only with the IP layer. The routing tables show IP routes, and titling the *Gateway* column *Router* instead would be more correct. However, many people associate *Router* with a dedicated IP router, so the less specific *Gateway* is used.

The information in the routing table determines how to get to a particular remote host or network, and shows the usage statistics for each route. The destination column shows the remote address; if it is a remote network, the address has a .0 suffix to indicate that it is a network number. Note that you can get to multiple networks through a single gateway. The gateway listed in the routing tables is just the first step that must be taken to reach the remote network; additional routing information on the first gateway directs a packet to another gateway if required.

The Flags column describes the gateway:

U   The gateway is up. If this flag appears in **netstat -r**, the gateway is probably up.

G   To get to the destination address, packets must go through a gateway. The gateway's name is in the second column.

H   The gateway is a "host gateway" and is directly connected to the network listed as the destination. In the first line of the routing table in the previous example, destination 131.40.191.1 is the IP address of *gatehost*, the gateway referenced in several other route table entries. Host gateways are always listed with their full IP addresses as the destination, and are generally at the far end of a point-to-point link.

D   The route was added after receiving an ICMP redirect message. The local host probably sent a packet to some other router, such as *gatehost*, with a destination network of 131.40.208.0. *gatehost* consulted its routing tables and found that the router to this network was *gatehost2*, and to get to *gatehost2* it had to send the packet back out on the same network interface on which it was received. The IP routing algorithm realizes that it should never have been handed a packet for this network in the first place, so it sends an ICMP redirect message to the originator informing it of a better route to network 131.40.208.0. Using static routes in a network with multiple gateways can lead to a steady stream of ICMP redirect requests unless the transmitting hosts update their route tables. Figure B-1 shows the generation of an ICMP redirect message.

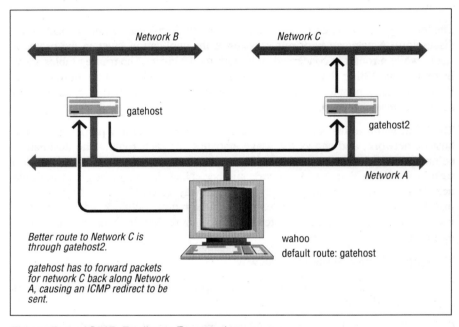

Figure B-1. ICMP Redirect Generation

The last column in the output of **netstat -r** shows the physical or pseudo device used to reach the gateway. The last three routes deserve some additional explanation. The route with *wahoo* as the gateway describes the local host's connection to the local network. The next entry shows the loopback device, which is listed as a host gateway. The last line is a *default* routing entry, which is used as a catchall if the destination IP network cannot be matched to any explicit route in the table.

The combination of the flags U, G, and H imply "This host is the gateway to this network": the U flag means the gateway is up, the G flag means the packets must go through a gateway, and the H flag indicates that the remote network is connected to the host listed in the route table. The gateway host has at least one network interface and one or more point-to-point links. A gateway listed with flags U and G has two or more network interfaces, and is acting as a routing host. The lack of the H flag means that the remote network isn't attached directly to the gateway; the gateway host listed in the routing table is merely a stepping stone on the way to that remote network.

Armed with the route tables, we can locate the host on our local network that can forward our packets to any destination host. However, our broadcasts reach only those hosts on our local IP network. There is no mechanism for sending an ARP broadcast to a remote IP host. Since we need the MAC address of the destination to send a packet, this presents a problem for the transmitter when the receiver is on another network. How do packets actually get to the remote network?

Let's assume that *wahoo*, at IP address 131.40.52.15, has mounted a filesystem through one or more gateways from the NFS server *bigguy* at IP address 131.40.208.10. To send a packet to *bigguy*, *wahoo* looks for its IP address in its routing table. It finds it, with *gatehost2* named as the gateway to this network. If the remote IP network was not matched to a destination in the routing tables, the default route, which uses *gatehost*, would be used. *wahoo* sends its packet to *gatehost2*, filling in the MAC address for *gatehost2* but the *IP address* for *bigguy*.

When *gatehost2* receives the packet, it realizes that the IP network in the destination field is not its own. It forwards the packet, using its own routing information to locate a gateway to network 131.40.208.0. *gatehost2* sends the packet to the next gateway, putting in the remote gateway's MAC address but leaving the destination IP address of *bigguy* intact. Eventually, the packet is received by a gateway that is on network 131.40.208.0; this gateway recognizes that its IP network and the destination IP network in the packet are the same, and it sends it along the local area network to *bigguy*. The last gateway to forward the packet is the one that inserts *bigguy*'s MAC address in the packet.

By default, hosts on more than one network forward IP packets from one network to another, based on information in their routing tables. In some cases, it's desirable to disable automatic IP forwarding, so that the host may communicate on multiple networks but it will not act as a transparent conduit between them. Refer back to the NIS security issues raised in "Making NIS More Secure," in Chapter 8, *Network Security*: if an NIS client can bind to an NIS server, it can dump the password map from the server. To protect the contents of your password file map, you may want to make it impossible for clients outside the local network to bind to a local NIS server. With IP forwarding enabled, any client can use **ypset** to get to any NIS server, but if IP forwarding is disabled on the host that connects the local network to other networks, **ypset** never makes it beyond this router host. It's also a good idea to disable IP forwarding on machines that join your company network to a larger network such as the Internet. This creates a firewall between your internal networks and the outside world: hosts outside the router cannot get packets into your company networks.

Disable IP forwarding by modifying the kernel variable **ip_forwarding** using **adb**:

```
# echo "ip_forwarding/W 0" | adb -k -w /vmunix /dev/mem
# echo "ip_forwarding?W 0" | adb -k -w /vmunix /dev/mem
```

The second command modifies the kernel image on disk, so that IP forwarding remains disabled even if you reboot the gateway.

C

NFS Problem Diagnosis

NFS Server Problems
NFS Client Problems
NFS errno values

Throughout this book, we've used the output of **nfsstat** on both NFS clients and servers to locate performance bottlenecks or inefficient NFS architectures. The first two sections in this appendix summarize symptoms of problems identified from the output of **nfsstat**. The last list contains typical values for the error variable **errno** that may be returned by file operations on NFS-mounted filesystems.

NFS Server Problems

Check the output of **nfsstat -s** for the following problems:

- *badcalls* > 0. RPC requests are being rejected out of hand by the NFS server. This could indicate authentication problems caused by having a user in too many groups, attempts to access exported filesystems as *root*, or an improper Secure RPC configuration.

- *nullrecv* > 0. NFS requests are not arriving fast enough to keep all of the **nfsd** daemons busy. Reduce the number of NFS server daemons until *nullrecv* is not incremented.

- *symlink* > 10%. Clients are making excessive use of symbolic links that are on filesystems exported by the server. Replace the symbolic link with a directory, and mount both the underlying filesystem and the link's target on the client.

- *getattr* > 60%. Check for possible non-default attribute cache values on NFS clients. A very high percentage of *getattr* requests indicates that the attribute cache window has been reduced or set to zero with the **noac** mount option.

- *null* > 1%. The automounter has been configured to mount replicated filesystems, but the timeout values for the mount are too short. The null procedure calls are made by the automounter to locate a server for the filesystem; too many *null* calls indicates that the automounter is retrying the mount frequently. Increase the mount timeout parameter on the automounter command line.

NFS Client Problems

Using the output of **nfsstat –c**, look for the following symptoms:

- *timeout* > 5%. The client's RPC requests are timing out before the server can answer them, or the requests are not reaching the server. Check **badxid** to determine the cause of the timeouts.

- *badxid ~ timeout*. RPC requests that have been retransmitted are being handled by the server, and the client is receiving duplicate replies. Increase the **timeo** parameter for this NFS mount to alleviate the request retransmission, or tune the server to reduce the average request service time.

- *badxid ~ 0*. With a large *timeout* count, this indicates that the network is dropping parts of NFS requests or replies in between the NFS client and server. Reduce the NFS buffer size using the **rsize** and **wsize** mount parameters to increase the probability that NFS buffers will transit the network intact.

- *badcalls* > 0. RPC calls on soft-mounted filesystems are timing out. If a server has crashed, then *badcalls* can be expected to increase, but if *badcalls* grows during "normal" operation then soft-mounted filesystems should use a larger **timeo** or **retrans** value to prevent RPC failures.

NFS errno values

The following system call **errno** values are the result of various NFS call failures:

EINTR
: A system call was interrupted when the **intr** option was used on a hard-mounted filesystem.

EACCES
: A user attempted to access a file without proper credentials. This error is usually caused by mapping *root* or anonymous users to *nobody*, a user that has almost no permissions on files in the exported filesystem. This error will be reported by **biod**.

EBUSY
: The superuser attempted to unmount a filesystem that was in use on the NFS client.

ENOSPC
: The fileserver has run out of room on the disk to which the client is attempting an NFS write operation. This error is reported by **biod** when a client write fails.

ESTALE
: An NFS client has asked the server to reference an inode that has either been freed or re-used by another client. This error may be reported by user applications (such as **ls**), or by **biod** if it attempts to write a file that was removed by another client.

EREMOTE
: An attempt was made to NFS-mount a filesystem that is itself NFS-mounted on the server. Multi-hop NFS-mounts are not allowed. This error is reported by **mount** on the NFS client.

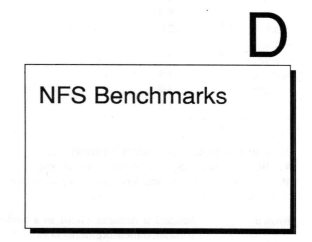

D

NFS Benchmarks

As we've seen in Chapter 12, *Performance Analysis and Tuning*, NFS performance is very dependent on the particular kinds of NFS RPC calls made by clients, as well as the sheer number and order of calls made. Benchmarking efforts on an NFS fileserver produce meaningful results only if the traffic patterns used in the benchmark match those of your computing environment. There are two popular choices for generating client loads: the **nhfsstone** utility available from Legato Systems, and suites of shell scripts that perform file operations.

Legato's **nhfsstone** is a *synthetic* traffic generator. That is, it simulates the RPC calls made by an NFS client over a typical usage period. The default RPC mixture used in traffic generation models a diskless client, and is somewhat heavily weighted toward write operations, as shown in Table D-1.

Table D-1. Legato NFS RPC Mixture

Operation	Representation
getattr	13%
setattr	1%
lookup	34%
readlink	8%
read	22%
write	15%
create	2%
remove	1%
readdir	3%
fsstat	1%

Networks with dataless clients typically perform 5-10% writes, and servers that handle only user files (and no boot service) may have write operations account for as little as 3% of the total RPC calls. Three other RPC mixtures model dataless and diskless clients:

Brown   Models a dataless client in a student laboratory, based on performance measurements done at Brown University.

SunMark   Models a dataless client running shell commands typically used in a software development environment.

NetBench   Models a diskful client running shell commands that use NFS-mounted files. This model performs a large percentage of writes as a result of file copying.

The RPC mixtures for these models are summarized in Table D-2.

Table D-2. Dataless and Diskful Client RPC Mixtures

Operation	Brown	SunMark	NetBench
getattr	23	41	26
setattr	1	0	0
lookup	45	29	7
readlink	8	5	7
read	13	5	21
write	2	1	24
create	1	1	2
remove	1	1	1
readdir	5	16	9
fsstat	1	1	3

The RPC mix used for traffic generation can be modified through benchmark configuration files to represent the actual breakdown of RPC calls you observe using **nfsstat -ns** on your servers.

The **nhfsstone** code should be run on your fastest client machine so that the request generation rate does not govern the benchmark results. If you are evaluating a server that will be on multiple networks, you should run **nhfsstone** on one client on each network to fully load the server. You can choose a sample period for the benchmark, and should use at least five minutes so that short-term cache effects are smoothed out of the measured results. Output from **nhfsstone** includes a measure of the total number of NFS operations handled by the server and the average server response time.

Additional information and the **nhfsstone** code can be obtained directly from Legato at the following address:

> Legato Systems, Inc.
> 260 Sheridan Avenue
> Palo Alto, CA 94306
> (415) 329-7880
> *nhfsstone-request@legato.COM*

One criticism of synthetic traffic generators is that they remove some randomness from the network. With a single client sending requests, there is no possibility of inter-client interface shaping the results, or of measuring server performance when a burst of similar packets—for example, several reads—arrives at once. Actual work-load traffic generation scripts attempt to solve these shortcomings by executing streams of actual UNIX filesystem operations.

Standard UNIX commands generate a variety of requests, as shown in Table D-3.

Table D-3. NFS Requests Generated by UNIX Commands

Command	NFS RPC Operations
find	*lookup, readdir, getattr*
cp	*read, write, setattr*
mv	*rename*
ls	*lookup, getattr, readdir, readlink*
ln	*symlink*

To emulate a mix of 30% read and 10% write operations, you can use a script that copies a file entirely within an NFS filesystem (doing *N* reads and *N* writes) and then does two copies of the file from the NFS filesystem to a local filesystem (doing 2*N* reads and no NFS writes). Running this script repeatedly generates 3*N* reads for every *N* write operations, modeling the 30/10 RPC mixture.

find and **ls** exercise the *getattr*, *readdir*, and *lookup* calls. **find** is primarily pathname oriented, and uses *getattr* less than **ls -l**, which is the classic *getattr* source. In addition, **ls -l** reads symbolic links, generating *readlink* RPC calls if the directory contains one or more symbolic links. For example, to model an RPC mixture of 35% *getattr* and 5% *readlink* operations, create a directory on the NFS server with 70 regular files and 10 symbolic links in it. Run **ls -l** in the directory to produce a 7:1 ratio of *getattr* to *readlink* RPC calls.

Several caveats apply to crafting your own NFS benchmark suite:

- Make sure that your benchmark script produces the same RPC mixture over time. Clients cache data, and you may find that some *read* operations turn into *getattr* cache consistency checks instead of disk operations on the server. If necessary, run a process in the background on the client traffic generator to keep the client's memory full and limit cache effects.

- Experiment with combinations of basic utilities to produce an RPC mixture that closely resembles your work load, but avoid commands that are CPU-bound on the client. Using the compiler to test NFS performance is not effective, because the client's NFS request generation is limited by the compiler's input parsing and code generation speeds.

- Make sure the test files used for *read* and *write* operations are sufficiently large, usually 2-3 Mbytes. Clients are able to cache small files and remove disk operations from the benchmark.

Above all else, evaluate benchmark results in the framework in which they were generated: a potentially quiescent network with well-defined traffic patterns. In the more random real world, file sizes show much greater variation, and clients will generate bursts of traffic that are hard to simulate.

Index

+, and maps, 32
& , and key values, 341

A

accelerated make, 131
access, transparent, 164-166
access=host, 94
acdirmax, 320
acdirmin, 320
acregmax, 320
acregmin, 320
add_client, 142
Address Resolution Protocol,
    (see ARP)
addresses, broadcast, 207-209
    classes, IP, 208
    Ethernet, 5, 207, 219
    host, 7
    IP, 7

MAC, 5, 207
    prefixes, 216
    station, 7
AFS, 137
aliases, file, 37;
        and NIS information, 33
    merging local and NIS, 201
    NIS, 197
    wide-area, 198
amd, 325
ampersand (&), and key values,
    341
Andrew File System, (see AFS)
anon export option, 94, 176
architecture, kernel and CPU, 140
archive file, 201
ARP, and broadcast addresses, 207
    converting IP to MAC
        addresses, 8
    duplicate replies, 262-264
    PC/NFS, 370

About the Author

Hal Stern is a Technical Consultant with Sun Microsystems, where he specializes in networking, performance tuning, and kernel hacking. Hal earned a Bachelor of Science degree from Princeton University in 1984.

Before joining Sun, Hal had been a member of the technical staff at Polygen Corporation, developing UNIX-based molecular modelling and chemical information system products. Hal also worked on the Massive Memory Machine project as a member of the Research Staff in Princeton University's Department of Computer Science. His interests include large installation system administration, virtual memory management systems, performance, local- and wide-area networking, interactive graphics, applications in financial services, cosmology, and the history of science. Hal is active in the Sun User's Group and has served on the advisory trustee board of the Princeton Broadcasting Service for seven years.

Hal and his wife Toby live in Burlington, MA. At home, Hal enjoys carpentry, jazz music, cooking, and watching the stock market.

More Titles from O'Reilly

Network Administration

Using & Managing PPP

By *Andrew Sun*
1st Edition March 1998 (est.)
400 pages (est.), ISBN 1-56592-321-9

Covers all aspects of PPP, including setting up dial-in servers, debugging, and PPP options. Also contains overviews of related areas, like serial communications, DNS setup, and routing.

Managing IP Networks with Cisco Routers

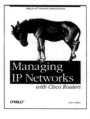

By *Scott M. Ballew*
1st Edition October 1997
352 pages, ISBN 1-56592-320-0

This practical guide to setting up and maintaining a production networ covers how to select routing protocols, configure protocols to handle most common situations, evaluate network equipment and vendors, and setup a help desk. Although it focuses on Cisco routers, and gives examples using Cisco's IOS, the principles discussed are common to all IP networks.

Virtual Private Networks

Charlie Scott, Paul Wolfe &
Mike Erwin
1st Edition February 1998 (est.)
184 pages (est.), ISBN 1-56592-319-7

Historically, only large companies could afford secure networks, which they created from expensive leased lines. Smaller folks had to make do with the relatively untrusted Internet. Nowadays, even large companies have to go outside their private nets, because so many people telecommute or log in while they're on the road. How do you provide a low-cost, secure electronic network for your organization?

The solution is a virtual private network: a collection of technologies that creates secure connections or "tunnels" over regular Internet lines—connections that can be easily used by anybody logging in from anywhere. This book tells you how to plan and build a VPN. It starts with general concerns like costs, configuration, and how a VPN fits in with other networking technologies like firewalls. It continues with detailed descriptions of how to install and use VPN technologies that are available for Windows NT and UNIX, such as PPTP and L2TP, the Altavista Tunnel, and the Cisco PIX Firewall.

sendmail, 2nd Edition

By *Bryan Costales & Eric Allman*
2nd Edition January 1997
1050 pages, ISBN 1-56592-222-0

This new edition of *sendmail* covers sendmail Version 8.8 from Berkeley and the standard versions available on most systems. It is far and away the most comprehensive book ever written on sendmail, the program that acts like a traffic cop in routing and delivering mail on UNIX-based networks. Although sendmail is used on almost every UNIX system, it's one of the last great uncharted territories—and most difficult utilities to learn—in UNIX system administration.

This book provides a complete sendmail tutorial, plus extensive reference material on every aspect of the program. Part One is a tutorial on understanding sendmail; Part Two covers the building, installation, and m4 configuration of sendmail; Part Three covers practical issues in sendmail administration; Part Four is a comprehensive reference section; and Part Five consists of appendices and a bibliography.

In this second edition an expanded tutorial demonstrates hub's cf file and nullclient.mc. Other new topics include the #error delivery agent, sendmail's exit values, MIME headers, and how to set up and use the user database, mailertable, and smrsh. Solution-oriented examples throughout the book help you solve your own sendmail problems. This new edition is cross-referenced with section numbers.

sendmail Desktop Reference

By *Bryan Costales & Eric Allman*
1st Edition March 1997
74 pages, ISBN 1-56592-278-6

This quick-reference guide provides a complete overview of the latest version of sendmail (V8.8), from command-line switches to configuration commands, from options declarations to macro definitions, and from m4 features to debugging switches—all packed into a convenient, carry-around booklet co-authored by the creator of sendmail. Includes extensive cross-references to *sendmail*, second edition.

Network Administration (continued)

DNS and BIND, 2nd Edition

By Paul Albitz & Cricket Liu
2nd Edition December 1996
438 pages, ISBN 1-56592-236-0

This book is a complete guide to the Internet's Domain Name System (DNS) and the Berkeley Internet Name Domain (BIND) software, the UNIX implementation of DNS. In this second edition, the authors continue to describe BIND version 4.8.3, which is included in most vendor implementations today. In addition, you'll find complete coverage of BIND 4.9.4, which in all probability will be adopted as the new standard in the near future.

In addition to covering the basic motivation behind DNS and how to set up the BIND software, this book covers many more advanced topics, including using DNS and BIND on Windows NT systems; how to become a "parent" (i.e., "delegate" the ability to assign names to someone else); how to use DNS to set up mail forwarding correctly; debugging and troubleshooting; and programming. Assumes a basic knowledge of system administration and network management.

Getting Connected: The Internet at 56K and Up

By Kevin Dowd
1st Edition June 1996
424 pages, ISBN 1-56592-154-2

A complete guide for businesses, schools, and other organizations who want to connect their computers to the Internet. This book covers everything you need to know to make informed decisions, from helping you figure out which services you really need to providing down-to-earth explanations and configuration instructions for telecommunication options at higher than modem speeds, such as frame relay, ISDN, and leased lines. Once you're online, it shows you how to set up basic Internet services, such as a World Wide Web server. Tackles issues for PC, Macintosh, and UNIX platforms.

Networking Personal Computers with TCP/IP

By Craig Hunt
1st Edition July 1995
408 pages, ISBN 1-56592-123-2

This book offers practical information as well as detailed instructions for attaching PCs to a TCP/IP network and its UNIX servers. It discusses the challenges you'll face and offers general advice on how to deal with them, provides basic TCP/IP configuration information for some of the popular PC operating systems, covers advanced configuration topics and configuration of specific applications such as email, and includes a chapter on on integrating Netware with TCP/IP.

TCP/IP Network Administration, 2nd Edition

By Craig Hunt

2nd Edition December 1997 (est.)
608 pages (est.), ISBN 1-56592-322-7

TCP/IP Network Administration, 2nd Edition, is a complete guide to setting up and running a TCP/IP network for administrators of networks of systems or lone home systems that access the Internet. It starts with the fundamentals: what the protocols do and how they work, how addresses and routing are used to move data through the network, and how to set up your network connection.

Beyond basic setup, this new second edition discusses advanced routine protocols (RIPv2, OSPF, and BGP) and the gated software package that implements them. It contains a tutorial on configuring important network services, including PPP, SLIP, sendmail, Domain Name Service (DNS), BOOTP and DHCP configuration servers, some simple setups for NIS and NFS, and chapters on troubleshooting and security. In addition, this book is a command and syntax reference for several important packages including pppd, dip, gated, named, dhcpd, and sendmail.

Covers Linux, BSD, and System V TCP/IP implementations.

How to stay in touch with O'Reilly

1. Visit Our Award-Winning Site

http://www.oreilly.com/

★ "Top 100 Sites on the Web" —*PC Magazine*
★ "Top 5% Web sites" —*Point Communications*
★ "3-Star site" —*The McKinley Group*

Our web site contains a library of comprehensive product information (including book excerpts and tables of contents), downloadable software, background articles, interviews with technology leaders, links to relevant sites, book cover art, and more. File us in your Bookmarks or Hotlist!

2. Join Our Email Mailing Lists

New Product Releases
To receive automatic email with brief descriptions of all new O'Reilly products as they are released, send email to:
listproc@online.oreilly.com
Put the following information in the first line of your message (*not* in the Subject field):
subscribe oreilly-news

O'Reilly Events
If you'd also like us to send information about trade show events, special promotions, and other O'Reilly events, send email to:
listproc@online.oreilly.com
Put the following information in the first line of your message (*not* in the Subject field):
subscribe oreilly-events

3. Get Examples from Our Books via FTP

There are two ways to access an archive of example files from our books:

Regular FTP
- ftp to:
  ftp.oreilly.com
  (login: anonymous
  password: your email address)
- Point your web browser to:
  ftp://ftp.oreilly.com/

FTPMAIL
- Send an email message to:
  ftpmail@online.oreilly.com
  (Write "help" in the message body)

4. Contact Us via Email

order@oreilly.com
To place a book or software order online. Good for North American and international customers.

subscriptions@oreilly.com
To place an order for any of our newsletters or periodicals.

books@oreilly.com
General questions about any of our books.

software@oreilly.com
For general questions and product information about our software. Check out O'Reilly Software Online at **http://software.oreilly.com/** for software and technical support information. Registered O'Reilly software users send your questions to:
website-support@oreilly.com

cs@oreilly.com
For answers to problems regarding your order or our products.

booktech@oreilly.com
For book content technical questions or corrections.

proposals@oreilly.com
To submit new book or software proposals to our editors and product managers.

international@oreilly.com
For information about our international distributors or translation queries. For a list of our distributors outside of North America check out:
http://www.oreilly.com/www/order/country.html

O'Reilly & Associates, Inc.
101 Morris Street, Sebastopol, CA 95472 USA
TEL   707-829-0515 or 800-998-9938
        (6am to 5pm PST)
FAX   707-829-0104

Titles from O'Reilly

Please note that upcoming titles are displayed in italic.

WEB PROGRAMMING
Apache: The Definitive Guide
Building Your Own Web
    Conferences
Building Your Own Website
Building Your Own Win-CGI
    Programs
CGI Programming for the World
    Wide Web
Designing for the Web
HTML: The Definitive Guide
JavaScript: The Definitive Guide,
    2nd Ed.
Learning Perl
Programming Perl, 2nd Ed.
Mastering Regular Expressions
WebMaster in a Nutshell
Web Security & Commerce
Web Client Programming with
    Perl
World Wide Web Journal

USING THE INTERNET
Smileys
The Future Does Not Compute
The Whole Internet User's Guide
    & Catalog
The Whole Internet for Win 95
Using Email Effectively
Bandits on the Information
    Superhighway

JAVA SERIES
Exploring Java
Java AWT Reference
Java Fundamental Classes
    Reference
Java in a Nutshell
Java Language Reference
Java Network Programming
Java Threads
Java Virtual Machine

SOFTWARE
WebSite™ 1.1
WebSite Professional™
Building Your Own Web
    Conferences
WebBoard™
PolyForm™
Statisphere™

SONGLINE GUIDES
NetActivism   NetResearch
Net Law   NetSuccess
NetLearning   NetTravel
Net Lessons

SYSTEM ADMINISTRATION
Building Internet Firewalls
Computer Crime: A Crimefighter's
    Handbook
Computer Security Basics
DNS and BIND, 2nd Ed.
Essential System Administration,
    2nd Ed.
Getting Connected: The Internet
    at 56K and Up
*Internet Server Administration
    with Windows NT*
Linux Network Administrator's
    Guide
Managing Internet Information
    Services
Managing NFS and NIS
Networking Personal Computers
    with TCP/IP
Practical UNIX & Internet
    Security. 2nd Ed.
PGP: Pretty Good Privacy
sendmail, 2nd Ed.
sendmail Desktop Reference
System Performance Tuning
TCP/IP Network Administration
termcap & terminfo
Using & Managing UUCP
Volume 8: X Window System
    Administrator's Guide
Web Security & Commerce

UNIX
Exploring Expect
Learning VBScript
Learning GNU Emacs, 2nd Ed.
Learning the bash Shell
Learning the Korn Shell
Learning the UNIX Operating
    System
Learning the vi Editor
Linux in a Nutshell
Making TeX Work
Linux Multimedia Guide
Running Linux, 2nd Ed.
SCO UNIX in a Nutshell
sed & awk, 2nd Edition
Tcl/Tk Tools
UNIX in a Nutshell: System V
    Edition
UNIX Power Tools
Using csh & tcsh
When You Can't Find Your UNIX
    System Administrator
Writing GNU Emacs Extensions

WEB REVIEW STUDIO SERIES
Gif Animation Studio
Shockwave Studio

WINDOWS
Dictionary of PC Hardware and
    Data Communications Terms
Inside the Windows 95 Registry
Inside the Windows 95 File
    System
Windows Annoyances
Windows NT File System Internals
Windows NT in a Nutshell

PROGRAMMING
Advanced Oracle PL/SQL
    Programming
Applying RCS and SCCS
C++: The Core Language
Checking C Programs with lint
DCE Security Programming
Distributing Applications Across
    DCE & Windows NT
Encyclopedia of Graphics File
    Formats, 2nd Ed.
Guide to Writing DCE
    Applications
lex & yacc
Managing Projects with make
Mastering Oracle Power Objects
Oracle Design: The Definitive
    Guide
Oracle Performance Tuning, 2nd
    Ed.
Oracle PL/SQL Programming
Porting UNIX Software
POSIX Programmer's Guide
POSIX.4: Programming for the
    Real World
Power Programming with RPC
Practical C Programming
Practical C++ Programming
Programming Python
Programming with curses
Programming with GNU Software
Pthreads Programming
Software Portability with imake,
    2nd Ed.
Understanding DCE
Understanding Japanese
    Information Processing
UNIX Systems Programming for
    SVR4

BERKELEY 4.4 SOFTWARE DISTRIBUTION
4.4BSD System Manager's Manual
4.4BSD User's Reference Manual
4.4BSD User's Supplementary
    Documents
4.4BSD Programmer's Reference
    Manual
4.4BSD Programmer's
    Supplementary Documents
X Programming
Vol. 0: X Protocol Reference
    Manual
Vol. 1: Xlib Programming Manual
Vol. 2: Xlib Reference Manual
Vol. 3M: X Window System User's
    Guide, Motif Edition
Vol. 4M: X Toolkit Intrinsics
    Programming Manual, Motif
    Edition
Vol. 5: X Toolkit Intrinsics
    Reference Manual
Vol. 6A: Motif Programming
    Manual
Vol. 6B: Motif Reference Manual
Vol. 6C: Motif Tools
Vol. 8 : X Window System
    Administrator's Guide
Programmer's Supplement for
    Release 6
X User Tools
The X Window System in a
    Nutshell

CAREER & BUSINESS
Building a Successful Software
    Business
The Computer User's Survival
    Guide
Love Your Job!
Electronic Publishing on CD-ROM

TRAVEL
Travelers' Tales: Brazil
Travelers' Tales: Food
Travelers' Tales: France
Travelers' Tales: Gutsy Women
Travelers' Tales: India
Travelers' Tales: Mexico
Travelers' Tales: Paris
Travelers' Tales: San Francisco
Travelers' Tales: Spain
Travelers' Tales: Thailand
Travelers' Tales: A Woman's
    World

O'REILLY™

TO ORDER: **800-998-9938** • **order@oreilly.com** • **http://www.oreilly.com/**
OUR PRODUCTS ARE AVAILABLE AT A BOOKSTORE OR SOFTWARE STORE NEAR YOU.
FOR INFORMATION: **800-998-9938** • **707-829-0515** • **info@oreilly.com**

O'REILLY WOULD LIKE TO HEAR FROM YOU

Which book did this card come from?

_____

Where did you buy this book?
- ❏ Bookstore   ❏ Computer Store
- ❏ Direct from O'Reilly   ❏ Class/seminar
- ❏ Bundled with hardware/software
- ❏ Other _____

What operating system do you use?
- ❏ UNIX   ❏ Macintosh
- ❏ Windows NT   ❏ PC(Windows/DOS)
- ❏ Other _____

What is your job description?
- ❏ System Administrator   ❏ Programmer
- ❏ Network Administrator   ❏ Educator/Teacher
- ❏ Web Developer
- ❏ Other _____

❏ Please send me O'Reilly's catalog, containing
a complete listing of O'Reilly books and
software.

Name _____ Company/Organization _____

Address _____

City _____ State _____ Zip/Postal Code _____ Country _____

Telephone _____ Internet or other email address (specify network) _____

Nineteenth century wood engraving
of a bear from the O'Reilly &
Associates Nutshell Handbook®
Using & Managing UUCP.

‖‖‖

BUSINESS REPLY MAIL
FIRST CLASS MAIL   PERMIT NO. 80   SEBASTOPOL, CA

Postage will be paid by addressee

O'Reilly & Associates, Inc.
101 Morris Street
Sebastopol, CA 95472-9902

‖‖‖‖‖‖‖‖‖‖‖‖‖‖‖‖‖‖‖‖‖‖‖‖‖‖‖‖‖‖‖‖‖‖‖‖